FOR THOSE WHO SLEEP IN THE DUST

FOR THOSE WHO SLEEP IN THE DUST

Essays on Archaeology and the Bible

William G. Dever

SBL PRESS

Atlanta

Copyright © 2026 by William G. Dever

All rights reserved. No part of this work may be reproduced or transmitted in any form or by any means, electronic or mechanical, including photocopying and recording, or by means of any information storage or retrieval system, except as may be expressly permitted by the 1976 Copyright Act or in writing from the publisher. Requests for permission should be addressed in writing to the Rights and Permissions Office, SBL Press, 825 Houston Mill Road, Atlanta, GA 30329 USA.

Library of Congress Control Number: 2025940086.

Contents

Original Publications	vii
Abbreviations	ix
Prologue	1
1. Yigael Yadin: Prototypical Biblical Archaeologist	5
2. Biblical Archaeology: Death and Rebirth?	21
3. Philology, Theology, and Archaeology: What Kind of History of Israel Do We Want, and What Is Possible?	51
4. On Listening to the Text—and the Artifacts	79
5. Histories and Nonhistories of Ancient Israel: What Archaeology Can Contribute	107
6. Israelite Origins and the "Nomadic Ideal": Can Archaeology Separate Fact from Fiction?	135
7. Merenptah's "Israel," the Bible's, and Ours	169
8. Ethnicity and the Archaeological Record: The Case of Early Israel	185
9. Archaeology, Urbanism, and the Rise of the Israelite State	219
10. Material Remains and the Cult in Ancient Israel: An Essay in Archaeological Systematics	249

11. The Silence of the Text	279
12. Archaeology and the Ancient Israelite Cult: How the Khirbet el-Qom and Kuntillet ʿAjrud Asherah Texts Have Changed the Picture	307
13. Folk Religion in Ancient Israel: The Disconnect between Text and Artifact	323
Index of Biblical References	343
Index of Ancient People(s), Places, and Objects	345
Index of Modern Authors	347

Original Publications

1. "Yigael Yadin: Prototypical Biblical Archaeologist." *ErIsr* 20 (1989): 44*–51*.
2. "Biblical Archaeology: Death and Rebirth?" Pages 706–22 in *Biblical Archaeology Today, 1990: Proceedings at the Second International Congress on Biblical Archaeology, Jerusalem, June 1990*. Edited by Avraham Biran and Janet Amitai. Israel Exploration Society, 1993.
3. "Philology, Theology, and Archaeology: What Kind of History of Israel Do We Want, and What Is Possible?" Pages 706–22 in *Biblical Archaeology Today, 1990: Proceedings at the Second International Congress on Biblical Archaeology, Jerusalem, June 1990*. Edited by Avraham Biran and Janet Amitai. Israel Exploration Society, 1993.
4. "On Listening to the Text—and the Artifacts." Pages 1–23 in *The Echoes of Many Texts: Reflections on Jewish and Christian Traditions: Essays in Honor of Lou H. Silberman*. Edited by William G. Dever and J. Edward Wright. BJS 313. Scholars Press, 1996.
6. "Israelite Origins and the 'Nomadic Ideal': Can Archaeology Separate Fact from Fiction?" Pages 220–37 in *Mediterranean People in Transition: Thirteenth to Early Tenth Centuries BCE*. Edited by Seymour S. Gitin, Amihai Mazar, and Ephraim Stern. Israel Exploration Society, 1998.
7. "Merenptah's 'Israel,' the Bible's, and Ours." Pages 90–96 in *Exploring the Longue Durée: Essays in Honor of Lawrence E. Stager*. Edited by J. David Schloen. Eisenbrauns, 2009.
8. "Ethnicity and the Archaeological Record: The Case of Early Israel." Pages 49–66 *The Archaeology of Difference: Gender, Ethnicity, Class and the "Other" in Antiquity; Studies in Honor of Eric M. Meyers*. Edited by Douglas R. Edwards and C. Thomas McCollough. American Schools of Oriental Research, 2007.

9. "Archaeology, Urbanism, and the Rise of the Israelite State." Pages 172–93 in *Urbanism in Antiquity: From Mesopotamia to Crete*. Edited by Walter E. Aufrecht, Neil A. Mirau, and Steven W. Gauley. JSOTSup 244. Sheffield Academic, 1997.
10. "Material Remains and the Cult in Ancient Israel: An Essay in Archaeological Systematics." Pages 571–87 in *The Word of the Lord Shall Go Forth: Essays in Honor of David Noel Freedman in Celebration of His Sixtieth Birthday*. Edited by Carol L. Meyers and M. O'Connor. Eisenbrauns, 1983.
11. "The Silence of the Text." Pages 143–68 in *Scripture and Other Artifacts: Essays on the Bible and Archaeology in Honor of Philip J. King*. Edited by Michael D. Coogan, J. Cheryl Exum, and Lawrence E. Stager. Westminster John Knox, 1994.
12. "Archaeology and the Ancient Israelite Cult: How the Khirbet el-Qom and Kuntillet ʿAjrud Asherah Texts Have Changed the Picture." *ErIsr* 2 (1999): 9*–15*.
13. "Folk Religion in Ancient Israel: The Disconnect between Text and Artifact." Pages 426–39 in *Berührungspunklte Studien zur Sozial- und Religionsgeschichte Israels und Seiner Umwelt: Festschrift für Rainer Albertz zu seinem 65. Geburtstag*. Edited by Ingo Kottsieper, Rüdiger Schmitt, and Jacob Wöhrte. AOAT 350. Ugarit-Verlag, 2008.

Abbreviations

AA	*American Anthropologist*
AB	Anchor Bible
ABD	Freedman, David Noel, ed. *Anchor Bible Dictionary*. 6 vols. Doubleday, 1992.
ABRL	Anchor Bible Reference Library
ABS	Archaeology and Biblical Studies
AJA	*American Journal of Archaeology*
ANEM	Ancient Near East Monographs
AOAT	Alter Orient und Altes Testament
AYBRL	Anchor Yale Bible Reference Library
BA	*Biblical Archaeologist*
BAR	*Biblical Archaeology Review*
BASOR	*Bulletin of the American Schools of Oriental Research*
BEATAJ	Beiträge zur Erforschung des Alten Testaments und des antiken Judentum
Bib	*Biblica*
BibInt	*Biblical Interpretation*
BibOr	Biblica et Orientalia
BibSem	The Biblical Seminar
BJS	Brown Judaic Studies
BMI	The Bible and Its Modern Interpreters
BN	*Biblische Notizen*
BRev	*Bible Review*
BZAW	Beihefte zur Zeitschrift für die alttestamentliche Wissenschaft
CurBS	*Currents in Research: Biblical Studies*
DDD	Toorn, Karel van der, Bob Becking, and Pieter W. van der Horst, eds. *Dictionary of Deities and Demons in the Bible*. 2nd ed. Eerdmans, 1999.

EAEHL	Avi-Yonah, Michael, ed. *Encyclopedia of Archaeological Excavations in the Holy Land*. 4 vols. Israel Exploration Society and Massada Press, 1975.
ErIsr	*Eretz-Israel*
FAT	Forschungen zum Alten Testament
GBS	Guides to Biblical Scholarship
HBAI	*Hebrew Bible and Ancient Israel*
HSM	Harvard Semitic Monographs
HSS	Harvard Semitic Studies
HTR	*Harvard Theological Review*
HUCA	*Hebrew Union College Annual*
IDBSup	Crim, Keith, ed. *Interpreter's Dictionary of the Bible: Supplementary Volume*. Abingdon, 1976.
IEJ	*Israel Exploration Journal*
Int	*Interpretation*
JAOS	*Journal of the American Oriental Society*
JARCE	*Journal of the American Research Center in Egypt*
JEOL	*Jaarbericht van het Vooraziatisch-Egyptisch Gezelschap (Genootschap) Ex oriente lux*
JESHO	*Journal of the Economic and Social History of the Orient*
JSOTSup	Journal for the Study of the Old Testament Supplement Series
JSSEA	*Journal of the Society for the Study of Egyptian Antiquities*
LAI	Library of Ancient Israel
LHBOTS	The Library of Hebrew Bible/Old Testament Studies
NEA	*Near Eastern Archaeology*
NEAEHL	Stern, Ephraim, ed. *The New Encyclopedia of Archaeological Excavations in the Holy Land*. 4 vols. Israel Exploration Society & Carta; Simon & Schuster, 1993.
OEANE	Meyers, Eric M., ed. *The Oxford Encyclopedia of Archaeology in the Near East*. 5 vols. Oxford University Press, 1997.
OIP	Oriental Institute Publications
OIS	Oriental Institute Seminars
OJA	*Oxford Journal of Archaeology*
OLA	Orientalia Lovaniensia Analecta
Or	*Orientalia*
OTL	Old Testament Library
PAe	Probleme der Ägyptologie

PEQ	*Palestine Exploration Quarterly*
QD	Quaestiones Disputatae
RB	*Revue biblique*
SBLMS	Society of Biblical Literature Monograph Series
SBLStBL	Society of Biblical Literature Studies in Biblical Literature
SBT	Studies in Biblical Theology
SHANE	Studies in the History (and Culture) of the Ancient Near East
SJLA	Studies in Judaism in Late Antiquity
SJOT	*Scandinavian Journal of the Old Testament*
SOTSMS	Society for Old Testament Studies Monograph Series
SWBA	Social World of Biblical Antiquity
SymS	Symposium Series
TA	*Tel Aviv*
TRu	*Theologische Rundschau*
UF	*Ugarit-Forschungen*
VT	*Vetus Testamentum*
VTSup	Supplements to Vetus Testamentum
ZAW	*Zeitschrift für die alttestamentliche Wissenschaft*
ZDPV	*Zeitschrift des deutschen Palästina-Vereins*

Prologue

This book, a collection of previously published essays, has been in the making for many years. The subjects reflect underlying essential themes in my work that go back more than fifty years.

In presuming to offer these essays, I should note my credentials for doing so. I was raised in the home of an evangelical pastor and was myself a seminary graduate and an ordained Congregational Christian minister for thirteen years. In graduate work at Harvard I majored in both biblical studies and Near Eastern archaeology. I lived in Israel for nearly twelve years, headed two American postdoctoral research institutes in Jerusalem, and directed excavations at several major sites for more than thirty seasons.

In retrospect, my goal was always to relate the archaeology of ancient Israel and its neighbors to the world of the Bible—not to theology, in which I was once interested, but rather to *history* as "the ground of faith." For me, archaeology can teach us moral lessons, and that explains my passion. These essays presented here, chosen from more than three hundred, are not disinterested, abstract, scholarly discussions for specialists. They are meant to share some of the exciting results of archaeology in the past fifty years with a broader public. (More background can be found in my autobiography, *My Nine Lives: Sixty Years in Israeli and Biblical Archaeology* (2020b).

The main title of this collection of essays, *For Those Who Sleep in the Dust*, is a partial quotation from Dan 12:2. These are the innumerable, ordinary, anonymous folk who have left us no history of their own. Their voice is heard nowhere in the Bible, which was written by a handful of elites in Jerusalem, concerned only with history as the public deeds of great men. It is only *archaeology* that illumines their lives. It brings them back and allows them to speak to us of their experiences and to enlighten us about what it meant to be fully human in that time and place. That is why I presume to offer these essays to a wider audience today.

Not all of the archaeology in Israel is about the Bible, of course. Indeed, much of my fieldwork and many of my publications are about much earlier events in the Bronze Age. Here, however, I have deliberately chosen essays that focus almost exclusively on the Iron Age, circa 1200–600 BCE, the period of the Israelite settlement and monarchy. On each topic, the essay is one of many, but one that I judged the most comprehensive yet the most readily accessible.

These are all period pieces, representative of mainstream scholarship of a particular time, some going back forty years. To put the essays into context, I introduce each one by describing how scholarly discussion went at the time and why I got involved. But I have not updated the essays themselves except to update bibliographical references and to add more recent bibliography to show how far we have come.

Another factor influenced my choices. Most of the essays were first published in relatively obscure places, in the proceedings of international symposia, in volumes honoring particular scholars, or in foreign-language periodicals. I thought that they might deserve wider circulation and renewed attention even if they are somewhat dated. For lay readers who want to pursue these topics further, I recommend several good resources: Freedman 1992; Meyers 1998; Master 2013; Silberman 2012; Steiner and Killebrew 2014; and Mazar 1990. Many of the topics treated here are also summarized conveniently in my *Has Archaeology Buried the Bible?*, which has many illustrations and much more accessible bibliography (2020a).

Finally, I owe too much to too many to express my gratitude properly. I have been unusually fortunate with my parents, teachers, mentors, family, colleagues, friends, and students, as well as generous and often anonymous sponsors. I owe much to Bob Buller and his colleagues at SBL Press, who once again have helped me to reach a wider audience. Above all, I am grateful for a long life that allows me to offer this work in my ninetieth year.

Works Cited

Dever, William G. 2020a. *Has Archaeology Buried the Bible?* Eerdmans.

———. 2020b. *My Nine Lives: Sixty Years in Israeli and Biblical Archaeology*. SBL Press.
Freedman, David Noel, ed. 1992. *Anchor Bible Dictionary*. 6 vols. Doubleday.
Master, Daniel M., ed. 2013. *The Oxford Encyclopedia of the Bible and Archaeology*. Oxford University Press.
Mazar, Amihai. 1990. *Archaeology of the Land of the Bible, 10,000–586 BCE*. Doubleday.
Meyers, Eric M., ed. 1998. *The Oxford Encyclopedia of Archaeology in the Near East*. 5 vols. Oxford University Press.
Silberman, Neil Asher, ed. 2012. *The Oxford Companion to Archaeology*. 2nd ed. 3 vols. Oxford University Press.
Steiner, Margreet, and Ann E. Killebrew, eds. 2014. *The Oxford Handbook of the Archaeology of the Levant, c. 8000–332 BCE*. Oxford University Press.

1

Yigael Yadin: Prototypical Biblical Archaeologist

This brief essay was an attempt to pay tribute to Yigael Yadin in the volume of *Eretz-Israel* dedicated to him shortly after his death in 1984, to try to put him in context as the principal figure of classic Israeli-style biblical archaeology of the 1950s–1960s. Since then, the doyen and the last of a group of pioneer archaeologists, Binyamin Mazar, has died, as has a lesser but quietly glowing light, Nahman Avigad. The current ranking generation of younger Israeli archaeologists of the Hebrew University of Jerusalem, Tel Aviv University, Bar-Ilan University, and Haifa University, now in their fifties and sixties, seem largely to revolt against their teachers, Yadin and Yohanan Aharoni (this is less true of those in Jerusalem). This is parallel to third-generation Albrightians such as myself and other American Palestinian (or now "Levantine") archaeologists, who have felt constrained to establish themselves over against their teachers. Such generational conflicts—Thomas Kuhn's paradigm shifts—may be painful, but they are necessary if scholarship is to progress. Besides, they teach us humility, or should do so; we, too, shall pass, but not before, I hope, we have time to acknowledge some of our own obsolescence.

Three developments since Yadin's death indicate to me the rejection of his fundamental views by many younger Israeli scholars. (1) First is the overwhelming consensus that the earliest Israelites were largely displaced, indigenous Canaanites, not invaders from Transjordan, much less Egypt. Yadin's reconstruction of an Israelite conquest that could be dated circa 1200 BCE at Hazor has been completely overturned. (2) The Solomonic kingdom that Yadin so confidently reconstructed at Hazor, Megiddo, and Gezer has been severely questioned and even rejected, together with his understanding of its stratigraphic basis. I happen to be a staunch defender of Yadin on this point, but the challenge cannot be ignored. (3) Finally, the dialogue between archaeology and biblical studies, which Yadin (with Aharoni, Amihai Mazar,

Reprinted with permission from *ErIsr* 20 (1989): 44*–51*.

and many Americans) took for granted as fundamental, does not seem to be high on the agenda of the younger generation of Israeli archaeologists, despite the fact that they are the ones producing the critical new data on the Bronze and Iron Ages. Their failure to take seriously the full-scale attack on the conventional understanding of the history and religion of ancient Israel, mounted more than ten years ago by biblical "revisionists," is a case in point. Although superb in their own discipline and growing rapidly in socioanthropological sophistication, Israeli archaeologists, in my opinion, do not engage most of the mainstream issues in biblical studies, with the exception of topics such as the tenth–ninth century BCE and the question of the united monarchy. This, incidentally, was one of my major points in 1989, namely, that they are not, *pace* Cross and others, biblical archaeologists in anything like the American, European, or traditional Israeli sense, despite their necessary concern with the history (at least in a relatively narrow scope) of ancient Israel. I would argue that the Israeli notion that they identify "directly and emotionally" (so Stern 1987) with the land of the Bible and ancient Israel is naïve. It is also possibly even dangerous, given the onslaught of both Israeli and American fundamentalists, a sort of "secular fundamentalism," as one Israeli himself (Anson F. Rainey) had dubbed it. In short, I suggest that this essay is more on the mark today than when I wrote it in 1989.

More recent bibliography will be found in chapter 2 below. Note also the critique of Stager 2006.

As a small measure of my personal admiration for the late Professor Yigael Yadin, I shall argue that he was not only one of the fathers of the distinctive Israeli national school of archaeology but also the country's prototypical "biblical archaeologist." In that respect, he was Israel's W. F. Albright, and such a comparison is not only well deserved but will also enable us to measure Yadin's stature in several ways.

1.1. American Biblical Archaeology

In using the term *biblical archaeology* and the various concepts behind it, we need to remember that it has been hotly debated, not only recently (as some suppose), but from the very beginning of the enterprise in the late nineteenth century. Especially pertinent to our discussion here is the development of classic American-style biblical archaeology from the

1920s through the 1960s by Albright and his disciples—part of the intellectual background out of which I believe Yadin emerged. Elsewhere I have analyzed this school in some detail.[1] To facilitate the comparisons I wish to make here, it will be sufficient to reiterate that *American* biblical archaeology was characterized by several distinctive, even unique, elements. (1) It was rooted in late nineteenth–early twentieth-century American religious life, specifically in the acrimonious fundamentalist-modernist controversy and the traumatic issue of the historicity of the Bible that this controversy brought to the fore. (2) The movement was reactionary from the beginning. In popular circles, both liberal and conservative camps claimed that the archaeology of the day vindicated their theological positions vis-à-vis the Bible. The academic scene, however, came to be dominated by Christian, Protestant Old Testament scholars, mostly of conservative or middle-of-the-road bent, but decidedly not fundamentalists. (3) The leaders of the school were almost exclusively clerics, and the pivotal issues in the debate were not so much archaeological as historical and theological.

It was Albright himself, of course, who was the mentor, if not the creator, of the distinctive American biblical archaeological school. And the issues upon which he focused—especially the historicity of the patriarchs and the Israelite conquest under Joshua—formed the battle lines for two generations. Into the same mold would have fit most other American archaeologists who specialized in Palestine (i.e., the Holy Land), such as James B. Pritchard, Nelson Glueck, G. Ernest Wright, Paul W. Lapp, James A. Callaway, Edward F. Campbell, Lawrence E. Toombs, Albert E. Glock, and others—in addition to almost the entire younger generation that grew out of the Shechem, Taʿanach, Gezer, and other representative projects (the present writer included). From at least the 1940s through the late 1960s, the parallel secular stream of American Palestinian archaeology seemed but a minor tributary. Now, of course, all of that has changed with the passing of the era of classic biblical archaeology and the ascendency of the New Archaeology in America in the 1970s and 1980s. But without an appreciation of its *theological* roots and background, American Palestinian archaeology remains incomprehensible, as several belated forays into the

---

1. See Dever 1985, with references there to several other treatments; see also Dever 1992.

discussion of biblical archaeology by both American and Israeli commentators have demonstrated.²

1.2. Some Thoughts on Israeli Biblical Archaeology

But is any of this relevant in attempting to assess the role and contribution of Yigael Yadin to our branch of archaeology? I believe that it is, if for no other reason than the fact that it is helpful to portray Yadin *by contrast* against this background. Yadin was, by his own or any other definition, a biblical archaeologist and certainly proud of it. But confusion results when it is assumed, as it usually is, that the definition of this term is self-evident or that American and Israeli biblical archaeology are identical. Since there has been virtually no discussion of these issues in the literature, I shall address them with a boldness of which I think Yadin would have approved.

Let us begin with a brief (and thus somewhat simplistic) résumé of the development of the Israeli school.³ It is much younger, of course. It has roots in the early work of Jewish archaeologists during the British Mandate, such as Yadin's own father, Eliezer Sukenik, and many others (including some of Israel's senior archaeologists, still active). As a national school it really emerged only after Yadin's own epochal project at Hazor in 1955–1958, and the school has matured only in the last decade or so. Here we face a severe handicap in our analysis. Due to its relative youth, and perhaps also its overwhelmingly pragmatic nature, Israeli archaeology has not yet rendered a comprehensive account of itself.⁴ The current

---

2. On the Israeli side, see the interview with Amihai Mazar in Shanks 1984b and with Yigal Shiloh in Shanks 1988; and add Stern 1987. Mazar and Stern dismiss the biblical archaeology controversy as an American problem, one they confess they do not understand, while Shiloh is more sympathetic but still retains the term. It is instructive to compare essays by Americans in Perdue, Toombs, and Johnson 1987, especially those by D. Glenn Rose and Lawrence E. Toombs, to see how far the discussion has progressed in America.

3. I have attempted fuller analyses in the works cited in n. 1 above, as well as in Dever 1980 and especially Dever 1989.

4. Virtually the only treatments of the development, methods, and aims of Israeli archaeology, *by Israelis*, are those cited in n. 2 above, supplemented by Ussishkin 1982; Bar-Yosef and Mazar 1982. Add now the perceptive and provocative paper of Magen Broshi 1987.

generation is understandably the first to demonstrate either the interest or the perspective requisite to such a reflective task, so we are deprived of the unique perspective of pioneers such as Yadin. We must therefore extrapolate from the record in order to discover what made the first generation or two "tick," presumptuous though this may be.

It seems evident in retrospect that Israeli archaeology, with Yadin himself in the forefront, has gone through a number of discernible stages in its growth. Without going into detail, one might sketch them as follows. (1) First was the period of stock-taking and consolidation immediately after the State was established in 1948, that is, founding a new Department of Antiquities and Museums, inventorying sites, and undertaking considerable salvage work in the wake of modern development. (2) Then in the 1950s there was the inauguration of new publication series, the fostering of the academic programs (initially only at the Hebrew University of Jerusalem but later elsewhere), and the production of the first generation of indigenous Israeli archaeologists—all the necessary foundation for sustaining the new school. (3) Also in the 1950s, extending through the 1960s, there came the first large cooperative projects such as Hazor, well organized and funded, often with international participation. These not only trained professional staff and built up popular support locally but also experimented deliberately with improved methodology. (4) Beginning in the 1960s, there was a period of rapid proliferation in fieldwork as well as in research and publication, with numerous and varied projects now in evidence. At the same time, growth resulted in rivalry, and thus new institutes were founded like that at Tel Aviv University (and later in Beersheva and Haifa). (5) Already in the 1960s, and certainly by the early 1970s, Israeli archaeology had attained international prominence. This attracted many foreign and so-called joint projects, but it also inevitably pointed up the growing dominance of the Israeli school. (6) By the late 1970s, the impetus had shifted entirely, one result being that *Israeli* archaeologists, not Americans or Europeans, now suddenly bore the burden of being the leading exponents of biblical archaeology. I say suddenly because I believe that this development was not planned or even anticipated. It was thrust upon the generation of men such as Yadin and Binyamin Mazar, who had always taken biblical archaeology for granted. Indeed, they had played a vital role in and had produced a good deal of fundamental data of the biblical archaeology movement. But they had never felt any compulsion to articulate, much less to defend, the basic conception and methodology of biblical archaeology, and this left them vulnerable to change.

Several factors had apparently been at work, all culminating in the early 1980s. (1) The death of the older-style biblical archaeology in America; it had been moribund for a decade, but the definitive obituaries had been written only recently. More importantly, the postmortems were only now coming to the attention of the Israeli archaeologists, who all throughout the 1970s, when the controversy over biblical archaeology was at its peak, ignored it or dismissed it as an American preoccupation.[5] Thus, even though aspects of the New Archaeology that was replacing biblical archaeology in America were adopted more or less readily by Israelis, they either did not appreciate or were not concerned with the *theoretical* challenge posed by the newer approach. More than any other single factor, this challenge brought about the demise of classical biblical archaeology by undermining its already-weakened historical and theological foundations. Yet the devastating impact of the secular revolution, as we may properly term it, was almost entirely lost on Israeli archaeologists. Why? I would argue that this was because Israeli archaeology, despite its appropriation of the language and style of American biblical archaeology, had really been exclusively secular in approach all along (see further below).

(2) The second factor in bringing about an identity crisis in Israeli biblical archaeology was admittedly less academic than it was pragmatic and political. The issue on the surface appeared to be simply the preferred term for our discipline, but there were obviously much more substantial issues having to do with the fundamental conception of the field itself. The term biblical archaeology had traditionally been used by Israelis as virtually synonymous with Palestinian archaeology—a kind of shorthand, especially in popular usage, or when speaking to audiences abroad. But the terms regularly used in *scholarly* publications in English were Palestine and archaeology of Palestine. And in Hebrew the accepted designation of the discipline had always been "the archaeology of Eretz-Israel" (a *very* significant difference, making the geographical area, not the Bible, the point of reference).[6] Even when this writer and other Americans began to favor

---

5. See nn. 2 an 4 above.

6. The translation of "biblical archaeology" into Hebrew as *arkeologia miqrait* is also common but usually denotes simply the archaeology of the First Temple period. For the continued use of *Palestine* over *Eretz-Israel*, despite the awkward-

Palestinian archaeology over biblical archaeology more deliberately, beginning in the early 1970s, there were few misgivings among Israelis. But after 1973, Israel's involvement in the modern Palestinian problem rendered the term *Palestinian* archaeology more and more problematical. In 1981, the Syrians sponsored a would-be international symposium on "Palestinian archaeology" in Aleppo, with offers of travel grants to archaeologists all over the world—ostensibly a straight-forward academic congress but (as is now known) subsidized by funds from the PLO. This was followed by other surveys of the Middle Eastern archaeological scene in which Arab scholars seemed either to ignore Israeli archaeology altogether or, worse still, to co-opt it as simply a subbranch of Levantine archaeology.[7] Biblical archaeology as Israel's unique cultural heritage seemed threatened to some.

Then in the spring of 1982, unfortunate timing saw a well-intentioned but doomed proposal for an international textbook on "Syro-Palestinian archaeology," at the very time of the Israeli intervention in Lebanon in direct confrontation with the Syrians and Palestinians. The tensions were reflected in the Annual Archaeological Conference that year, as well as in heated conversations of the writer with Yadin, Mazar, and others during his sabbatical in Israel. One outcome of all this was reflected in the planning of the First International Congress on Biblical Archaeology, held later in Jerusalem, in April 1984. Neither the conception nor the title was coincidental, as was later admitted by more than one Israeli observer.[8] Yadin was one of the guiding sprits behind this somewhat reactionary attempt to showcase Israeli archaeology as biblical archaeology. And his keynote address is most revealing—especially since it turned out to be the only public statement Yadin was to make on a topic that had clearly been growing in urgency in his thinking.[9]

---

ness, see Mazar 1987, 33 n. 1, where he explains that "Palestine" is used as the point of reference, citing the consistent usage of the *Israel Exploration Journal*.

7. See, for example, the treatment of Masry 1982 and the inclusion of Israeli archaeology in this issue of *World Archaeology* only as a separate entry (Bar-Yosef and Mazar 1982).

8. This was common knowledge and was constantly in the background of the sessions; it is correctly reflected even in the account in the popular magazine (Shanks 1984a). See also specifically Stern's remarks at 1987, 35.

9. See the printed version, Yadin 1985. The other opening speakers were Frank M. Cross and Binyamin Mazar; no younger archaeologists or American archaeologists at all were included, nor was any discussion allowed.

Yadin's characteristic fervor in his defense of biblical archaeology comes through even in cold type and is admirable, but closer examination reveals little substantive argument. He retains the term and even applies it to the whole archaeological history of Israel, partly just because others are rejecting it out of what he feels are political motivations or simple revisionist views. He does not define biblical archaeology, however, in either content or method, beyond the obvious (i.e., the scope being all of Israel, in all periods, as the "Land of the Bible"; the need for interdisciplinary methods, including the analysis of biblical and other texts; etc.). Yadin's principal objection seems to be directed against the concept of *Syro-Palestinian archaeology*, introduced by Albright and recently revived by this writer and others, as an overarching rubric for the field. He argues, rather, for the historical connection of Palestine with Egypt. This point is, of course, well taken, but underlying the discussion is clearly the fear that ancient Israel may come to be comprehended simply as a southern province of Syria, and thus the archaeology of modern Israel simply subsumed under the archaeology of the Levant. (This fear is groundless, I believe, but it has become a factor in the minds of others as well.)[10] In short, Yadin's offhand and somewhat polemical remarks are tantalizing, but they fail to reveal either the logical force or the subtlety with which he alludes here. Meanwhile, younger students of Yadin, such as Yigal Shiloh, Ephraim Stern, and Amihai Mazar, had taken up his belated defenses of biblical archaeology in a rather desultory way. But it is evident, as we shall see, that the fashion in which these and other younger Israelis actually *do* their fieldwork and research is a far cry from the old style of biblical archaeology, either American or Israeli. And Yadin's own case study of the Israelite "conquest" as a triumph of biblical archaeology's methodology is the best example of how newer and more powerful explanatory paradigms have prevailed (below).

1.3. A Comparison of Two Approaches to Biblical Archaeology

We must now undertake a more precise distinction between the *two* biblical archaeologies, not least of all to evaluate properly the role of Yadin

---

10. See not only Yadin's specific remarks (1985, 26) but Stern 1987, 35.

and his generation. The Americans, up to (and even including) the present generation, had almost all been clerics and professors of religion; none of the Israeli archaeologist had been, nor would a rabbi-archaeologist have been conceivable. In America, Palestinian archaeology was taught almost entirely in seminaries or in programs in religious studies, and even when occasionally in an ancient Near Eastern department the theological connection was presumed; in Israeli universities, the strict separation of such academic programs is the rule. Until the 1970s, most American projects were supported with funds from religious sources, and such is still often the case; in Israel, the religious establishment is notorious for its adamant and often violent opposition to archaeology. Finally, American Palestinian archaeology until fairly recently has been narrowly concerned with the biblical period (especially the Old Testament or First Temple period), with clearly identifiable biblical sites and with specific events described in the biblical texts, and with problems growing largely out of difficulties in theological interpretation of the Bible (the old, unresolved "faith and history" issue). Israeli archaeology, despite critics in some quarters, has always been *much* less parochial (!) in outlook and overwhelmingly secular in outlook (below).

In spite of obvious differences, it is often asserted (even by Israelis themselves) that the Israelis are biblical archaeologists precisely in the American sense.[11] Furthermore, some think that their continuing prowess (and, finally, their vocal approval) validate traditional American-style biblical archaeology. No less a scholar than Frank Cross has advanced such an argument. That is, the Bible is fundamental in the archaeology of Israel, and to their credit, the Israelis, unlike many younger American spokesmen for the New Archaeology, who have ceased to be humanists and have become mere technicians, recognize this.[12] That simply misses the point: it is not a question of *whether* to use the Bible but *how*. The issue is not biblical archaeology and in what relationship it stands to the larger discipline of Palestinian (or Syro-Palestinian) archaeology.

Another point of confusion exists, but it may be dismissed as mere semantics, namely, the debate over the term biblical archaeology itself. Again, it is not a question of using the term or not using it, but *how*—both

---

11. See, for example, the treatments cited in nn. 2 and 4 above.
12. See his address before the congress discussed (Cross 1985, 9–15). See also Cross's earlier response, specifically to my views, in Cross 1973.

the content and the intent. *Whose* Bible—Christian, Jewish, secularist, or other? Where is the *New* Testament? And how does using *biblical* as an adjective modify our understanding (and promotion) of archaeology? That brings us to what may be the most crucial distinction between American and Israeli usage. In America, as we have seen, *biblical* has an inevitable theological connotation, in popular circles no doubt something of an advantage, given the quasi-religious climate of the culture, but in academic and professional circles it is a barrier to acceptance. This is a point that Israelis may find rather difficult to grasp,[13] for in Israel the term biblical carries few if any of the negative overtones that it may have elsewhere. In Israel the Bible is universally accepted simply as the *founding document of the nation's history*. Therefore, the *use* made of the Bible by Israeli archaeologists is not confessional but secular, in the sense that the objectives of research are historical rather than theological. It is sometimes overlooked that nearly all Israeli archaeologists are nonreligious, some of them outspokenly so, and their audience is overwhelmingly secular. As Ephraim Stern has recently said, in one of the few published statements on Israeli-style biblical archaeology, "our ties with Bible are direct and emotional."[14] His further remarks, as well as the similar observations of Amihai Mazar, underline the point that in Israel the identification with the Bible is fundamental, but it is intuitive rather than formal, a matter of ethnic national consciousness rather than religious commitment. Such a stance does not, of course, make the Israeli biblical archaeologist necessarily any more "objective" than an American counterpart who may be more religiously motivated. The Israeli may, in fact, have an even more powerful emotional commitment: an existential involvement with the Bible and the land that few non-Israelis will likely experience. Of course, both Jews and Christians, as well as many others, also tend to share such sentiments: few would claim to be neutral about the Bible and the Holy Land—one of the peculiar difficulties of our branch of archaeology. But these subjective feelings must be kept under rigid control if archaeology aspires to be anything like a true science. Certainly emotional appeals are neither sufficient motivation or justification for biblical archaeology as an academic enterprise, much less for its bid to dominate this branch of archaeology as a whole.

---

13. See the references in nn. 2 and 4 above.
14. Stern 1987, 35; see also Mazar in Shanks 1984b, 60–61. But cf. the more astute and pertinent observations of Broshi 1987, 26–30.

1.4. Yigael Yadin as the Prototypical Israeli Biblical Archaeologist

We are now in a position to evaluate the role of Yadin himself in the development of both biblical and Palestinian archaeology.

1. Yadin's background and training fitted him superbly for biblical archaeology. He grew up in Palestine as the son of a distinguished archaeologist of the *yishuv*, steeped in the intense nationalism of the period, the ideology of which was based in large part on the notions of the Bible and the return of the Land. This was also the classic era of biblical archaeology, and Yadin as an archaeological student in the 1940s and 1950s no doubt came under the influence of Albright, whom he later claimed as his mentor. In that regard, he absorbed biblical archaeology as a natural part of his environment. Yet it is clear from his writings that Yadin was oblivious to the *theological* controversies that grew out of this movement somewhat later, in America and Europe in the 1950s–1960s, particularly under the influence of protégés of Albright such as G. Ernest Wright.[15] In that sense, he was prototypical, that is, in the classic mold of Albright, and if his last remarks hearken back to the early days of the movement rather than pointing the way toward the future, that was perhaps inevitable.

2. By temperament and talent and breadth of interests, Yadin was uniquely representative among Israeli scholars of biblical archaeology. Without detracting in any way from Yadin's distinctive individual genius or his celebrated personal flair, we may point out that his career paralleled that of Albright in many ways. He coupled artifactual studies with detailed textual analyses, devoting almost disproportionate energies to authoritative publications of the Dead Sea Scrolls and other ancient documents. Yadin also consistently saw the land of the Bible in the broadest ancient Near Eastern context, as his many stimulating historical and cross-cultural papers amply demonstrate. Finally, he focused again and again on some of the same basic problems of biblical archaeology that exercised Albright and his followers, notably the Israelite conquest and settlement, and the era of the monarchy. Even projects such as the caves in the Judean wilderness and Masada were related to the biblical period, albeit late (what others might term New Testament archaeology or, perhaps better, the archaeology of late antiquity). In all this Yadin was a brilliant and innovative leader, again the prototype.

---

15. See Dever 1985, 53–59.

3. Finally, Yadin's spirited defense of biblical archaeology, although it was rather reactionary and came after the movement had waned, entitles him to the role of senior Israeli spokesman for the cause. In this, as in so many other things, it is true that he may have no successors, but that is a tribute to the fact that, like Albright, he was sui generis.

With all due respect to Yigael Yadin's towering stature in the field and his final heroic efforts to reshape Israeli archaeology in the classical mold, there are several cautions to be drawn from his commitment to biblical archaeology. First, reactionary movements are by nature short-lived, because the trends against which they define themselves soon change, leaving them without sufficient rationale. In the case of the newer archaeology that Yadin resisted, it has become so well accepted that it is already beginning to be dismissed as the old archaeology. Even the debate about terminology (i.e., biblical archaeology or Palestinian archaeology) is somewhat passé. And Yadin's parade example of archaeology's ability to confirm the historicity of biblical texts—his confident reconstruction of a military conquest of Canaan under Joshua—has been completely overturned by his younger pupils and colleagues. Today newer evidence and theories not only call into question the conquest model of Yadin (and Albright) but seriously undermine one of the very foundations of the biblical archaeology movement. This challenge is likely to become even more acute as it dawns on more and more biblical scholars that the current generation of archaeologists, working with socioanthropological theories and vastly more varied and sophisticated archaeological data, is radically rewriting the early history of Israel. This time, however, I would hazard the guess that archaeology may take precedence over the biblical texts.[16]

Second, the Bible is indeed an indispensable tool for the archaeologist specializing in Iron Age (and even Bronze Age) Israel, as Yadin staunchly maintained. But it is tempting to be hasty and simplistic in seizing upon a biblical text to explain an archaeological find. At worst, this results in a tautology, and even at best the argument usually remains unconvincing. As a single example, until recently the Solomonic date of the Gezer fortifications, advanced by both Yadin and the writer, seemed obvious, and indeed

---

16. Yadin's views will be found in many places, but see, for example, Yadin 1979. But papers in the other sessions of this same congress overwhelmingly *reject* this model. The most recent current treatment, with full references to recent literature, is Finkelstein 1988.

firmly established by the reference in 1 Kgs 9:15–17. But today this correlation is coming under determined attack, mostly from younger Israeli archaeologists who reject Yadin's premises concerning archaeology's relation to biblical texts and even suggest that this writer (!) had succumbed to the methodological weaknesses of biblical archaeology.[17]

It is important for all of us to remember that the Hebrew Bible is simply not history in the modern sense. Neither is it an ancient *Baedeker* that the pilgrim or scholar can take as a reliable guide in re-creating the original biblical landscape. There is simply no way to avoid confronting the Bible critically, that is, with all the tools of modern interdisciplinary and comparative scholarship. For today's highly specialized and compartmentalized archaeologist, the task probably entails collaboration with experts in biblical (and other textual) studies. Again, Yadin, with his broad command of the ancient texts, was prototypical, but his successors will almost certainly have to resort to greater teamwork. Yet one of the most conspicuous weaknesses in our branch of archaeology today, both in Israel and America, remains the *lack of integration* between Palestinian archaeology and biblical studies. To their everlasting credit, Yadin and the biblical archaeologists firmly insisted on the integral relationship of artifactual and textual studies.

Before the Bible can be properly utilized as a source of history, however, or even as a commentary on material culture remains, the cautions set forth above must be reinforced. The typical noncritical use of the Bible as an ally to archaeology in Israel (and in America) all too easily disregards the fact that this is radically *theocratic* history. Thus one falls into the trap of a kind of secular fundamentalism—a literalistic and mechanical way of reading the texts, as though simply through the eyes of the ancient writers, at face value, as it were. It is either naïve or disingenuous, however, to suppose that: (1) the texts were written or originally used by synagogue and church with our kind of history in mind; or (2) that we can approach the ancient texts directly without being biased by modern interpretations (or, for that matter, apart from modern theological controversies, whether we are interested in them or not).

---

17. See the 1990 issue of *BASOR* that includes articles by G. J. Wightman, David Ussishkin, and Israel Finkelstein, with responses from John S. Holladay, Lawrence E. Stager, and William G. Dever.

The principal challenge of biblical archaeology all along was to avoid the dangers of Biblicism, and if Biblicism comes to be coupled with a certain brand of archaeology, and the whole is then imbued with nationalism, the danger is compounded. Yadin saw the danger, and so do most Israelis who are fascinated by archaeology today. The pressures of the modern political situation, however, may tempt the abuse of the Bible, and of archaeology—ironically, not just by religious extremists, but perhaps even more so by well-intentioned secularists.

1.5. Conclusion

In retrospect, one cannot help but think that Yigael Yadin's last attempt to retain certain aspects of the conception and terminology of biblical archaeology were due to the traditional and convenient usage of the term itself, as well as to a somewhat sentimental attachment to the Bible that many share. Also at work, I think, was a nostalgia for a simpler time, when Middle Eastern archaeology was less politicized, and a certain apprehension for the future of Israeli archaeology in particular. Yet the strength of Israeli archaeology has always been its secular and indigenous nature. It has remained free from entanglements with the sterile theological debates of American and Europe and more recently free from the perilous religious situation in Israel. It has developed its own distinctive and appropriate aim, namely, the reconstruction of the whole history of the Land of Israel, not merely of the biblical period and its literature.

Israeli archaeology today is vigorous, restive, thrusting out dramatically in all directions. It is truly coming of age. It would be tragic if some sought to perpetuate a concept and terminology that are borrowed, anachronistic, inaccurate, needlessly polemical, restrictive. If Yigael Yadin was indeed a prototypical figure, he was also the authentic precursor of a *new* style of the Israeli archaeology, biblical and other, for in any case the next generation will build on the foundations he laid. Let him, then, be remembered for his vision and his courage.[18]

---

18. I myself have recently called for a new style of biblical archaeology, i.e., of *relating* the newer scientific and interdisciplinary Palestinian archaeology and its socioanthropological models to current trends in biblical studies. However, much

Works Cited

Bar-Yosef, Ofer, and Amihai Mazar. 1982. "Israeli Archaeology." *World Archaeology* 13:310–25.
Broshi, Magen. 1987. "Religion, Ideology, and Politics and Their Impact on Palestinian Archaeology." *Israel Museum Journal* 6:17–32.
Cross, Frank Moore. 1973. "W. F. Albright's View of Biblical Archaeology." *BA* 36:2–5.
———. 1985. "Biblical Archaeology Today: The Biblical Aspect." Pages 9–15 in *Biblical Archaeology Today: Proceedings of the International Congress on Biblical Archaeology, Jerusalem, April 1984*. Edited by Janet Amitai. Israel Exploration Society.
Dever, William G. 1980. "Archaeology in Israel: A Continuing Revolution." *BA* 43:41–48.
———. 1985. "Syro-Palestinian and Biblical Archaeology." Pages 31–74 in *The Hebrew Bible and Its Modern Interpreters*. Edited by Douglas A. Knight and Gene M. Tucker. BMI 1. Scholars Press.
———. 1989. "Archaeology in Israel Today: A Summation and Critique." Pages 143–52 in *Recent Excavations in Israel: Studies in Iron Age Chronology*. Edited by Seymour Gitin and William G. Dever. American Schools of Oriental Research.
———. 1990. "Of Myths and Methods." *BASOR* 277–278:121–30.
———. 1992. "Archaeology, Syro-Palestinian and Biblical." *ABD* 1:354–67.
Finkelstein, Israel. 1988. *The Archaeology of the Israelite Settlement*. Israel Exploration Society.
———. 1990. "On Archaeological Methods and Historical Considerations: Iron Age II Gezer and Samaria." *BASOR* 277–278:109–19.
Glock, Albert E. 1985. "Tradition and Change in Two Archaeologies." *American Antiquity* 50:464–77.
Holladay, John S., Jr. 1990. "Red Slip, Burnish, and the Solomonic Gateway at Gezer." *BASOR* 277–278:23–70.
Masry, Abdullah H. 1982. "Traditions of Archeological Research in the Near East." *World Archaeology* 13:222–39.
Mazar, Amihai. 1990. *Archaeology of the Land of the Bible, 10,000–586 B.C.E.* ABRL. Doubleday.

---

groundwork is necessary before that relation can be redefined, as it must be. See, provisionally, the comments of Glock 1985; Rose 1987.

Perdue, Leo G., Lawrence E. Toombs, and Gary L. Johnson, eds. 1987. *Archaeology and Biblical Interpretation: Essays in Memory of D. Glenn Rose*. John Knox.

Rose, D. Glenn. 1987. "The Bible and Archaeology: The State of the Art." Pages 53-64 in *Archaeology and Biblical Interpretation: Essays in Memory of D. Glenn Rose*. Edited by Leo G. Perdue, Lawrence E. Toombs, and Gary L. Johnson. John Knox.

Shanks, Hershel. 1984a. "Jerusalem Rolls Out Red Carpet for Biblical Archaeology Congress." *BAR* 10.4:12-18.

———. 1984b. "A New Generation of Israeli Archaeologists Comes of Age." *BAR* 10.3:46-48, 54-61.

———. 1988. "Yigal Shiloh—Last Thoughts, Part II." *BAR* 14.3:38-46.

Stager, Lawrence E. 1990. "Shemer's Estate." *BASOR* 277-278:93-107.

———. 2006. "Yigael Yadin and Biblical Archaeology." Pages 13-27 in *In Memory of Yigael Yadin, 1917-1984: Lectures Presented at the Symposium on the Twentieth Anniversary of His Death*. Edited by Joseph Aviram. Israel Exploration Society.

Stern, Ephraim. 1987. "The Bible and Israeli Archaeology." Pages 31-40 in *Archaeology and Biblical Interpretation: Essays in Memory of D. Glenn Rose*. Edited by Leo G. Perdue, Lawrence E. Toombs, and Gary L. Johnson. John Knox.

Toombs, Lawrence E. "A Perspective on the New Archaeology." Pages 41-52 in *Archaeology and Biblical Interpretation: Essays in Memory of D. Glenn Rose*. Edited by Leo G. Perdue, Lawrence E. Toombs, and Gary L. Johnson. John Knox.

Ussishkin, David. 1982. "Where Is Israeli Archaeology Going?" *BA* 45:310-25.

———. 1990. "Notes on Megiddo, Gezer, Ashdod, and Tel Batash in the Tenth to Ninth Centuries B.C." *BASOR* 277-278:71-91.

Wightman, G. J. 1990. "The Myth of Solomon." *BASOR* 277-278:5-22.

Yadin, Yigael. 1979. "The Transition from a Semi-nomadic to a Sedentary Society in the Twelfth Century B.C.E." Pages 57-68 in *Symposia Celebrating the Seventy-Fifth Anniversary of the Founding of the American Schools of Oriental Research (1900-1975)*. Edited by Frank Moore Cross. American Schools of Oriental Research.

———. 1985. Biblical Archaeology Today: The Archaeological Aspect. Pages 21-27 in *Biblical Archaeology Today: Proceedings of the International Congress on Biblical Archaeology, Jerusalem, April 1984*. Edited by Janet Amitai. Israel Exploration Society.

2

Biblical Archaeology: Death and Rebirth?

The theme of this essay—the possibility of a "new" biblical archaeology—grew out of developments following my initial attack on traditional Albright-Wright style biblical archaeology in the 1970s. My *Archaeology and Bible Studies: Retrospects and Prospects* (1974) was a revolution. It met with a counterrevolution in the early 1980s, aired in an issue of *The Biblical Archaeologist*. The issue was now clear: the old, positivist biblical archaeology was not sustainable. I wrote a full obituary in 1985. What would take its place?

Meanwhile, I had discovered Ian Hodder's 1986 *Reading the Past: Current Approaches to Interpretation in Archaeology,* which was also a revolution, against the processualist New Archaeology and advocating a postprocessual approach. While my approach was not actually radical—all about a better dialogue with biblical studies—I now explored a way of reconciliation. Thus, building on the First International Congress on Biblical Archaeology in Jerusalem in 1990, where Yadin's plenary address castigated my views, I determined that I would propose a "rebirth" of biblical archaeology. Published in 1993, that was this paper.

Shlomo Bunimovitz and several others applauded my effort, the former noting that it indicated a new phase that was "both timely and attractive" (1995). But there the discussion remained. Pragmatic as always, old and new American and Israeli biblical archaeologists went on with business as usual. Some aspects of the reactionary "cognitive archaeology" in the general field of world archaeology were appealing, but they were never followed up.

Developments from about 1995 on are outlined in Dever 2003a. Bibliography from circa 1980 on brings the discussion up to date. It is now clear

---

Originally published as pages 706–22 in *Biblical Archaeology Today, 1990: Proceedings at the Second International Congress on Biblical Archaeology, Jerusalem, June 1990.* Edited by Avraham Biran and Janet Amitai. Israel Exploration Society, 1993. Reprinted by permission.

that, as in general in archaeology today, pragmatism has won out over any particular ideological theory (see Pruecel and Mrozowski 2010; Levy 2010). Yet evangelicals, now more active than ever, may explore prospects for their own "new archaeology."

For bibliography since about 1985, when this article was first conceived, see the Updated Bibliography (arranged chronologically) at the end of the Works Cited.

For much of its first one hundred years, Syro-Palestinian archaeology was dominated by biblical interests, but as we celebrate its centennial it should finally be clear that biblical archaeology of the traditional style is dead. In the opening session of the First International Congress six years ago, some of us here were accused of killing biblical archaeology. I'm flattered, but in truth we simply observed the passing of the movement in the early 1970s and wrote its obituary by about 1980.

2.1. A Brief Inquest into the Death of Biblical Archaeology

The older biblical archaeology met its demise as a significant force because of many deficiencies: its amateur status and unprofessional standards of fieldwork and excavation; its theological naïveté; its parochial research interests; its inability to compete for secular funding; its reactionary character and failure to meet the challenge of newer interdisciplinary approaches and the rise of national schools in the Middle East. These weaknesses would ultimately have been fatal anyway, but the death blow finally came when the movement was unable to achieve the major objective of its agenda.[1]

As set forth, for instance, by its founding father, W. F. Albright, this objective was the establishment of the essential historicity of the biblical narratives, particularly those of the patriarchal and conquest eras. The Albrightian synthesis in both cases, however, has been almost completely dismantled. By the late 1970s, archaeological proofs of the patriarchal age were passé, and during the 1980s Israeli archaeologists and others demonstrated conclusively that there was no overwhelming military conquest

---

1. On the passing of biblical archaeology, see Dever 1985.

and that the early Israelites were largely indigenous Canaanites.² In religion, another area of Albright's concern, archaeology in recent years has shown that Israel's cult was not unique, was anything but monotheistic, and was indeed syncretistic from start to finish.³ As though that were not revolutionary enough, in the last few years even the archaeological documentation of the Solomonic era—one of biblical archaeology's proudest achievements—has come under sustained attack. A number of Israeli archaeologists now maintain that the tenth-century BCE city walls and gates at Hazor, Megiddo, and Gezer, apparently confirming 1 Kgs 9:15–17, must all be moved down to the ninth century BCE. Such a radical redating of the basic stratigraphy of Palestinian archaeology would leave us with almost no monumental remains of the united monarchy. Here I find myself in the paradoxical position of defending at least this position of biblical archaeology against "young Turks" who are apparently determined to bring down its last bastions.⁴

Where do we go from here? The old style of relating archaeology and biblical studies, using both as prooftexts for historical and theological propositions, is no longer possible or desirable. In that sense, then, we must conclude that the New Archaeology has triumphed. But I shall argue that there are current trends in general archaeology that provide us with an unprecedented opportunity for developing, rather, a new style of biblical archaeology (although I shall suggest another term for the enterprise).

2.2. Toward a Dialogue between Many Disciplines

Let me begin by reminding us all of what is often overlooked, namely, that the call twenty years ago for the separation of Syro-Palestinian archaeology from biblical studies, and the concomitant professionalization and secularization of the former, was largely for the purposes of inaugurating

---

2. See Dever 1977; Finkelstein 1988.

3. On archaeology and the Israelite cult, see most recently Dever 1987, 1989; Holladay 1987.

4. See the entire issue of *BASOR* 277–278 (1990), with articles defending a Solomonic date for Gezer's defenses by Dever, Holladay, and Stager and opposing that date by Finkelstein, Ussishkin, and Wightman. For the issues, see especially Dever 1990.

a new, more productive dialogue between two disciplines, each with its own methods, objectives, and integrity. It was never my intention, as some critics maintained, to sever Syro-Palestinian archaeology from literary sources, biblical or other, that is, from history and history writing. In the 1970s it was necessary, however, to clear the ground of such accumulated rubbish before the foundations for a new structure could be laid over the ruins of the old. Unfortunately, because of the emotional overreaction of scholars in both disciplines, clearing the ground took nearly twenty years, during which time much energy was wasted on semantic arguments over the name of our discipline and on sterile controversies about theory and method where both were misunderstood. I confess that my own youthful rhetoric, like that of many of today's "newer archaeologists," may have been too strident. We also became enamoured of technical advances in archaeology for their own sake and got bogged down in a morass of data often collected with no notion of what we were trying to learn. All of us tended to lose sight of the goal: to use both texts and artifacts, in a larger environmental and sociocultural context, in order to understand, if possible, how it was in the human past and in the biblical world. Today I want to redefine and reemphasize that goal in the light of what has happened to archaeology, particularly in the last few years. I also hope to show that, rather than returning to unilateral approaches, we shall have to be more interdisciplinary than ever in this quest. In that sense, we do not reject the New Archaeology but build upon it.[5]

2.3. Entering the Postprocessualist Era

One of the most exciting and promising recent trends in archaeology has been the effort of many to move beyond the New Archaeology of the 1970s and 1980s, to what is being called postprocessual or contextual archaeology. This movement is associated particularly with Ian Hodder of Cambridge, who has set forth the principles in several works, especially *Reading the Past: Current Approaches to Interpretation in Archaeology* (1986).[6]

---

5. For and early plea for dialogue, see Dever 1974 The terms and concept of a new biblical archaeology were introduced in Dever 1989b.

6. See Hodder 1986.

Postprocessual or contextual archaeology is characterized by several trends, which I would define as follows: (1) a disenchantment with elegant theory per se, especially with the borrowing of positivist philosophies of science and notions of testing "universal laws" of cultural change (thus Hodder's "postprocessualist," below); (2) a return to more traditional data-based inquiries into the past and to models drawn from material culture itself rather than from other disciplines; (3) a revival of interest in chronology and history writing, indeed what I would call an ambitious new *Kulturgeschichte*; (4) an ecological thrust that stresses context in its broadest sense, factoring into the study of change not only the natural environment but also society and culture; (5) a rejection of determinist and materialist paradigms and a reassessment of the role of symbol, of ideology, even of religion, in the shaping of society, that is, an unabashedly idealist approach; and (6) a reaffirmation of the place of archaeology's study of culture in modern social consciousness: archaeology as neither antiquarianism nor rhetoric but as moral value in an endangered world.

In summary, postprocessual or contextual archaeology now bids fair to replace the New Archaeology as an overall paradigm. It would be folly, however, to dismiss this approach as the latest fad. The newer archaeology represents, rather, a critical balance of the best of the old and new in archaeological theory and method. Its advent is a sign that archaeology has truly come of age as a discipline, and I would argue that contextual archaeology is likely to guide the growth of the field well into the next generation. Ironically, the New Archaeology is already obsolete at the very moment when our branch of archaeology is finally about to adopt it as the latest word! We confront the sad spectacle of one discipline belatedly borrowing another's outmoded methodology in a superficial effort at interdisciplinary inquiry. Let us stop facing resolutely backward into the future and move truly ahead—in this case, as I shall show, to a bright future.

2.4. Toward a New Style of Correlating Artifactual and Textual Approaches to History Writing

The trends I have just sketched are clearly more congenial to many of us than were the more extreme and controversial aspects of the New Archaeology of the past two decades.[7] Lest we congratulate ourselves, however, on successfully resisting a generation of secular heresy and rejoice in the triumph of orthodoxy, I point out that, unless we actually participated in the growing pains of the New Archaeology, we missed a vital opportunity to see the discipline and ourselves mature. A further caveat: postprocessual or contextual archaeology (henceforth I shall follow Hodder's term, contextual archaeology) will likely be truly revolutionary for biblical studies. Ultimately, of course, it must augur well for us, but how?

First, the newest archaeology calls for archaeologists to take a fresh look at the potential of the biblical texts as historical sources. There are problems, of course. I think it is axiomatic now, both in archaeological and biblical circles, that the literary tradition in the Hebrew Bible as we now have it is much later than the events it purports to describe, that it is idealist and elitist in the extreme, that it is largely propagandistic in nature, and that it is not history at all in the modern sense but rather a late, minority construct imposed upon a few genuinely historical materials.[8]

For the above reasons, the current generation of Palestinian archaeologists—both American and Israeli, I would insist—has failed to achieve a proper balance in interpretation. Many have tended to reject biblical texts as capable of illuminating archaeological discoveries or as sources of history in themselves. Others have tried simply to mine the Bible arbitrarily for a few nuggets of historical fact, in total disregard of the radically theocratic nature of the biblical tradition. In our rush to secularism, we have been blind to the fact that the Bible, if not history, is nevertheless ideology, and ideology is a powerful clue to cultural change. An explanation of what happened in history cannot be reduced, as contextual archaeology reminds us, to adaptation, to materialist or determinist schemes that look only at such factors as environment, technology, and subsistence. It is culture itself that is paramount in cultural change, because it is uniquely human, just as the very concept of history is. It is not the predictable, the human propensity for the novel, the concrete freedom of the individual in actual historical circumstances to make choices, the cohesiveness of

---

7. I advanced a number of criticisms and cautions regarding the New Archaeology, while applauding many of its features in general, in Dever 1981.

8. The bibliography on archaeology and biblical historiography is vast, but for orientation see Dever 1990; see also Dever 1991e, 1994.

society. Finally, in fact, it is the unfathomable mystery of life and of the universe that we must confront.

For all these reasons, an explanation of what really took place in ancient Israel in the Iron Age must look not only at the material remains of that culture but also at those ideals, spiritual and secular (and the distinction is modern), that motivated those who were the bearers of that culture. We must be careful, of course, not to impose our own modern cultural notions and values on the past. Instead, we must listen patiently and respectfully to what those who lived through the events thought they meant—even if we, from our perspective, are convinced that they were wrong. As Hodder says, "To study history is to try to get at purpose and thought."[9] Here lies the newest archaeology's imperative to look at "the inside of events" (as Hodder puts it, following Collingwood), and this can only be read from texts in conjunction with artifacts, both being reflections of the culture that produced them (Hodder's "context," or event with text).

Now, since the biblical texts are our only extensive internal source, however fragmentary and unrepresentative for the thought world of ancient Israel, they can, if properly interpreted, provide an indispensable datum. If so, then it follows that every archaeologist who deals with the Iron Age must either be conversant with the entire apparatus of modern, critical study of biblical texts or must resort to cooperation with specialists who are (the necessary dialogue again). Here we are all at fault: postreligious Americans who jettison the literary tradition rather than undertaking to master it; and Israeli secular fundamentalists who read the ancient text mechanically and suppose that they understand it simply because they are native speakers of Hebrew or live in the Land of the Bible.[10]

A respectable new biblical archaeology is now possible, but it will require an earnest grappling with the biblical texts, which takes them seriously as ideology, if not as history, and which gives equal weight to archaeological-historical context and to culturally derived interpretations, both ancient and modern.

---

9. Hodder 1986, 94.

10. For American views on archaeology's contribution to the study of the biblical text, see references in works cited in notes 3, 5, and 8 above. Israeli archaeologists have rarely expressed themselves on theory in this matter, being largely pragmatic in approach, but see Stern 1987.

This leads me to the second challenge posed by contextual archaeology: it gives us, at last, the possibility of writing a more adequate history of ancient Israel, based on both artifactual and textual data. Archaeology as history, not only anthropology, is once more in vogue. As is well known, the New Archaeology had reacted theoretically against a *Kulturgeschtlich* approach that it regarded as inadequate because it was merely descriptive and classificatory and not truly explanatory. But in practice, the New Archaeology movement went to the extreme of rejecting history altogether as a legitimate goal of archaeology. The "timeless cultural process" became the focus. As Lewis Binford put it, as recently as 1987:

> The attempt to use history as the model for archaeological investigation is ... totally inappropriate.... The archaeologist sees no past events, only contemporary phenomena.[11]

In other words, only the manipulation of theory and data—the testing of scientific method—mattered to many "new archaeologist." That has now changed.

At the very heart of the new cooperative task of contextual archaeology and biblical studies will be a renewed examination of historiography. Biblical scholars are far ahead of us here, as witness the recent works of Thomas L. Thompson (1992), Norman K. Gottwald (1979), Niels Peter Lemche (1985), Robert B. Coote and Keith W. Whitelam (1987), Frank S. Frick (1985), Giovanni Garbini (1988), John Van Seters (1983), Baruch Halpern (1988), David L. Hopkins (1985), and others—all of whom have made some attempt to utilize archaeological data (without much help from us, I fear). Yet few Syro-Palestinian archaeologists, while assuming that they are doing history (what else should they be doing?), have read or reacted to these pioneering efforts of biblical scholars to analyze the materials and methods of history writing. What kind of truly historical archaeology can result from archaeologists who have never reflected seriously on the nature of history, who have no philosophy of history themselves, and who are ignorant of the vast literature on modern historiography?[12]

---

11. Binford 1987, 401. See the entire article.

12. See the references in the works cited in notes 8, 10, and 14. On the biblical side, the principal historians who at least attempt to use archaeological data include Gösta Ahlström, James W. Flanagan, Frank S. Frick, Giovanni Garbini,

It is here that we suffer most grievously from the isolation of the disciplines of archaeology and biblical studies and the lack of dialogue, both in America and in Israel. In America, however, there is at least a growing interest in dialogue among professional scholars, while in Israel I see little more than a populist interest in connecting archaeology with the Bible.

Fundamental as the theoretical underpinnings of history writing are, however, it is the practical aspect that concerns us here. How shall we write a history of ancient Israel that does justice to all that we can now know of artifacts and texts? It all depends, of course, on what kind of history we want. Which is better: history written from the top down or from the bottom up? In the past, biblical scholars, basing themselves almost exclusively on biblical texts, produced what I would call political history, largely an account of the deeds of great men and of public events. This was, of course, what the biblical writers were interested in and what they recorded, and for reasons that we cannot assess here most modern Jewish and Christian historians simply adopted that bias. In contrast to Hodder's "inner history of events" or Fernand Braudel's *la longue durée,* this school of historians, who were preoccupied with the literary tradition, produced an "outer" history, one that was elitist, episodic, and superficial. Such a flat history of ancient Israel may have been acceptable to religionists because of their own view of history as the result of divine intervention. But to others, and to secular historians, this history was ultimately unsatisfying because it could not adequately comprehend ancient Israel in its totality.

Archaeology, on the other hand, because it deals with artifacts rather than with text and ideology, aspires not to political history but rather to socioeconomic and cultural history. The basic data with which archaeologists work—thanks largely to the more beneficial, interdisciplinary aspects of the New Archaeology—are ecological setting, settlement types and patterns, subsistence, trade, technology, art and architecture, demography, and, especially, larger social structure. These are subjects upon which the biblical writers are almost totally silent—not inaccurate, simply uninterested. Such data—vital to historical reconstruction and complementary to the history of ideas derived from texts—is obtainable only through archaeological investigation of material culture remains.

Norman K. Gottwald, B. Halpern, David C. Hopkins, Niels Peter Lemche, John Van Seters, and Thomas L. Thompson. The results, however, are often minimal or even largely negative.

Now if we could envision an ideal, synthetic history of ancient Israel, it would, of course, embrace both categories of data, both emphases. In the meantime, however, we may have to be content with two parallel histories: a "sacred history" based largely upon biblical texts and embodying an account of the development of Israel's unique religious life and institutions and a "secular history" that attempts to place Palestine in the Iron Age in the larger context of the ancient Near East and seeks to illuminate its overall culture in a comparative and evolutionary sense.

Is the latter—a sort of history without texts of Palestine—like Pliny's *Natural History*, really feasible on the basis of current archaeological data? I believe that it is and, indeed, that it is overdue. Will the two histories be compatible or contradictory? Again, I am optimistic. All histories are partial, in that they stress some truths at the expense of others; none is able to tell us "Wie es eigentlich gewesen war" (as Ranke supposed). History writing is a product of the intellectual and social environment of the writers, whether ancient or modern. Thus, we need more than one kind of history of ancient Israel, each kind focusing upon some aspect of what transpired in the past and each true insofar as it adheres to its own appropriate objectives and methods. That is all we can ask of history writing, and today's sophisticated archaeology can certainly deliver that.[13] In summary, it is sometimes asked: Which class of data—textual or artifactual—takes precedence? That is posing the question wrongly, for both are essential to a balanced, richly textured, and ultimately satisfying history. Yet we have a long way to go toward that goal!

2.5. Brave New World: Harbingers?

Are there any signs in recent literature of the dialogue that I am advocating between biblical historians and archaeologists? On the biblical side, I have noted above a handful of current works on Israelite history that at least appear open to prospects—almost wistfully looking to us, it seems, for new sources of data, now that the analysis of the purely literary tradition

---

13. Elsewhere I have proposed a "secular" or "natural history of ancient Palestine," with archaeological data being equal with texts or even taking precedence. See further in note 34 below.

may be nearing the point of diminishing returns.[14] On the archaeological side, however, there has been little response from Americans and virtually none that I can see from Israelis. The call for a new biblical archaeology often falls on deaf ears.

I would cite, however, a few tentative feelers that have been put out, perhaps hinting at a rapprochement. The late Joe Callaway, staunch Baptist biblical scholar and seminarian that he was, nevertheless took some bold steps in our direction late in life when he came to grips with the disturbing archaeological evidence from his own site of 'Ai. In a paper read in 1984 at the First International Congress on Biblical Archaeology in Jerusalem, Callaway stated:

> For many years, the primary source for the understanding of the settlement in Canaan of the first Israelites was the Hebrew Bible, but every reconstruction based upon the biblical traditions has foundered on the evidence from archaeological remains.... The primary source has to be archaeological remains because ultimately every hypothesis based upon the Bible, extra-biblical texts, inscriptions, or historical analogy has to find support in the material remains of the time.

Callaway concluded that Albrecht Alt was correct when he argued that "repeated editing of the biblical traditions throughout the Old Testament period made a reconstruction of Israel's history from those early traditions impossible."[15] Apart from his negative view on the specific episode of the so-called conquest, Callaway's statements suggest a radical methodological shift in the war in which archaeological and textual evidence had been balanced in his own traditional upbringing in the biblical archaeology movement. He was clearly moving in the direction of our broader contextual archaeology.

Working again on the 'Ai materials and the problem of the Israelite settlement, Lawrence Stager, however, has recently provided an especially fruitful example of the dialogue between newer approaches in archaeology and biblical history. Basing himself primarily on survey data and excavation of early Iron I highland villages, especially house form and vil-

---

14. An example of a recent standard history that is disappointing because it uses almost no archaeological data would be Miller and Hayes 1986. See further my remarks in Dever 1991b.

15. Both quotations from Callaway 1985, 72.

lage layout, Stager summarizes innovations in material culture, shifts in demography, and changes in socioeconomic structure. Noting a remarkable correlation of these data with descriptions of family life in texts in Joshua, Judges, and Samuel, Stager concludes that these early Iron I villages can be connected with the first attempts of the biblical Israelites to settle central Canaan, not by conquest but peacefully. While he is wary of claiming this as an exercise in biblical archaeology, he does suggest the potential of this kind of interdisciplinary research, and I strongly concur. Indeed, Stager's article is an excellent prolegomenon to the contextual archaeology that I advocate. One might say that, despite the ideological bias of the writers of the Bible (or perhaps because of it?), Stager has been able to wring a surprising amount of cultural information and, indeed, of authentic history from the biblical texts.[16] More such studies are needed.

Thus on certain specific issues—like the origins of Israel—we can occasionally find a prolegomenon to a dialogue between archaeology and biblical studies. Here one might also cite the fuller-scale work of Israel Finkelstein, *The Archaeology of the Israelite Settlement* (1988)—although I suggest that while this is a pioneering synthesis of the archaeological data, it is not sufficiently conversant with recent work done on early Israelite history by biblical scholars and seems almost oblivious to the critical theological issues involved.[17]

The above treatments by archaeologists may seem promising, but they are ad hoc. They are responses to a particular problem rather than the radical, theoretical revolution that we need to make real progress. Few archaeologists have been begun to think about the overall issues of theory and method regarding a dialogue between archaeology and biblical studies. In particular, the fundamental epistemological dilemma has not been faced: How can textual facts, artifacts, and ecofacts be integrated and interpreted so as to constitute meaningful data, and what can we actually hope to know, at best, about the way it was in the past?[18] Above all, what are the most crucial and hopeful areas for interdisciplinary research in the future, as archaeology seeks to illuminate the biblical world?

I can point to only a handful of essays on these larger topics. Stager has made a few theoretical comments in passing. Lawrence Toombs has also

---

16. Stager 1985.
17. See Finkelstein 1988 and my review of his work at Dever 1991a.
18. See Dever 1994 and cf. the brief remarks of Rast 1990.

made several very perceptive observations, not only on the adaptation of the New Archaeology in Palestinian archaeology, but also on its application to biblical studies. Having surveyed several current trends, Toombs concludes that there has been "a reorientation of Syro-Palestinian archaeology from merely methodological interests toward a more synthetic examination of its theoretical base, particularly in the areas of research design and interpretation theory." For Toombs, the best prospect is that "by presenting Biblical scholars with cultural interpretations refined to their highest degrees of probability, archaeology in Bible lands may be performing the greatest possible service to those whose main task is literary interpretations."[19]

In the same volume as Toombs's essay, *Archaeology and Biblical Interpretation*, the only other theoretical essay on our subject is by Glenn Rose (to whose memory the volume is dedicated). Rose, like Callaway and Toombs, a biblical scholar converted to the New Archaeology, concludes that "we need to free archaeology of the debate over whether there is a biblical archaeology or not and allow it to pursue a method which produces an understanding of the past which is broader than the term biblical suggests."[20] Rose does not elaborate, however, on the theory of method of such an approach, except for brief allusions to structuralism; indeed, most of his essay, "The Bible and Archaeology: The State of the Art," is concerned only with recent methodological trends in biblical studies.

Carol and Eric Meyers have recently followed some preliminary observations of mine on a new style of biblical archaeology with a programmatic essay of their own. They appear to be more concerned with the larger theoretical concerns in either America or Israel. They do, however, attempt to define a growing interest in the social world of antiquity, arguing that the best hope for further dialogue with biblical studies lies in the use of social-science models, which offers an opportunity for a higher level of synthesis thanwas previously possible. For them, the frontiers of biblical archaeology today lie in what they call socioarchaeology, taking as their model Colin Renfrew's *Approaches to Social Archaeology* (1984). It is significant, however that Meyerses can cite, as examples, a number of sociological approaches among recent American biblical scholars but none among Palestinian archaeologists (except for some forthcoming

---

19. Toombs 1987, 49–50.
20. Rose 1987, 60.

dissertations of their own students).²¹ While the direction in which the Meyerses' point is similar to mine, it seems to me that they do not go nearly far enough. Furthermore, their stress on the importance of social context, while sound, lacks specificity.

Ephraim Stern, in one of the few published statements on Israeli theory and method, has declared of the American debate on biblical archaeology that Israelis find it "sterile and unintelligible." He argues that for them "Palestinian and biblical archaeology are synonymous terms which it would be unthinkable to separate"; as he puts it, "our ties with the Bible are direct and emotional."²²

This statement appears naive, but I suspect that it does indeed reflect the view of most Israeli archaeologists. They may regard the Bible as Israel's Magna Carta, but they have little interest in confirming its historicity and even less in its religious significance. That is what I mean by "secular fundamentalism." Stern's statements merely underline my contention that, despite the convenient use of the term, Israelis are not biblical archaeologists in any but the most minimalist sense (the exceptions being Yohanan Aharoni, Yigael Yadin, and perhaps Amihai Mazar). While that characteristic has helped the Israeli national school to avoid the theological controversies of Europe and America, it is not very promising for the dialogue I envision, nor for a full illumination of the biblical world. Israeli archaeologists will no doubt provide mush of the future data for contextual archaeology, but, unless the new generation experiences a theoretical revolution and undertakes serious commitment to modern critical biblical scholarship, I believe that the real frontiers of biblical archaeology or its replacement will lie elsewhere.²³

2.6. Case Studies for Contextual Archaeology and Biblical Studies

Throughout this paper, I am, like Binford's book, unabashedly "for theory-building."²⁴ However, archaeologists in our field are often impatient with talk about theory, being inclined to dismiss it as philosophy or mere

---

21. Meyers and Meyers 1989, especially 143.
22. Stern 1987, 35.
23. See Dever 1989b.
24. Binford 1977.

speculation. They pride themselves, rather, on being data-based. This is especially true of Israeli archaeologists, who are characteristically pragmatic, as the few published state-of-the-art treatments freely acknowledge. Underlying this view, however, is an unfortunate misunderstanding of terms. It seems to be unclear that by *theory* we mean simply a body of principles to guide research, without which no discipline can be systematic, thrive, or hope to grow. Lacking a theoretical, that is, an intellectual and interpretive, framework, archaeology is little more than treasure-hunting. It can never answer fundamental questions about the human past because it never asks them in such a way as to obtain meaningful answers.

Here and elsewhere I have tried to show that the older style of biblical archaeology had little theory of its own, merely an agenda borrowed from theology, and from a parochial school of theology at that. The New Archaeology, which supplanted it, was more concerned with formulating a body of appropriate archaeological theory that could foster the growth of archaeology as a discipline; it was inimical to history writing but stressed, rather, the cultural process and was thus frustrating for many in our fields of inquiry. In this paper I have argued that recent contextual archaeology offers more opportunities for historical archaeology, largely because its theoretical base is more substantial, more sophisticated, and more congenial to a new style of relating archaeology to biblical studies. Beyond theory, however, I do agree that results are what count, so I wish to conclude this paper by giving a few examples of how contextual archaeology offers superior insights into historical problems. Let us begin with research into the problem of the Israelite settlement, where recent archaeological data have already disposed of conquest models and have required us to rethink Israelite origins entirely. A beginning has been made, of course, in works cited above by archaeologists such as Callaway, Stager, Finkelstein, and a generation of younger Israeli archaeologists, as I have shown in several treatments elsewhere.[25] These studies, following the ecological and processual orientation of the newer archaeology, have correctly sought to emphasize the role of environment, subsistence, and technology as factors in the emergence of early Israel. Thus, for the first time we have begun to collect and assess adequate data on settlement types and distribution, to quantify demographic changes, to specify

---

25. I have dealt with the archaeology of the Israelite settlement in Dever 1990 and 1992a. The standard work now, of course, is Finkelstein 1988.

agriculturally based subsistence systems, to analyze a new technology based on terrace-farming, the use of silos, and cisterns for storage of surplus commodities, and iron implements. We have even begun to try to reconstruct, for early Israel, a limited social context, if not the entire social system. Nevertheless, it is striking that archaeologists of all persuasions have been reluctant to address two issues that the new contextual archaeology would consider essential: (1) ideology, including art, symbol, and religion; and (2) larger systemic contexts, in this case the setting provided by the collapse of the Late Bronze Age Canaanite culture in the mid-thirteenth to late twelfth centuries BCE. It is my conviction that we now can and must address these questions if we are to elucidate Israelite origins further.

On the first point, ideology, we specialists in material culture have been so derelict that we have not even responded to a number of biblical historians who have sought to utilize cultic remains, such as Cornelius C. H. J. de Geus, Norman K. Gottwald, Baruch Halpern, Niels Peter Lemche, Gösta Ahlström, and others. Since this silence can only be partially excused by lack of data, I must conclude either that we archaeologists have unwittingly subscribed to the materialist paradigm of the New Archaeology, that we are ignorant of the recent literature on symbolic and structuralist archaeology, or that we are interested in ideology but afraid of being labeled Marxists, on the one hand, or religionists, on the other.

A beginning would be to note the material remains of the early Iron I cult that we do happen to have (twelfth–eleventh centuries BCE). These would include a number of remarkable terra-cotta offering stands, such as those from ʿAi, Beth-shean, and elsewhere—some of them known for fifty years, including kraters with zoomorphic handles and spouts and other vessels. No comprehensive, synthetic study of this material exists, yet surely it could clarify the extent of continuity between Canaanite and Israelite religion, especially with reference to the pervasiveness of themes from the old fertility cults of the Late Bronze Age in early Israelite religion. Apart from the ideological components of Yahwism as set forth in the literary tradition, what were its material and behavioral correlates; that is, what role did folk religion play in the emergence of early Israel? Only archaeological investigation can answer this vital question.[26]

---

26. See the references in note 3. A number of essay in Miller, Hanson, and McBride 1987 other than those cited will also be found useful.

2. Biblical Archaeology: Death and Rebirth?

A second avenue of inquiry into ideology in assessing those cultural changes that spawned early Israel would be to note the overwhelming absence of shrines and sanctuaries in the twelfth–eleventh centuries BCE, in contrast to the proliferation of temples and cult installations in the preceding Late Bronze Age. In my judgment, only Amihai Mazar's Bull Site would qualify as a Yahwistic shrine (not Adam Zertal's Ebal altar, so-called), and here the bull image is in full continuity with the old El iconography of Late Bronze Age Canaan. Yet this isolated sanctuary is thus far simply the exception that proves the rule: early Israelite sites do not typically produce any evidence of a popular or official organized cult. What does this datum signify? Is it, for instance, corroboration of Gottwald's notion of a radically egalitarian social revolution that was the catalyst that formed Israel out of a struggling band of displaced Canaanite peasants? Or is the lack of cultic installations merely the result of accidents of excavation, and, if so, how might new research strategies redress the imbalance?

The contextual archaeology that I advocate here will seek to confront the above questions. Furthermore, it will do so within the framework of a dialogue with biblical texts, however recalcitrant and overlain they are with later royalist and priestly propaganda. For without some better understanding of the ideology of early Israel, we shall never come to grips with the real reasons for its emergence or appreciate the actual variety and vitality of its cultural experience. Yet the converse is true, for ideology and material culture are inextricably bound up. As Gottwald aptly puts it, "Only as the full materiality of ancient Israel is more securely grasped will we be able to make proper sense of its spirituality."[27]

Gottwald's observation leads me to note yet another shortcoming of recent research. Gottwald himself, de Geus, Stager, Hopkins, and others have all tried to elucidate the role of technology and subsistence in the emergence of early Israel.[28] Yet they have not managed to integrate the increasing data on an Iron I agrarian economy with the ideological factors that must surely have been part of the total system. Here we could learn from Marshall Sahlins's *Stone Age Economics*. Sahlins builds upon Marx's

---

27. Gottwald 1979, xxv.
28. For various, preliminary attempts at describing an early Israelite agrarian society and economy, see de Geus 1976; Gottwald 1979; Stager 1985; Lemche 1985; and Hopkins 1985.

Asiatic or Oriental mode of production in order to elaborate a "Domestic Mode of Production," which, like Marx's, includes such factors as environment, technology, political structure, class relations, conceptual systems, and even religion. Sahlins analyzes this total mode by describing prestate or chiefdom levels of social organization in terms of the basic household social and economic units around which they are typically organized. At this level, families are self-sufficient, labor and skills are more important than technology, and production, largely agricultural, is geared to use rather than surplus or exchange. Such a mode of production tends to be antiautocratic by nature, yet it obliges household groups to enter into compacts. As Marshall Sahlins puts it, "As the domestic economy is in effect the tribal economy in miniature, so politically it underwrites the conditions of primitive society—society without a Sovereign."[29] Is this not an astonishingly apt description of early Israel? Later Sahlins argues that technology does not create culture but that it is the other way around.[30] If so, we have new possibilities in contextual archaeology for truly historical explanations of the unique character of early Israel, stressing not simply mechanistic but also cultural and ideological factors. The first Israelites were indeed farmers and stock-breeders, perhaps of peasant background, but they possessed a social vision, one that ought to be reflected not only in the biblical texts but also in the remains of their material culture.

The second deficiency of current archaeological approaches to the question of Israelite origins is the failure to place early Israel in a wider cultural context, that is, in the multiethnic society that emerged in the aftermath of the collapse of Canaanite culture in the twelfth century BCE, in the so-called Dark Age. We have, as yet, no full-scale, synthetic treatment of this former Dark Age in the eastern Mediterranean, despite the fact that the Late Bronze/Iron I horizon is rapidly being illuminated by a series of startling discoveries. (A symposium on this theme in May 1990 at Brown University, at which Trude Dotham and I represented Palestine, should help to remedy the lack of studies.[31]) Yet without Hodder's context—artifacts with texts—we can hardly hope to assess continuity and change in the early Iron I period in Palestine in proper perspective. Nor can we appreciate the exceedingly complex cultural environment in which

---

29. Sahlins 1972, 95.
30. Sahlins 1976, 30.
31. See Dever 1992b.

Israel came to exist as a separate ethnic identity, in which it had to struggle long and hard before it eventually prevailed. Again, ideology is one of the essential variables we must seek to identify, both textually and archaeologically, for ideology, religious or otherwise, shaped ancient Israel at least as much as natural setting. Even Israel's distinctive material culture cannot be understood apart from the behavior and the ethnic consciousness that produced it.

Now, I am as aware as anyone of the limitations of the recent behavioral approach and even more mindful of Binford's caution that archaeologists are poorly equipped to work as paleopsychologists." Nevertheless, we can and must aim at nothing less than the isolation of what constitutes ethnicity, on the basis of the material correlates of behavior, that is, the recognition and definition of peoplehood by means of the traces those people left behind in the archaeological record. That is an admittedly ambitious and difficult goal for contextual archaeology, but it is not impossible, and again it is context that may enable us to identify ethnicity archaeologically. It is not enough to look simply at isolated traits such as pottery or even at trait lists like those drawn up by a former generation. Rather, we must attempt to see the culture of early Israel whole and in systemic context, in this case within the cultural heterogeneity of twelfth- to eleventh-century BCE Canaan. I suggest that, despite the formidable difficulties of this task, we can make a start by comparing presumably early Israelite sites with early Iron I sites that are demonstrably Philistine, as well as those that appear to represent continuing Canaanite influence and culture. Today we have sites in each of these categories, and we could devise deliberate research strategies for excavating them with the full range of ecological and multidisciplinary methods now available, then comparing the material directly. Thus we could begin to test propositions about Israelite ethnicity, and, beyond that, we could also move toward isolating and identifying archaeologically those unique cultural traits that gave rise to the later literary traditions about what constituted biblical Israel. Here the dialogue between artifacts, ecofacts, and textual facts could come to full fruition.[32]

---

32. I have dealt with ethnicity in the archaeological record in Dever 1991e; see also London 1989.

2.7. Conclusion

Throughout this paper I have proposed a new contextual archaeology that is postorthodox, post-Marxist, postpositivist, and postprocessualist. I have suggested its potential for biblical studies by referring to a single issue, the Israelite settlement in Canaan. Other historical issues to be addressed by contextual archaeology, however, might include:

1. the rise of the Israelite state;
2. the Assyrian and Babylonian destructions;
3. religion and cult in the monarchy; and
4. the exile and return

We now have rich archaeological documentation for these eras, yet even a glance at recent histories of Israel or archaeologies of ancient Palestine will show how little synthesis has been done, how isolated biblical scholars and archaeologists still are from each other.[33]

The other areas for future investigation through contextual archaeology must be singled out. The first is obviously archaeology and New Testament studies. The older-style biblical archaeology was so biased toward a few eras of Israelite history (notably patriarchs and conquest) that it ignored the Second Temple and New Testament periods almost entirely. (Properly speaking, the enterprise should have been called Old Testament archaeology rather than archaeology and the Hebrew Bible, because most practitioners were Protestant Old Testament scholars.) There are now a few encouraging signs of an emerging archaeology of late antiquity that focuses on the origins of Judaism and early Christianity, notably in the research projects of Eric and Carol Meyers, with James Strange and others.

---

33. The two most recent textbooks are Mazar 1990 and Weippert 1988. I reviewed Mazar in Dever 1991c, Weippert in Dever 1991d. Both are admirably thorough and up-to-date, in the style of the *Handbuch*, yet neither offers anything approaching a real synthesis of ancient Israel. In order to remedy this deficiency, a biblical scholar, Susan Ackerman (Dartmouth College), and I are planning to develop a radically new "History of Ancient Palestine in the Iron Age," including, of course, the history of the Israelite monarchy. In this work, the material cultural and ecological data will loom as large as the textual data. For the limitations of current text-based histories of Israel, see above and note 14.

Much more can be done, however, to illuminate the cultural backgrounds of the New Testament and early rabbinic sources, if the tools of contextual archaeology are utilized fully.

Finally, with some hesitation I venture a step back to one of the original concerns of the biblical archaeology movement: the implications of history, and therefore of archaeology, for questions of faith. Admittedly, it was the theological weakness of biblical archaeology, as much as anything else, that brought it into discredit. Yet the fundamental intention to make archaeology relevant to both history and religion was not, I daresay, mistaken. The inadequacy was rather the parochial view of archaeology, the positivist bias, the amateurishness of excavation and publication, and, above all, the special pleading for a certain tradition of Judeo-Christian belief.

I think that the time is ripe for a new look at the most basic of biblical archaeology's concerns. One recalls G. Ernest Wright's dictum, "In Biblical faith, everything depends upon whether the central events [i.e., exodus and conquest] actually occurred."[34] That presupposition was dangerously close to fundamentalism, as Wright's critics pointed out, and he himself later repudiated it. What actually occurred, of course, is no more accessible to us moderns than it was to the biblical writers, filtering events, as we all must, through later experience. Yet what matter is not events-in-themselves but the meaning imputed to them by those who experience them. Here, there is a point of contact with contextual archaeology, which, like many other movements in current archaeology, no longer pretends to be objective or value free. It recognizes that, unless archaeology today can make itself relevant in terms of eliciting the moral value of the human past, it ought rightly to be dismissed as unworthy of our attention.[35]

I would go further in drawing contextual archaeology and biblical studies together. At the very heart of biblical faith is the assertion that the land is sacred trust, that humans are meant to live in harmony with one another and with nature, that there is meaning beyond the tangible

---

34. See Wright 1952, 126–27. For a critique of Wright in this regard, see Dever 1981.

35. There is considerable recent literature on the contemporary relevance of archaeology, some of it rather radically neo-Marxist, other schools more structuralist in orientation, still others allied with critical theory in other social science disciplines. See, for example, Marcus and Fisher 1987 and, more specifically, Shanks and Tilley 1987, 1–16, 19–34, 63–73, 89–102.

and the present. Archaeology's fundamental concerns today are understanding the environment and humanity's relationship to it, elucidating both the material and ideological dimensions of culture, and grasping the meaning of the long trajectory of human experience. These two avenues of enquiry may be parallel paths to enlightenment. If that is so, then we stand at a critical juncture in the growth of archaeology as a discipline, as well as in its relation to biblical and religious studies.

Let the new inquiry into the biblical world via texts and artifacts begin now, as we celebrate the centennial of Palestinian archaeology, and let it emanate from Jerusalem.

Works Cited

Binford, Lewis R. 1977. *For Theory Building in Archaeology: Essays on Faunal Remains, Aquatic Resources, Spatial Analysis, and Systemic Modeling.* Academic Press.

———. 1987. "Data, Relativism and Archaeological Science." *Man* 22:391–404.

Bunimovitz, Shlomo. 1995. "How Mute Stones Speak: Interpreting What We Dig Up." *BAR* 21.2:58–67, 96–100.

Callaway, Joseph A. 1985. "Response." Pages 72–78 in *Biblical Archaeology Today: Proceedings of the International Congress on Biblical Archaeology, Jerusalem, April 1984.* Edited by Janet Amitai. Israel Exploration Society.

Coote, Robert B., and Keith W. Whitelam. 1987. *The Emergence of Early Israel in Historical Perspective.* SWBA 5. Almond.

Dever, William G. 1974. *Archaeology and Biblical Studies: Restrospects and Prospects.* The Winslow Lectures, Seabury-Western Theological Seminary, 1972. Seabury-Western Theological Seminary.

———. 1977. "Palestine in the Second Millennium B.C.E: The Archaeological Picture." Pages 70–120 in *Israelite and Judean History.* Edited by John H. Hayes and J. Maxwell Miller. Fortress.

———. 1981. "Biblical Theology and Biblical Archaeology: An Appreciation of G. Ernest Wright." *HTR* 73:1–15.

———. 1985. "Syro-Palestinian and Biblical Archaeology." Pages 31–74 in *The Hebrew Bible and Its Modern Interpreters.* Edited by Douglas A. Knight and Gene M. Tucker. BMI 1. Scholars Press.

———. 1987. "The Contribution of Archaeology to the Study of Canaanite and Israelite Religion." Pages 209–47 in *Ancient Israelite Religion: Essays in Honor of Frank Moore Cross.* Edited by Patrick D. Miller, Paul D. Hanson, and S. Dean McBride. Fortress.

———. 1989a. *Recent Archaeological Discoveries and Biblical Research.* The Stroum Lectures, University of Washington. University of Washington Press.

———. 1989b. "Yigael Yadin: Prototypical Biblical Archaeologist." *ErIsr* 20:44*–51*. Republished as chapter 1 in this volume.

———. 1990. "Of Myths and Methods." *BASOR* 277–278:121–30.

———. 1991a. "Archaeological Data on the Israelite Settlement: A Review of Two Recent Works." *BASOR* 284:77–90.

———. 1991b. "Archaeology, Material Culture and the Early Monarchial Period in Israel." Pages 103–15 in *Fabric of History: Text, Artifact and Israel's Past.* Edited by Diana Vikander Edelman. JSOTSup 127. JSOT Press.

———. 1991c. Review of *Archaeology of the Land of the Bible, 10,000–586 B. C. E.*, by Amihai Mazar. *AJA* 1995:546.

———. 1991d. Review of *Palästina in vorhellenistischer Zeit*, by Helga Weippert. *JAOS* 111:645–46.

———. 1991e. "Unresolved Issues in the Early History of Israel: Toward a Synthesis of Archaeological and Textual Reconstructions." Pages 195–208 in *The Bible and the Politics of Exegesis: Essays in Honor of Norman K. Gottwald on his Sixty-Fifth Birthday.* Edited by David Jobling. Pilgrim.

———. 1992a. "Archaeology, Syro-Palestinian and Biblical." *ABD* 1:354–67.

———. 1992b. "The Late Bronze-Early Iron I Horizon in Syria-Palestine: Egyptians, Canaanites, Sea Peoples, and Proto-Israelites." Pages 99–110 in *The Crisis Years: The Twelfth Century B.C.; From beyond the Danube to the Tigris.* Edited by William A. Ward and Martha S. Joukowsky. Kendall/Hunt.

———. 1994. "Archaeology, Texts, and History-Writing: Toward an Epistemology." Pages 105–17 in *Uncovering Ancient Stones: Essays in Memory of H. Neil Richardson.* Edited by Lewis M. Hopfe. Eisenbrauns.

Finkelstein, Israel. 1988. *The Archaeology of the Israelite Settlement.* Israel Exploration Society.

———. 1990. "On Archaeological Methods and Historical Considerations: Iron Age II Gezer and Samaria." *BASOR* 277–278:109–19.

Frick, Frank S. 1985. *The Formation of the State in Ancient Israel: A Survey of Models and Theories*. SWBA 4. Almond.

Garbini, Giovanni. 1988. *History and Ideology in Ancient Israel*. Crossroad.

Geus, Cornelius C. H. J. de. 1976. *The Tribes of Israel: An Investigation Into Some of the Presuppositions of Martin Noth's Amphictyonic Hypothesis*. Van Gorum.

Gottwald, Norman K. 1979. *The Tribes of Yahweh: A Sociology of the Religion of Liberated Israel, 1250-1050 B.C.E.* Orbis Books.

Halpern, Baruch. 1988. *The First Historians: The Hebrew Bible and History*. Harper & Row.

Hodder, Ian. 1986. *Reading the Past: Current Approaches to Interpretation in Archaeology*. Cambridge University Press.

Holladay, John S., Jr. 1987. "Religion in Israel and Judah under the Monarchy: An Explicitly Archaeological Approach." Pages 249-99 in *Ancient Israelite Religion: Essays in Honor of Frank Moore Cross*. Edited by Patrick D. Miller, Paul D. Hanson, and S. Dean McBride. Fortress.

———. 1990. "Red Slip, Burnish, and the Solomonic Gateway at Gezer." *BASOR* 277-278:23-70.

Hopkins, David C. 1985. *The Highlands of Canaan: Agricultural Life in the Early Iron Age*. SWBA 3. Almond.

Lemche, Niels Peter. 1985. *Early Israel: Anthropological and Historical Studies on the Israelite Society before the Monarchy*. VTSup 37. Brill.

London, Gloria. 1989. "A Comparison of Two Contemporary Lifestyles of the Late Second Millenium B.C." *BASOR* 273:37-55.

Marcus, George E., and Michael M. J. Fischer. 1987. *Anthropology as Cultural Critique*. University of Chicago Press.

Mazar, Amihai. 1990. *Archaeology of the Land of the Bible, 10,000-586 B.C.E.* Doubleday.

Meyers, Carol, and Eric Meyers. 1989. "Expanding the Frontiers of Biblical Archaeology." *ErIsr* 20:140*-47*.

Miller, J. Maxwell, and John H. Hayes. 1986. *A History of Ancient Israel and Judah*. Philadelphia: Westminster.

Miller, Patrick D., Paul D. Hanson, and S. Dean McBride, eds. 1987. *Ancient Israelite Religion: Essays in Honor of Frank Moore Cross*. Fortress.

Rast, Walter E. 1990. "Editorial." *BASOR* 277-278: 2-3.

Renfrew, Colin. 1984. *Approaches to Social Archaeology*. Harvard University Press.

Rose, D. Glenn. 1987. The Bible and Archaeology: The State of the Art. Pages 53-67 in *Archaeology and the Biblical Interpretations: Essays*

in Memory of D. Glen Rose. Edited by Leo G. Perdue, Lawrence E. Toombs, and Gary L. Johnson. Scholars Press.
Sahlins, Marshall. 1972. *Stone Age Economics*. Aldine.
———. 1976. *Culture and Practical Reason*. University of Chicago Press.
Shanks, Michael, and Christopher Tilley. 1987. *Re-constructing Archaeology: Theory and Practice*. Cambridge University Press.
Stager, Lawrence E. 1985. "The Archaeology of the Family in Ancient Israel." *BASOR* 200:1–35.
———. 1990. "Shemer's Estate." *BASOR* 277–278:93–107.
Stern, Ephraim. 1987. "The Bible and Israeli Archaeology. Pages 31–40 in *Archaeology and the Biblical Interpretation: Essays in Memory of D. Glen Rose*. Edited by Leo G. Perdue, Lawrence E. Toombs, and Gary L. Johnson. Scholars Press.
Thompson, Thomas L. 1992. *Early History of the Israelite People: From the Written and Archaeological Sources*. SHANE 4. Brill.
Toombs, Lawrence E. 1987. "A Perspective on the New Archaeology." Pages 49–52 in *Archaeology and Biblical Interpretation: Essays in Memory of D. Glen Rose*. Edited by Leo G. Perdue, Lawrence E. Toombs, and Gary L. Johnson. Scholars Press.
Ussishkin, David. 1990. "Notes on Megiddo, Gezer, Ashdod, and Tel Batash in the Tenth to Ninth Centuries B.C." *BASOR* 277–278:71–91.
Van Seters, John. 1983. *In Search of History: Historiography in the Ancient World and the Origins of Biblical History*. Yale University Press.
Weippert, Helga. 1988. *Palästina in vorhellenistischer Zeit*. Hanbuch der Archäologie Vordwerasien 2/1. Beck.
Wightman, G. J. 1990. "The Myth of Solomon." *BASOR* 277–278:5–22.
Wright, G. Ernest. 1952. *God Who Acts: Biblical Theology as Recital*. SBT 1/8. SCM.

Updated Bibliography

Broshi, Magen. 1987. "Religion, Ideology, and Politics and Their Impact on Palestinian Archaeology." *Israel Museum Journal* 6:17–32.
Drinkard, Joel. F., Gerard L. Mattingly, and J. Maxwell Miller, eds. 1988. *Benchmarks in Time and Culture: An Introduction to Palestinian Archaeology*. ABS 1. Scholars Press.

Dever, William G. 1989. "Archaeology in Israel Today: A Summation and Critique." Pages 143–52 in *Recent Excavations in Israel: Studies in Iron Age Chronology*. Edited by Seymour Gitin and William G. Dever. American Schools of Oriental Research.

Stager, Lawrence E. 1989. "A Personal Remembrance of Yigael Yadin as Biblical Archaeologist and Historian." *ErIsr* 20:14–16.

Moorey, P. R. S. 1991. *A Century of Biblical Archaeology*. Westminster John Knox.

Dever, William G. 1992. "Archaeology, Syro-Palestinian and Biblical." *ABD* 1:354–67.

Kempinski, Aaron. 1994. "The Influence of Archaeology on Israeli Culture." Pages 179–90 in *Landscape of Israel: Azaria's Alon Jubilee Volume*. Edited by Gabriel Barkay and E. Schiller. Ariel.

Ben-Yehuda, Nachman. 1995. *The Massada Myth: Collective Memory and Mythmaking*. University of Wisconsin Press.

Bunimovitz, Shlomo. 1995. "How Mute Stones Speak: Interpreting What We Dig Up." *BAR* 21.2:58–67, 96–100.

Dever, William G. 1995. "The Death of a Discipline." *BAR* 21.5: 50–55, 70.

———. 1996. "Biblical Archaeology." *OEANE* 1:315–19.

Elon, Amos. 1997. "Politics and Archaeology." Pages 34–47 in *The Archaeology of Israel: Constructing the Past, Interpreting the Present*. Edited by Neil Asher Silberman and David Small. Sheffield Academic.

Finkelstein, Israel. 1998. "Bible Archaeology or the Archaeology of Palestine in the Iron Age?" *Levant* 30:167–74.

Thompson, Thomas L. 1999. *The Mythic Past: Biblical Archaeology and the Myth of Israel*. Basic Books.

Barr, James. 2000. *History and Ideology in the Old Testament: Biblical Studies at the End of a Millennium*. Oxford University Press.

Benvenisti, Meir. 2000. *The Buried History of the Holy Land since 1948*. University of California Press.

Dever, William G. 2000. "Biblical and Syro-Palestinian Archaeology: A State-of-the-Art Assessment at the Turn of the Millennium." *CurBS* 8:91–116.

Hallote, Rachel, and Alex H. Joffe. 2002. "The Politics of Israeli Archaeology." *Israel Studies* 7:84–116.

Zevit, Ziony. 2002. "Three Debates about Bible and Archaeology." *Bib* 83:1–27.

Clark, Douglas R., and Victor Matthews, eds. 2003. *100 Years of Ameri-*

can Archaeology in the Middle East. American Schools of Oriental Research.

Dever, William G. 2003a. "Syro-Palestinian and Biblical Archaeology: Into the Next Millennium." Pages 513–27 in *Symbiosis, Symbolism, and the Power of the Past: Canaan, Ancient Israel, and Their Neighbors from the Late Bronze Age through Roman Palestina*. Edited by William G. Dever and Seymour Gitin. Eisenbrauns.

———. 2003b. "Why It's So Hard to Name Our Field." *BAR* 29.4:57–61.

Provan, Ian, V. Phillips Long, and Trevor Longman III. 2003. *A Biblical History of Israel*. Westminster John Knox.

Davis, Thomas W. 2004. *Shifting Sands: The Rise and Fall of Biblical Archaeology*. Oxford University Press.

Hoffmeier, James K., and Alan Millard, eds. 2004. *The Future of Biblical Archaeology: Reassessing Methodologies and Assumptions*. Eerdmans.

Collins, John J. 2005. *The Bible after Babel: Historical Criticism in a Postmodern Age*. Eerdmans.

Ortiz, Steven. 2005. "Archaeology, Syro-Palestinian." Pages 60–79 in *Dictionary of the Old Testament*. Edited by Bill T. Arnold and H. G. M. Williamson. InterVarsity Press.

Hallote, Rachel. 2006. *Bible, Map and Spade: The American Palestine Exploration Society, Frederik Jones Bliss and the Forgotten Story of Early American Biblical Archaeology*. Gorgias.

Kletter, Raz. 2006. *Just Past? The Making of Israeli Archaeology*. Equinox.

Faust, Avraham. "2007. Forum: Rural Settlements, State Formation, and 'Bible and Archaeology.'" *NEA* 70:4–25.

Mazar, Amihai. 2007a. "On Archaeology, Biblical History, and Biblical Archaeology." Pages 21–33 in *The Quest for the Historical Israel: Debating Archaeology and the History of Early Israel*. Edited by Brian B. Schmidt. ABS 17. Society of Biblical Literature.

———. 2007b . "The Spade and the Text: The Interaction Between Archaeology and Israelite History Relating to the Tenth-Ninth Centuries BCE." Pages 143–71 in *Understanding the History of Ancient Israel*. Edited by H. G. M. Williamson. Proceedings of the British Academy 143. Oxford University Press.

Ussishkin, David. 2007. "Archaeology of the Biblical Period: On Some Questions of Methodology and Chronology of the Iron Age." Pages 131–41 in *Understanding the History of Ancient Israel*. Edited by H. G. M. Williamson. Proceedings of the British Academy 143. Oxford University Press.

Dever, William G. 2010. "Does 'Biblical Archaeology' Have a Future?" Pages 349–60 in *Historical Biblical Archaeology and the Future: The New Pragmatism*. Edited by Thomas E. Levy. Equinox.

Joffe, Alex H. 2010. "The Changing Place of Biblical Archaeology: Exceptionalism or Normal Science?" Pages 328–48 in *Historical Biblical Archaeology and the Future: The New Pragmatism*. Edited by Thomas E. Levy. Equinox.

Dever, William G. 2012. "Reflections on the Death of Biblical Archaeology." *Buried History* 48:3–10.

———. 2017a. *Beyond the Texts: An Archaeological Portrait of Ancient Israel and Judah*. SBL Press.

———. 2017b. "A Critique of Biblical Archaeology." Pages 141–57 *The Old Testament in Archaeology and History*. Edited by Jennie Ebeling, J. Edward Wright, Mark Elliott, and Paul V. M. Flesher. Baylor University Press.

Ben-Yosef, Erez. 2019. "The 'Architectural Bias' in Current Israeli Archaeology." *VT* 69:361–87.

Dever, William G. 2023. "Pragmatism in Archaeology: The End of Theory?" Pages 1789–199 in vol. 2 of *"And in Length of Days Understanding" (Job 12:12): Essays in Archaeology in the Eastern Mediterranean and Beyond in Honor of Thomas E. Levy*. Edited by Erez Ben-Yosef and Ian W. N Jones. 2 vols. Springer.

Thomas, Zachary. 2023. "What Is the Name of Our Discipline? Or, the Onomastic Stew That Is Archaeology in the Southern Levant." Pages 555–71 in vol. 1 of *"And in Length of Days Understanding" (Job 12:12): Essays in Archaeology in the Eastern Mediterranean and Beyond in Honor of Thomas E. Levy*. Edited by Erez Ben-Yosef and Ian W. N Jones. 2 vols. Springer.

Biographies

Brown, Jonathan M., and Laurence Kutler. 2005. *Nelson Glueck: Biblical Archaeologist and President of Hebrew Union College*. Hebrew Union College Press.

Davis, Miriam C. 2008. *Dame Kathleen Kenyon: Digging Up the Holy Land*. Left Coast Press.

Feineman, Peter D. 2004. *William Foxwell Albright and the Origins of Biblical Archaeology*. Andrews University Press.

Silberman, Neil Asher. 1993. *A Prophet amongst You: The Life of Yigael Yadin; Soldier, Scholar, and Mythmaker of Modern Israel.* Addison-Wesley.

For bibliography on general archaeological theory and method since circa 1985, consult the following, all with full references and arranged in chronological order.

Shanks, Michael, and Christopher Tilley. 1987. *Re-constructing Archaeology: Theory and Practice.* Cambridge University Press.
Hodder, Ian. 1986. *Reading the Past: Current Approaches to Interpretation in Archaeology.* Cambridge University Press.
Pinsky, Valerie, and Alison Wylie, eds. 1989. *Critical Traditions in Contemporary Archaeology: Essays in the Philosophy, History, and Socio-politics of Archaeology.* Cambridge University Press.
Preucel, Robert W., ed. 1991. *Processual and Postprocessual Archaeologies: Multiple Ways of Knowing the Past.* Southern Illinois University Press.
Renfrew, Colin, and Ezra B. Zubrow, eds. 1994. *The Ancient Mind: Elements of Cognitive Archaeology.* Cambridge University Press.
Hodder, Ian, ed. 1995. *Interpreting Archaeology: Finding Meaning in the Past.* Routledge.
Preucel, Robert W., and Ian Hodder, eds. 1996. *Contemporary Archaeology in Theory.* Blackwell.
Whitley, David S., ed. 1998. *Reader in Archaeological Theory: Post-processual and Cognitive Archaeology.* Routledge.
Meskell, Lynn, ed. 1999. *Archaeology under Fire: Nationalism Politics and Heritage in the Eastern Mediterranean and Middle East.* Routledge.
Preucel, Robert W., and Stephen A. Mrozowski, eds. 2010. *Contemporary Archaeology in Theory: The New Pragmatism.* Wiley-Blackwell.
Bintliff, John L., and Mark Pearce, eds. 2011. *The Death of Archaeological Theory?* Oxbow.

For general handbooks, see:

Renfrew, A. Colin, and Paul Bahn. 2019. *Archaeological Theories, Methods and Practices.* 8th ed. T&T Clark.
Trigger, Bruce G. 2006. *A History of Archaeological Thought.* 2nd ed. Cambridge University Press.

3
Philology, Theology, and Archaeology: What Kind of History of Israel Do We Want, and What Is Possible?

As the historiographical crises described above deepened toward the mid-1990s, I came to feel strongly that much of the impasse that we seemed to have reached was due to a fundamental flaw: none of us had defined what we meant by *history*. Thus when the Philip and Muriel Berman Center for Jewish Studies at Lehigh University convened an international symposium in 1994 on the theme of "Imagining the Past: Archaeology and Ancient Israel" (see now Silberman and Small 1997), I knew immediately what my paper would attempt to do. I envisioned various kinds of history but would focus more closely on how an *archaeologically based* history of ancient Israel might differ. Here I drew again on my original interest and training in biblical theology in the 1950s so as to include that discipline—or, more precisely, to exclude it. At the close of the symposium, several of my Israeli colleagues, who seemed quite mystified, admonished me to "leave theology and philosophy alone and get back to archaeology." But I have always been convinced that if archaeology does not grapple with the big questions—especially history and history writing—it will be little more than antiquarianism. The broader intellectual aspects of archaeology is a theme that recurs repeatedly in the chapters below.

Bibliography on Israelite historiography since this essay was written in 1995 will be found in the Updated Bibliography (arranged chronologically) at the end of the Works Cited. The Leheigh symposium was in my mind a

---

Originally published as pages 706–22 in *Biblical Archaeology Today, 1990: Proceedings at the Second International Congress on Biblical Archaeology, Jerusalem, June 1990.* Edited by Avraham Biran and Janet Amitai. Israel Exploration Society, 1993. Reprinted by permission.

landmark gathering of peoples and papers. It was published as follows, the title reflecting the postmodern notion already in the air then, that is, that everything is constructed.

For the past twenty years or so there has been increasing scholarly discussion of issues in Israelite historiography, yet there is a growing sense of uneasiness that has now reached crisis proportions. Given the problematic nature of our sources in the Hebrew Bible, is it possible to write a satisfactory history of ancient Israel? Or, as Max Miller (1991) has put it recently, "Is it possible to write a history of Israel without relying on the Hebrew Bible?"

In earlier stages of the discussion, it was largely a matter of competing approaches or models, the assumption being apparently that a deliberate choice among various alternatives was necessary but would then enable the historian to get on with the task. Somewhat later there appeared the first full-scale analyses of the Hebrew Bible as a specifically "historical" work, in the comparative context of ancient Near Eastern and Greek historiography: John Van Seters's *In Search of History: Historiography in the Ancient World and the Origins of Biblical History* (1983); and Baruch Halpern's *The First Historians: The Hebrew Bible and History* (1988).

In the past decade, scholars have brought forth several new histories of ancient Israel that mark a turning away from the era of Martin Noth and John Bright, with its sharp polarization of nihilistic and positivist histories. Fullscale works of the new school would include J. Alberto Soggin, *A History of Israel* (1985); Niels Peter Lemche, *Early Israel: Anthropological and Historical Studies on the Israelite Society before the Monarchy* (1985), and his more popular *Ancient Israel: A New History of Israelite Society* (1988); J. Maxwell Miller and John H. Hayes, *A History of Ancient Israel and Judah* (1986); and Giovanni Garbini, *History and Ideology in Ancient Israel* (1988), the latter more an essay on historiography than a history. One could add to this list a number of introductions that included historical sketches of a sort.

These more recent histories of Israel, despite wide divergence, are characterized, I believe, by a rather remarkable consensus, not usually spelled out but recognizable in several common traits, all of course interrelated. (1) The overall assumption is that the texts of the Hebrew Bible are late postexilic, or even Hellenistic, not only in their present edited form but in content as well; that is, the literary tradition is largely "unhistorical." (2) Much more attention must thus be paid to the role of ideology in history writing—theirs and ours—including religion and cult. (3) A history of *Israel* can begin only with the period of the judges, or even the monarchy, since any prehistory is unrecoverable; however, coverage at the other end may extend to the Second Temple period and the formation of rabbinic Judaism. (4) Since the tradition is a literary one, not historical, the most fecund approach may be through newer literarycritical methods (narrative history, symbolic-structuralist and other forms of discourse analysis, folklore and ethnohistory, etc.), and the most appropriate models may be those drawn from anthropology. (5) The newer, more comprehensive rubric should be social history, rather than religious or political history. (6) Archaeology is acknowledged as a potential source of historical information (usually unexploited, however). (7) The question of the "emergence" of Israel is one of the most pressing yet controversial issues. (8) Finally, several of the most recent works hint at the possibility of a new "secular history" of ancient Israel or Palestine that will mark the next major scholarly departure—indeed, I think, a new era in Israelite historiography (below).

In the following remarks, I want to look briefly at three basic approaches to writing a history of ancient Israel, with special emphasis on the unique contribution that I think Syro-Palestinian archaeology as a mature discipline can now make.[1]

3.1. The Philological Approach to the History of Ancient Israel

In many ways philology has been the basic tool of modern critical biblical scholarship. The fundamental flaw in the philological approach, however, lies in its unexamined positivist presuppositions. It simply assumes (1) that the texts of the Hebrew Bible as they have come down to us, despite the seemingly intractable nature of some passages, taken together consti-

---

1. For orientation and bibliography on recent trends in Syro-Palestinian archaeology, see Dever 1985, 1993; for archaeology and problems of Israelite historiography, see Dever 1995a and the review of issues in 1995b. Add Preucel 1991 and, for possible application to Syro-Palestinian and biblical archaeology, Dever 1993.

tute an accurate witness to the actual phenomenon of life in ancient Israel; and (2) that the rapid progress of comparative Semitic philology would enable us to read these texts correctly and comprehend their meaning. As Morton Smith put it in his 1968 Presidential Address to the Society of Biblical Literature: "For a correct history of the Israelites we must have the archeological facts determined quite objectively and independently by competent archeologists, and the biblical facts likewise determined by competent philologians, and then can we begin to compare them."[2]

In other words, philologians were confident that they really could penetrate behind the obfuscation of centuries of theological interpretation to *das Ding an sich*—if not to historical and religious truth then at least to an "exegetical truth," based not on correct belief but on a correct reading of the texts. Much of the vaunted optimism of classic Protestant liberalism in its heyday regarding the task of reconstructing Israelite history and religion rested upon the assumed superiority of such an objective approach, largely philological (what Burke Long terms the logocentric approach).

Today this seems naïve, wistful, and rather sad. Already in the late nineteenth century, as Baruch Halpern points out, the Greek philologian Burckhardt had castigated then-burgeoning classical philology for its "spiritual bankruptcy."[3] It is not simply that the texts—Greek, Latin, Hebrew, or ancient Near Eastern—are not truly representative of the whole gamut of ancient society and culture or even that such texts are highly symbolic, cryptic encoded messages about past human thought and behavior that can never be fully deciphered.

The more intransigent problem with "mere philology" is that such an excessively rationalistic, and ultimately literalistic, approach to history can never grasp its inner reality, if I may phrase it thus. Or to put it another, less impressionistic way: literature is not life but rather the product of the intellectual and literary imagination of a creative few. Thus the study of elitist texts of the "great tradition" alone can never enlighten us fully on many matters. In short, in this postmodern, postpositivist era, we ought to acknowledge at last that, even in possession of abundant textual data, we cannot really reconstruct the past. The past is gone irretrievably, and, whatever our data, as Lewis Binford reminds us, we can only draw

---

2. Smith 1969, 34.
3. Halpern 1988, 23.

inferences about "what it was like in the past."[4] All these inferences are indirect and partial; most are untestable; and many are simply modern notions, not derived at all from that past but imposed upon it. What we think we know reveals more about us and our ignorance than about the past that we are proposing to investigate. To counter von Ranke's familiar phrase, we can never really know *wie es eigentlich gewesen war*, historically or archaeologically.

The minimalist view of Israelite historiography espoused here is not as radical as it would have seemed a generation ago. Indeed, current trends in England and on the Continent are much more extreme. This was borne out for me in January 1993 at a Bern symposium on monotheism in ancient Israel, where the consensus of leading European scholars was that the texts of the Hebrew Bible, in their present edited form, are all late and tendentious, of little or no value for the historian.[5] That is a view vigorously championed also by Philip R. Davies in his recent book *In Search of "Ancient Israel"* (1992). Though I find this work curious, and certainly not persuasive, Davies does typify the ultimate absurdity to which the exclusive use of the philological method (i.e., his) leads. Davies contends that there was no "ancient Israel." This is simply a literary construct that has been invented by later rabbinic Judaism (perpetuated by Christianity as well), by a postexilic community seeking an identity, seeking to vindicate itself in the aftermath of national tragedy. Davies's real villains are those he calls a scribal class, who finally shaped the literary tradition, who he thinks were temple personnel. But they are not consciously producing Scripture, or even a Bible, just propaganda. Even the language of these scribal schools is artificial—not a Hebrew that was ever actually spoken during the monarchy but an archaizing *Bildungssprache*. In short, all the literature of the Hebrew Bible, based on Davies's philological analysis (certainly not his amateurish theology or historiography), is Hellenistic, even the prophetic books, a Hasmonean phantasmagoria, worthless as sources of history for any other period. There is no ancient Israel, but Davies is its chronicler.

Davies's nihilism is echoed in both most recent, comprehensive attempts to write a history of ancient Israel: Thomas L. Thompson's *Early*

---

4. Binford 1983, 31–32.
5. The proceedings are published in Dietrich and Klopfenstein 1995.

History of the Israelite People from the Written and Archaeological Sources (1992); and the late Gösta Ahlström's *The History of Ancient Palestine from the Paleolithic Period to Alexander's Conquest* (1993). These recent works do not, in my opinion, signal a new approach, much less a breakthrough in writing a history of Israel. Rather, they mark a return full circle to Wellhausen; they simply confirm the intellectual exhaustion, after a century and a half, of the philological method and the classic literary-critical apparatus that accompanied it. In this pessimistic view, I as an archaeologist am neither beyond the pale nor alone. Rolf Rendtorff, in the inaugural issue of the journal *Biblical Interpretation*, in an article entitled "The Paradigm is Changing: Hopes—and Fears," points out that the classic Documentary Hypothesis is dead. "The question is rather whether the texts are Pre-Exilic or Post-Exilic," and the consensus is for the latter dating. "We will have to redesign our image of Israel's history and the history of its religion."[6] Indeed! But *how*?

3.2. The Theological Approach to the History of Ancient Israel

A second traditional approach to the history and religion of ancient Israel has been through theology, either so-called biblical theology or systematic and dogmatic theology. Whatever the merits of this approach, I would argue that theology is ill-suited to a productive investigation of ancient Israel's history.

Despite a historical thrust of some sort or another, the fact is that the vast majority of Old Testament theologies in the last two centuries have had a frankly confessional character; that is, their goal has been to reconstruct a normative religion of ancient Israel as a foundation for modern belief and morality, largely within the Christian community. That category would certainly include the works of most influential twentieth-century Old Testament theologians.[7]

1. The theological approach may best be characterized as *Heilsgeschichte*: ancient Israel viewed primarily as the first chapter in the history of salvation, that is, the story of God's redemption of his people Israel and

---

6. Rendtorff 1993, 50.

7. For orientation to the vast literature, see Hasel 1991, written from a conservative perspective but a good review of the literature and the issues.

then of the Christian church as the new Israel. The dilemma posed by this perspective on Scripture, however, has been with the church since Marcion in the second century of the Common Era: what to *do* with the Old Testament? Even in its most benign form, reading the Bible as salvation history overlooks most of the *real* (i.e., secular) history of ancient Israel. Furthermore, when Christians appropriate the Hebrew Bible and Scripture as their own tradition—denying the validity of the tradition for those who created it—this is an enormous piece of hutzpah.

2. In its more extreme forms, however, this kind of "spiritualizing" leads to typology, which, although vigorously opposed by Rudolph Bultmann, Friederich Baumgärtel, G. Ernest Wright, James Barr, and others, is a methodology with which numerous Old Testament scholars have flirted, either coyly or overtly, among them Walther Eichrodt, Gerhard von Rad, Wilhelm Vischer, and others. Typology may take the form of simply seeing the Old Testament as the prophecy (*Verheissung*) of which the New Testament is the fulfillment (the familiar Pauline and Lutheran dichotomy of law versus gospel). Or it may become truly pernicious in the form of allegorical interpretation, which denies the literary tradition—and thus the experience and faith of ancient Israel—any historical reality at all. In this view, not only were the interpretations of events upon which the writers of the Hebrew Bible based their faith wrong, but any actual events themselves are called into question. That is, they had no intrinsic reality but were merely prototypes, foreshadowings of the gospel. Secular or profane history, since it is not *Heilsgeschichte*, is not a true history, is in fact no history at all. In this apocalyptic perspective, the *eschaton* in which we are living reduces all that precedes it to meaninglessness; *Urzeit* is swallowed up in *Endzeit*. The Christ event becomes the only authentic event because it alone is revelatory. But this makes the *real* history of ancient Israel a mere charade.

3. Another way in which Christian Old Testament theology devalues the history of ancient Israel and its religion is an outgrowth of the salvation-history approach, namely, the appropriation of the Old Testament as simply the starting point of a *Vergegenwärtigung*, or re-presentation. What is involved here is the attempt not merely to retell the story (*nacherzählen*), and thus to contemporize God's saving acts on behalf of Israel, but to actualize these events in the proclamation so as to re-create the (supposedly) biblical faith that was originally inspired by the events. This method of *Vergegenwärtigung* as the most appropriate form of theological discourses

was pioneered by Gerhard von Rad, followed by Claus Westermann, Norman Porteous, Peter R. Ackroyd, Bernhard W. Anderson, James A. Sanders, and many others. The concept is perhaps most accessible in G. Ernest Wright's popular *God Who Acts: Biblical Theology as Recital* (1952). (I still remember the surge of excitement I felt upon discovering that little book as a seminarian nearly forty years ago.)

Sometimes regarded as an aspect of the traditio-historical method, this approach actually begs the question of historicity, as James Barr has pointed out trenchantly of Wright's work. The story eclipses the facts. What really may have happened in ancient Israel is preempted by the question: What should I do? History is less significant than repetition of the biblical writers' interpretations (and ours) of the supposed events. Now, confessional recital may be effective theology, but can it claim to be history? Is it even interested in the mundane event? It seems to me that seeing history only *sub specie aeternitatis* may depreciate it to the point where factual history is not worth recovering at all. Allegory makes a farce of history, reduces ancient Israel to a morality play.

4. Whatever and however a selection is made from the many strands of literary traditions regarding Israel's history and religion, the results tend to say more about a given scholar's predilections than the reality. Christian Old Testament theology, for instance, has overwhelmingly preferred the prophetic tradition—despite the fact that it clearly presents a late and perhaps minor tradition within ancient Israel, the Hebrew Bible, and later Judaism—and has pointedly ignored or rejected the priestly tradition with its emphasis on ritual and cult. The Deuteronomistic tradition has been favored by Old Testament scholars secondarily, in my opinion, largely because its theological program, masked by quasi-historical intentions, suits the political history orientation stemming from the Reformation heritage of the Protestant scholars who have dominated Old Testament theology. Indeed, I would argue that the characteristically Protestant mode of Old Testament theology explains many things: its excessively rationalistic preoccupation with ideology, theology, and systematics; its philological penchant in exegesis, stemming from the doctrine of *sola scriptura*; a verbal gestalt that results in a bias against ritual and cult and in favor of the proclamation of the word; a disproportionate emphasis upon faith that stems from Pauline and Lutheran antinomianism, rejects law out of a false dichotomy with gospel, and tends to justify faith by appeals to history and historical proofs; its obsession with what Jon Levenson calls

"repristinization,"[8] which must always find its biblical origins, its continuity with an earlier and thus presumably more authentic religion. Why this compulsion of Old Testament theologians to baptize ancient Israel and the Hebrew Bible, to make Moses and Paul proper Lutherans? Is it not mostly wishful thinking—a nostalgia for a biblical past that never was—and perhaps also a chronic crisis of faith, despite the prevalent slogan *sola fide*?

An observation of Jon Levenson is eloquent: "In part, biblical theology results from the fact that Christians read the Hebrew Bible through a logic of displacement. It draws much of its energy from the anxieties of the younger sibling."[9] Levenson also compares Judaism's typical stance with Protestantism's quest for historical certitude and for the systematization of religious beliefs in theology, concluding that Jews today approach the past, even the biblical past, partly in imitation of non-Jews. They do so, however, "not because of faith, but because of the lack of it, not in hopes of defining a theology, but of finding a replacement for theology." To be sure, the late Moshe Goshen-Gottstein (1987), a brilliant and seminal Jewish thinker, has proposed a Tanak theology alongside Christian Old Testament theology. But he conceived this quite frankly as a confessional enterprise, like most Old Testament theology, with no pretensions to descriptive-historical objectivity, more typically Jewish philosophy than theology. He also acknowledges that in this enterprise he is entirely alone among Jewish scholars, a maverick. The near total absence of biblical theologies among Jewish scholars—the community that surely represents the mainstream of continuity with the various tributaries of the Hebrew Bible—should at least give us pause.

3.3. Key Issues in the Current Debate and the Role of Archaeology

3.3.1. The Historiographical Dilemma

That there is currently a crisis in Israelite historiography is widely acknowledged by many biblical scholars, and related epistemological issues are at last beginning to be addressed by Syro-Palestinian archaeologists. In the latter field, the replacement of the materialist-functionalist paradigms of

---

8. Levenson 1987, 296.
9. Levenson 1987, 296.

the New Archaeology of the 1970s and 1980s by today's postprocessual archaeology brings those of us who deal with the archaeology of ancient Israel squarely to face again with ideology and *history*. Meanwhile, we have noted Rolf Rendtorff's conclusion that we will have to redesign our image of Israel's history and the history of its religion. Indeed, but archaeology will then have to play a vital, even dominant role. And very few biblical scholars seem to be aware of that fact or willing to face its consequences. That is apparently because most biblical scholars still do not understand what today's archaeology is. If not, then we archaeologists are largely at fault.

It is not so much our sources that are flawed, but our approach. Better histories will require better historians, as well as new data and new models. The mere increase in new information will not, in itself, bring a concomitant increase in our understanding of the past, that is, in genuine historical knowledge. Facts must be converted into data by being placed within a context of meaningful questions.

A beginning might be made by isolating the historiographical questions that biblical philology and exegesis, the writing of Israel's history and religion, and Syro-Palestinian archaeology have in common. What is history, and above all what *kind* of history do we want? What are the appropriate, and obtainable, goals and purposes of history writing? How do we distinguish primary and secondary data; that is, what is the legitimate and most fruitful relationship between textual data and archaeological evidence? What constitutes a workable balance of probability or adequate verification of historical facts? How do we achieve a balance between an empirically based, disinterested, objective history, on the one hand, and a dynamic, sympathetic, relevant history, on the other? These questions are especially urgent when that history is biblical, Judeo-Christian, and fundamental to so much of the Western tradition—*our* history.

It is to the credit of recent biblical scholars such as Thomas L. Thompson, Gösta Ahlström, and Philip R. Davies—and such radical predecessors as Lemche, Garbini, Soggin, Norman K. Gottwald, and others—that they have raised these historiographical issues so sharply. Of all the above questions, however, I believe that the most crucial is: What *kind* of history do we want? Everything else hinges on that. (1) Clearly the biblical texts, on any other than a minimalist reading, can yield a history of ideas, or ideology, as well as an outline of religious-political history—at least for the postexilic period, and I would argue even for much of the monarchy (although not for "proto-Israel" in the twelfth–eleventh centuries BCE). (2) Modern, interdisciplinary archaeology, on the other hand, as a mature discipline itself, is now poised to begin writing a techno-environmental and socio-economic history—my secular history of ancient Palestine (including ancient Israel), Thompson's larger-scale "historical (human) geography of Palestine," or Ernst Axel Knauf's provocative notion of an extension of natural history into the specific realm of *homo sapiens*. It is worth noting also that Knauf has picked up the emphasis of Fernand Braudel and the Annales school on *la longue durée*, which several of us have toyed with, suggesting that we combine Braudel's long-term history (structures) and his medium-term history (conjunctures) into a processual history, an approach that he says "cannot do without archaeology".[10]

At issue in many recent discussions, at least *implicitly*, is the role of archaeology in writing a history of ancient Israel. But it is curious that that issue has been raised almost exclusively by nonarchaeologists. There are, for example, at least brief, tentative discussions of archaeology's role in writing a history of Israel in several works of biblical scholars, in addition to those reviewed above. Among Syro-Palestinian archaeologists, however—American, European, or Israeli—one can point to only a handful of discussions of archaeology, Bible, and history, none much more than dilettantish and nearly all confined to the early settlement horizon. Until Syro-Palestinian archaeologists who fancy themselves historians engage historiographical issues seriously, there can be no productive dialogue with biblical studies. And archaeologists must contribute precisely *as* historians. Clearly our training is too specialized to allow us any longer to be biblical philologians or exegetes; we rightly eschew theology as a means of appropriating the past on its own terms; and we are, even at best, self-taught as ethnographers, anthropologists, or social theorists. We are thus historians. If Americanist archaeology is "anthropology or nothing," then Syro-Palestinian archaeology is "history or nothing." With all the salutary emphasis today in archaeology on interdisciplinary approaches, the use of socioanthropological models, and the borrowing of analytical and statistical techniques from the natural sciences, we must not forget that basically we archaeologists working in the historical periods of Israel and the ancient Near East are simply historians who work more with material

---

10. Knauf 1991, 44.

culture remains than with texts. This brings us to a second issue, that of models drawn from other disciplines and their use.

3.3.2. Appropriate Models in History Writing

Socioanthropological approaches to the study of ancient Israel have been in vogue for some time now and are too well known to need documentation here. In particular, sociological models have been employed for the earlier periods, such as the settlement era and the rise of the monarchy, as in recent works of George E. Mendenhall (1973), Gottwald (1979), Lemche (1985), Frank S. Frick (1985), James W. Flanagan (1988), Israel Finkelstein and Nadav Na'aman (1994), and others. These newer approaches are certainly refreshing, and their specifically anthropological bent makes them congenial, at least in theory, to much of the newer archaeology, especially among the younger generation. Thus there would seem to be a methodological confluence that would bode well for a future dialogue. Yet one can point to only a few studies among archaeologists or biblical scholars that make what I would consider *appropriate* use of socioanthropological models. Furthermore, the tendency of these efforts to float in the ratified atmosphere of pure theory, the endless controversy, the lack of demonstrable results, and especially the dreadful jargon all tend to vitiate what might be fruitful approaches and only increase resistance to models among the many remaining skeptics.

We need to remember what models, as used elsewhere in the social and natural sciences, are. They are only abstractions, not drawn from the data but imposed upon them in order to manipulate those data experimentally, that is, heuristic devices. As Baruch Halpern says in a devastating critique of Mendenhall (and less so of Gottwald): "Models teach questions that one might ask, not answers that one must give."[11] And as Ziony Zevit points out in a recent review of Davies's *History*, "[models] cannot be used to infer unattested data. The shoehorning of archaeological data into a social-theoretical Procrustean bed and using the mangled results to render a verdict on 'historical Israel' is unsophisticated, to say the least."[12] In short, models are rarely explanatory.

---

11. Halpern 1992, 66.
12. Zevit 1995.

It is interesting that Syro-Palestinian archaeologists have made much less use of extreme socioanthropological models, but in as much as that is probably due to their backwardness in general, it does them little credit. Recent models, where employed at all, tend to be simply statistical, as in current Israeli surveys, are drawn from more traditional sources, such as the study of Middle Eastern pastoral nomadism, or are still resolutely (and somewhat naively) confused with historical explanations. I am convinced that sophisticated, modern, interdisciplinary social science models *can* be employed to elucidate textual-historical and archaeological data successfully, just as models from the natural sciences have helped to generate enormous quantities of useful techno-environmental data on the ancient Near East. But we have a long way to go. Meanwhile, inchoate social theories of scholars such as Flanagan and Davies, or crypto-theological agendas such as that of Robert G. Boling (1988), get us nowhere. Recently some scholars, increasingly pessimistic about any textual facts, have turned to sociolinguistics and faddish theories to address the issues. By contrast, I point out that any *new* hard data in ancient Israel will come, by definition, out of the ground—artifacts or texts—not out of the Hebrew Bible, which is a closed corpus. In that sense, if in no other, archaeological data will take precedence and will constitute a large proportion of the primary data in the future, especially for the premonarchic period (as some biblical scholars already recognize). To that issue we now turn.[13]

3.3.3. Archaeology and the Question of Secondary Sources

Another issue where archaeology can play a role has to do with the nature of the sources: primary or secondary? The first issue is primarily whether the textual sources in the Hebrew Bible are largely of secondary value (if any) for writing the history of the periods of the Judges and the monarchy, since in their final edited form they date to the Persian and Hellenistic eras. In short, what we have here is a *literary*, not a genuinely historical, tradition. Increasingly, biblical scholars such as those reviewed here, and especially those on the Continent, conclude that late

---

13. Halpern 1992, 65; On the possibilities of a secular history, see Dever 1991, 108–15; Knauf 1991, 44; Thompson 1992, 402–5; add now the extended discussion in Dever 1995b.

redaction means late *composition* and thus sources that are *post factum*, of little historical value.

No responsible scholar today doubts the late date of the final redaction of the tradition. But the question remains whether or not there may be a core within the tradition that comprises earlier, genuinely historical material—some of it possibly contemporary with the events the tradition purports to describe. No one would argue more forcefully than I that archaeology cannot be used to prove the Bible. Nevertheless, there are a number of points at which datable Iron Age archaeological evidence and literary reference in the Bible do converge in such a way as to suggest contemporaneity, a fact that responsible historians cannot deny. If not proof, there is weight here on the side of the balance of probability, which is what the historian always must work with.

Of the many hundreds of such convergences that might be listed, I mention only a few. (1) Nearly three hundred early Iron Age or "proto-Israelite" villages are now known in the hill country, the settlement type and distribution of which, along with artifactual evidence, provide an archaeological assemblage that agrees remarkably well with conditions described in Joshua–Samuel, as Finkelstein (1988) and Stager (1985) have shown, and enable us to reconstruct a very plausible twelfth–eleventh century socioeconomic and cultural setting for the core of these narratives, folk history or not. (2) The twelfth- to eleventh-century BCE biblical Philistines are now so well documented archaeologically that we can confidently describe their origins, material culture, and sociopolitical organization. That all this fits the many biblical allusions so well, with no major accommodations needed, shows that a postexilic editor cannot simply have invented these passages, that they are genuinely archaic. (3) The same can be said for the rise of the Israelite state under Solomon (if not David), where the overwhelming indication of the archaeological evidence is for precisely the kind of urbanization and centralization that accompanies the emergence of a state in virtually all cross-cultural comparisons.[14] (4) A fact not often noted is that almost every detail of the sometimes enigmatic descriptions of the Solomonic temple in 1 Kgs 6–9 can now be directly illustrated by reference to actual Bronze and Iron Age temples and

---

14. See Flanagan 1988 and Boling 1988; for further critique, see Dever 1995a, 1995b.

their furnishings elsewhere in the southern Levant. A later writer who had never seen the temple could not possibly have given such accurate, detailed descriptions. (5) Finally, we have noted above the emergence of what we may call archaeologically a homogeneous Israelite-Judean culture under the divided monarchy. First, this very well documented material culture is clearly the expression of a well-defined, ethnically distinct "national character," that is, a people and a nation-state that we can readily distinguish as Israel (precisely the entity that Davies thinks never existed). The evidence is massively documented elsewhere (yet is never surveyed adequately by any biblical scholar):[15] settlement type and distribution; defensive and domestic architecture; household furnishings; ceramic, lithic, and metal implements; ivories, seals, and bullae with biblical names; shekel weights; ostraca and inscriptions; distinctive burials and grave goods; temples, shrines, and cult paraphernalia of all kinds; and so on. Again, the point is that this rich panoply of items accords so well with *both* the biblical descriptions of daily life in Israel-Judah and the overall conditions we know in Iron Age Palestine that it simply cannot have been contrived by writers living in the Persian or Hellenistic period—as though to provide a pseudo-historical setting for their theocratic propaganda and program for reform. Any archaeologist could multiply these examples on the ground many times over. These are properly *historical* data, and in the future no historian of ancient Israel can afford to ignore them.

3.3.4. What Constitutes a *Sitz im Leben*?

As is well known, both form and redaction criticism since Gunkel have sought to comprehend smaller or larger units of biblical texts by attempting to place them in their original context, or *Sitz im Leben*. The notion of context, of course, is vital, indeed essential, for every archaeologist, and therefore we readily applaud the search for *Sitz im Leben*. Yet I would observe that in practice the search produced little more than a *Sitz im Lit-*

---

15. For a review of state formation processes in early Israel and a critique of some the literature, see Dever 1994. The latest work is Finkelstein and Na'aman 1994—certain to be the point of departure for all subsequent studies, despite what in my view is an exaggerated emphasis upon nomadic origins. The view that monarchic Israel basically saw a revival of the old Bronze Age Canaanite city-state system was already elaborated in Fritz 1995.

eratur, a setting that reflected much more the history of the *literature* and its transmission than of real life or history in the usual sense.

To be sure, a few biblical scholars have sensed this deficiency. Rolf Knierim's incisive critique of recent literary criticism of the Hebrew Bible points out:

> For form criticism, the societal settings behind the text are assumed to be the decisive generative forces for the emergence of generative texts. The assumption, however, has always meant that a comprehensive sociological picture of Israel's history is indispensable for form-critical work. The only problem is that we have never had such a comprehensive picture.[16]

Knierim goes on to decry "dubious reconstructions of settings via dubiously identified text patterns," which I would characterize simply as a classic circular argument. He concludes:

> A new direction would evolve, however, if the sociological study of Israel's history and the study of the genres of the OT literature, each in its own right, would be programmatically correlated. Of such a programmatic correlation we have at best embryonic indications, but neither a program nor an execution.[17]

Exactly, but how about including in that program *archaeology*, the only source of information on society independent of the Hebrew Bible, indeed, I would argue, our best source for a real "sociology of biblical Israel" (contra Davies).

Thompson has also addressed this point, although obliquely, in observing that the postexilic setting usually delineated for the final redaction and composition of the Hebrew Bible as a whole is the work of what he terms only "a handful of tradents." "One ought not to assume, however, that such *Sitze im Leben* lie *im Leben des Volkes*. Rather we are dealing with scholarly bibliophiles."[18]

---

16. Knierim 1985, 144.
17. Knierim 1985, 144.
18. Davies cites as his principal archaeology "authority" Thomas L. Thompson (1992), another historian and biblical scholar who knows the archaeological data only second- or third-hand and who furthermore is as nihilistic as Davies. For my own critique of both, see Dever 1995a, 1995b. For excellent, authorita-

I would say simply that we are dealing with literature, a literary rather than a real-life setting. The essential point that many philologians (and theologians) seem to overlook is that literature does not necessarily mirror real life, at least not the life of the masses, but only of the literati. The texts reflect the creative, literary imagination of a very few of the elite classes. In ancient Israel, pre- and postexilic, these classes constituted a mere handful of priests, intellectuals sometimes attached to the court, writing prophets, and probably scribes. *These* were the people who wrote the Bible for others like themselves. And while they could write disinterested history or include details on ordinary day-to-day activities when they chose to do so, the fact is that they were simply not interested in what the vast majority of people in ancient Israel thought or did. Only archaeology, as some Annales historians argue, can give history back to the people.

Perhaps the point is simply: Who *makes* history? And who *writes* it? Which count more, the principal actors, countless individuals over the slow-moving millennia, as with Braudel, or those few who rationalize events, who are often makers of myth more than of history. (If history is written by the winners, what constitutes winning?) While I have argued here that there is much more genuine historical information in the biblical texts than supposed by many nowadays (especially if we read skillfully between the lines), the fact is that we are nevertheless almost totally dependent upon *archaeological* data for most of what we shall ever know about most of the people of ancient Israel most of the time.

3.4. Toward a Nontheological Agenda?

We have assessed the theological approach above, so only a few further comments are necessary here. The case against Old Testament theology as a surrogate for the study of the history of Israel has also recently found forceful expression in Jon D. Levenson's 1987 essay "Why Jews Are Not Interested in Biblical Theology," noted above. Another devastating critique, aimed partly at Mendenhall's and Gottwald's supposedly sociological models, is that of Baruch Halpern, who concludes:

---

tive summaries of the archaeological evidence for an Israelite material culture, see Weippert 1998, 417–681 (already available to Davies); Mazar 1990, 368–530; and Ben-Tor 1992, 303–73.

> The study of Israel has bleached, not obliterated, its theological spots.... Biblical history is not, as Mendenhall claimed, in transition. It remains biblical, not Syro-Palestinian, Canaanite, or Israelite.... What is wanted is a liberation of Israelite history from modern theology.... Israelite history can engage a disciplined historical imagination. It wants one abjuration for it to do so: an abjuration of external doctrine, theological or sociological, in favor of the authority of intrinsic data.[19]

My own methodological preferences have been stated in a recent paper entitled "Archaeology, Philology, Theology and the Pursuit of Ancient Israelite Religion."[20] One could simply substitute History for Religion. The point is that these more recent nontheological approaches to ancient Israel reveal a shared if largely unarticulated notion that it is possible, and desirable, to write some sort of secular history—history without the Bible—rather than the typical *Heilsgeschichte* that does such violence to the biblical texts in their context, as well as to the socioeconomic and cultural context for which archaeology increasingly provides empirical data. Despite my criticism here of several biblical scholars who have recently addressed the issues of Israelite historiography, I agree with all of them (and others) on one basic point. We need a fresh approach to the phenomenon of ancient Israel that is truly critical, comparative, generative, synthetic, and ecumenical. In short, let us aspire to truer histories, in the sense of *better* histories—histories, not theologies.[21]

The intent here is not to delegitimize theology but simply to segregate it, so as to keep the historical, exegetical, and theological enterprises honest—all of them, each true to its own interests. In approaching the biblical tradition, we should follow Krister Stendahl's (1992) well-known insistence upon separating the question of What *does* it mean? from the question of What *did* it mean? I think it is possible to add a third, deeper level of inquiry: What really happened? Despite all the well-taken precautions mentioned above, that we can never know *wie es eigentlich gewesen war*, if we do not presuppose that there is some objective real-

---

19. Halpern 1992, 54, 66, 67.

20. This paper was delivered at the 1993 inaugural meeting of a new American Schools of Oriental Research five-year consultation on Archaeology and the Religion of Israel.

21. Susan Ackerman of Dartmouth College and I are working on a volume tentatively entitled *A Social History of Iron Age Palestine and Ancient Israel*.

ity out there, we shall never be moved to investigate and therefore shall learn nothing of what may have transpired. Even the more skeptical archaeologists of the processualist school, for whom history was a bad word, have finally yielded on this point, thanks to the withering critique of Ian Hodder and other postprocessualists.[22] Something *did* happen in the past, quite apart from either our conceptualization of its meaning or even of the perceptions of the original participants in the events. It is our task as historians and archaeologists to penetrate as deeply as possible into past realities, with all means at our disposal, to learn if possible something of how it was.

3.5. Conclusion

Baruch Halpern has recently observed of the current state of biblical studies: "Today the welter of competing claims, the cacophony of methods, betrays the cumulation of the decades. The synthetic eschaton promised in the apocalypse of philological positivism has not arrived."[23]

The age of positivism in archaeology is similarly over in this post-Albrightian era. Perhaps it is time to liberate the writing of the history of ancient Israel, as well as its literature and religion, from all external dogmas. In particular, we must redefine the relation between our two best sources of information—texts and artifacts—not subsuming one under the dominant paradigm of the other or leap-frogging back and forth between narrative and archaeology, which will only produce what Knauf aptly calls "a pseudohistory of nonevents."[24] The point of departure must be a mutual, honest, critical dialogue between textual studies and the best that archaeology can offer—one that above all is humble, fully aware of what we do not know and thus open to new insights about the past. Otherwise, as Santyana observed, we are doomed to repeat the mistakes of the past, as well as those of past scholarship.

It is my contention that it is *only* in the dialogue between texts and artifacts—pursued rigorously by scholars committed to interdisciplinary inquiry—that we can hope for more comprehensive, better balanced,

---

22. See Hodder 1986; Preucel 1991.
23. Halpern 1992, 65.
24. Knauf 1991, 49.

ultimately more satisfying histories of ancient Israel in all its variety and vitality. The fixed textual data, although of somewhat restricted value historically, can yield an outline of political and theocratic history, of ethnic and religious ideology, together with numerous details of real life embedded in the older materials now incorporated into the literary traditions of the Hebrew Bible, an "internal history." The archaeological data—theoretically almost unlimited in extent and variety, more flexible, and less deliberately biased—can yield a broader techno-environmental and socioeconomic history, an external, secular history that is parallel, complementary in many ways, and often corrective. *Both* histories of ancient Israel are now essential, and possible—if scholars in several disciplines are willing to set aside conventional approaches and cooperate in a true dialogue between texts and artifacts.

Let us heed the sage advice of my esteemed colleague, Professor Lou Siberman, to "listen" to both text and artifact. That means that as historians, when we have been able to read both texts and artifacts as accurately as possible with all means at our disposal, assessing all the data as disinterestedly as possible, we must then be content to sit back and listen—intently, patiently, with a disciplined but sympathetic imagination, and above all with humility. As Ian Hodder reminds us, in the quest for meaning in history, there are always these subjective elements. The role of history is "to understand human action, rather than events.... To get at action is to get at subjective meanings, at the *inside* of events."[25] By listening perceptively to the human past as it speaks to us today, we may indeed imagine, and thus appropriate, that past, and so gain the only insights that we shall ever have into the future.

Works Cited

Ahlström, Gösta W. 1993. *The History of Ancient Palestine from the Paleolithic Period to Alexander's Conquest*. JSOTSup 146. JSOT Press.

Ben-Tor, Amnon, ed. 1992. *The Archaeology of Ancient Israel*. Yale University Press.

Binford, Lewis R. 1983. *Pursuit of the Past: Decoding the Archaeological Record*. Thames & Hudson.

---

25. Hodder 1986: 79.

Boling, Robert G. 1988. *The Early Biblical Community in Transjordan.* SWBA 6. Almond Press.

Davies, Philip R. 1992. *In Search of "Ancient Israel."* JSOTSup 148. JSOT Press.

Dever, William. G. 1985. "Syro-Palestinian and Biblical Archaeology." Pages 31–74 in *The Hebrew Bible and Its Modern Interpreters.* Edited by Douglas A. Knight and Gene M. Tucker. BMI 1. Scholars Press.

———. 1991. "Archaeology, Material Culture and the Early Monarchial Period in Israel." Pages 103–15 in *Fabric of History: Text, Artifact and Israel's Past.* Edited by Diana Vikander Edelman. JSOTSup 127. JSOT Press.

———. 1993. "Biblical Archaeology—Death and Rebirth?" Pages 706–22 in *Biblical Archaeology Today, 1990: Proceedings of the Second International Congress on Biblical Archaeology, Jerusalem, June 1990.* Edited by Avraham Biran and Joseph Aviram. Israel Exploration Society.

———. 1994. "From Tribe to Nation: A Critique of State Formation Processes in Ancient Israel." Pages 213–38 in *Nuove fondazioni nel Vicino Oriente antico: Realtà e ideologia.* Edited by Stefania Mazzoni. University of Pisa.

———. 1995a. "Archaeology and the Current Crisis in Israelite Historiography." *ErIs* 25:18*–27*.

———. 1995b. "'Will the Real Israel Please Stand Up?' Archaeology and Israelite Historiography: Part 1." *BASOR* 297:61–80.

———. 2002. "Theology, Philology, and Archaeology: In the Pursuit of Ancient Israelite Religion." Pages 11–34 in *Sacred Time, Sacred Place: Archaeology and the Religion of Israel.* Edited by Barry M. Gittlen. Eisenbrauns.

Dietrich, Walter, and Martin Klopfenstein, eds. 1995. *Ein Gott allein? JHWH-Verehrung und biblischer Monotheismus im Kontext der israelitischen und altorientalischen Religionsgeschichte.* Universitätsverlag; Vandenhoeck & Ruprecht.

Finkelstein, Israel. 1988. *The Archaeology of the Israelite Settlement.* Israel Exploration Society.

Finkelstein, Israel, and Nadav Na'aman, eds. 1994. *From Nomadism to Monarchy: Archaeological and Historical Aspects of Early Israel.* Israel Exploration Society.

Flanagan, James W. 1988. *David's Social Drama: A Hologram of Israel's Early Iron Age.* SWBA 7. JSOT Press.

Frick, Frank S. 1985. *The Formation of the State in Ancient Israel: A Survey of Models and Theories*. JSOT Press.

Fritz, Volkmar. 1995. *The City in Ancient Israel*. BibSem 29. JSOT Press.

Garbini, Giovanni. 1988. *History and Ideology in Ancient Israel*. Crossroad.

Goshen-Gottstein, Moshe. 1987. "Tanakh Theology: The Religion of the Old Testament and the Place of Jewish Biblical Theology." Pages 617–44 in *Ancient Israelite Religion: Essays in Honor of Frank Moore Cross*. Edited by Patrick D. Miller, Paul D. Hanson and S. Dean McBride. Fortress.

Gottwald, Norman K. 1979. *The Tribes of Yahweh: A Sociology of the Religion of Liberated Israel, 1250–1050 B.C.E.* Orbis Books.

Halpern, Baruch. 1988. *The First Historians: The Hebrew Bible and History*. Harper & Row.

———. 1992. "Sociological Comparativism and the Theological Imagination: The Case of the Conquest." Pages 53–67 in *Sha'arei Talmon: Studies in the Bible, Qumran and the Ancient Near East Presented to Shemaryahu Talmon*. Edited by Michael Fishbane and Emmanuel Tov. Eisenbrauns.

Hasel, Gerhard. 1991. *Old Testament Theology: Basic Issues in the Current Debate*. Eerdmans.

Hodder, Ian. 1986. *Reading the Past: Current Approaches to Interpretation in Archaeology*, Cambridge University Press.

Knauf, Ernst Axel. 1991. "From History to Interpretation." Pages 26–64 in *The Fabric of History: Text, Artifact and Israel's Past*. Edited by Diana V. Edelman. JSOTSup 127. JSOT Press.

Knierim, Rolf. 1985. "Criticism of Literary Features, Form, Tradition, and Redaction." Pages 123–65 in *The Hebrew Bible and Its Modern Interpreters*. Edited by Douglas A. Knight and Gene M. Tucker. Fortress; Scholars Press.

Lemche, Niels Peter. 1985. *Early Israel: Anthropological and Historical Studies on the Israelite Society before the Monarchy*. VTSup 37. Brill.

———. 1988. *Ancient Israel: A New History of Israelite Society*. BibSem 5. Sheffield Academic.

Levenson, Jon D. 1987. "Why Jews Are Not Interested in Biblical Theology." Pages 281–307 in *Judaic Perspectives on Ancient Israel*. Edited by Jacob Neusner. Fortress.

Mazar, Amihai. 1990. *Archaeology of the Land of the Bible, 10,000–586 B.C.E.* Doubleday.

Mendenhall, George E. 1973. *The Tenth Generation: The Origins of the Biblical Tradition.* Johns Hopkins University Press.

Miller, J. Maxwell. 1991. "Is it Possible to Write a History of Israel without Relying on the Hebrew Bible?" Pages 93-102 in *The Fabric of History: Text, Artifact and Israel's Past.* Edited by Diana V. Edelman. JSOTSup 127. JSOT Press.

Miller, J. Maxwell, and John H. Hayes. 1986. *A History of Ancient Israel and Judah.* Westminster.

Preucel, Robert W., ed. 1991. *Processual and Postprocessual Archaeologies: Multiple Ways of Knowing the Past.* Southern Illinois University Press.

Rendtorff, Rolf. 1993. "The Paradigm is Changing: Hopes—and Fears." *BibInt* 1:34-53.

Smith, Morton. 1969. "The Present State of Old Testament Studies." *JBL* 88:19-35.

Soggin, J. Alberto. 1985. *A History of Israel.* Westminster

Stager, Lawrence E. 1985. "The Archaeology of the Family in Ancient Israel." *BASOR* 200:1-35.

Stendahl, Krister. 1992. *Early History of the Israelite People from the Written and Archaeological Sources.* Brill.

Thompson, Thomas L. 1992. *Early History of the Israelite People: From the Written and Archaeological Sources.* SHANE 4. Brill.

Van Seters, John. 1983. *In Search of History: Historiography in the Ancient World and the Origins of Biblical History.* Yale University Press.

Weippert, Helga. 1988. *Palästina in vorhellenistischer Zeit.* Hanbuch der Archäologie Vordwerasien 2/1. Beck.

Wright, G. Ernest. 1952. *God Who Acts: Biblical Theology as Recital.* SBT 1/8. SCM.

Zevit, Ziony. 1995. Review of *In Search of "Ancient Israel,"* by Philip R. Davies. *AJS Review* 21:153-56.

Updated Bibliography

Since this essay was written in 1995, the following publications have updated the discussion, all with full references.

Millard, Alan R., James K. Hoffmeier, and David W. Baker, eds. 1994. *Faith, Tradition, and History: Old Testament Historiography in Its Ancient Near Eastern Context.* Eisenbrauns.

Brettler, Marc Zvi. 1995. *The Creation of History in Ancient Israel*. Routledge.

Davies, Philip R. 1995. "Method and Madness: Some Remarks on Doing History with the Bible." *JBL* 114:699–705.

Halpern, Baruch. 1995. "Erasing History: The Minimalist Assault on Ancient Israel." *BRev* 11.6:26–35, 47.

Provan, Ian W. 1995. "Ideologies Literary and Critical: Reflections on Recent Writing on the History of Israel." *JBL* 114:585–606.

Thompson, Thomas L. 1996. "Historiography of Ancient Palestine and Early Jewish Historiography: William G. Dever and the Not So New Biblical Archaeology." Pages 26–43 in *The Origins of the Ancient Israelite States*. Edited by Volkmar Fritz and Philip R. Davies. JSOTSup 228. Sheffield Academic.

Whitelam, Keith W. 1996. *The Invention of Ancient Israel: The Silencing of Palestinian History*. Routledge.

Grabbe, Lester L., ed. 1997. *Can a "History of Israel" Be Written?* JSOTSup 245. Sheffield Academic.

Iggers, Georg G. 1997. *Historiography in the Twentieth Century: From Scientific Objectivity to the Postmodern Challenge*. Wesleyan University Press.

Long, Burke O. 1997. *Planting and Reaping Albright: Politics, Ideology, and Interpreting the Bible*. Pennsylvania State University Press.

Silberman, Neil Asher, and David Small, eds. 1997. *The Archaeology of Israel: Constructing the Past, Interpreting the Present*. JSOTSup 237. Sheffield Academic.

Finkelstein, Israel. 1998. "The Rise of Early Israel: Archaeology and Long-Term History." Pages 7–39 in *The Origin of Early Israel—Current Debate: Biblical, Historical and Archaeological Perspectives*. Edited by Shmuel Ahituv and Eliezer D. Oren. Ben-Gurion University of the Negev Press.

Lemche, Niels Peter. 1998. *The Israelites in History and Tradition*. LAI. Westminster John Knox.

Thompson, Thomas L. 1999. *The Bible in History: How Writers Create a Past*. Cape.

Amit, Yairah. 1999. *History and Ideology: Introduction to Historiography in the Hebrew Bible*. Sheffield Academic.

Römer, Thomas. 2000. *Israel Constructs its History. Deuteronomic Historiography in Recent Research*. JSOTSup 306. Sheffield Academic.

Dever, William G. 2001. *What Did the Biblical Writers Know and When Did They Know It? What Archaeology Can Tell Us about the Reality of Ancient Israel*. Eerdmans.

Finkelstein, Israel, and Neil Asher Silberman. 2001. *The Bible Unearthed: Archaeology's New Vision of Ancient Israel and the Origins of Its Sacred Texts*. Free Press.

Thompson, Thomas L. 2002. *The Historicity of the Patriarchal Narratives: The Quest for the Historical Abraham*. BZAW 133. Trinity Press International.

Garbini, Giovanni. 2003. *Myth and History in the Hebrew Bible*. JSOTSup 362. Sheffield Academic.

Provan, Ian, V. Phillips Long, and Trevor Longman III. 2003. *A Biblical History of Israel*. Westminster John Knox.

Albertz, Rainer. 2003. *Israel in Exile: The History and Literature of the Sixth Century B.C.E.* SBLStBL 3. Society of Biblical Literature.

Day, John. ed. 2004. *In Search of Pre-exilic Israel: Proceedings of the Oxford Old Testament Seminar*. JSOTSup 106. T&T Clark.

Hendel, Ronald. 2005. *Remembering Abraham: Culture, Memory, and History in the Hebrew Bible*. Oxford University Press.

Collins, John J. 2005. *The Bible after Babel: Historical Criticism in a Postmodern Age*. Eerdmans.

Kofoed, Jens B. 2005. *Text and History: Historiography and the Study of the Biblical Text*. Eisenbrauns.

Liverani, Mario. 2005a. *Israel's History and the History of Israel*. Equinox.

———, ed. 2005b. *Recenti Tendenze nella Ricostrozione della Storia Antica D'Israele*. Accademia Nazionale de Lincei.

Banks, Diane. 2006. *Writing the History of Israel*. T&T Clark.

Knight, Douglas A. 2006. *Rediscovering the Traditions of Israel*. 3rd ed. SBLStBL 16. Society of Biblical Literature.

Davies, Philip R. 2007. *The Origins of Biblical Israel*. LHBOTS 485. T&T Clark.

Schmidt, Brian B., ed. 2007. *The Quest for the Historical Israel: Debating Archaeology and the History of Early Israel*. ABS 17. Society of Biblical Literature.

Grabbe, Lester L. 2007. *Ancient Israel: What Do We Know and How Do We Know It?* T&T Clark.

Williamson, Hugh G. M., ed. 2007. *Understanding the History of Ancient Israel*. Proceedings of the British Academy 143. Oxford University Press.

Barstad, Hans M. 2008. *History and the Hebrew Bible: Studies in Ancient Israelite and Ancient Near Eastern Historiography*. FAT 61. Mohr Siebeck.

Davies, Philip R. 2008. *Memories of Ancient Israel: An Introduction to Biblical History—Ancient and Modern*. Westminster John Knox.

Grabbe, Lester L., ed. 2008. *Israel in Transition 1: From Late Bronze II to Iron IIa (c. 1250–850 B.C.E.); The Archaeology*. LHBOTS 491. T&T Clark.

Lemche, Niels P. 2008. *The Old Testament between Theology and History: A Critical Survey*. Westminster John Knox.

Davies, Philip R., and Diane V. Edelman, eds. 2010. *The Historian and the Bible: Essays in Honour of Lester L. Grabbe*. LHBOTS 530. T&T Clark.

Grabbe, Lester L., ed. 2010. *Israel in Transition 2: From Late Bronze II to Iron IIa (c. 1250–850 B.C.E.); The Texts*. LHBOTS 521. T&T Clark.

Halpern, Baruch, and Andre Lemaire, eds. 2010. *The Book of Kings: Sources, Composition, Historiography and Reception*. VTSup 129. Brill.

Kratz, Reinhard G., and Herman Spieckermann, eds. 2010. *One Cult—One Nation: Archaeological and Historical Perspectives*. BZAW 405. De Gruyter.

Grabbe, Lester L. 2011. *Enquire of the Former Age: Ancient Historiography and Writing the History of Israel*. LHBOTS 554. T&T Clark.

Moore, Megan B., and Brad E. Kelle. 2011. *Biblical History and Israel's Past: The Changing Study of the Bible and History*. Eerdmans.

Fleming, Daniel. 2012. *The Legacy of Israel in Judah's Bible: History, Politics, and the Reinscribing of Tradition*. Cambridge University Press.

Hoffmeier, James K., and Dennis E. Magary, eds. 2012. *Do Historical Matters Matter to Faith? A Critical Appraisal of Modern and Postmodern Approaches to Scripture*. Crossway.

Arnold, Bill T., and Richard S. Hess, eds. 2013. *Ancient Israel's History: An Introduction to Issues and Sources*. Baker Academic.

Finkelstein, Israel. 2013. *The Forgotten Kingdom: The Archaeology and History of Northern Israel*. ANEM 5. SBL Press.

Niemann, Hermann M. 2015. *History of Ancient Israel, Archaeology, and Bible: Collected Essays*. AOAT 418. Ugarit-Verlag.

Dever, William G. 2016. "History from Things: On Writing New Histories of Ancient Israel." Pages 3–20 in *Le-ma'an Ziony: Essays in Honor of Ziony Zevit*. Edited by Frederick E. Greenspahn and Gary A. Rendsburg. Cascade.

———. 2017. *Beyond the Texts: An Archaeological Portrait of Ancient Israel and Judah*. SBL Press.

Elliot, Mark, and Paul W. M. Flesher. 2017. "Introduction to the Old Testament and Its Character as Historical Evidence." Pages 45–81 in *The Old Testament in Archaeology and History*. Edited by Jennie Ebeling, J. Edward Wright, Mark Elliott, and Paul V. M. Flesher. Baylor University Press.

Faust, Avraham. 2023. "Between the Biblical Story and History: Writing an Archaeological History of Ancient Israel." Pages 67–87 in *The Ancient Israelite World*. Edited by Kyle H. Keimer and George A. Pierce. Routledge.

4

On Listening to the Text—and the Artifacts

This essay was written as a contribution for the 1996 Festschrift I coedited for my esteemed Arizona colleague of twenty years, Lou H. Silberman. Here I tried to show the surprising degree to which the fundamental methodology of both mainstream biblical studies and Syro-Palestinian archaeology has been similar, although the various "schools" had not always been contemporary, and they were seldom mutually interactive (the lack of dialogue again). I cite no new literature at the end of this chapter because I am not aware that anyone else has attempted to draw such parallels except passing. On schools in biblical studies per se, see conveniently James Barr, *History and Ideology in the Old Testament: Biblical Studies at the End of a Millennium* (2000); and John J. Collins, *The Bible after Babel: Historical Criticism in a Postmodern Age* (2005).

This essay, buried in yet another Festschrift, has attracted little attention, yet I regard it as one of the most mature expressions of my lifelong agenda and even more pertinent than it was when written twenty years ago. In particular, I note the principal themes: (1) epistemology; (2) history writing; (3) the challenge of postmodernism and biblical revisionism; (4) archaeology as a primary source; (5) and the need for a knowledge of critical studies, and especially for dialogue. Many of these desiderata have come to fruition, at least partially in later books such as my *The Lives of Ordinary People in Ancient Israel: Where Archaeology and the Bible Intersect* (2012) and *Beyond the Texts: An Archaeological Portrait of Ancient Israel and Judah* (2017).

Originally published as pages 1–23 in *The Echoes of Many Texts: Reflections on Jewish and Christian Traditions: Essays in Honor of Lou H. Silberman*. Edited by William G. Dever and J. Edward Wright. BJS 313. Scholars Press, 1996. Reprinted by permission.

In this tribute to an esteemed friend, colleague, and mentor, Professor Lou H. Silberman, I would like to respond as an archaeologist and historian to the theme of his 1982 SBL Presidential Address: "On Listening to the Text."[1] What I shall attempt to show in this essay is (1) that the textual and artifactual data now available concerning ancient Israel are remarkably similar in character; (2) that the history of scholarly interpretation of both classes of data runs surprisingly parallel; and (3) that these convergences point to an interdisciplinary dialogue that holds the best hope yet for writing an adequate history of ancient Israel. How, then, shall we listen to both texts and artifacts?

4.1. How the Textual Record and the Archaeological Record Compare

We may begin by noting that the corpus of individual texts and artifacts constitutes in each case what we may call a record of the past. That the texts of the Hebrew Bible are a record of sorts is obvious, although the nature of that record is disputed. On the other hand, archaeologists have also been seeking to define a phenomenon known as the archaeological record since the dawn of the New Archaeology some three decades ago. By general consensus today, the archaeological record may be said to consist of (1) all those physical remains that survive from past human actions, that is, not only artifacts or objects strictly speaking; (2) any observable traces of human impact upon the external world and the natural environment or cultural deposits of many kinds (including the burials of the humans themselves); (3) the above remains situated in their larger spatial and temporal context; and (4) the whole of the evidence seen in the light of the intellectual and social matrix that we moderns inevitably bring to the task of interpretation. Need it be stressed that biblical texts must be seen as constituting a parallel and very similar kind of record of the past—indeed, with the same scope, complexity, and limitations?

Before proceeding, we may attempt in the interests of brevity to list some of the essential characteristics of both texts and artifacts in a simplified chart form, noting similarities and differences.

---

1. Silberman 1983.

	Biblical Texts (as preserved)	Archaeological Artifacts (as preserved)
1.	Concretize thought and behavior	Concretize thought and behavior
2.	Symbolic, encoded messages of past	Symbolic, encoded messages of past
3.	Express deliberate intent, imagination	Express deliberate intent, imagination
4.	Selective, elitist by nature	Broadly representative, populist
5.	Heavily edited in transmission	Constitute random sample
6.	Reflect principally ideology	Reflect common practice
7.	Closed corpus	Dynamic, expanding source of data
8.	Continuous tradition	"Broken" tradition
9.	Only a residue of past	Only a residue of past
10.	Curated artifacts	Curated artifacts
11.	Refract the past	Refract the past
12.	Literature	Real life

Of these twelve diagnostic characteristics, fully half are the same for both texts and artifacts, and a number of others are similar or overlap. Further, as I shall argue, even those characteristics that differ share something, in the fact that the same *interpretive methods* are required of the historian who works with these two types of data. Specifically, both texts and artifacts are objective, yet require subjective interpretation if the record is to be read correctly. Both contain valid information about the past, but only in the form of inferences we make that must be tested against some external criteria. These facts, when established as such, come to constitute true *data* only when placed within an intellectual framework that gives them meaning in relation to specific questions that are appropriate to history writing. Furthermore, the use of both classes of data requires an interpretive methodology that is fundamentally genetic, evolutionary, and comparative. Finally, if reading both the textual and archaeological record is the appropriate metaphor, then it is obvious that the interpreter must master the peculiar vocabulary, grammar, and syntax of each class of data. Otherwise, the text will remain as "mute" as some misguided biblical scholars maintain that the artifacts are.

4.2. Parallel Schools of Interpretation until Recently

We shall return shortly to this notion of a common hermeneutic that may be developing. First, however, we need to look at how texts and artifacts have, in fact, already been interpreted in various scholarly schools over the past century or so that have taken similar approaches, although not deliberately or explicitly so. Indeed, no one to my knowledge, writing on the history of either biblical or archaeological scholarship, has ever pointed out these parallels. Here I simply note some of the more obvious.[2]

1. Lower or textual criticism. This earliest manifestation of modern biblical criticism in the mid- to late nineteenth century sought to establish, as nearly as possible, an *Urtext* (a *Hebraica Veritas*), so as to isolate the fundamental body of data with which the historian could then work. This approach had its counterpart in nineteenth- and early twentieth-century Syro-Palestinian archaeology in the attempt of pioneers such as Edward Robinson, the explorers of the survey of western Palestine, and others to make the first modern site maps and to clarify the existence and nature of tells or stratified mounds, the raw source materials of the archaeological record. Philology as the basic tool of textual studies was matched in archaeology by learning the "language" of the landscape. In both disciplines the foundations were thus laid for all subsequent research (although, of course, these efforts must still continue, even if with diminishing and less revolutionary results).

2. Higher or literary criticism. Building upon better manuscript traditions and a more secure text, higher or literary criticism of the Hebrew Bible was able to turn to the analysis of individual books and larger literary units, raising questions of composition, sources, authors/redactors, date, historical circumstances and intent, as well as the essential question of historicity. This effort was paralleled almost exactly in the "stratigraphic revolution" of Syro-Palestinian archaeology's second generation, following Flinders Petrie in the 1890s and extending through Kathleen Kenyon's

---

2. In the following discussion I shall give references only for more recent schools of biblical interpretation, since earlier schools are well known. Recent histories of interpretation in general archaeology, with full bibliography, are Lamberg-Karlovsky 1989; and Trigger 2006. For the history of interpretation in Syro-Palestinian archaeology, see Dever 1985 and references there to earlier works. See also Dever 1991c and nn. 3, 10, 12, 37, 40, 42 below.

work in the 1950s–1960s. Here the questions addressed of the Palestinian tell were very much like those posed of the biblical texts: how to understand, separate, and date the complex layers of a typical mound and how to explain the origins and significance of these strata and their contents. In both disciplines, although they still operated mostly independently, the larger objective was to work out a chronological-cultural history, based upon a proper ordering and comprehension of the basic data in texts and artifacts.

It is not, I think, a coincidence that typologies of sorts played a prominent role in both disciplines—J, E, D, and P in biblical studies and soil layers and ceramic and other artifact types in archaeology—or that a typologist such as W. F. Albright could contribute simultaneously to both disciplines. More than anything else, it was a common methodology, although largely unacknowledged as such, that enabled biblical archaeology in its heyday to relate to Protestant Old Testament biblical studies during its floruit in the 1920s–1950s.[3]

3. Form criticism. Beginning early in the twentieth century, form criticism (*Formgeschichte* or *Gattungsgeschichte*) began to focus on individual subunits or pericopes of the text, attempting to classify literary forms. These smaller traditions, with their own history of transmission, were thought to derive largely from folk literature and to have been handed down orally for long periods in cultic circles or other social institutions. Thus following Hermann Gunkel there were efforts to place such literary forms as myth, sagas, cult legends, legal material, and other genres in an original setting—or *Sitz im Leben*—so as to understand them better. Unfortunately, as I shall show, an incipient historical thrust was usually blunted by the literary bias of form critics, who settled for what was in fact merely a *Sitz im Literatur* and who indeed were often poorly informed by a knowledge of *actual* socioeconomic conditions in ancient Palestine, such as archaeology might have provided. This deficiency of form criticism has finally been acknowledged by a few current biblical scholars, with at least lip service paid to archaeology.[4]

---

3. On Albright's use of typology, see Dever 1993c and references there. For the Protestant bias in biblical and archaeology scholarship, see Dever 1987, 210–17.

4. For tacit acknowledgements of the limitations of traditional searches for a *Sitz im Leben* in biblical scholarship, see Knierim 1985, 144; Thompson, 1992, 391–92.

The archaeological parallel to form criticism of the early to mid-twentieth century was the further development of typology as an *explicit* method. This aimed not simply at classifying artifacts but included the beginning attempts to explain recurrent patterns (either individual traits or larger assemblages) in the light of cultural and technological factors (and, later, environmental factors). Thus the discussion in the 1940s–1960s focused more and more on typical archaeological genres in their overall context. It could be argued that this approach in both disciplines was fundamentally a further attempt to get at the *prehistory* of the basic record as we now have it, either textual or artifactual. Yet there was a tendency to beg the question of any *actual* history to be derived from either source.

4. Tradition and redaction criticism. These approaches, often combined (as *Überlieferungsgeschichte*), moved further in order to study the nature and development of the individual genres that form criticism had sought to isolate. The questions were: How did these genres grow from oral to written traditions? How were they combined into larger literary units? How did they grow by stages into *the* tradition? Finally, how was this larger tradition transmitted and finally transformed into the Hebrew Bible as we have it? In short, how did oral and literary genres/traditions become text (or, in this case, Scripture)? Here we are dealing not simply with the prehistory of the biblical text but with the development of the final (or, shortly, canonical) form of the text itself. Again, however, establishing the history of the formation of the *text* as record did not necessarily lead to grappling with the issue of how one might derive any history per se from that record. That omission would lead ultimately to the present crisis in biblical historiography, to which we return below.

An uncannily exact parallel to the *Überlieferungsgeschichte* of the 1960s–1970s came in Syro-Palestinian archaeology in the 1960s–1980s in what was often called formation processes of the archaeological record.[5] At first, this approach was mainly an outgrowth of the stratigraphic revolution of the 1950s. This had been spearheaded by Kenyon at Jericho, then followed up by American excavations at Shechem, Gezer, and other sites in the 1960s. Prompted initially by the pragmatic question of how best to excavate and record a stratified Palestinian mound, excavators soon real-

---

5. For general orientation, see Schiffer 1987. Only scant literature exists with specific reference to Palestinian archaeology, although there is considerable experience with tell formation and a kind of common "oral tradition."

ized that they had first to grasp the complex natural and cultural factors that make up the depositional history of a typical mound. In short, how did a tell, like a text or textual tradition, take shape? Neither the textual nor the archaeological record can be read properly until we possess an adequate understanding of the process of its original formation, *plus* its long transformation over time until it comes into our hands today.

5. *Religionsgeschichte.* Overlapping and closely related to the above schools of biblical criticism was a school of historical and comparative religion (*Religionsgeschichte*, or religio-historical criticism) that was influential up until the 1940s and still has some proponents. Here the focus was upon what seemed to be the dominant role of religion and cult in ancient Israel on the shaping of the literary traditions of the Hebrew Bible. This school extended the critical, historical, and comparative methods already in vogue specifically to Israelite religion, often with the positivist presuppositions of that period. Occasionally, ethnographic and folkloric parallels from other religions were employed, even some archaeological evidence as it was understood at the time.

It is instructive to note parallels to *Religionsgeschichte* in archaeology of the same era. Indeed, the interest in ancient Israelite religion and cult had prevailed from the very beginning of Syro-Palestinian, and especially "biblical," archaeology, to the extent that the early literature abounds in attempts to explain nearly everything that seemed "exotic" as evidence of religious belief and practice. The one effort, however, to completely rewrite the history of Israel's religion in the light of archaeological discoveries was in Walter C. Graham and Herbert G. May's *Culture and Conscience: An Archaeological Study of the New Religious Past in Ancient Palestine.*[6] It is no accident that May, a distinguished biblical scholar, was also a member of the staff of the Oriental Institute of Chicago excavations at Megiddo and collaborated with Graham in another work entitled *Material Remains of the Megiddo Cult.*[7] The positive and lasting contribution of the "cultic school" in archaeology was limited, however, by the fact that the field was then dominated by biblical scholars. Thus it was dependent upon the naïveté of conservatives, on the one hand, and upon the equally naive evolutionary optimism of liberal scholars, on the other hand. The result was

---

6. Graham and May 1936. See further Dever 1987.
7. May 1935.

that all these early reconstructions of Israelite religion have been overturned by modern scholarship, both biblical and archaeological, which in the last decade has returned to the subject of religion and cult with a wealth of new data and vastly superior models, much of the evidence drawn from archaeology. It is no exaggeration to say that this fledgling dialogue implies that we are currently in the process of rewriting the entire history of ancient Israelite religion.[8]

6. The ethnographic approach. Closely related to *Religionsgeschichte* with its commitment to empirical method and comparative religion was a school of biblical studies that was never perhaps formalized but that utilized universal folklore and ethnographic data from primitive societies past and present to illuminate the cultural and religious background of the Hebrew Bible. This approach, often called the anthropological school, goes all the way back to W. Robertson Smith's 1909 *Lectures on the Religion of the Semites*[9] and continues in the well-known works of J. G. Frazer in the early twentieth century. Part of this approach's momentum continued in later *Religionsgeschichte*, particularly in the Scandinavian and British "myth and ritual" schools, and it was felt later still in modern socioanthropological approaches (below).

The parallel to this early school of biblical studies in archaeology was obviously ethnoarchaeology. This, however, did not break upon the scene in Near Eastern archaeology until the 1970s, as a strong component of the New Archaeology, and even today ethnoarchaeology has made little impact upon Syro-Palestinian archaeology.[10] That is partly because few practitioners of our discipline have been trained in anthropology, much less ethnography; in any case, the rapid modernization of pastoral nomads and other marginal groups in the Middle East and the politicization of the whole area have made productive ethnographic fieldwork virtually impossible.

7. Old Testament theology. Old Testament theology has had a venerable tradition within biblical studies since the eighteenth century, and

---

8. See further Dever 1987; Holladay 1987.
9. Smith 1927.
10. For convenient orientation, see Kramer 1979; Hodder 1982. The literature on pastoral nomadism is vast, but references will be found in Bar-Yosef and Khazanov 1992.

despite frequent obituaries it remains vigorous in some circles even today.[11] Its primary objective, whether in its dogmatic or its supposedly descriptive-historical guise, has been to describe the normative religion of the Old Testament (*sic*) and to systematize this theologically in terms of binding religious beliefs and practices for the modern Christian community. We may specify *Christian*, since biblical theology has never had any appeal for Jewish scholars of the Hebrew Bible. Indeed, Old Testament theology may best be described not as a historical (or even exegetical) discipline at all but as a branch of Christian apologetics. As I have recently shown,[12] it is scarcely interested in the history of ancient Israel per se, unable to grasp the actual vitality and diversity of Israelite religion, especially the popular cults, and of little interest to comparative religionists or Syro-Palestinian archaeologists today.

Nevertheless, Old Testament theology had its direct counterpart in previous generations in the classic school of biblical archaeology. Though now defunct as a serious intellectual enterprise, much less an academic discipline, biblical archaeology dominated much of the history of American Syro-Palestinian and even broader Near Eastern archaeology from its beginnings in the nineteenth century up until the 1970s. Since I have discussed this movement in detail elsewhere,[13] here I shall only point out briefly the similarities between biblical theology and biblical archaeology, which not by chance ran their courses concurrently. Again, at the risk of oversimplifying, we may chart the convergences, which in every case are direct.

Biblical Theology	Biblical Archaeology
The biblical text taken as starting point	The biblical text taken as starting point
"Historical" agenda actually drawn from theological issues	"Historical" agenda actually drawn from theological issues
Conservative, tendentious throughout in basic method	Conservative, tendentious throughout in basic method
Drew heavily on popular religious mentality in the U.S.	Drew heavily on popular religious mentality in the U.S.

---

11. See Hasel 1991.

12. On the implications for archaeology and the history of Israelite religion, see Dever 2002; see also Dever 1980, 1987.

13. See n. 12 above.

Operated with positivist presuppositions	Operated with positivist presuppositions
Actually begged the broader historical questions	Actually begged the broader historical questions
Resisted newer interdisciplinary methods	Resisted newer interdisciplinary methods
Could not accommodate "secular" approaches	Could not accommodate "secular" approaches
Gradually became parochial or obsolete	Gradually became parochial or obsolete

Even though factors other than these were operative in the demise of biblical archaeology in the 1970s—such as competition from foreign "national schools" and a crisis in funding—two facts remain clear. (1) As Albright and Wright, with their peculiar *combination* of biblical studies and archaeological research, passed from the scene in the early 1970s, so did biblical archaeology, which had in many ways always been uniquely Protestant and American.[14] (2) At the very same time, Brevard S. Childs could write an obituary of the biblical *theology* movement, *Biblical Theology in Crisis*.[15] Both movements had construed the history of ancient Palestine and of Israel as a sort of religio-political history that was thought to yield a universal, self-evident cultural meaning. The effort was perhaps noble, but it was doomed to failure.

8. Socioanthropological approaches. Partly continuing but expanding the older *Religionsgeschichte* and ethnographic approaches, several newer ways of looking at the Hebrew Bible and ancient Israel have drawn upon modern sociological studies and various anthropological models and case studies (social-scientific criticism). From Max Weber in the 1920s–1930s to current studies by Norman K. Gottwald, Frank S. Frick, James W. Flannagan, Robert B. Coote, Niels Peter Lemche, Robert R. Wilson, and many others, the value of the socioanthropological approach, while never dominant, has been clear—never moreso than today, I would argue.

Not only does this approach produce many exciting new insights; it also draws biblical studies closer methodologically to Syro-Palestinian archaeology, which has been moving in similar directions because of its own rapprochement with general and especially with New World archaeology. For the latter discipline, at least as practiced by Americans, nearly all

---

14. See references in nn. 2, 12 above. See Further Dever, 1985, 1992.
15. Childs 1970.

the underlying theory, the working hypotheses, and the analytical methods are drawn not from history (certainly not theology) but from anthropology in one fashion or another. The recent volume *The Archaeology of Society in the Holy Land*, edited by Thomas E. Levy, will mark the beginnings of a more self-conscious archaeology of society in our discipline.[16]

4.3. Recent Interpretive Approaches: Toward a New Hermeneutic?

The foregoing sketch of parallel schools of interpretation in biblical and archaeological studies up until some twenty years ago is suggestive. I would argue, however, that more recent trends in both disciplines pave the way for the first dialogue *between* texts and artifacts, with unique possibilities for illuminating the past in general and the phenomenon of ancient Israel in particular.

1. Structuralism. Structuralism as a putative method, much less a school, is nearly impossible to define, but the approach as applied sporadically in recent biblical studies has sought to penetrate behind the texts to comprehend the underlying mental construct as a whole, as a closed system yet one capable of transformation (the deep structure). Often the analysis focuses on bipolar opposites that constitute universal themes in the myths and often function as symbols or signs: male/female; life/death; good/bad; nature/culture; immanence/transcendence; and so on. Structuralism originated not, of course, in biblical studies, but in cultural anthropology, especially in linguistics. Because of its interest in the structure of society, structuralism is sometimes allied with Marxist notions of the social relations of production, and the relation of these to ideology, as they shape society (Marx was not simply a "vulgar materialist").

Structuralism has had little if any impact on Syro-Palestinian archaeology, although it has had its advocates in the general field of archaeology. Yet if there is a discernible deep structure in texts, then it is reasonable to suppose that some such structure exists in artifactual remains as well; furthermore, it is evident that artifacts, like texts, are signs and have symbolic meaning.

---

16. Levy 1995. For socioanthropological approaches to the Hebrew Bible, see Rogerson 1978; Gottwald 1979; Wilson 1984; Culley 1985; Flanagan 1991; La Bianca 1988.

2. *Structuralism, semiotics, and new literary criticism.* Similar in many ways to structuralism is semiotics—a "science of how language works as a set of symbols"—and several related approaches that sometimes go under the banner of New Literary Criticism.[17] The effort of the latter is directed toward a formal description of the fundamental structure of a text as discourse. Obviously this discourse is associated with some meaning, but the question is not primarily what texts mean but rather what makes meaning possible. In short, how is the text *able* to say what it says, how does it "signify," and to whom? The basic tool of the newer literary approaches is often metalanguage, a special language of description that focuses on the play among "signifying elements" in the text—mostly opposites/contrasts that are said to make meaning possible.

At the heart of these varied approaches is the notion of *symbol*, understood as a primary language that emerges directly and simultaneously out of experience. In a secondary stage, this symbolic language comes to be arranged in narrative form as myth, but this is not, however, yet at the stage of reflective thought. These symbolized myths, in turn, must be analyzed by the interpreter in terms of a double structure, as: conveying obvious, literal meaning and as analogies. Texts, then—biblical or other—do refer to a "reality," but in different and special ways. They do say something to somebody; they offer at least the possibility of re-creating the world that was real to their authors and/or editors, if not an "objective" reality.

New Literary Criticism, with its emphasis on narrative history and the intent of the text, is clearly related to older approaches, as well as more recent schools such as rhetorical and canonical criticism, and therefore it seems accessible to many biblical scholars (at least in its less extreme forms). Unfortunately, New Literary Criticism falls easily into a deconstructionist mode: the text itself means nothing, and we must supply whatever meaning we choose, largely in terms of our own contemporary needs. There are no truths about the past to be learned; our supposed knowledge of the past is conditioned entirely by the modern context of the quest, mostly political. Ultimately, there is no history, only propaganda—theirs and ours. Thus the extremes of New Literary Criticism—often in the guise of the radical new critical theory of the Frankfurt school (below)—

---

17. On various aspects of New Literary Criticism, including semiotics, see Alter 1981; Culley 1985; Ricoeur, 1980.

may tend to discredit it. In that case, few biblical historians or historical archaeologists will find this approach congenial or productive.

Despite these caveats, a few Syro-Palestinian archaeologists (this writer and one or two others) are beginning to show an interest in semiotics, structuralism, and New Literary Criticism, if for no other reason than the fact that it is instructive to view the textual record and the archaeological record as parallel "texts to be read." Indeed, one of the emergent trends in today's postprocessualist archaeology, after the long reign of the New Archaeology, is epitomized in Ian Hodder's *Reading the Past: Current Approaches to Interpretation in Archaeology*.[18]

The main title is significant. Moving substantially beyond the New Archaeology, with its largely functionalist notion of culture as ecological/technological adaptation, as well as his own previous structuralist models, Hodder advocates a more idealist and historical approach that he calls contextual—literally artifacts "with texts." But he goes even further in defining the archaeological record itself as a text and conversely written texts as artifacts. Thus both can and must be "read," indeed in similar ways, if a common "generative grammar" can be developed. Hodder says that such a notion "has long been tacitly assumed in archaeology," but he gives few examples, and he does not expand much on this fecund idea, beyond saying that artifacts are not necessarily mute, if we can work out suitable principles of interpretation. At the Second International Congress on Biblical Archaeology in Jerusalem in 1990, I called attention to the work of Hodder and other current postprocessualist archaeologists as possibly heralding a return to the concept of history in Syro-Palestinian archaeology—with wide-ranging implications for a new biblical archaeology (although I prefer another name).[19] Yet it is now possible to go much further.

3. Toward a new hermeneutic. The foregoing list of parallels between interpretive schools in biblical studies and Syro-Palestinian archaeology, while already impressive, could be expanded. For instance, canonical criticism (noted above) addresses the Hebrew Bible as a complete witness, a literary corpus closed for good reasons at a given point in time, as though

---

18. Hodder 1986; for critical assessment of Hodder and other postprocessual archaeologists, see Dever 1996.
19. Dever 1993a.

religious authorities then knew best.[20] Studies of the formation processes of the archaeological record (above) seek similarly to address the question of why a tell is the way we confront it today and whether it is possible to penetrate behind human and cultural transformations over time to reveal an alternative or more comprehensive view of past realities, no longer easily visible in the mound itself. Or again, in current biblical studies several marginal movements such as radical feminism, liberation theology, new critical theory, and new hermeneutics have had some impact, even on mainstream scholarship.[21] Parallels to all these approaches to biblical texts can be found in world archaeology,[22] although only sporadically in Syro-Palestinian archaeology. Some women's issues, however, have been raised in the call for a shift of attention from the prevailing political history to a new family or domestic archaeology, which would include the study of popular and women's cults in the light of archaeological evidence.[23] Also significant is the willingness of a few Syro-Palestinian archaeologists to confront the role of modern ideology in shaping archaeological research, including not only religion and politics but elitism, economic considerations, nationalism, and even racism.[24] Such protests are, however, little more than murmurs compared to the bold views of writers such as Michael Shanks and Christopher Tilley, whose work *Re-constructing Archaeology: Theory and Practice*[25] regards archaeology as a powerful tool for "cultural critique." A considerable radical, postpositivist, postmodern literature of this sort is now appearing, especially in Britain, in both archaeology and anthropology, some of it Neo-Marxist, all of it controversial. Yet the hubbub surrounding the "new nihilism" could serve as a timely reminder of the value and relevance of archaeological investigation—of the uses of the past—one that might be heartening to Syro-Palestinian and "biblical" archaeologists who have always thought of themselves as being in the

---

20. On canonical criticism, see Sanders 1984; Sheppard 1992.

21. On some of the most recent trends in biblical criticism, see Culley 1985; Gottwald 1993; and several of the essays in Jobling, Day, and Sheppard 1991.

22. For other references, see, for instance, Shanks and Tilley 1987; Marcus and Fischer 1987; Dever 1996; the latest and best are Pinski and Wylie 1989; Preucel 1991.

23. See Meyers 1988.

24. See, for instance, Broshi 1987.

25. See n. 22 above.

humanist tradition. The continuing dilemma, however, is simply: What, if anything, can we know with certainty of the past?

4. Back to epistemology. Most encouraging of all recent parallel developments in both biblical and archaeological studies is the growing concern with epistemological and historiographical issues, what might be called the new hermeneutics.[26] The maturation of both disciplines, and particularly the interdisciplinary thrust, has brought us to the point where we *must* ask basic methodological questions. In particular, the question of how to write an adequate history of ancient Israel and it religion, *of sources*, is one that both biblical scholars and archaeologists (at last) are beginning to confront. Indeed, it is not too much to speak of a crisis in current scholarship that is fundamentally hermeneutical. As Rolf Rendtorff recently put it, "The question is rather whether the texts are pre-exilic or postexilic.... We will have to redesign our image of Israel's history and the history of its religion."[27]

Above I noted some of the problems and possibilities of semiotics, structuralism, and New Literary Criticism for developing a common hermeneutic. It may be useful to expand that discussion at this point. These and related newer approaches, which in anthropology may simply be called interpretive anthropology, may be congenial to archaeologists because they tend to use the metaphor of culture as a text to be read, a notion popularized by Clifford Geertz.[28] It is obviously only one step further to extend the notion of text to that which is enmeshed with culture and gives it concrete expression, namely, material culture. Furthermore, despite the unfortunate antihistorical bias of some of its practitioners, structuralism is attractive because focusing on structure means looking critically at society and culture, which are the basic phenomena that the archaeologist seeks ultimately to comprehend, as well as being the "context" (Hodder's phrase) within which all material culture remains must be understood. Finally, both structuralist and archaeological (as well as biblical/textual) studies today must grapple with the fundamental problem of the meaning of symbols and symbolic actions, that is, not merely with materialist but with idealist explanations of culture and culture change (including religion).

---

26. See Culley 1985; Knierim 1985; and several essays in Jobling, Day, and Sheppard 1991.
27. Rendtorff 1993, 44, 50. See further Dever 1995.
28. See, for example, Geertz 1973.

Here Hodder's "cognitive" archaeology, or "archaeology of mind"—which to many New Archaeologists signals a return to the prescientific and subjective *Kulturgeschichte*, or historical particularism, of the past—is actually a positive sign of anthropology and archaeology's coming of age.[29] Partly as a reaction to the reductionist paradigms of the previous generation, it is now being recognized once again, and with a new sophistication, that *ideology* is not a mere epiphenomenon but instead is a basic component of all cultures. Thus we may speak of archaeological (and historical) data as consisting of (1) artifacts, (2) ecofacts, (3) textual facts, and (4) ideofacts. All these facts, and the culture they make up, are indeed texts to be read.

Yet as Hodder has observed, somewhat ruefully, there are no grammars and dictionaries of material culture language. What is offered in the following is a first, tentative outline of a "grammar of artifacts," based on the parallels that I am presupposing here with texts, where such grammars exist in abundance. Since I presented the similarities between texts and artifacts above in chart form, I use that device again, to list what we must know in order to "read" or interpret texts and artifacts, both as objects and as signs.

Texts	Artifacts
Writing system	"Language" of material culture
Vocabulary	Artifacts of all types
Grammar	Formation processes
Syntax	Ecological, sociocultural context
Author, composition, date	Date, technology
Cultural context (*Sitz im Leben*)	Overall historical setting
Intent	"Mental template" of makers
Later transmission, interpretation	Natural-cultural transformations
What the text "symbolizes"	What the artifact "symbolizes"
How its "meaning" is relevant today	How its "meaning" is relevant today

---

29. On archaeology of mind, see especially Hodder 1986; Binford 1989; see also the works cited in n. 22 above. For a positive reaction, see see Dever 1996. On the new respectability of ideology as a factor in cultural change, see Gilman 1989; Demarest 1989; and Conkey 1989.

Once again, the parallels in reading the two types of texts are striking. Although I am sanguine about the possibilities for eventually reading the archaeological record as effectively as the textual record in the Hebrew Bible has been read in the past century of critical scholarship, examples of such readings—what have been called formalist-structuralist interpretations—are still relatively rare. One thinks, however, of New World examples such as James Deetz's analysis of early New England houses and their furnishings, Henry Glassie's similar study of folk housing in Georgia, Jon Muller's study of the American Southwest, Dorothy Washburn's of ceramic design, Robert L. Hall's interpretation of Indian peace pipes, and even of the revealing studies of modern discard patterns by my colleague William Rathje and his fellow "garbologists." All these are studies in "reading" material culture texts.[30]

In Old World prehistory, André Leroi-Gourhan has elucidated what appear to be underlying structural principles that can be useful in understanding Paleolithic cave art. This is a sort of vocabulary, grammar, and syntax for reading the "statements" made by the various representations and arrangements of animal drawings—what Leroi-Gourhan considers a "cave-as-text," or "mythogram." Here is a striking example of the potential of poststructuralist archaeology of mind for doing prehistory, if not history itself. It is from such challenges to realism and naturalism that the reader of cultural texts—such as literary myths, visual images, and archaeological artifacts—can profit. But as Terence Hawkes points out, the textual-artifactual record is not simply a static one-to-one representation of an underlying reality in the natural world but is dynamic in nature, subject interacting with object. Thus, he says, all art (and, I would add, texts and artifacts) "acts as a mediating, molding force in society rather than an agency which merely reflects or records."[31] The conclusion might be that in the structuralist view, as opposed to the empiricist/rationalist view, reality is not expressed by culture (or language) but *produced* by it. Yet I think we need not go that far. There is a real, tangible world "out there," but intervening between us and our perceptions of it are always ideas, beliefs, and meanings, both individual and cultural.[32] Nevertheless, as George Cowgill, a leading formalist, puts it, "I believe it is possible to

---

30. See Hodder 1986, 34, 39, 51, 135; Rathje 1974.
31. See Leroi-Gourhan in Conkey 1989, 140–46; Hawkes in Conkey 1989, 139.
32. Hawkes in Conkey 1989, 139.

construct models of the world that increasingly approximate how it really is, even if we never get beyond approximations."[33] On this positivist note, I cannot help remarking how ironic I find it that at the very time when biblical historians, basing themselves on texts, are rejecting von Rankian notions of *wie es eigentlich gewesen war*—despairing of writing a genuinely historical picture of ancient Israel—some archaeologists are about to take up the challenge.[34] How is that possible?

4.4. "History from Things": Why Neither Texts Nor Artifacts are Mute for the Sensitive Historian

One of the enduring canards regarding archaeology, perpetuated by certain schools of biblical historians (beginning apparently with Martin Noth), is that "archaeological data without texts are mute."[35] But is that true? If so, the dialogue between texts and artifacts as equals envisioned here is obviously impossible; archaeology would be merely a silent partner. The charge, however, is patently false, as every archaeologist knows—and not just prehistorians who have no texts and yet espouse legitimately to write history. After all, in Palestine the whole of the remains of the Paleolithic, Neolithic, Chalcolithic, and Early-Middle Bronze Ages are anepigraphic. Does that mean that we cannot give a connected account of cultural and historical developments throughout these eras? Certainly not! As we shall see, the controversy revolves around what we mean by *history*, although the issue is rarely posed as such. As for archaeological data being mute, Ernst Axel Knauf has pointed out that both sources of data for history writing are similar; for the scholar who does not know Hebrew, the Hebrew Bible is mute.[36]

Part of the failure of communication lies in the fact that most biblical scholars who address the issues are *not* historians broadly trained but philologians and secondarily theologians. Further, they tend by tempera-

---

33. Cowgill 1989, 79.
34. See also n. 37 below.
35. Noth 1960, 47–48. The term mute (German *dumm*) is perpetuated in the works of Rolf Rendtorff, J. Alberto Soggin, Gösta W. Ahlström, and several others; see Miller 1991.
36. Knauf 1991.

ment, training, and profession to overvalue texts, while at the same time they are woefully ignorant of the nature and potential of parallel material culture remains. (Texts, like artifacts, are metaphors, not objective reports on the way it really was in the past.) It must also be admitted that few Syro-Palestinian archaeologists today, highly specialized as they must be, are conversant enough with ancient Near Eastern and biblical texts to be able to use the textual data critically.[37] Thus there is little true dialogue, only the monologues of scholars in each discipline talking to each other rather than daring to cross disciplinary boundaries.

Thomas L. Thompson's *Early History of the Israelite People from the Written and Archaeological Sources* and Gösta W. Ahlström's *The History of Ancient Palestine from the Paleolithic Period to Alexander's Conquest* both purport to be syntheses of the archaeological and cultural history of ancient Palestine, by *biblical* scholars who have no training or experience in archaeology. Meanwhile, few American, European, or Israeli Palestinian archaeologists (especially the latter) are even aware of the current crisis in Israelite historiography or see their research as contributing to a solution.[38] If ever a dialogue between texts and artifacts were needed, it is now—not just for the sake of the promising results but in order to keep *both* disciplines healthy. Precisely because the two classes of data with which we both work as historians are so similar, we depend upon each other methodologically. Yet this raises the issue of whether or not either source of data is indeed properly historical.

Biblical scholars have wrestled with this question from the beginning, with renewed vigor in the last decade or so, as seen in the works of John Van Seters, Baruch Halpern, and others and now in the fierce debate over the origins of Israel—the latter involving archaeologists as well, since it is they who have produced the compelling new data. Yet there is no consensus. The Hebrew Bible is "theocratic history" (Miller and Hayes 1986),

---

37. Dever 1993a and references there to earlier published remarks going back twenty years. Others in both disciplines (most recently Åhlström and Thompson) seem to assume that some sort of dialogue may be beneficial or even essential, but one sees few specific calls for it in print among biblical specialists.

38. The literature is vast, but for orientation see Dever 1991a, 1993b. The standard work is Finkelstein 1988. On current historiographical issues in Syro-Palestinian archaeology, see several of my treatments cited in nn. 12, 18, 27 and add Dever 1991b, 1994b.

historicized myth or mythologized history (many scholars), "rationalized myth" (Garbini 1988), simply myth (Oden 1976), texts possessed only of a certain "historicality" (Knierim 1985), "history-like" (Frei 1974), "tradition" (Knight 2006), the "final form of narrative history" (Childs 1970), *kerygma* or *Heilsgeschichte* (von Rad, Wright, and many others); story (Barr 2000 and others), "prose fiction" (Alter 1981), or simply "fiction" (Davies 1992).[39] No wonder there is currently a crisis in Israelite historiography! Of late, the rather desperate question is being raised: Is it possible to write a history of ancient Israel without the Bible? The answer usually given by biblical scholars, textually biased as they are, is no. But it is possible and even desirable to write such a history; it all depends upon what *kind* of history one wants: *Heilsgeschichte*? political history? socioeconomic history? Thomas L. Thompson has seen this point in several programmatic statements, but his own recent attempt at such a history (above) must be judged a failure—in my judgement precisely because he is unable, despite his efforts, to utilize critically the rich archaeological data now available.[40]

Archaeological evidence, I would maintain, constitutes *primary* data, and indeed such evidence is often more useful than the textual data in the Hebrew Bible for purposes of historical reconstruction. For example, Syro-Palestinian archaeology at its present stage of refinement as an autonomous, professional, and academic discipline[41] can comment, often extensively, on the following cultural-historical categories.

1. Environmental setting
2. Settlement types and patterns
3. Subsistence
4. Technology

---

39. Davies 1992. Davies's position, however, is too extreme for most American biblical scholars, as reviews have indicated.

40. Miller 1991; see also the responses in the same volume by Knauf (1991) and Dever (1991b, 1991c). Further on the possibilities of a parallel secular history of ancient Israel, see my remarks in the works cited in nn. 12, 18, 27, and 38 above. Thompson has expressed similar views in 1992, 108–16, 158–70, 316; and already remarks in 1987, 25–28. See my reaction to Thompson 1992, however, in Dever 2002.

41. This assessment of the current status of Syro-Palestinian archaeology is by now too well known—to both biblical scholars and archaeologists—to need further defense. For earlier characterizations, see Dever 1985 and works cited there.

5. Demography
6. Socioeconomic structure
7. Political organization
8. Architecture, ceramics, and other aspects of material culture
9. Daily life
10. Art, ideology, and cult
11. Trade and international relations
12. Chronology

These categories, or subsystems in a General Systems Theory approach, taken together actually *constitute* culture in its manifold expressions, and what is history writing if not the analysis of culture change? Yet a moment's reflection will reinforce the point that most of the information we now have concerning the above categories has to do with matters not described explicitly anywhere in the Hebrew Bible, nor capable of being derived from the texts as they now stand except by reading between the lines.[42] The omissions should not be surprising. The biblical writers and editors could be competent historians when they chose, but their steadfastly fixed view *sub specie aeternitatis* did not usually concede much importance to such mundane matters as the daily life of the masses. Yet Braudel and historians of the Annales school have shown forcefully that this is the *real* stuff of history. Such an approach, over *la longue durée*, is only belatedly making an impact on archaeologists, but it seems to have been neglected almost entirely by biblical historians.[43] Is the latter fault because the parochial, elitist, theocratic biases of the writers and final editors of the Hebrew Bible have been (unconsciously?) adopted by most modern biblical scholars?[44]

---

42. See Dever 1994a, 1994b.

43. On the Annales approaches in general, see Bintliff 1991; Knapp 1992. Specifically in Syro-Palestinian archaeology, see Dever 1988 and references there. Few references to Braudel and the Annales school can be found among biblical scholars—perhaps because of their turning away recently from history to literature—but note Coote and Whitelam 1987; Knauf 1991, 42–43 and references there; Thompson 1992, 149–70, 371–94; Ahlström 1993, 20–24.

44. See the scathing, but not entirely undeserved, critique of most biblical "historians" in Garbini 1988, 10–20, 170–78; see also Knauf 1991, passim; and Lemche 1985, passim.

Since there is no such thing as an objective history of ancient Israel (or anything else), it may be necessary to cultivate a certain empathy with the biblical text and the world of its writers, but it is not admissible for the modern historian to blur the boundaries between confessional history and critical historical *scholarship*. Unfortunately, we get the kind of history we deserve, and most histories of Israel are hopelessly inadequate. They are either little more than paraphrases of the biblical story or else so minimalist (like Thompson's) that they are no histories at all.

It is my contention that it is *only* in the dialogue between texts and artifacts—pursued rigorously by scholars committed to interdisciplinary inquiry—that we can hope for more comprehensive, better balanced, ultimately more satisfying histories of ancient Israel in all its variety and vitality. The fixed textual data, although of somewhat restricted value historically, can yield an outline of political and theocratic history, of ethnic and religious ideology, together with numerous details of real life embedded in the older materials now incorporated into the literary traditions of the Hebrew Bible—an "internal history." The archaeological data—theoretically almost unlimited in extent and variety, more flexible, and less deliberately biased—can yield a broader environmental and socioeconomic history, an external, secular history that is parallel, complementary in many ways, and often corrective. Both histories of ancient Israel are now essential, and possible—if scholars in several disciplines are willing to set aside conventional approaches and cooperate in a true dialogue between texts and artifacts.[45]

4.5. Conclusion

Let us return to the point at which we began, attempting to heed Professor Silberman's sage advice to listen. That means that as historians, when

---

45. There are only a few articles on theory and method by Israeli archaeologists, and none betrays any significant interest in a *critical* dialogue between archaeology and biblical studies. See my critique in ch. 1 above; add now Shay 1989. For prospects in the archaeology of Judaism and early Christianity, see Meyers and Meyers 1989. Among the very few pioneering attempts by archaeologists at dialogue for the period of ancient Israel, one might cite my 1994c; and Stager 1985.

we have been able to read both texts and artifacts as accurately as possible with all means at our disposal, assessing all the data as disinterestedly as possible, we must then be content to sit back and listen—intently, patiently, with a disciplined but sympathetic imagination, and above all with humility. As Hodder reminds us, in the quest for meaning in history there are always these subjective elements. The role of history is "to understand human action, rather than events.... To get at action is to get at subjective meanings, at the inside of events."[46] By listening perceptively to the human past as it speaks to us today, we may appropriate that past, and thus we gain the only insights that we shall ever have into the future.

Works Cited

Ahlström, Gösta W. 1993. *The History of Ancient Palestine from the Paleolithic Period to Alexander's Conquest.* JSOTSup 146. JSOT Press.

Alter, Robert.1981. *The Art of Biblical Narrative.* Basic Books.

Barr, James. 2000. *History and Ideology in the Old Testament: Biblical Studies at the End of a Millennium.* Oxford University Press.

Bar-Yosef, Ofer, and Anatoly Khazanov eds. 1992. *Pastoralism in the Levant: Archaeological Materials in Anthropological Perspectives.* Prehistory Press.

Binford, Lewis R. 1989. "The 'New Archaeology,' Then and Now." Pages 50–62 in *Archaeological Thought in America.* Edited by Carl C. Lamberg-Karlovsky. Cambridge University Press.

Bintliff, John. 1991. *The Annales School and Archaeology.* Leicester University Press.

Broshi, Magen. 1987. "Religion, Ideology, and Politics and Their Impact on Palestinian Archaeology." *Israel Museum Journal* 6:17–32.

Childs, Brevard S. 1970. *Biblical Theology in Crisis.* Westminster.

Collins, John J. 2005. *The Bible after Babel: Historical Criticism in a Postmodern Age.* Eerdmans.

Conkey, Margaret W. 1989. "The Structural Analysis of Paleolithic Art." Pages 135–54 in *Archaeological Thought in America.* Edited by Carl C. Lamberg-Karlovsky. Cambridge University Press.

---

46. Hodder 1986, 94.

Coote, Robert B., and Keith W. Whitelam. 1987. *The Emergence of Early Israel in Historical Perspective.* SWBA 5. Almond.

Cowgill, George L. 1989. "Formal Approaches in Archaeology." Pages 74-88 in *Archaeological Thought in America.* Edited by Carl C. Lamberg-Karlovsky. Cambridge University Press.

Culley, Robert C. 1985. "Exploring New Directions. Pages 184-89. In *The Hebrew Bible and Its Modern Interpreters.* Edited by Douglas A. Knight and Gene M. Tucker. Fortress; Scholars Press.

Davies, Philip R. 1992. *In Search of "Ancient Israel."* JSOTSup 148. JSOT Press.

Demarest, Arthur A. 1989. "Ideology and Evolution in American Archaeology: Looking Beyond the Economic." Pages 89-102 in *Archaeological Thought in America.* Edited by Carl C. Lamberg-Karlovsky. Cambridge University Press.

Dever, William G. 1980. Biblical Theology and Biblical Archaeology. *HTR* 73:1-16.

———. 1985. "Syro-Palestinian and Biblical Archaeology." Pages 31-74 in *The Hebrew Bible and Its Modern Interpreters.* Edited by Douglas A. Knight and Gene M. Tucker. BMI 1. Scholars Press.

———. 1987. "The Contribution of Archaeology to the Study of Canaanite and Israelite Religion." Pages 209-47 in *Ancient Israelite Religion: Essays in Honor of Frank Moore Cross.* Edited by Patrick D. Miller, Paul D. Hanson, and S. Dean McBride. Fortress.

———. 1988. "Impact of the 'New Archaeology.'" Pages 337-52 in *Benchmarks in Time and Culture: Introduction to Palestinian Archaeology.* Edited by Joel F. Drinkard Jr., Gerald L. Mattingly, and J. Maxwell Miller. Scholars Press.

———. 1991a. "Archaeological Data on the Israelite Settlement: A Review of Two Recent Works." *BASOR* 284:77-90.

———. 1991b. "Archaeology, Material Culture and the Early Monarchial Period in Israel." Pages 103-15 in *Fabric of History: Text, Artifact and Israel's Past.* Edited by Diana Vikander Edelman. JSOTSup 127. JSOT Press.

———. 1991c. "Unresolved Issues in the Early History of Israel: Toward a Synthesis of Archaeological and Textual Reconstructions." Pages 195-208 in *The Bible and the Politics of Exegesis: Essays in Honor of Norman K. Gottwald on his Sixty-Fifth Birthday.* Edited by David Jobling. Pilgrim.

———. 1992. "Archaeology, Syro-Palestinian and Biblical." *ABD* 1:354-67.

---. 1993a. "Biblical Archaeology—Death and Rebirth?" Pages 706–22 in *Biblical Archaeology Today, 1990: Proceedings of the Second International Congress on Biblical Archaeology, Jerusalem, June 1990*. Edited by Avraham Biran and Joseph Aviram. Israel Exploration Society.

---. 1993b. "Cultural Continuity: Ethnicity in the Archaeological Record and the Question of Israelite Origins." *ErIsr* 24:23–33.

---. 1993c. "What Remains of the House That Albright Built?" *BA* 56:25–36.

---. 1994a. "Ancient Israelite Religion: How to Reconcile the Differing Textual and Archaeological Portraits." Pages 105–25 in *Ein Gott allein? JHWH-Verehrung und biblischer Monotheismus im Kontext der israelitischen und altorientalischen Religionsgeschichte*. Edited by Walter Dietrich and Martin A. Klopfenstein. Universitätsverlag; Vandenhoeck & Ruprecht.

---. 1994b. "Archaeology, Texts, and History-Writing: Toward an Epistemology." Pages 105–17 in *Uncovering Ancient Sources: Essays in Memory of H. Neil Richardson*. Edited by Lewis F. Hopfe. Eisenbrauns.

---. 1994c. "The Silence of the Text: An Archaeological Commentary on 2 Kings 23." Pages 143–68 in *Scripture and Other Artifacts. Essays in Honor of Phillip J. King*. Edited by Michael D. Coogan, Cheryl Exum, and Lawrence E. Stager. Westminster John Knox.

---. 1995. "Archaeology and the Current Crisis in Israelite Historiography." *ErIs* 25:18*–27*.

---. 1996. "Archaeology and the Current Crisis in Israelite Historiography." *ErIsr* 25:18*–27*.

---. 2002. "Theology, Philology, and Archaeology: In the Pursuit of Ancient Israelite Religion." Pages 11–34 in *Sacred Time, Sacred Place: Archaeology and the Religion of Israel*. Edited by Barry M. Gittlen. Eisenbrauns.

---. 2012. *The Lives of Ordinary People in Ancient Israel: Where Archaeology and the Bible Intersect*. Eerdmans.

---. 2017. *Beyond the Texts: An Archaeological Portrait of Ancient Israel and Judah*. SBL Press.

Finkelstein, Israel. 1988. *The Archaeology of the Israelite Settlement*. Israel Exploration Society.

Flanagan, James W. 1991. "New Construction in Social World Studies." Pages 209–23 in *The Bible and the Politics of Exegesis: Essays in Honor of Norman K. Gottwald on His Sixty-Fifth Birthday*. Edited by David Jobling, Peggy L. Day, and Gerald T. Sheppard. Pilgrim.

Frei, Hans W. 1974. *The Eclipse of Biblical Narrative: A Study in Eighteenth and Nineteenth Century Hermeneutics.* Yale University Press.

Garbini, Giovanni. 1988. *History and Ideology in Ancient Israel.* Crossroad.

Geertz, Clifford. 1973. *The Interpretation of Cultures.* Basic Books.

Gilman, Antonio. 1989. "Marxism in American Archaeology." Pages 50–73 in *Archaeological Thought in America.* Edited by Carl C. Lamberg-Karlovsky. Cambridge University Press.

Gottwald, Norman K. 1979. "Sociological Method in the Study of Ancient Israel." Pages 69–81 in *Encounter with the Text: Form and History in the Bible.* Edited by Martin J. Buss. Fortress.

———. 1993. *The Bible and Liberation: Political and Social Hermeneutics.* Rev. ed. Orbis Books.

Graham, Walter C., and Herbert G. May. 1936. *Culture and Conscience: An Archaeological Study of the New Religious Past in Ancient Palestine.* University of Chicago Press.

Hasel, Gerhard. 1991. *Old Testament Theology: Basic Issues in the Current Debate.* Eerdmans.

Hodder, Ian. 1982. *Symbols in Action: Ethnoarchaeological Studies of Material Culture.* Cambridge University Press.

———. 1986. *Reading the Past: Current Approaches to Interpretation in Archaeology.* Cambridge University Press.

Holladay, John S., Jr. 1987. "Religion in Israel and Judah under the Monarchy: An Explicitly Archaeological Approach." Pages 249–99 in *Ancient Israelite Religion: Essays in Honor of Frank Moore Cross.* Edited by Patrick D. Miller, Paul D. Hanson, and S. Dean McBride. Fortress.

Jobling, David, Peggy L. Day, and Gerald T. Sheppard, eds. 1991. *The Bible and the Politics of Exegesis: Essays in Honor of Norman K. Gottwald on his Sixty-Fifth Birthday.* Pilgrim.

Knapp, A Bernard. 1992. *Archaeology, Annales, and Ethnohistory.* Cambridge University Press.

Knauf, Ernst Axel. 1991. "From History to Interpretation." Pages 26–64 in *The Fabric of History: Text, Artifact and Israel's Past.* Edited by Diana V. Edelman. JSOTSup 127. JSOT Press.

Knierim, Rolf. 1985. "Criticism of Literary Features, Form, Tradition, and Redaction." Pages 123–65 in *The Hebrew Bible and Its Modern Interpreters.* Edited by Douglas A. Knight and Gene M. Tucker. Fortress; Scholars Press.

Knight, Douglas A. 2006. *Rediscovering the Traditions of Israel.* 3rd ed. SBLStBL 16. Society of Biblical Literature.

Kramer, Carol, ed. 1979. *Ethnoarchaeology: Implications for Archaeology*. Columbia University Press.

La Bianca, Østein S. 1988. "Sociocultural Anthropology in the Study of Ancient Israel." Pages 69–81 in *Benchmarks in Time and Culture: An Introduction to Palestinian Archaeology*. Edited by Joel F. Drinkard, Gerald L. Matting, and J. Maxwell Miller. Scholars Press.

Lemche, Niels Peter. 1985. *Early Israel: Anthropological and Historical Studies on the Israelite Society before the Monarchy*. VTSup 37. Brill.

Levy, Thomas E., ed. 1995. *The Archaeology of Society in the Holy Land*. Leicester University Press.

Marcus, George E., and Michael M. J. Fischer. 1987. *Anthropology as Cultural Critique*. University of Chicago Press.

May, Herbert G. 1935. *Material Remains of the Megiddo Cult*. OIP 26. University of Chicago Press.

Meyers, Carol. 1988. *Discovering Eve: Ancient Israelite Women in Context*. Oxford University Press.

Meyers, Carol, and Eric Meyers. 1989. "Expanding the Frontiers of Biblical Archaeology." *ErIsr* 20:140*–47*.

Miller, J. Maxwell. 1991. "Is it Possible to Write a History of Israel without Relying on the Hebrew Bible?" Pages 93–102 in *The Fabric of History: Text, Artifact and Israel's Past*. Edited by Diana V. Edelman. JSOTSup 127. JSOT Press.

Miller, J. Maxwell, and John H. Hayes. 1986. *A History of Ancient Israel and Judah*. Westminster.

Noth, Martin. 1960. *The History of Israel*. Harper & Row.

Oden, Robert. 1976. "The Persistence of Canaanite Religion." *BA* 39:31–36.

Pinski, Valerie, and Alison Wylie, eds. 1991. *Critical Traditions in Contemporary Archaeology*. Cambridge University Press.

Preucel, Robert W., ed. 1991. *Processual and Postprocessual Archaeologies: Multiple Ways of Knowing the Past*. Southern Illinois University Press.

Rathje, William J. 1974. "The Garbage Project: A New Way of Looking at the Problems of Archaeology." *Archaeology* 27:236–41.

Rendtorff, Rolf. 1993. "The Paradigm is Changing: Hopes—and Fears." *BibInt* 1:34–53.

Ricoeur, Paul. 1980. *Essays on Biblical Interpretation*. Translated by Lewis S. Mudge. Fortress.

Rogerson, John W. 1978. *Anthropology and the Old Testament*. Blackwell.

Sanders, James A. 1984. *Canon and Community: A Guide to Canonical Criticism*. Fortress.

Schiffer, Michael B. 1987. *Formation Processes of the Archaeological Record*. University of New Mexico Press.

Shanks, Michael, and Christopher Tilley. 1987. *Re-constructing Archaeology: Theory and Practice*. Cambridge University Press.

Shay, Talia. 1989. "Israeli Archaeology—Ideology and Practice." *Antiquity* 63:768–72.

Sheppard, Gerald T. 1992. "Canonical Criticism." *ABD* 1:861–66.

Silberman, Lou H. 1983. "Listening to the Text." *JBL* 102:3–26.

Smith, W. Robertson. 1927. *Lectures on the Religion of the Semites*. A&C Black.

Stager, Lawrence E. 1985. "The Archaeology of the Family in Ancient Israel." *BASOR* 200:1–35.

Thompson, Thomas L. 1987. The Origin Tradition of Ancient Israel. JSOTSup 55. JSOT Press.

———. 1992. *Early History of the Israelite People: From the Written and Archaeological Sources*. SHANE 4. Brill.

Trigger, Bruce G. 2006. *A History of Archaeological Thought*. 2nd ed. Cambridge University Press.

Wilson, Robert R. 1984. *Sociological Approaches to the Old Testament*. Fortress.

5
Histories and Nonhistories of Ancient Israel: What Archaeology Can Contribute

In introducing chapter 3, I dealt with the general issue of historiography and provided some basic bibliography on the "revisionist" school of biblical history since that chapter was written in the mid-1990s. That was hardly the last word; if anything, my interest in revisionism has grown since then. Thus I read papers (some still unpublished) attacking revisionism in 1997 at Bar-Ilan University in Israel (appearing opposite Niels Peter Lemche; see Dever 1998a; Lemche 1998c); in 1998 at the "First International Congress on Near Eastern Archaeology" in Rome; again in 1998 at the reopening of the Ancient Canaan and Israel Gallery at the University Museum in Philadelphia (opposite Israel Finkelstein); once again in 1998 at Hartford; and in 1999 at a symposium at Northwestern University (opposite Philip R. Davies and Thomas L. Thompson). Then for the Second International Congress on Near Eastern Archaeology in Copenhagen in 2000, I proposed a panel including myself and Lawrence Stager of Harvard University on "our" side and Lemche and Thompson on the other side. My paper, previously unpublished, is reproduced here. Then in 2003, a symposium was convened in Rome on revisionism by European scholars. The only Americans invited were Peter Machinist of Harvard and me. I resolved to beard the lions in their own den, the result being the paper republished here, obviously a prolegomenon to my forthcoming history. Davies was so outraged that he was almost foaming at the mouth. Other exchanges were equally heated, but, in my judgment, no progress toward a consensus was made. We should have agreed beforehand on a specific agenda and assigned specific topics. Again, there was little constructive dialogue. Even so, the European biblical revisionists may be fading from the scene (along with their postmodern mentors). But meanwhile, the Western cultural tradition has come under attack from *other* quarters, especially in the rise of radical Islam, which is further evidence of how little we have learned from archaeology in the Middle East.

Bibliography after about 1990 will be found in chapter 3. In addition, see Dever 1998a and Lemche 1998c in the Works Cited below.

5.1. Introduction

In light of the trauma that we have experienced recently—nothing less than a threat to the Western cultural tradition—it may seem trivial to raise the question of whether a history of ancient Israel, a petty West Asian kingdom, can any longer be written. But ancient Israel is not trivial, and that is because the Western tradition, the dominant cultural force that has driven the free world for centuries and may forge its destiny into this millennium, derives essentially from the biblical worldview. In particular, that tradition rests on the premise of history as purposeful and individual rights and responsibilities as the foundation of a moral and just society. (I am not speaking here of the perversion of the Western cultural tradition, or American pop culture.)[1]

I affirm that cultural tradition unapologetically. The biblical "revisionists," and now a few naïve archaeologists who have become their followers, undermine it. In their increasingly strident claims that we Jews, Christians, and modern scholars have "invented" ancient Israel, they make of the Hebrew Bible a pious fraud, the greatest literary hoax of all time.

5.2. History, Ideology, and the Past: Why We Cannot Give In to Nihilism

Can a history of ancient Israel be written? That is the urgent question of the hour. Of course, it can—if one happens to be a historian, and there's the rub. More than a dozen years ago, Giovanni Garbini's penetrating but largely ignored critique of Old Testament scholarship, *History and Ideology in Ancient Israel* (1988), pointed out that few biblical scholars have any real training as historians. And Baruch Halpern has made an eloquent

---

1. For a convenient and positive orientation to the Western cultural tradition (previously, but inaccurately, the Judeo-Christian tradition), see Tarnas 1991; Gress 1998. For postmodernism, which is essentially a wholesale rejection of the Western cultural tradition, see n. 4 below.

case that the typical formula of "philology plus theology" hardly adds up to history writing.

After all, these "minimalists" are not real historians. They have typically been trained in either nonhistorical theological seminaries or department of Near Eastern studies or religion. Their exposure to history as it is practiced with respect to other times and other places is almost always marginal.[2]

As for Syro-Palestinian archaeologists, the other potential partners in the much-needed dialogue, who increasingly control the primary data for history writing, most are little better than technicians. The larger intellectual (i.e., epistemological) questions in all our related disciplines are rarely raised, indeed rarely even conceptualized.[3]

5.2.1. The Challenge of Israel's Past

Hundreds of putative histories of ancient Israel have been written in the past 2,500 years, from those implicit in the Hebrew Bible itself, to rabbinical and medieval commentaries, to modern critical reinterpretations of the Bible, mostly Christian. But in the past decade or so, all "positivist" histories have been repudiated, and the concept of history itself called into question. A recent collection of essays edited by Lester Grabbe, entitled *Can a "History of Israel" Be Written?* (1997), may be a bellwether. Here the majority of the members of the European Seminar on Methodology in Israel's History, presumably representative of Continental scholarship, corroborate recent observations that many of these scholars are not really minimalists; for them, there is nothing left to minimalize.[4]

---

2. Halpern, 1995, 28.

3. For a recent state-of-the-art discussion of Syro-Palestinian (and so-called biblical) archaeology, see Dever 2000, with full references; see also the revealing response in Davies 2000. Add now Dever 2003b, with reference to theory, or the lack of it, in our discipline. On the general lack of dialogue with biblical studies, see Halpern 1997.

4. The literature on biblical revisionism is too extensive to cite here. The primary works would include Davies 1992; Whitelam 1996; Grabbe 1997; Lemche 1998a, 1998b; and Thompson 1999. For a full-scale discussion and critique of these and other revisionist works from an archaeological perspective, see Dever 2001a and full references there; add now Levine and Mazar 2001. For a critique from mainstream biblicists, see Barr 2000; Deist 2000. For conservative reactions, see

As I argued years ago, at the beginning of the maximalist-minimalist controversy, the revisionists are, practically speaking, nihilists. The leaders of the movement—Davies, Lemche, Thompson, and Keith W. Whitelam—all proclaim that our ancient as well as biblical Israel was invented, that is, not discovered (which is what the word *invented* should mean) but "made up," that is, a fiction. *Israel* is simply a modern social and scholarly construct.

5.2.2. Postmodernism and the New Nihilists

I have charged that the biblical revisionists are not simply skeptics, as scholars should be generally, but thinly disguised postmodernists. If one doubts that, one has only to note that their assertion that all claims to knowledge are simply social constructs parrots the *fundamental* epistemological assertion of postmodernism, sometimes called constructivism. Such a nihilist notion, however, is scarcely novel or innovative, since it derives from one of nihilism's founders, Nietzsche, who announced more than a century ago that "there are no facts, only interpretations." This denial of any objective reality "out there" explains why Jean Francois Lyotard, the French Marxist and one of postmodernism's leading lights, insisted in *The Postmodern Condition* on maintaining an "incredulity toward metanarratives."[5] They are all social constructs, that is to say, fictitious. Therefore, they must be deconstructed, that is, discredited.

Obviously the *great* metanarrative of the Western tradition under skepticism here is the Hebrew (and Greek) Bible's vision of a universal, manifest destiny for humankind, which has been dominant in the West until the postmodern era. (I hasten to say, I do not mean the cultural impe-

---

the essays in Long, Baker, and Wenham 2002. On the concept of historiography—fundamental to discussions from all across the methodological spectrum—see references in n. 17 below.

5. Lyotard 1984, xxiv. For a sympathetic orientation to postmodernism, see Lemert 1997; with particular reference to biblical studies, Adam 1995. For documentation of the fact that the revisionists really are belated, thinly disguised postmodernists, see Dever 2001b, especially 254–66. Postmodernism tends inevitably toward nihilism; see Gress 1998, 475–80. For a devastating critique of the specific postmodern technique of deconstruction, see Ellis 1989. Examples of *revisionist* deconstruction of biblical texts are too numerous to cite; it is their typical approach to the texts.

rialism that has too often resulted from the perversion of this vision, much less a crude form of Christian supersessionism that we would all deplore.) Yet if the Bible's vision does not grow out of some actual historical experience of the people of Israel in the Iron Age, as the Hebrew Bible clearly presents it, if it is nothing but a late Hellenistic phantasmagoria, then the Hebrew Bible is indeed simply political propaganda, a shaky foundation on which to erect any ethical or moral edifice. That is why history, and the possibility of writing a reliable history, matter in this case.

Needless to say, most revisionists do not think that it is possible to write a factual history of ancient Israel, at least not anything that I would call history. Again, they echo Michel Foucault, another guru of postmodernists, who claimed to be a historian of many things yet declared in his book *Power/Knowledge* that "I am well aware that I have never written anything but fiction."[6] He goes on to say that "one 'fictions' history on the basis of a political reality that makes it true." Truth, for Foucault, is not a reality that one must acknowledge but merely what counts as true within a particular realm of discourse. This is what is popularly known as political correctness. The folly—indeed, the hypocrisy—of these pseudo-sophisticates has nowhere been more mercilessly exposed than in Keith Windschuttle's *The Killing of History: How Literary Critics and Social Theorists Are Murdering Our Past*. Of Foucault, Windschuttle says:

> Foucault's histories of institutions, therefore are demonstrations of the falsity of his own theories. History is not fiction, nor is it merely perspective. The core of history—the basis for the conclusions that individual historians reach, and the basis of the debates that historians conduct between each other—is factual information. Despite the speculations of Foucault and his followers, history remains a search for truth and the construction of knowledge about the past.[7]

5.2.3. Rewriting History: Who Owns the Past?[8]

1. Philip R. Davies. Of course, the revisionists have complained angrily about the charge of historical nihilism leveled against them, claiming that I

---

6. Focault 1980, 193.
7. Windschuttle 1996, 154.
8. This epistemological issue—how we "shape" the past and that it shapes us—looms large in current archaeology. I would point out that it is simply another

have deliberately misrepresented them. This whole controversy is about our side's penchant for personal polemics, our ideological bias. For instance, Davies now states that he has never denied the possibility of writing a history of ancient Israel. Yet read his *In Search of "Ancient Israel"* (1992). Here Davies distinguishes three "Israels." The entire burden of Davies's book, however, is that one searches in vain for ancient Israel because it never existed, any more than biblical Israel did; both are simply social constructs. Davies is forced to acknowledge, of course, that some "historical" Israel may have existed in the Iron Age, but this is a counsel of despair, because for him archaeological data would constitute our only reliable source of information, and these are either too scant or too subject to varying interpretation to yield any real history. In fact, despite paying lip service to archaeology, Davies does not reference *any* standard archaeological handbook, except that of Mazar 1990, whom he cites once, in a footnote, and that only to dismiss this work because it ends before coming to the Hellenistic era—Davies's "biblical world."[9] The only pertinent data are eliminated or discredited at the outset. This is not only disingenuous; it is biased scholarship. The result? The Hebrew Bible is held guilty until proven innocent, which it cannot be because the pertinent evidence is ruled out beforehand.

2. Keith W. Whitelam. Whitelam collaborated with Robert Coote in 1987 to produce an innovative prolegomenon to a history of ancient Israel

---

dimension of postmodernist discourse, which typically asserts that all claims to knowledge are ultimately issues of race, class, gender, power, and especially politics. See, for instance, the discussions of archaeology and nationalism in Meskell 1999, with an essay by Silberman 1999 specifically on our branch of archaeology. To his credit, Davies (1995) has raised this issue of "who owns the past" with regard to the Hebrew Bible.

9. Chapter 4 of Davies 1992 reputedly deals with "historical Israel," but in fifteen pages Davies simply acknowledges the *possibility* of some such a "political entity." He does not have so much as a brief outline, and he makes no reference whatsoever to actual archaeological data except for a footnote citing Finkelstein 1988. Davies's failure to utilize virtually any archaeological data contradicts his own statement that such data constitutes "primary evidence" (1992, 60). But in fact Davies does not seem serious about either archaeology or any history whatsoever of the Iron Age. At best, Davies might write a history of "Jewish ideas in the Persian-period province of Yehud." For a penetrating critique of Davies's "Yehud context" for the Hebrew Bible, see Deist 2000, 55–77 (in a Sheffield Academic volume edited in part by Davies himself).

from the perspective of long-term settlement history, making frequent and generally sound use of archaeological data as a primary source (Coote and Whitelam 1987). Yet less than a decade later, working alone and apparently having had an ideological conversion of some sort, now he published a work entitled *The Invention of Ancient Israel: The Silencing of Palestinian History* (1996). Whitelam argued that *all* histories of Israel—including his own—had been invented. Moreover, every such an effort at history writing was improper and indefensible. All along, we should have been writing a history of the "Palestinian peoples" in all periods, not that of some imaginary ancient Israel in the Iron Age. I suggest that it is his Israel that has been invented, not ours.[10]

Even his fellow revisionist Lemche protested that there were no "Palestinians" in the Iron Age. And I once asked Whitelam after his paper at an ASOR Annual Meeting: "Where have you been? We archaeologists have devoted ourselves for more than a century now to writing just such 'history of Palestine' (not the modern Palestinians, of course), in all periods from the Lower Paleolithic to the Ottoman Empire." Whitelam's history, by his own definition, is no history of ancient Israel because he thinks such a history is not only impossible but illegitimate in principle. Thus Whitelam is clearly a nonhistorian where ancient Israel is concerned.[11]

3. Niels Peter Lemche. Lemche, a well-trained and once-mainstream biblical scholar, produced in the 1980s two versions of a history of ancient Israel, utilizing both rather sophisticated anthropological theory and a commendable amount of then-current archaeological data (Lemche 1985,

---

10. Whitelam's pro-Palestinian bias is obvious in such statements as this: "Biblical scholarship is not just involved in 'retrospective imperialism,' it has collaborated in an act of dispossession" (of the Palestinian people; 1996, 224). See further n. 11 below.

11. See, for instance, Whitelam 1996, 220–37. Zevit has underlined my charge that Whitelam cannot write any history of Israel. As Zevit observes, "his book, a cleverly written rhetorical polemic, is all negative criticism. It presents neither a positive agenda nor any 'how to' formulae of its own nor does it suggest how unsuppressed history might look.…There is no historical revisionism here, only a preference for silence" (2002, 18 n. 29) It is no coincidence that Whitelam's book has been translated into Arabic, published by Cadmus Press in Beirut, and is popular in East Jerusalem bookstores. (Cadmus Press confirms that they consulted Whitelam but says that he did not initiate the Arabic version; nevertheless, he apparently acquiesced.)

1988). By the late 1990s, however, Lemche had also undergone an ideological about-face—apparently stemming from his increasing conviction that the composition (not merely the editing) of the Hebrew Bible must be down-dated to the Hellenistic era. Thus there could be no history of an Iron Age or biblical Israel derived from the biblical texts; they are too far removed, both chronologically and ideologically. Recently Lemche produced two new full-scale works: *The Israelites in History and Tradition* (1998a) and *Prelude to Israel's Past: Background and Beginnings of Israelite History and Identity* (1998b). Several reviewers have pointed out, however, that neither of these works is little more than a critique of past histories of Israel, plus a poorly articulated prolegomenon for a history that the new Lemche is apparently unable to write.

Here is a typical disclaimer of Lemche, in his *Israelites in History and Tradition*, one that I find astonishing.

> The Israel(s) of the Old Testament showed itself to be a product of a literary imagination. It history was not one of the real world, but in its organization was directed by the requirements of the two foundation myths, the first of the Exodus, and the second of the Babylonian exile. (Whether or not parts of this history really happened in the "real" world is to the mind that formed his history immaterial.[12]

At the very end of the book—presumably about an "Israel in history"—Lemche concludes:

> The Israel of the Iron Age proved to be most elusive, in historical documents as well as in material remains, where hardly anything carries an ethnic tag that helps the modern investigator to decide what is Israelite and what is not. Not even the kingdom known in some contexts to have been called Israel seems to have been generally known under this name.

---

12. Lemche 1998a, 129. Lemche, like Thompson (below), consistently refers to Israel by any other name he can think of, ignoring the fact that the very *first* mention of the northern kingdom—in the Assyrian annals recording Shalmaneser III's Battle of Qarqar in 853 BCE—refers specifically to "Ahab, the Israelite" (Pritchard 1969, 279). The ninth-century BCE Dan inscription (which Thompson has declared a forgery) refers to "Israel" even earlier (as does the Mesha Stela). The reluctance of some of the revisionists even to *refer* to an Iron Age Israel seems to me an indication of their basic historical nihilism. See further below on Thompson.

5. Histories and Nonhistories of Ancient Israel

Instead of Israel, the dynastic name of the state, "the House of Omri," and the name of the capital Samaria seem to have been more widely used, except of course in the Old Testament imagery of this Palestinian Kingdom.[13]

At the end we have a situation where Israel is not Israel, Jerusalem not Jerusalem, and David not David. No matter how we twist the factual remains from ancient Palestine, we cannot have a biblical Israel that is at the same time the Israel of the Iron Age.[14]

The latter may be true, but it is irrelevant. It is obvious to all but the most naive that the Hebrew Bible's portrait of ancient Israel is often idealistic, yet that does not mean that it contains no history. Finally, it is noteworthy that Lemche also regards archaeology as a *primary* source for writing any history of Israel but a source that he is no longer willing to try to use.[15]

4. Thomas L. Thompson. Thompson has been the most extreme of the revisionists. In 1987 he had advocated a sort of "secular history" of ancient Palestine and Israel, using archaeology as an independent source. This was similar to the research program that I had been advocating for some time.[16] True to his word, Thompson produced an attempt at such a history in his 400-plus-page *Early History of the Israelite People: From the Written and Archaeological Sources* (1992). Despite its idiosyncratic use of the archaeological data, Thompson's 1992 work gave some promise of both a dialogue and the true revisionist history that is indeed much needed. But only five years later, Thompson repudiated his magnum opus almost entirely, declaring that it "was after all hardly history, but rather just another rationalistic paraphrase for biblical history," that his "colleagues

---

13. Lemche 1998, 166–67.
14. Lemche 1998, 166. Neither Lemche 1998a nor 1998b has a reference to "archaeology" in the index. Both of Lemche's "histories" deal almost exclusively with the ideology of the biblical texts (as myths, of course), not with any historical realities, and they cite virtually no archaeological data. Lemche only refers to standard archaeological handbooks (e.g., Mazar 1990) in passing. If there were any doubts about Lemche as a working historian of ancient Israel, note that he has now repudiated his earlier, real histories (i.e., 1985, 1988; see the rejection in 1997, 146–48).
15. Lemche 1988, 166.
16. See Dever 1995, 62 and references there; add 1997d.

in Copenhagen allow only a remnant of this historiographic scenario to survive: namely, my *a quo* dating in the Persian period ... for the development of the ... biblical concept of Israel." And now he has abandoned that for a Hellenistic date.[17]

In 1999, Thompson produced another large volume, entitled *The Mythic Past: Biblical Archaeology and the Myth of Israel*. This work had little to do with archaeology, apart from an occasional ill-informed diatribe against a style of biblical archaeology that had been dead for twenty-five years. What is significant here is that Thompson does not even attempt a history of ancient Israel. He cannot. He knows little about current archaeological theory, method, or results, and he discards virtually all the biblical texts as devoid of genuine historical information. So he is a historian with no data.

As Thompson puts it in another place, "It may perhaps appear strange that much of the Bible deals with the origin tradition of a people that never existed as such."[18] He admits that there are, of course, the biblical king lists, which are fully corroborated by synchronisms with known Neo-Assyrian and Neo-Babylonian texts and are thus certainly historical. Yet of these, Thompson declares:

> The central questions regarding the Bible and history do not in fact concern issues of history so much as how texts work. When we are dealing with the hypothetical lists of kings for the states of Israel and of Judah which presumably were used in writing the Book of II Kings, the interests are issues of legitimacy and continuity, epitomizing balance.[19]

There are, of course, the nonbiblical texts. Thompson usually "privileges" them (another typical postmodern term), as though they were not propaganda. But even here, he is skeptical—skepticism elevated to the position of a method. Thus of the Mesha Stela—an *independent* witness to Omri—Thompson says:

> The literary nature of the Mesha Stela needs to be taken seriously. It is quite doubtful that it refers to an historical person when it refers to

---

17. See Thompson 1997, 178–79. As assumed throughout, for instance, in Thompson (e.g., 1999, xv: "It is only a Hellenistic Bible that we know"). Further on the supposed Hellenistic date, see nn. 29 and 32 below.
18. Thompson 1999, 34.
19. Thompson 1999, 23.

Israel's king. "Omri, king of Israel," eponym of the highland patronate, *Bit Humri*, belongs to the world of stories.[20]

In the whole of his 347-page treatise on the myth of Israel, Thompson devotes only thirty-one pages to a description of the entire period of the settlement and monarchy, and even here he rarely deigns to call this entity Israel, speaking rather of "the Iron Age population of Syria's southern marginal fringe." Thompson would, of course, deny that he is a nihilist regarding ancient Israel. But what else can one make of such statements as: "There is no more 'ancient Israel.' History no longer has room for it."[21]

5. Israel Finkelstein. The only archaeologist beside myself to have entered the revisionist fray, Israel Finkelstein is a minimalist on such topics as the biblical patriarchs and the exodus/conquest (as virtually all archaeologists are). But, although a revisionist on the topic of the tenth century BCE, he is not a nihilist, since he does allow for at least a sort of "highland patronate" headed by a quasi-historical "Solomon" in the tenth century BCE. Finkelstein argues, however, that the biblical united monarchy is a fiction created by the Deuteronomistic Historians in Judah in the seventh century BCE as survival literature. Further, Jerusalem became a political capital only after the Assyrian destructions in the north, Judah for the first time now in the ascendency.

Finkelstein's views are now developed fully in *The Bible Unearthed: Archaeology's New Vision of Ancient Israel and the Origin of Its Sacred Texts* (2001, with Silberman). He obviously thinks of this book as a major effort at rewriting ancient Israel's history, as well as a significant contribution to biblical studies. But leading biblical scholars with whom I have consulted have all said that *The Bible Unearthed* has not been taken seriously by mainstream scholarship. The reasons given are as follows: (1) It is cleverly structured and well written, but it is a popular book with inadequate documentation for its many sweeping claims. (2) Its arguments are directed

---

20. Thompson increasingly speaks of "stories" and "how stories work," of "how texts are able to say what they say"—as typical devices of semiotics and postmodernist deconstruction as one could imagine. This suggests to me that he is not really interested in any possible historical events *behind* the stories; he has become a narratologist (like Mieke Bal and others). For a devastating exposé of Thompson, see now Provan 2002.

21. Thompson 1995, 697.

mostly against straw men, not the crucial historiographical issues. (3) Its authors are not well grounded in critical biblical scholarship. (4) Finally, its biblical and its archaeological stance is idiosyncratic. Yet I applaud the effort, the teamwork, and the attempt at dialogue.[22]

Since not only laypeople but some biblicists may be taken in by Finkelstein's revisionist history, I must point out that *everything* in his "new vision" of ancient Israel hinges on his "low chronology," that is, moving the monumental architecture that for most of us reflects statehood down to the ninth century BCE.[23] But it is significant that no mainstream archaeologist has come out in print in support of Finkelstein's low chronology, despite his claims. There is simply no indisputable empirical evidence for it as yet—neither stratigraphy, comparative ceramic chronology, nor carbon 14 dates. Recently Amihai Mazar (2003) stated the consensus view succinctly and forcefully. And if Finkelstein's low chronology collapses, so does his new vision of ancient Israel's history—for it is only a vision, and merely one man's vision at that.[24]

5.3. Can a History of Ancient Israel Any Longer Be Written?

Before ascertaining whether or not the revisionists, or their antagonists, whom they deride as "positivists" and "historicists," can write any history of ancient Israel, we need to outline some prerequisites for history writing itself.

---

22. See further my review of Finkelstein and Silberman 2001 in Dever 2001a and their response in Finkelstein and Silberman 2002.

23. The concept of statehood is obviously fundamental to much of revisionist discourse, but it is rarely defined, even by moderates such as Finkelstein (even in 1999), nor do revisionists seem to be conversant with the extensive literature in anthropology on state-formation processes. The sole exception is Schäfer-Lichtenberger 1996. For orientation, see Dever 1997a.

24. Mazar 2003. I offer a thoroughly documented refutation of Finkelstein's low chronology in Dever 2004. Meanwhile, see some of the critical carbon 14 evidence supporting the conventional chronology in Mazar 2003. Further details have appeared now in Bruins, van der Plicht, and Mazar 2003, which completely discredits Finkelstein and his low chronology.

5.3.1. Essential Assumptions

1. A working definition of history, which, oddly enough, is often lacking in the current controversy on both sides.[25]
2. A systematic, rigorous, critically developed historiographical methodology.
3. A presumption that there exist "out there" some empirical truths about the past that can be recovered.
4. A disinterested approach, however, as objective as humanly possible.
5. Accessible and pertinent facts, established as such independently of the hypotheses being tested and accepted by consensus.
6. An interpretation that takes into account all possible variables, including its own limitations.
7. The best probabilistic narrative of the actual course of events, their interpretation by contemporary witnesses, and the most likely explanation of what really happened.

5.3.2. Why the Revisionists Are Nonhistorians

How do the revisionists measure up against these historiographical criteria? They do not, as we shall see by examining the above points one by one.

(1) and (2) For all their pretense to having provoked a historiographical crisis, none of the revisionists has offered more than a rudimentary definition of history or of historical method. (3) The revisionists appear to presume not that there may be historical truths waiting to be discovered but that there are not. (4) Theirs is not, by their own admission, a disinterested approach, since they insist that that is not possible. They agree essentially, if not openly, with postmodernists in holding that that "all readings of texts are political"—inexorably conditioned (read "compromised") by contemporary issues of race, class, and gender. Objectivity

---

25. For all the current historiographical crisis, there are few attempts even to define history and history writing even in such works as Grabbe 1997. See, however, Halpern 1988; Brettler 1995; many of the essays in Long 1999; and some essays on the Deuteronomistic History in Knoppers and McConville 2000. For representative conservative works, see Millard, Hoffmeier, and Baker 1994; Long, Baker, and Wenham 2002 (with special reference to the revisionists).

is an illusion, a Marxian mask that always betrays a hidden ideological agenda (although they deny that they have any such ideology).[26] (5) As for facts, with Nietzsche the revisionists declare that there are no facts, only interpretations. (6) and (7) Finally, no one cares what really happened, for that went out with von Ranke; all that matters is the brave new world to come, what Thompson hails as *Wissenschaft* at last, a science of biblical study (a science without facts, it seems).[27]

If the revisionists are not, and cannot be, historians of ancient Israel, what *are* they? Literary critics? Despite their jettisoning the category of history for literature, they have no adequate theory of literary production. For them, the Hebrew Bible did not grow out of any real, extended history or an interpretation of events over time. It just happened overnight, the product of the fevered imagination of a few confused Jews searching for their identity in the Persian–Hellenistic era in Palestine.

That the revisionists are not leading Hebraists hardly needs documentation. If they understood the historical development of the Hebrew language better, they would know that the language of the Deuteronomistic History and of the classical prophets is not, as Davies asserts, a *Bildungssprache*, a late, artificial scribal argot. It is rather a living language of the Iron Age, attested in many hundreds of securely dated ostraca, seals, inscribed objects, tomb inscriptions, and even a few monumental inscriptions. To put it succinctly, Biblical Hebrew is not an archaizing dialect; it is genuinely archaic. Nor is the Siloam Tunnel inscription "Hellenistic."[28]

As for the presumption of the revisionists that they are competent to speak for the disciplines of anthropology and archaeology, that scarcely

---

26. Nothing is more fundamental to revisionist discourse than ideology and its role in culture and the production of knowledge—another clue to their postmodernist orientation. A helpful recent discussion of ideology, sympathetic to some aspects of revisionism yet incisive in its critique, is Deist 2000, 78–117. The point is that everything is *not* about ideology, that of the ancient writer and editors of the Hebrew Bible or their modern interpreters. If it were, "scholarly" discussion would be a farce.

27. Thompson 1995, 698.

28. On "archaic/archaizing Hebrew," see Davies 1992, 102–5; cf. the critique of Hurvitz 1997; Dever 2001b, 273–77. On the supposed Hellenistic date of the Siloam Tunnel inscription, see Rogerson and Davies 1996; cf. the overwhelming refutation in Hendel 1996; Hackett et al. 1997 (including Cross, Eshel, Hurvitz, Lemaire, McCarter, Yardeni).

deserves a response. All they can do when challenged by me and others is to engage in character assassination—the last, desperate resort of those who have no facts.[29]

What are the revisionists, then? As the polemics escalate and the issues are increasingly obscured, it becomes clear that all along the revisionists were not dispassionate scholars searching for the truth. They were and are *ideologues*, and their publications are nearly all ideological manifestos. I suggested that at the beginning of the controversy, and now no less an authority than James Barr, Regius Professor Emeritus at Oxford, has corroborated this charge in his recent *History and Ideology in the Old Testament: Biblical Studies at the End of a Millennium* (2000).

Barr does several things in this state-of-the-art assessment. (1) He focuses primarily on historiography as the major issue today in biblical studies. (2) He selects the revisionists for his main thrust. (3) He situates the revisionists within the context of postmodernism in a thoroughgoing discussion. (4) Finally, Barr refutes most of the revisionists' assertions and documents the fact that they are indeed ideologues. These are precisely the points that I as an archaeologist have been making in lectures and in print for the past several years. Lemche has already responded to Barr's critique (2000), but he simply protests, without attempting to refute any of Barr's specific charges. He does acknowledge their seriousness, however, since Barr is for him the recognized "Dean of Old Testament scholars."[30]

Barr specifically cites my work and implies that he agrees with my charge that the revisionists are nihilists where the history of ancient Israel is concerned. He states specifically that Davies's views are "too absurd to be taken seriously," that Whitelam's arguments are without any "factual evidence," and that throughout revisionist discourse one observes "the alacrity with which hostile ideology is adopted as the obvious explanation." Of the repeated insistence on a Hellenistic date for the composition of the Hebrew Bible, Barr concludes that this simply shows how "desperate for evidence" the revisionists are.[31]

---

29. As a single example, see Davies's review of Dever 2001a in Davies 2002. See also n. 30 below.

30. See Lemche 2000, where he dismisses me as a "rustic" (presumably because I am not a European scholar). This is polemics, not scholarship.

31. Barr 2000, 61, 71, 73, 85, 101.

5.3.3. The Fundamental Issue: The Date of the Biblical Sources

The barrage of confrontational rhetoric from the revisionists in the past decade often distracts us not only from their underlying ideological agenda but also from the fact that their *entire* program rests on an assertion that when examined proves to be without factual basis. The underlying presupposition of virtually everything the revisionists have published is that the Hebrew Bible was written—not simply edited and composed—in the Hellenistic period, specifically in the course of the identity crisis that Jews in Palestine experienced during the conflict with Hellenism and in the Hasmonean wars. The revisionists' rejection of the biblical texts as a source of genuine information about an ancient Israel in the Iron Age rests almost entirely on the notion that those texts are all much later and are thus nothing but pious propaganda. That has been their contention from the very beginning, starting with Davies's *In Search of "Ancient Israel"* in 1992, through Lemche's early articles, to Thompson's conversion to this view in the mid-1990s.[32]

More recently, the revisionists' Hellenistic date has not even been argued: it is simply presumed. Yet it cannot be stated too strongly that there is not a shred of evidence for such a late date. Biblical scholars such as Avigdor Hurowitz, Baruch Halpern, Kyle McCarter, Ronald Hendel, Ziony Zevit, Sara Japhet, and others have pointed out that the linguistic evidence alone renders a Hellenistic date for the composition of the Hebrew Bible impossible.[33] My book *What Did the Biblical Writers Know and When Did They Know It? What Archaeology Can Tell Us about the Reality of Ancient Israel* (2001b) documents in detail how archaeology shows that the context within which the biblical stories were composed and make sense is overwhelmingly that of the Iron Age, in fact betraying no Hellenistic influ-

---

32. See nn. 9, 17, and 28 above. Lemche's Hellenistic date is continuously quoted be many revisionists, but a review of the literature reveals that his only evidence is a single footnote in an early article (1993), declaring without presenting any data that the historiography of the writers of the Hebrew Bible most closely resembles that of Pliny. The question of dating the composition (not simply the final redaction) of the biblical texts—especially the Deuteronomistic History—is discussed in Knoppers and McConville 2000 and most recently in Grabbe 2001.

33. See nn. 9, 17, 28, and 32 above.

ences whatsoever. But the revisionists have never responded to any of this mass of evidence; they simply vilify those of us who present it.³⁴

5.4. Toward Real Revisionist Histories of Ancient Israel

The revisionists are right, however, about one thing. Historiography is indeed the critical issue now in biblical studies and, I might add, in archaeology as well. Further, they do us all a service in insisting that we do not need any more of what Garbini aptly termed "rational paraphrases of the Bible." But it is we who are the real revisionists, not they. We historical archaeologists, working together with mainstream biblical scholars who have mastered their texts as we have our material culture remains, control the only real sources for writing the bold, innovative histories of ancient Israel that we need today. It is not an increasingly shrill ideology that will provide the impetus for the revolution but scholarly competence, a painstaking return to the analysis of basic data, and, above all, the courage and patience to engage in an honest dialogue between text and artifact. Let us get on optimistically with our teamwork as historians, leaving the rhetoric to those few, isolated ideologues who can only talk to each other.

5.4.1. What Archaeology Can Contribute to Rewriting Israel's History

I would maintain that the basic data upon which the rewriting of the history of ancient Israel can proceed must come in the future from archaeology, now our primary source for any genuinely new information. Indeed, we archaeologists, not waiting for our colleagues in biblical studies, have already produced revisionist histories of several epochs in ancient Israel in the past decade. Among them would be (1) the early settlement of protoIsraelites in Canaan, (2) the rise of the Israelite state, and (3) the evolution of the Israelite cult, especially popular religion.³⁵ These archaeological syntheses may be provisional and still largely programmatic, but

---

34. See nn. 30 and 32 above.
35. On early Israel, see Dever 1997b, 1998b, 2003b; cf. Finkelstein and Silberman 2001, 72–122, all with extensive references. On the rise of the Israelite state, see Holladay 1995; Dever 1997a; cf. Finkelstein 1999, again with full references. On archaeology and cult, see Dever 1999a; 2001b, 188–98; Hadley 2000; Nakhai

they mark a turning point. You have only to review the standard literature of fifteen years ago on the exodus and conquest or the age of Solomon or Israelite monotheism and then compare the current literature to see the revolution, a revolution that Albright had predicted, although hardly with the consequences that he hoped. In every case, it is the new *archaeological* data that have proven decisive. That revolution can only continue. We will never again be able to write traditional histories of ancient Israel, but we can write newer and better histories.

Why do I argue that archaeology is now a primary source for history writing? After all, this is not a very popular notion among some of our colleagues, who are accustomed to privileging the biblical and other texts, some of whom still repeat the old canard that "archaeology is mute." There are many reasons for my confidence.

(1) The goal of mainstream archaeology has always been history, that is, empirically based accounts of past events. As we archaeologists put it, this constitutes a "history from things," written from artifacts and the patterns of thought and behavior that they reflect. For the New Archaeology of the 1980s and 1990s, with its functionalist biases and scientific pretensions, history was a bad word. But the postprocessual archaeology of the new millennium has refurbished history as an appropriate goal of archaeology and with it a new appreciation of the role of ideology and even religion in cultural change. Furthermore, archaeology provides uniquely for the perspective of ecology and of Braudel's *la longue durée*, long-term settlement history. It is in this broad context that we must see ancient Israel.[36]

(2) Archaeology in particular has unique capacities for writing various histories: a history of settlement patterns and of demographic change; a history of technology; a socioeconomic history; a history of international relations; and even, to some extent, a history of aesthetics and religion. All of these histories powerfully supplement the rather narrow political and theocratic history that is often the preoccupation of the biblical writers, as well as the authors of other ancient Near Eastern texts.

2001; Zevit 2001; and several essays in Gittlen 2002, all with extensive references to earlier literature.

36. On postprocessualism, see Dever 2003a and references there to the scant literature in our field. On the Annales school, see Dever 1988, 339–40; 1997c, 22; and update by reference to Finkelstein 1988 (an application to long-term settlement patterns and the emergence of early Israel).

(3) The most promising approach to history writing in current archaeology is that pioneered in the work of Ian Hodder, namely, the notion of "reading" material culture remains in much the same way that we have always read texts. It is clear that the artifacts and texts are "encoded messages" from the past. With an adequate understanding of the unique vocabulary, grammar, and syntax of each category of data and with proper hermeneutical principals, we can read with understanding, if not perfect then at least instructive.[37] But if the revisionists are skeptical about finding meaning in their texts, they are completely mystified by the notion of reading artifacts. When it comes to archaeology, to which they must perforce appeal, the revisionists are nearly illiterate. Archaeology *is* mute for them, because they cannot read artifacts, and their arrogant skepticism prevents them from learning.

(4) Finally, archaeology is a primary source for history writing because of the unique qualities of the data that it produces. Archaeological data are more abundant, more varied than the available textual data; more dynamic, more open-ended, potentially almost limitless; more representative, less deliberately biased, and in any case easier to control in interpretation; and, finally, more factual in the sense of being more tangible.

Many will contest this, but I think that after two thousand years we have approached the natural point of diminishing returns from textual exegesis, no matter how ingenious, how much in touch with the latest hermeneutical fads. What the biblical texts alone can tell us, they probably have. But the archaeological revolution has barely begun. I like to underscore this by pointing out that 90 percent of what I teach in advanced seminars was unknown—and unimaginable—when I was a graduate student.

5.4.2. A Case Study: The Eighth Century BCE

As a single example of the new histories that can now be written, I offer here the example of the eighth century BCE, an "axial age," to use Karl Jasper's phrase. It was in this crucial century that ancient Israel faced continuing social, economic, and class conflict; the internal crisis of civil war; the deadly threat posed by the advance westward of the Neo-Assyrian

---

37. See originally Hodder 1986; cf. the application of this model to Syro-Palestinian and "biblical" archaeology in Dever 1997c.

Empire; and the call of the classical prophets to religious and cultural reforms.[38]

Our textual sources for the eighth century BCE, both in the Hebrew Bible and in the Neo-Assyrian archives, are relatively abundant, but they are limited in scope. They constitute political history by and large: selective, elitist, highly tendentious. With reference to the northern kingdom in particular, the Deuteronomic Historians indulge mostly in polemics, and when Samaria finally falls in 721 BCE, they devote only one chapter to the disaster. What matters to the nationalist parties who wrote and edited the Hebrew Bible is that Jerusalem—the City of David and the temple housing Yahweh's presence—was spared. By contrast, I would point out that today archaeology could easily write a three-hundred-page account of the Neo-Assyrian campaigns in the north, the destruction of most sites, and the widespread devastation and aftermath in the eighth century BCE.

Beyond illuminating eighth-century BCE episodes such as the fall of the northern kingdom, archaeology can shed new light on other aspects of the axial age. We now possess enough factual information to portray the daily life of the masses in ancient Israel—those countless anonymous folk whom Daniel has in mind in honoring "those who sleep in the dust," from cradle to grave. The texts of the Great Tradition, the Hebrew Bible included, write history from the top down. Archaeology writes history from the bottom up. We need both.

5.5. Conclusion

Some years ago Max Miller asked, not altogether rhetorically: "Is it possible to write a history of ancient Israel without the Hebrew Bible?"[39] Of course it is. Such a reconstruction—based on archaeological data, including the

---

38. When this chapter was originally published, I planned a book of some four hundred pages on this subject, tentatively entitled *Archaeology and an "Axial Age": The Eighth Century B.C. in Israel and Judah*. It was to be based largely on archaeology and extrabiblical texts, but it was to integrate biblical texts where they can be shown to contain factual historical information. This is the kind of history that the revisionist cannot or will not write, and it is only the beginning of real revisionist, archaeologically informed history. See now Dever 2017.

39. Miller 1991.

extrabiblical texts recovered by excavation—would now be possible. But it would be a truncated history, anonymous with regard to most of the principal actors and lacking in ideological dimensions, including the role of religion. It would be a somewhat materialistic and reductionist history of things rather than a history of ideas.

Fortunately, there is no need to resort to such impoverished histories of ancient Israel. Contrary to the ill-informed claims of skeptics, we have adequate sources. One source consists of the biblical texts, critically analyzed to sort out what I would call a core history of events, which although minimal will prove reliable.[40] The other source is the archaeological data now available, which despite minor controversies provides us with a vast array of empirical information on the Iron Age and the real-life context of biblical Israel.

Giving the revisionists the benefit of the doubt and assuming that their search for some ancient Israel may be sincere, it seems that their major difficulty is that the historical Iron Age Israel increasingly illuminated by archaeology does not appear to correspond with the texts' portrait of a biblical Israel. Why should it? But the dichotomy is not as great as they think, and in any case it is irrelevant, unless we read the Hebrew Bible naively as a comprehensive and completely factual historical account, and no one does that. It is evident that the Bible never *claims* to be such an objective history; it provides an admittedly idealistic portrait. Caricaturing the Hebrew Bible is easy, but Bible bashing is reprehensible, unworthy of historians who seek the truth.

Our challenge is to eschew radicalism, moral relativism, and the sort of fashionable nonsense that passes for scholarship in today's postmodern malaise. Let us get back to basics, to *data*. Then we shall be able to write the multifaceted, balanced, satisfying histories of ancient Israel that we want and need.

As the British historian Eric Hobsbawn once observed, there are facts, facts matter, and some facts matter a great deal. Ancient Israel is just such a fact, and we must not allow it to be erased from history.

---

40. Dever 2001a, 2001b.

Works Cited

Adam, A. K. M. 1995. *What Is Postmodern Biblical Criticism?* GBS. Fortress.

Barr, James. 2000. *History and Ideology in the Old Testament: Biblical Studies at the End of a Millennium.* Oxford University Press.

Brettler, Marc Zvi. 1995. *The Creation of History in Ancient Israel.* Routledge.

Bruins, Hendrik J., Johannes van der Plicht, and Amihai Mazar. 2003. "14C Dates from Tel Rehov: Iron Age Chronology, Pharaohs, and Hebrew Kings." *Science.* 300:315–18. doi: 10.1126/science.1082776.

Coote, Robert B., and Keith W. Whitelam. 1987. *The Emergence of Early Israel in Historical Perspective.* SWBA 5. Almond.

Davies, Philip R. 1992. *In Search of "Ancient Israel."* JSOTSup 148. JSOT Press.

———. 1995. *Whose Bible Is It Anyway?* JSOTSup 204. Sheffield Academic.

———. 2000. "Corrigenda." *CurBS* 8:117–23.

———. 2002. Review of *What Did the Biblical Writers Know and When Did They Know It? What Archaeology Can Tell Us about the Reality of Ancient Israel,* by William G. Dever. *Shofar* 21:158–60.

Deist, Ferdinand E. 2000. *The Material Culture of the Bible: An Introduction.* BibSem 70. Sheffield Academic.

Dever, William G. 1988. "Impact of the New 'Archaeology.'" Pages 337–52 in *Benchmarks in Time and Culture: Introduction to Palestinian Archaeology.* Edited by Joel F. Drinkard, Gerald L. Mattingly, and J. Maxwell Miller. ABS 1. Scholars Press.

———. 1995. "'Will the Real Israel Please Stand Up?' Archaeology and Israelite Historiography: Part 1." *BASOR* 297:61–80.

———. 1997a. "Archaeology and the 'Age of Solomon': A Case Study in Archaeology and Historiography." Pages 217–51 in *The Age of Solomon: The Scholarship at the Turn of the Millennium.* Edited by Lowell K. Handy. SHANE 11. Brill.

———. 1997b. "Archaeology and the Emergence of Early Israel." Pages 20–50 in *Archaeology and Biblical Interpretation.* Edited by John Bartlett. Routledge.

———. 1997c. "On Listening to the Texts—and the Artifacts." Pages 1–23 in *The Echoes of Many Texts: Reflections on Jewish and Christian Tra-*

ditions. Edited by William G. Dever and J. Edward Wright. Scholars Press. Republished as chapter 4 in this volume.

———. 1997d. "Philology, Theology, and Archaeology: What Kind of History of Israel Do We Want, and What Is Possible?" Pages 290–310 in *The Archaeology of Israel: Constructing the Past, Interpreting the Present*. Edited by Neil Asher Silberman and David Small. JSOTSup 237. Sheffield Academic. Republished as chapter 3 in this volume.

———. 1998a. "Archaeology and State Development in Ancient Judah: Why the 'Revisionists' Are Wrong." Pages 84–96 in *New Studies on Jerusalem: Proceedings of the Third Conference, December 11, 1997* [Hebrew]. Edited by A. Faust and E. Baruch. Ingeborg Rennert Center for Jerusalem Studies.

———. 1998b. "Archaeology, Ideology, and the Quest for 'Ancient' or 'Biblical Israel.'" *NEA* 61:39–52.

———. 1999a. "Archaeology and the Israelite Cult: How the Kirbet el-Qôm and Kuntillet 'Ajrûd 'Ashera' Texts Have Changed the Picture." *ErIsr* 26:9*–15*. Republished as chapter 12 in this volume.

———. 1999b. "Histories and Nonhistories of Ancient Israel." *BASOR* 316:89–109.

———. 2000. "Biblical and Syro-Palestinian Archaeology: A State-of-the-Art Assessment at the Turn of the Millennium." *CurBS* 8:91–116.

———. 2001a. "Excavating the Bible, or Burying Again?" *BASOR* 322:67–77.

———. 2001b. *What Did the Biblical Writers Know and When Did They Know It? What Archaeology Can Tell Us about the Reality of Ancient Israel*. Eerdmans.

———. 2003a. "Syro-Palestinian and Biblical Archaeology: Into the Next Millennium." Pages 513–27 in *Symbiosis, Symbolism, and the Power of the Past: Canaan, Ancient Israel, and Their Neighbors from the Late Bronze Age through Roman Palestina*. Edited by William G. Dever and Seymour Gitin. Eisenbrauns.

———. 2003b. *Who Were the Early Israelites and Where Did They Come From?* Eerdmans.

———. 2004. "Histories and Non-histories of Ancient Israel: The Question of the United Monarchy." Pages 65–94 in *In Search of Pre-exilic Israel: Proceedings of the Oxford Old Testament Seminar*. Edited by John Day. JSOTSup 406. T&T Clark.

———. 2017. *Beyond the Texts: An Archaeological Portrait of Ancient Israel and Judah*. SBL Press.

Ellis, John M. 1989. *Against Deconstruction*. Princeton University Press.
Finkelstein, Israel. 1988. *The Archaeology of the Israelite Settlement*. Israel Exploration Society.
———. 1999. "State Formation in Israel and Judah: A Contrast in Context, a Contrast in Trajectory." *NEA* 62:35–52.
Finkelstein, Israel, and Neil Asher Silberman. 2001. *The Bible Unearthed: Archaeology's New Vision of Ancient Israel and the Origin of Its Sacred Texts*. Free Press.
———. 2002. "*The Bible Unearthed*: A Rejoiner." *BASOR* 327:63–73.
Foucault, Michel. 1980. *Power/Knowledge: Selected Interviews and Other Writings*. Edited by Colin Gordon. Pantheon.
Garbini, Giovanni. 1988. *History and Ideology in Ancient Israel*. Crossroad.
Gittlen, Barry M., ed. 2002. *Sacred Time, Sacred Place: Archaeology and the Religion of Israel*. Eisenbrauns.
Grabbe, Lester L., ed. 1997. *Can a "History of Israel" Be Written?* JSOTSup 245. Sheffield Academic.
———, ed. 2001. *Did Moses Speak Attic? Jewish Historiography and Scripture in the Hellenistic Period*. JSOTSup 317. Sheffield Academic.
Gress, David. 1998. *From Plato to NATO: The Idea of the West and Its Opponents*. Free Press.
Hackett, Jo Ann, Frank Moore Cross, P. Kyle McCarter Jr., Ada Yardeni, André Lemaire, Esther Eshel, and Avi Hurvitz. 1997. "Defusing Pseudo-Scholarship: The Siloam Ain't Hasmonean." *BAR* 23.2:41–50, 68.
Hadley, Judith M. 2000. *The Cult of Asherah in Ancient Israel and Judah: Evidence for a Hebrew Goddess*. Cambridge University Press.
Halpern, Baruch. 1988. *The First Historians: The Hebrew Bible and History*. Harper & Row.
———. 1995. "Erasing History: The Minimalist Assault on Ancient Israel." *BRev* 11.6:26–35, 47.
———. 1997. "Text and Artifact: Two Monologues." Pages 311–41 in *The Archaeology of Israel: Constructing the Past, Interpreting the Present*. Edited by Neil Asher Silberman and David Small. JSOTSup 237. Sheffield Academic.
Hendel, Ronald S. 1996. "The Date of the Siloam Inscription: A Rejoinder to Rogerson and Davies." *BA* 59:233–37.
Hodder, Ian. 1986. *Reading the Past: Current Approaches to Interpretation in Archaeology*. Cambridge University Press.

Holladay, John S. 1995. "The Kingdoms of Israel and Judah: Political and Economic Centralization in the Iron IIA-B (ca. 1000–750 BCE)." Pages 368–98 in *The Archaeology of Society in the Holy Land*. Edited by Thomas E. Levy. Facts on File.

Hurvitz, Avigdor. 1997. "The Historical Quest for 'Ancient Israel' and the Linguistic Evidence of the Hebrew Bible: Some Methodological Observations." *VT* 47:301–5.

Knoppers, Gary N., and J. G. McConville., eds. 2000. *Reconsidering Israel and Judah: Recent Studies on the Deuteronomistic History*. Sources for Biblical and Theological Study 8. Eisenbrauns.

Lemche, Niels Peter. 1985. *Early Israel: Anthropological and Historical Studies on the Israelite Society before the Monarchy*. VTSup 37. Brill.

———. 1988. *Ancient Israel: A New History of Israelite Society*. BibSem 5. Sheffield Academic.

———. 1993. "The Old Testament—A Hellenistic Book?" *SJOT* 7:163–93.

———. 1997. "Clio Is Also among the Muses! Keith W. Whitelam and the History of Palestine: A Review and Commentary." Pages 123–55 In *Can a History of Israel Be Written?* Edited by Lester L. Grabbe. JSOTSup 245. Sheffield Academic.

———. 1998a. *The Israelites in History and Tradition*. LAI. Westminster John Knox.

———. 1998b. *Prelude to Israel's Past: Background and Beginnings of Israelite History and Identity*. Hendrickson.

———. 1998c. "The Origin of the Israelite State: A Copenhagen Perspective on the Emergence of Critical Historical Studies of Ancient Israel in Recent Times." *SJOT* 12:44–63.

———. 2000. "Ideology and the History of Ancient Israel." *SJOT* 14:165–93.

Lemert, Charles. 1997. *Postmodernism Is Not What You Think*. Blackwell.

Levine, Lee I., and Amihai Mazar, eds. 2001. *Controversy over the Historicity of the Bible* [Hebrew]. Yad Yitzhak Ben Zvi Center for the Land of Israel Studies.

Long, V. Phillips, ed. 1999. *Israel's Past in Present Research: Essays on Ancient Israelite Historiography*. Sources for Biblical and Theological Study 7. Eisenbrauns.

Long, V. Phillips, David W. Baker, and Gordon J. Wenham, eds. 2002. *Windows into Old Testament History: Evidence, Arguments, and the Crisis of "Biblical Israel."* Eerdmans.

Lyotard, Francois. 1984. *The Postmodern Condition: A Report on Knowl-*

edge. Translated by Geoff Bennington and Brian Massumi. University of Minnesota Press.

Mazar, Amihai. 1990. *Archaeology of the Land of the Bible, 10,000–586 B.C.E.* Doubleday.

———. 2003. "Does Amihai Mazar Agree with Finkelstein's 'Low Chronology'?" *BAR* 29.2:60–61.

Meskell, Lynn, ed. 1999. *Archaeology under Fire: Nationalism, Politics and Heritage in the Eastern Mediterranean and the Middle East*. Routledge.

Millard Alan R., James K. Hoffmeier, and Dwight W. Baker, eds. 1994. *Faith, Tradition, and History: Old Testament Historiography in Its Near Eastern Context*. Eisenbrauns.

Miller, J. Maxwell. 1991. "Is it Possible to Write a History of Israel without Relying on the Hebrew Bible?" Pages 93–102 in *The Fabric of History: Text, Artifact and Israel's Past*. Edited by Diana V. Edelman. JSOTSup 127. JSOT Press.

Nakhai, Beth Alpert. 2001. *Archaeology and the Religions of Canaan and Israel*. ASOR Books 7. American Schools of Oriental Research.

Pritchard, James B., ed. 1969. *Ancient Near Eastern Texts Relating to the Old Testament*. 3rd ed. Princeton University Press.

Provan, Ian W. 2002. "In the Stable with the Dwarves: Testimony, Interpretation, Faith, and the History of Israel." Pages 161–97 in *Windows into Old Testament: Evidence, Arguments and the Crisis of "Biblical Israel."* Edited by V. Phillips Long, David W. Baker, and Gordon J. Wenham. Eerdmans.

Rogerson, John, and Philip R. Davies. 1996. "Was the Siloam Tunnel Built by Hezekiah?" *BA* 59:138–49.

Schäfer-Lichtenberger, Christa. 1996. "Sociological and Biblical Views of the Early State." Pages 78–105 in *The Origins of the Ancient Israelite States*. Edited by Volkmar Fritz and Philip R. Davies. JSOTSup 228. Sheffield Academic.

Silberman, Neil Asher. 1999. "Whose Game Is It Anyway? The Political and Social Transformations of American Biblical Archaeology." Pages 175–88 in *Archaeology under Fire: Nationalism, Politics and Heritage in the Eastern Mediterranean and the Middle East*. Edited by Lynn Meskell. Routledge.

Tarnas, Richard. 1991. *The Passion of the Western Mind: Understanding the Ideas That Have Shaped Our World View*. Ballantine Books.

Thompson, Thomas L. 1987. *The Origin Tradition of Ancient Israel I: The Literary Formation of Genesis and Exodus 1–23.* JSOTSup 55. Sheffield Academic.

———. 1992. *Early History of the Israelite People: From the Written and Archaeological Sources.* SHANE 4. Brill.

———. 1995. "A Neo-Albrightian School of History and Biblical Scholarship?" *JBL* 114:683–705.

———. 1997. "Defining History and Ethnicity in the Southern Levant." Pages 166–87 in *Can a "History of Israel" Be Written?* Edited by Lester L. Grabbe. JSOTSup 245. Sheffield Academic.

———. 1999. *The Mythic Past: Biblical Archaeology and the Myth of Israel.* Basic Books.

Whitelam, Keith W. 1996. *The Invention of Ancient Israel: The Silencing of Palestinian History.* Routledge.

Windschuttle, Keith. 1996. *The Killing of History: How Literary Critics and Social Theorists Are Murdering Our Past.* Free Press.

Zevit, Ziony. 1995. Review of *In Search of "Ancient Israel,"* by Philip R. Davies. *AJS Review* 21:153–56.

———. 2001. *The Religions of Ancient Israel: A Synthesis of Parallactic Approaches.* Continuum.

———. 2002. "Three Debates about Bible and Archaeology." *Bib* 83:1–27.

6

*Israelite Origins and the "Nomadic Ideal":
Can Archaeology Separate Fact from Fiction?*

One question that still lingers as more recent scholars have attempted to revive various theories of pastoral origins for early Israel (i.e., Avraham Faust, Israel Finkelstein, Anson F. Rainey, and Adam Zertal) is whether the nostalgic biblical notion of a return to "purer nomadic ideals" represents a genuine early historical memory. The only specific treatment in the literature, however, is a brief essay by Hiebert in 2009 in the Stager Festschrift (see below), which does not cite my 1998 article republished here.

The paper republished here further carried several themes already evident in earlier publications, among them defining early Israel ethnically and the necessity for a dialogue between text and artifact. In particular, my agrarian model for early Israel is spelled out here in more detail, comparing it with the pastoral-nomadic model of the other scholars and defining pastoralism more adequately. Obviously this chapter, written in 1996, turned out to be a prolegomenon to a later book, *Who Were the Early Israelites and Where Did they Come From?* (2003). Later bibliography will be found in chapter 8 and in the updated bibliography (arranged chronologically) at the end of the Works Cited.

Originally published as pages 220–37 in *Mediterranean People in Transition: Thirteenth to Early Tenth Centuries BCE.* Edited by Seymour S. Gitin, Amihai Mazar, and Ephraim Stern. Israel Exploration Society, 1998. Reprinted by permission.

6.1. Introduction

In his epochal *The Tribes of Yahweh: A Sociology of the Religion of Liberated Israel, 1250–1050 B.C.E.,* Norman K. Gottwald takes as his point of departure the observation that prior to 1960 virtually all commentators on Israelite origins, regardless of whether they espoused conquest or immigration models, viewed the earliest Israelites as former pastoral nomads from the desert who penetrated Canaan and became sedentarized there.[1]

Today all that has changed. The conquest and immigration models of biblical scholars, along with Gottwald's own peasants' revolt model, are now passé.[2] Further, in the past decade a formidable array of revolutionary new archaeological data has brought about a near consensus in support of indigenous origins, or what I would call, with Volkmar Fritz, symbiosis models.[3] Yet conventional notions of Israelite pastoral nomadic origins in the thirteenth century BCE and tribal origins in the twelfth–eleventh century BCE still persist among both biblical scholars and archaeologists. This is so despite the lack of any substantial data and what I regard as massive theoretical contradictions. Indeed, the major work that I shall review here, Israel Finkelstein's and Nadav Na'aman's edited volume of essays, *From Nomadism to Monarchy: Archaeological and Historical Aspects of Early Israel* (1994), may signal a return to the outmoded idea of nomadic origins for early Israel. If so, the basis of the argument of the various authors must be subjected to the most critical scrutiny from both archaeological and historical perspectives.

---

1. Gottwald 1979, 435.

2. The statement that all previous models are passé is so obvious that it needs no documentation, as a review of any of the recent literature will show. Proponents of these earlier models are barely represented in the current dialogue (such as it is) because they have not responded to the challenge of the newer archaeological data. Notable exceptions would be Bimson 1989, 1991, who still, however, holds to an impossible fifteenth-century BCE date for an "exodus"; and Gottwald 1993a, 1993b, who now eschews "egalitarian" in favor of "communitarian" but still upholds the critical ideological role of "Yahwism" in the emergence of early Israel, which, unfortunately, is not easily recognizable, if at all, in the material culture remains. Thus "indigenous" or "symbiosis" models prevail, if only by default (below), most tending toward functionalist explanations of one sort or another.

3. Fritz 1981, 1987.

I offer the following critique of my colleagues at Tel Aviv in the same spirit that they have often challenged me—as a compliment, a sign that I regard them as sufficiently innovative to take them seriously.

6.2. The Nomadic Ideal

6.2.1. The History of a Notion

What biblical scholars and others have called the nomadic ideal has a venerable history.

1. The ideal of the priority and superiority of "desert origins" seems regnant, indeed almost the integrating rubric, in the diverse strands of the tradition in the Hebrew Bible, from the patriarchs in Genesis to the Rechabites in the Latter Prophets.

2. The biblical notion of descent from the desert has many parallels in folklore and the ethnohistory of other peoples, even though it can rarely be documented in actual historical events.[4]

3. The use of various versions of the nomadic ideal has a long history in both ancient Near Eastern studies and biblical scholarship, from the early nineteenth century to the present.

4. The notion of nomadic origins can claim (and has claimed) support from any and all of the textual and archaeological models of Israelite origins that have been advanced.

5. Finally, the nomadic ideal would appear to offer the only overarching framework that might harmonize the often-conflicting data; that is, it makes good sense.

---

4. For the fact that memories of supposed nomadic origins and fictions of tribal organization prevail among many sedentary and even urban peoples, without any actual historical basis, see especially Gottwald 1979, 237–386; Lemche 1985, 164–406; Rogerson 1986; Neu 1992; for the wider ethnographic perspective, see the essays of Lois Beck, Albert Hourani, Richard Tapper, and Bassam Tibi in Khoury and Kostiner 1990. See also nn. 5 and 6 below.

6.2.2. A Critique of the Notion

Despite the obvious attractions of the nomadic ideal, I would argue that there are many reasons why it has outlived its usefulness.

1. More recent biblical scholarship is almost unanimously agreed that the literary tradition, largely shaped by the final Deuteronomistic and Priestly redactors, presents a portrait of Israel that is late, tendentious, and highly idealistic. Thus the nomadic ideal is just that: an ideal projected back upon a theoretical Israel that never existed (at least not in the form imagined by the biblical writers and editors).[5]

2. Meanwhile, ancient Near Eastern scholars, anthropologists, and ethnographers and Syro-Palestinian archaeologists have come universally to reject invasion hypotheses and notions of forceful penetration of nomads in what we may call *Siedlungsgeschichte*, or the long-term settlement history of the Levant. Earlier treatments of nomads and ethnic movements were based on nineteenth-century Eurocentric romanticism, misleading readings of the Mari and other texts dealing with ancient pastoralists, simplistic theories of culture change, and the lack of first-hand acquaintance with modern Middle Eastern nomads and tribal peoples.

3. In the past twenty years or so, the death knell should have been given to the nomadic ideal by developments in mainstream scholarship in biblical and Near Eastern studies. Most biblical scholars have long since rejected Noth's once-influential amphictyony, or tribal confederation, hypothesis. With that, most assumptions about any actual tribal structure in premonarchic Israel should have been given up.[6] In addition, most Syro-Palestinian archaeologists agree that the rich archaeological data we

---

5. On the nomadic ideal in the Bible and in biblical scholarship, see the classic article of Flight 1923; see also, more recently, Hauser 1978; Mendenhall 1973; Gottwald 1974, 1979, 1993a; de Geus 1976; Rogerson 1986; Martin 1989; Thompson 1992b; Dever 1995b, 1995c. Such notions are an aspect of later political realities and ideological conflicts, mostly in the period of monarchical Israel, and in no way reflect an actual pastoral nomadic background in the Middle–Late Bronze Age. See also n. 4 above.

6. Gottwald (1979, 333) argues that the whole notion of tribalism was "the last social entity in Israel to reach a relatively fixed form" and that in early Israel the family was the basic social unit; that is, we have simply a kin-based society, not a true tribal structure that derived from nomadic backgrounds. See also Coote 1991, 40–42, as well as nn. 4 and 5 above.

now possess effectively dispose of conquest and external origin models for early Israel. In my view, this consensus on indigenous origins should have eliminated "pastoral" (or any other) nomads as any more than a minor component in the early Iron I highland population, which I regard here as Proto-Israelite.[7]

4. Finally, as I shall try to show, outside biblical traditions of doubtful historical worth, there never was, and is not now, any conclusive empirical data to support the notion of nomadic origins for the Iron I or Proto-Israelite ethnic groups.

What I propose in the following is simply to carry to their logical conclusions more recent evidence and insights from biblical and archaeological scholarship regarding Israelite origins, however radical that may appear to be. I should note in passing that many scholars (most of them, significantly, nonarchaeologists) are now skeptical as to archaeology's ability to recognize ethnicity in the archaeological record.[8] But as I have argued in detail elsewhere on the basis of both textual and artifactual remains, I am sure that we can confidently identify those folk I prefer to call Proto-Israelites with both the references to Israel in the Merenptah Stela and the early Iron I highland village complex that is now well known archaeologically. Presuming this, the issue I have chosen to address here is not who these new settlers were but simply from where within Late Bronze Age Canaan they mostly came.[9]

---

7. I introduced this term (Dever 1990b, 46, 55; 1991, 87, 88) as a cautious, compromise measure, even though I think that the more explicit term "Israelite" would be (and will be) justifiable. Finkelstein approves of the term (1992b, 64); Whitelam (1994, 84) rejects it, without, however, giving any reasons. I came to "Proto-Israelite" independently, but since then I see that several German biblical scholars had used similar terms earlier, as has McCarter (1992).

8. As evidence of the growing trend of biblical scholars toward rejecting archaeological data as reflecting Israelite (or any other) ethnic identity, see Whitelam 1994 and the earlier treatments by Ahlström 1986, 1991; Lemche 1991: Skjeggestad 1992; Thompson 1992a, 1992b. For responses to these biblical scholars on ethnicity in the archaeological record, see n. 13 below. For specific references to the broader historiographical issue posed by those I call the "new nihilists," see n. 45.

9. Dever 1990a, 1990b, 1991, 1992a, 1993, 2001.

6.3. A Critique of Israel Finkelstein's Theory of Pastoral Nomadic Origins

We are all deeply indebted to Israel Finkelstein. The publication of his 'Izbet Ṣarṭah excavations in 1986, and especially his 1988 synthesis, *The Archaeology of the Israelite Settlement*, have marked a pivotal turning point in all our discussions of early Israel. In these initial treatments Finkelstein by and large simply assumed that the Iron I village complex he surveyed so persuasively could be labeled "early Israelite"—a methodological deficiency for which many reviewers, including myself, criticized him.[10] Yet I think that he was quite right in his basic conclusion, namely, that the term *Israel* could be appropriately used at least as a heuristic device. He simply failed to document that usage, as he might have done.

In the last few years, however, instead of following up on his own excellent early intuition, Finkelstein has backed away entirely from the idea that we can identify an early Israel, or for that matter any other ethnic group, in the Iron I highland villages. As he has put it recently, "There was no political entity named Israel before the late-eleventh century." Lest we suppose that he means to stress only that it was merely the political structure that was lacking, he has declared elsewhere that "any effort to distinguish between 'Israelite' and 'nonIsraelite' hill country sites during the twelfth eleventh centuries BCE according to their finds is doomed to failure" and, furthermore, that methodologically "the material culture of the Iron I sites in the hill country should not be viewed in ethnic perspectives." Elsewhere he says that he would now be "more nihilistic in the treatment of material culture."[11] On these specific points, Finkelstein has challenged my presumably more positivist position in several treatments in which I have defended the idea of an archaeologically based Israelite ethnicity.[12] Several others have now entered the fray on the question of ethnicity, most, like Niels Peter Lemche, Marit Skjeggestad, Keith W. Whitelam, and Gösta Ahlström, on the negative side, but some, like Lawrence E. Stager, Gloria London, Robert B. Coote, Zeev Herzog, and Shlomo Bunimovitz, on the cautiously optimistic side. There the debate on ethnicity rests at the

---

10. Dever 1991.
11. Finkelstein 1991, 56; see also 1994, 169; 1991, 53.
12. Dever 1990b, 1991, 1993.

moment, although several papers are in the press by myself, Finkelstein, Bunimovitz, Brian Hesse and Paula Wapnish, and others.[13]

Meanwhile, Finkelstein, having abandoned the quest for "Israelite ethnicity," has taken up a new notion: the pastoral nomadic origin of the now-anonymous Iron I hill-country settlers. By the time of his 1992 synthesis in the volume edited by Ofer Bar-Yosef and Anatoly M. Khazanov, *Pastoralism in the Levant: Archaeological Materials in Anthropological Perspectives*, Finkelstein was arguing that the Iron I occupation in the highlands was simply the "third wave of settlement" in the long-term cyclical settlement history of the area. The previous demographic shifts in Late Chalcolithic/Early Bronze I, and Early Bronze IV/Middle Bronze I were, in his view, closely comparable—even in several categories of material culture—and were also caused largely by pastoral nomads in the process of becoming sedentarized.

Finkelstein argues that, after the destructions and disruptions that ended the Middle Bronze Age, the second established urban phase of Palestine, around 1500 BCE, large elements of the local hill-country population were displaced. Thus they reverted to pastoral strategies of survival, remaining *nomadic* throughout the succeeding Late Bronze Age. It was from this highland group, not the lowlands and urban Canaanite centers, as I have maintained (below), that most of the Iron I village population derived. Specifically, these local pastoral nomads had been roaming along the semiarid eastern flanks of the central Samaria and Judah mountain ranges and out into the desert fringes, or Finkelstein's "ecological frontier zone." Then in Iron I they penetrated the hillier forested areas and intermontane valleys. They spread from east to west and shifted gradually from

---

13. See Stager 1985, 1989; London 1989; Coote 1990, 1991; Herzog 1994; Bunimovitz 1994, 1995; Dever 2001; Finkelstein 1995; Hesse and Wapnish 1997. See n. 8 above for some current views of biblical scholars, all of whom, however, are minimalists and thus not necessarily representative of mainstream scholarship. For better balance, see McCarter 1992; Gottwald 1974. For the views of archaeologists on ethnicity in the archaeological record, a discussion still in its infancy, see London 1989; Finkelstein 1995; Dever 1993, 2001; Bunimovitz 1995; Killebrew and MacKay 1995. The 1995 papers were presented at a special session on "pots and peoples" at the Annual Meetings of ASOR/SBL in Chicago in 1994, chaired by Jodi Magness; some have been excerpted in a 1995 issue of *Biblical Archaeologist*.

pastoralism to mixed agro-pastoralism as they became more sedentary by the late twelfth–early eleventh century BCE.

The archaeological evidence that Finkelstein cites for a pastoral background from which the Iron I settlers emerged consists largely of: (1) ecological considerations, changing shifts in Late Bronze II–Iron I; (2) the nature of the material remains of the Iron I villages, especially pottery and house form; and (3) the layout of some early Iron I oval village plans, which he thinks is reminiscent of Bedouin-like tent circles and "which seem to preserve the tent and camp traditions of the presedentary phase."

Elsewhere Finkelstein specifically disavows the technological arguments of Stager, myself, and others that pillared houses, terraces, and cisterns were a significant factor in the early waves of settlement.[14] Thus he dismisses what I believe to be a very well grounded presumption, one that is easily more defensible than Finkelstein's and is potentially decisive. It is that most of the hill-country settlers in Iron I must have come from a largely sedentary background in rural Late Bronze Age Canaan, where they were already familiar with the difficult conditions of intensive agriculture and specialized stock-breeding (below).

Given the restrictions of time and space here, I can only list in summary form the numerous objections that can be raised against Finkelstein's 1992 hypothesis of pastoral origins.

1. He still appears to be unduly under the influence of Alt's peaceful infiltration model, as he was in 1988.

2. He has uncritically adopted the biblical nomadic ideal, although mainstream biblical scholarship has shown that it is a literary construct and has little or no historical foundation (see, for example, Gottwald as long ago as 1974 and 1979, whose works Finkelstein barely quotes but from which he could nevertheless learn much).

3. He never really defines pastoralism (except to note that it refers mainly to animal husbandry) or cites the copious anthropological and ethnographic literature on pastoralism as a socioeconomic strategy, and thus

---

14. Finkelstein 1992a, 137; 1995, 364. On technology as a factor in the emergence of early Israel, see Finkelstein 1988, 308–14; 1989, who here and in subsequent treatments plays down the role of technology in favor of ecological and socioeconomic factors (although how can one separate them?). For more positive assessments, see Stager 1985 and references there; Dever 1990b, 46; 1991, 82–84; for agricultural technology, see Hopkins 1985.

6. Israelite Origins and the "Nomadic Ideal"   143

he confuses pastoralism with nomadism (he has the same difficulty with tribal). In particular, Finkelstein does not use the more precise term *seminomadism*, nor does he note, except in passing (using Michael B. Rowton's dimorphic chiefdom), the strongly symbiotic relationships between pastoralists and sedentary populations in both the ancient and the modern Middle East.[15] His adoption of the notion of a "nomadic-sedentary continuum" (recognized as significant by virtually all scholars today) is helpful, but he does not specify where along this continuum his pastoralists lie; that is, are they really nomads?

4. Finkelstein assumes, without consulting the critical literature, that pastoral nomads readily settle, especially in crisis periods, "as when urban civilizations and centralized social systems periodically collapse, as they did toward the end of the Late Bronze Age."[16] In fact, just the opposite is usually true: nomads typically settle only under considerable duress from the urban authorities, mainly in periods when central government is strong rather than weak (or nonexistent, as in the Late Bronze) and in times of general prosperity when they can easily convert their capital on the hoof. Fredrik Barth, Anatoly Khazanov, and many other ethnographers have documented these trends in the sedentarization of modern nomads many times over, as have J. Tracey Luke, Victor Matthews, and others for the Mari tribespeople.[17] Finkelstein has neither motive nor rationale for his pastoralists becoming sedentary in Iron I.

---

15. There is a vast literature on pastoral nomadism and specifically on nomadism versus sedentism; for earlier works, see references in Dever 1977; for broader orientation, add Rowton 1977 and references to his previous works; see also the several papers in Khoury and Kostiner 1990 and Bar-Yosef and Khazanov 1992 and references there. Virtually all authorities now agree on the symbiotic nature of nomads and sedentary people. Finkelstein's isolated and autochthonous Late Bronze Age "nomads" are an anomaly, since he sees almost no urban centers or even villages in the hill country. This observation alone is enough to question his entire hypothesis; see further n. 17 below. On the archaeology of nomads, see n. 30 below.

16. Finkelstein 1992a, 136–38.

17. See n. 15 above generally. On the mechanism of sedentarization specifically, see Barth 1973; Bates and Lees 1977; Salzman 1980; Khazanov 1984; Rafferty 1985; Lemche 1985, 136–42; and, most recently, Finkelstein and Perevolotsky 1990 and references there. Finkelstein, of course, is aware of and quotes some of this literature (as early as 1988, 345–47), but he draws from it what in my opin-

5. Positing pastoralist movements into the highlands in Iron I cannot account for the sudden demographic increase that Finkelstein himself has documented so ably. As his and other surveys have shown, the number of sites in the hill country goes from 29 in the Late Bronze to 254 in the early Iron I and the total occupied area from 47 to 219 hectares.[18] Such dramatic growth obviously cannot be explained by natural increase alone, and it also cannot be explained by "nomads settling down." Finkelstein has estimated that the population of the entire hill-country area in the twelfth century BCE was about 55,000 (using an estimate of 250 per hectare). Yet the total population of the area in the Late Bronze Age was no more than perhaps 12,000 (using Finkelstein's own reasonable estimate of ca. 250 per hectare). Estimates of the percentage of pastoral nomads among the sedentary population run no more than 10–15 percent,[19] leaving us a total of some 1,200–1,800 nomads at most in the Late Bronze Age. How did 1,200–1,800 pastoralists multiply to 55,000 in a couple of generations? Obviously, Late Bronze Age pastoral nomads—even if they all settled in Iron I—can have constituted no more than a small component (5 percent) of the total population. The majority of the Iron I highland villagers clearly came from other elements of Canaanite society and economy, as I will argue, probably former city and town dwellers together with a sizeable rural population, all displaced by the drastic upheavals at the end of the Late Bronze Age (below).

6. Finkelstein minimizes the cultural and ethnic diversity that common sense would dictate and that both the biblical and the archaeological data strongly suggest in the makeup of the earliest hill-country population. He does allow for some degree of diversified subsistence strategies among his first-generation "pastoralists," that is, "short-distance herding" combined with "seasonal agriculture."[20] But he does not seem to think that fully sedentarized agriculturists played any role, perhaps because that

---

ion is unwarranted support for his own theories of nomadic sedentarization. See further n. 30 below. For the process of sedentarization of pastoralists and tribespeoples at ancient Mari, see Luke 1965; Matthews 1978.

18. Finkelstein 1994, 154.

19. For the estimate of 10–15 percent pastoral nomads in modern Middle Eastern societies, see Na'aman 1994, 233–35 and references there; Finkelstein (1988, 343) uses the same estimate.

20. Finkelstein 1992a, 134.

6. Israelite Origins and the "Nomadic Ideal"

would require him to account for their previous background as farmers rather than pastoralists. To show how Finkelstein's preconceptions color his view, one should note that twelfth- to eleventh-century Tel Masos, in the northern Negev, where the animal bones were over 25 percent cattle, is dismissed by him as a "non-Israelite" site. Why? Apparently because it does not fit the picture. Yet the village layout, individual house form, occupational history, and many of the pottery forms are nearly identical to his hill-country sites. I have argued that extensive cattle breeding in the marginal northern Negev is not typical of pastoralists and would have required prior agricultural experience.[21]

7. The arguments of Finkelstein that are based on actual archaeological data (rather than on questionable theoretical constructs) are all either debatable or inconsequential. Thus the shift in settlement patterns, in village layout, and in house form in Iron I reveal only an emergent agrarian society and economy. The changes say little about where the pioneers of the hill-country frontier came from, unless suggesting that many had been villagers, peasant farmers, and rural folk elsewhere in Canaan (below). The supposed oval plans of ʿIzbet Ṣarṭah Stratum III, Tel Masos II, Arad XII, and Beersheba VII are all 90 percent reconstructions, without any basis in excavated remains. In any case, the Bedouin-style tent circle that this plan is supposed to evoke is so exceptional that Finkelstein is hard pressed to find a single illustration.[22] Most Bedouin camps feature relatively distant individual tents, all oriented toward the east. The notion that the typical Iron I pillar or four-room house, with its open central courtyard, is reminiscent of pastoralism is disingenuous.[23] These are simply ideal, functional

---

21. Dever 1990a, 93.

22. For easy reference and illustration of these oval and elliptical plans, see Herzog 1994, 133–37; Finkelstein 1988, 238–59. In addition to the obvious problem that these are all projections based on scant excavated remains, it may be observed that nearly all urban tell sites in Palestine are also oval or elliptical; are they, too, reflections of nomadic origins? The fact is that virtually all individual structures and village-town layouts in less-developed sites universally, in all time periods, are subrectangular, simply because this is the most obvious and most efficient plan. As for Finkelstein's (1988, 245–58) concurrence with the views of Fritz (1977, 1980), Kempinski (1978), and Herzog (1984) that the oval layout reflects the direct continuation of the lifestyle of tents and tent circles, that argument is far-fetched and seems to have persuaded almost no one; see Stager 1985, 17.

23. Finkelstein 1995, 365.

farmhouses of the type still found all around the Mediterranean, into which stables, mangers, and other facilities for stock breeding are naturally incorporated. We are dealing here simply with animal husbandry, which is not exclusively identified with pastoral nomadism.

Happily, Finkelstein does not employ Fritz's attempt to connect the plan of the typical courtyard house with the living arrangement of bedouin tents—a novel idea that has convinced no one. Finally, Finkelstein ignores the implication of the floral and faunal data from his own excavations at ʿIzbet Ṣarṭah. There his specialist in food systems, Baruch Rosen, has concluded that the founders of the settlement were very successful farmers and stock breeders capable of producing even sizeable surpluses.[24] They hardly look to me like "recently sedentarized pastoral nomads." Indeed, Finkelstein has never replied to the provocative paper of his own field supervisor at ʿIzbet Ṣarṭah, Zvi Lederman, entitled "Nomads They Never Were" (1990), or, for that matter, to my own similar criticisms.[25]

Finkelstein's remaining archaeological arguments can be easily dismissed. Thus the increase in ovine versus cattle bones from the Middle Bronze into the Late Bronze at the single site of Shiloh is hardly evidence of an increase in pastoralism. Like the relatively larger number of small Late Bronze Age sites found in the surveys, it is simply an indication of the predominance of a rural rather than urban society in this period, that is, of very much the same sort of village network that we see in the subsequent Iron I period. There were probably no more true nomadic pastoralists than in the Middle Bronze, just fewer urbanites. As for the supposed parallel of "isolated cult places" in both the Late Bronze and Iron I, the Tananir shrine is the Middle Bronze II–HI, the Amman Airport shrine is completely enigmatic, the Lachish Fosse temples are not "isolated" at all but are on the slopes of the tell, the Shiloh shrine cannot really be said to be rural, and only one clear Iron I shrine is known, the Bull Site.[26]

8. Much of Finkelstein's theory of "stages of pastoralist sedentarization" is based on the pattern of progressive east-to-west movement that

---

24. Rosen 1986, 156–85.

25. Lederman 1990; Dever 1990a, 93–95; 1991, 78–83.

26. Finkelstein's dating of the Tananir shrine to the Late Bronze without giving any reasons is extraordinary. As for his own Shiloh "isolated cult place," so little of Late Bronze Stratum VI was excavated that this conclusion is scarcely warranted.

he has attempted to reconstruct in the twelfth- to eleventh-century BCE settlement process. Thus, he argues that fully 75 percent of the earliest Iron I settlements are on the eastern flanks and desert steppes, that is, in areas well adapted to seasonal pastoralism and some dry farming but poorly suited to intensive agriculture. But he apparently is basing this argument entirely on survey sites (which, incidentally, are not yet published).[27] If one looks at the ten to twelve excavated hill-country sites north of the Jerusalem area that Finkelstein himself originally summarized, it is evident that none is located on the eastern flanks of the central ridge, much less out in the desert steppes. Furthermore, all these sites were founded in the thirteenth/twelfth or the twelfth century BCE and are thus among Finkelstein's early phases of the settlement process. Ironically, Finkelstein's own extremely important site of 'Izbet Ṣarṭah is not only (1) the earliest of all the settlement sites, dated by him to the late thirteenth century BCE, but it is also (2) the farthest west in location. So much for east-to-west waves of settlement, that is, pastoral nomads from the hinterland penetrating the area better suited to sedentarism.

Here we come to Finkelstein's related argument that knowledge of terrace agriculture—which is, of course, a hallmark of sedentary agriculture

---

27. Nowhere in his many publications does Finkelstein face the many problems of random sampling and statistical probability adequately, as these are treated in voluminous literature elsewhere in general archaeology. See, for example, Mueller 1979. Furthermore, the discussion of the identity of the hill-country settlers has grown so rapidly that few seem to have noticed that the basic survey data remain unpublished. In 1988 Finkelstein presented site statistics and discussed pottery, but he only published ten of his Iron I sherds! In his 1991, 1992a, 1994, and 1995 treatments there is no pottery and no discussion except for brief generalizations. Now the full survey material is presented fully in Finkelstein and Magen 1993. Yet here (1) the survey area is only 500 square kilometers, a fraction of Finkelstein's Ephraim survey, i.e., the Jerusalem-Ramallah area; (2) fewer than forty Iron I sites are discussed, without any further distinctions; (3) some four hundred Iron I sherds are mentioned, but only some sixty are published, the majority of them are rarely diagnostic, even for the expert; and (4) there are virtually none of the collar-rim jars or cooking pots published here, although Finkelstein has always maintained that these are the properly diagnostic Iron I types. Perusal of this first final report of the hill country surveys (which few will read in Hebrew anyway) hardly inspires much confidence. How did the discussion of origin and ethnicity get this far without exhaustive analysis and critical comparison of the pottery, still our best clue? See further nn. 36 and 43 below.

in the hill country—was not a factor in the choice of areas first to be settled. Yet all the ten to twelve excavated hill-country sites noted above are located in areas of extensive terracing. Finkelstein attempts to get around the terrace issue by arguing that terracing is not intimately connected with the sudden expansion of settlement activity in the hill country precisely in the Iron Age, as several have argued, but was introduced as early as the Early Bronze Age. When one looks, however, at the actual evidence for dating terraces that early, the argument is extremely weak. Finkelstein simply observes that "there is good reason to believe" that terracing was widespread before the Iron Age, but he cites no evidence.[28]

Turning to another line of argument, on what does he base his absolutely critical dates for the east-to-west direction of settlement? Only on cooking-pot rims, it turns out, and of course these have been collected only from surface surveys. I agree that the typology of thirteenth- to eleventh-century BCE cooking pots is well enough worked out to yield some reliable chronological information, and I have used such data myself. But surely more evidence is needed from other ceramic forms. Furthermore, Finkelstein's cooking-pot argument is statistical, and surface surveys are notorious for yielding results that are statistically invalid or even at best somewhat misleading. Here Finkelstein's ceramic arguments are identical to those of Zertal, which I have refuted elsewhere, the ultimate conclusions to which (i.e., migrations from even farther east, in Transjordan) Finkelstein himself rejects.[29]

---

28. Finkelstein 1995, 364. On terraces and their implications for the origin of the hill-country settlements, see n. 14 above and references there. The terrace systems at Sataf that Finkelstein (1992b, 64–65) tries to date as early as the Early Bronze Age are all in an overall Roman-Byzantine landscape. There is still no hard evidence to show that extensive agricultural terrace systems predate the early Iron Age (see de Geus 1975; Stager 1982).

29. Zertal 1991, 1994; Finkelstein 1992b, 67. See Dever 1991, 85–87; 1993, 26*–27*; 2001. The crucial point is that Finkelstein's and Zertal's early Type A cooking-pot rims, which I would also date to the late thirteenth/early twelfth centuries BCE, and the later Type B rims do not have the mutually exclusive distribution pattern that would be necessary to support their claim that the earlier are to the east and the later to the west. Finkelstein's own ʿIzbet Ṣarṭah, among the earliest sites, has both types. Furthermore, as I have argued, even if the earliest sites were all on the eastern fringes of the central ridge, that could be explained if refugees from the lowland urban sites were involved, as I argue, among the early

9. Finally, Finkelstein would need to document many Late Bronze Age pastoral encampments in the highlands to reconstruct a population reservoir of nomads capable of providing the large numbers of Iron I settlers he postulates. He claims to have found some such sites, but he publishes none of the raw data. The difficulties of locating pastoral nomads in the archaeological record, duly noted by Finkelstein, are well known and may be in his favor. Further, of course, there must have been sizeable numbers of pastoral nomads around in the Late Bronze Age, as in all periods. But Finkelstein does not have the definitive archaeological proof that he would need.[30]

In conclusion, the comparative cross-cultural and theoretical foundations of Finkelstein's pastoral nomadic origins are extremely weak, and his archaeological data are scant or better interpreted in other ways. Further, if he has little archaeological data to support his highland pastoralist origin theory, he has even less to oppose my suggestion of a partly lowland derivation. He simply asserts that the Late Bronze Age lowlands and urban centers as possible sources for deriving the Iron I hill-country settlers can be safely written off. There are no "direct roots to the Late Bronze Age lowlands." "There is absolutely no undisputed archaeological evidence for a *direct* shift of significant population from the lowlands to the highlands in the Late Bronze–Iron I transition."[31]

Yet what are Finkelstein's reasons for these assertions? He does not say, directly, but I suggest the following.

1. Finkelstein says that there is no archaeological evidence for pastoral nomadic encampments in the lowlands. But as he himself notes, little would be found because of heavy later occupation of sites and areas, deep alluviation, and disturbances due to modern development. Thus the absence of pastoralists is simply an argument, however justified, from silence.

2. Finkelstein is not predisposed even to look for such pastoral sites, since as he says, "I do not see why the lowland urban centers of the six-

---

settlers. Where better to seek refuge? See also the skepticism of Esse (1989) on east-to-west movements.

30. Finkelstein 1992a, 134. For recent discussion on the problem of invisible nomads in the archaeological record, see Banning 1993; Rosen and Avni 1993; and especially Cribb 1991. See also many of the essays in Bar-Yosef and Khazanov 1992.

31. Finkelstein 1995, 363, 365, emphasis original.

teenth–fourteenth centuries would have consented to the presence of the pastoral groups on the fertile grounds immediately adjacent to their dwelling."[32] Yet elsewhere he acknowledges that the Amarna letters and Egyptian texts prove that there were such pastoral and nomadic groups in the area—that is, in the lowland countryside surrounding the urban centers—such as the well-known Habiru and Shasu. He even endorses Rowton's models of "enclosed nomadism" and "dimorphic society," which draw precisely such a picture of closely interrelated groups of pastoral nomads, sedentary agriculturalists, and urban dwellers. Thus the implied dichotomy—urbanites and rural folk in the lowland, pastoralists in the hill country—cannot be maintained. I suggest rather that urbanites, rural agriculturalists, and pastoral nomads were all involved in the early Iron I colonization of the hill country, and they probably came from most areas of Canaan, not exclusively from the eastern flanks and desert steppes of the hill country (below).[33]

3. Finkelstein's failure to see any "direct connection" in material culture between lowland Late Bronze sites and hill-country Iron I sites, and thus continuity of population elements, is due to the fact that he concentrates on the admittedly disjunctive traits such as settlement location and type, house form, silos, and the like. He has consistently ignored or minimized the obvious continuities in pottery, universally perceived by archaeologists as our most sensitive medium for recognizing cultural contact and change. He is able only to say that there is a "sharp contrast" between the standard Late Bronze Age Canaanite repertoire and that of the Iron I hill-country sites, only a "certain degree of continuity," only "certain influence from Iron I lowland sites."[34] Yet as it turns out, Finkelstein's argument for discontinuity rests almost exclusively on the basis of relative percentages of certain relative forms, that is, a more limited general repertoire, and especially more collar-rim jars and cooking pots in the hill-country sites. But as London and I have both pointed out, that is to be expected.[35] The phenomenon simply reflects the predictable, functional differences between urban and rural sites (although I think that the difference has ethnic implications as well). Finkelstein has never answered this argument. Nor has he

---

32. Finkelstein 1991, 55.
33. See Finkelstein 1992, 136–39; 1994, 175; 1995, 353.
34. Finkelstein 1988, 274, 312–14.
35. London 1989; Dever 1991, 84.

ever responded to the several publications in which I have documented in detail the direct continuity of most of the Late Bronze–Iron I ceramic forms.[36] If Finkelstein allowed himself to see the typical Late Bronze Age ceramic repertoire as the immediate background out of which his Iron I hill-country pottery developed, he would be much more open to recognizing among his settlers various peoples from all over Canaan, not just "fringe-area pastoralists." These would be my "displaced Canaanites" (below).

4. Finally, one cannot help but conclude from Finkelstein's scathing critique of George E. Mendenhall and Norman K. Gottwald, and specifically his general obliviousness to Gottwald's epochal *Tribes of Yahweh*, that he is so predisposed against the sociological schools that he cannot see what valuable insights they have brought to the study of early Israel's history.[37] He also overlooks two simple facts: (1) they all wrote before any of the current, revolutionary archaeological data were available; and (2) they nevertheless were the first to propose indigenous origin theories, operating on an intuition into the social process and a sophisticated reading of the texts that we should all applaud.

6.4. Toward a Reformulation

6.4.1. Why Finkelstein's Synthesis Must Be Dismantled

On the basis of the foregoing critique (which could easily be expanded),[38] it should be obvious that Finkelstein's portrait of the Iron I hill-country

---

36. I have stressed the overall continuity of Late Bronze–Iron I ceramics in several studies (Dever 1990a, 1991, 1992b, 1993, 2001). See further Kempinski 1985; Wood 1990. This continuity is now generally acknowledged, but Finkelstein minimizes its significance for understanding processes of cultural change.

37. Finkelstein 1988, 305–10.

38. A number of biblical scholars, such as those cited in n. 8 above, have rejected Finkelstein's connection of the early Iron I hill-country settlements with any ethnic group, Israelite or other. I do not agree at all, of course, with their negative assessments, which are ill-founded (if at all) archaeologically, even though they may invoke various socioanthropological models. (Much better balanced are Coote 1990; Gottwald 1993b.) My criticisms are much more in line with those of

settlers is inadequate, and of course that of early Israel nonexistent, for many reasons.

1. Several of Finkelstein's own colleagues in *From Nomadism to Monarchy*, basing themselves on the same data, disagree with him on vital points. Thus Herzog stresses that "the settlement process encompassed varied groups of pastoral nomads, sedentary farmers and possibly also urban families" and that, because of the continuity with later regional developments, these people "may be considered Israelites."[39] Avi Ofer calls for a "reevaluation" of the pastoral background assumed by Finkelstein and Zertal, and although he believes that the archaeological data on origins are too scant to be conclusive, he states specifically that the available data "make it difficult to accept the assumption that many of the Iron I hill country people were pastoral nomads who settled down as a result of shortage in grain supply."[40] Mazar argues that archaeology can and must supply critical data on the question of the "emergence of Israel" and that the settlers, whatever their origin and self-identity at this early stage, "are certainly part of the population group that provided the nucleus for the rise of the Israelite state, and thus they can be identified as Israelites, in the broadest meaning of the term."[41] Finkelstein's coeditor, Nadav Na'aman, concludes that the overall archaeological evidence for pastoral groups in Late Bronze II Canaan is poor and that it supports his own estimate that they constituted no more than 7,000 to 10,000 of the total population, the 10–15 percent that is typical for most periods, ancient and modern. Finally, Bunimovitz advances a model of "shifting frontiers" that is in my opinion far more satisfactory, arguing that a picture "much different" from Finkelstein's now emerges. Following the collapse of the urban Middle Bronze Age, during the Late Bronze Age, "when an increase in pastoral activity could be expected ... the evidence for pastoral activity decreases" (contradicting Finkelstein directly). He notes, as I have done, that Finkelstein cannot have it both ways theoretically, that is, arguing that the collapse at the end of the Middle Bronze Age urban culture led to subsequent "nomadization" but that at the end of the Late Bronze Age led to the opposite, or

---

other archaeologists, such as Esse 1989, as well as those of several of Finkelstein's colleagues in Finkelstein and Na'aman 1994 as noted here.

39. Herzog 1994, 148–49.
40. Ofer 1984, 108–9.
41. Mazar 1994, 91.

large-scale sedentarization of nomads in Iron I. He concludes that in Iron I a "considerable pastoral population" probably accompanied by "other non-sedentary elements ... deprived of their former sources of livelihood in the *lowlands* reoccupied the hillcountry."[42] This region was now open because of the "vanished frontier," and it later became the heartland of the Israelite monarchy. Bunimovitz's arguments are in fact so persuasive that Finkelstein has softened his approach to "nomadism" somewhat, based on Bunimovitz's initial presentation of his model in his 1989 dissertation.[43]

2. My point here is not that there were no pastoral nomads in the ethnic mix (below) but that Finkelstein has outstripped the archaeological evidence, although it is not as meager as many maintain. Thus he has misunderstood and exaggerated the role of nomads in the settlement process; furthermore, he has minimized the historical, cultural, and socioeconomic diversity of the Iron I settlers (below).

3. By using inappropriate or outworn anthropological and ethnographic theory, he has compromised the newer archaeology that we both advocate, and thus he has raised questions about archaeology's ability to deal persuasively with larger mechanisms of cultural derivation and cultural change. There is too much speculation here, not enough analysis of the basic data that Finkelstein himself has so ably assembled, such as pottery.[44]

4. By giving up entirely on his original "Israelite ethnicity" in his 1992 and subsequent publications, while falling back on dubious notions of pastoral nomadism, Finkelstein threatens to rob Syro-Palestinian as well as the "new biblical archaeology" of one of its potentially greatest successes. Now he has nothing left to say in the crucial dialogue between archaeology and biblical scholars that I have advocated for twenty-five years, which finally is about to begin. He is abandoning the critical role that he ought to be playing in this dialogue, a role in which he himself began so courageously. Worse still, he has left the burgeoning field of early Israelite history to the new nihilists such a Lemche, Thompson, Davies, Whitelam,

---

42. Bunimovitz 1994, 193–202, emphasis added.
43. See Finkelstein 1991, 54–55 but not followed up in 1994, 1995.
44. On Finkelstein's minimal use of pottery see above and n. 27. I suspect that Finkelstein's reluctance to present and discuss the survey pottery in full stems from his recognition that it will not support his larger hypotheses. Note that of all the recent Israeli surveys, only Gal's (1992) treats the Iron I pottery extensively.

and others for whom there is no history to be recovered, no early Israel.⁴⁵ By eschewing a centralist position, Finkelstein concedes the discussion to extremists—the minimalists and the maximalists, archaeologists who are mere technicians, and social theorists masquerading as historians.

6.4.2. What Was Early Israel?

Assuming, for reasons argued above (and in much more detail elsewhere) that the Iron I hill-country archaeological complex can be at least tentatively identified as Proto-Israelite, can we come up with a more satisfactory portrait than Finkelstein's sedentarized nomads? With several other scholars, I suggest that we can and that the constitutive elements would include the following.⁴⁶

---

45. I designate as new nihilists such revisionist scholars as Jamieson-Drake 1991; Thompson 1992a; Davies 1992; and Whitelam 1994—not without justification, I think, since they do argue that nothing whatsoever can be said with confidence of earliest Israel. I find Lemche (1985), Ahlström (1986, 1993), Coote (1990), and Miller (1991) more balanced, thus more satisfactory. Knauf's (1991) skepticism is provocative, but I have learned much more from him. Weippert and Weippert (1991) are similarly skeptical but provide a trenchant review of recent literature. The present flap about the new Tel Dan inscription and the "house of David" controversy simply confirms for me the suspicion that many biblical scholars, while paying lip service to the newer archaeology, are in fact deconstructionists. No new archaeological evidence will convince them because their minds are already made up: there cannot be an early Israel.

46. For my earlier attempts to formulate a statement covering early Israelite diversity, see Dever 1990a, 93–95; 1990b; 1991, 84–88; 1992a, 54; 1993, 30*–31*. My views are close to Fritz's 1981, 1987 symbiosis model. Coote's similar emphasis on cultural diversity and on the positive role of archaeology in defining this diversity is welcome. But he exaggerates the role of relationships with Egyptian hegemony, now in decline, and in my judgment he minimizes the connection of the highland complex with later, biblical Israel (Coote 1990, 113–39; see also 1991). Several of the authors in Finkelstein and Na'aman 1994 also make a point of cultural diversity, as noted here, continuing the emphasis of Gottwald 1979, 1993a; Ahlström 1986; Coote 1990, 1991; and several others. Finkelstein himself (1991, 56; 1994, 177) has recently allowed for some "low-land," "withdrawing," and "foreign" elements. See n. 50 below. A summary and bibliography of other views will be found conveniently in Na'aman 1994, 231–32. The latest statement, that of Whitelam 1994, does not even attempt a definition of either the hill-country complex or of early Israel, indeed cautions throughout that efforts at

6. Israelite Origins and the "Nomadic Ideal"   155

1. Large numbers of those described in the fourteenth-century BCE Amarna letters as Habiru were still around in the early Iron Age. They were not situated mainly in the frontier zones, as Finkelstein thinks, but were to be found everywhere on the fringes of urban society, the rural areas, and the hinterland.[47] Already displaced and disaffected, as many scholars have pointed out, they would have provided a ready pool of mobile people, prospective highland pioneers. While "Habiru" and "Hebrew" may not be etymologically equivalent, the two are partly identifiable socioeconomically.[48]

2. The Shasu nomads known from Papyrus Anastasi and texts of Ramesses II are portrayed not only as pastoralists in Transjordan but also as a sizeable nonnucleated element in Cisjordan. As several scholars have suggested,[49] elements of the Shasu may have joined new settlers in the highlands, perhaps even contributing the nucleus of early "Yahwism," the roots of which have long been sought in southern Transjordan or northwestern Arabia.

3. Many former urbanites, fleeing from the chaos of the Late Bronze Age Canaanite city-states, now so well documented, must have withdrawn or been "displaced" both geographically and ideologically (to use Mendenhall's and Gottwald's still-apt phrases). They could have been conscripted readily by any new movement that offered alternatives, a niche somewhere else.

4. A substantial, impoverished rural population was dispersed throughout Canaan by the thirteenth century BCE, not just on the desert

---

the latter are only an "obstruction," a "distraction." For whom? I plan to reply to Whitelam's outdated and ill-formed use of archaeology in a forthcoming review article, hopefully in *JSOT* (which regularly airs this discussion but almost never publishes anything by archaeologists).

47. Finkelstein 1992a, 139.

48. The literature on the Habiru is vast, but see Na'aman 1986; Lemche 1985; and Weippert and Weippert 1991. Chaney 1983 is still useful and not necessarily made obsolete by the more recent archaeological data. Gottwald (1979, 419–25, 489–97; 1993a), Ahlström (1986, 16–19), Coote and Whitelam (1987, 108–38), and Weippert and Weippert (1991) argue for some Habiru role in the origins of early Israel.

49. Recently several scholars, such as Weippert (1976), Coote (1990, 75–85), and especially Hopkins (1993, with bibliography), have attempted to connect the Shasu with the ancestors of Israel. Contra this view, however, see Yurco 1986, 1990.

fringes. In my opinion, they would have provided the bulk of the population elements, that is, a group substantial enough to create and sustain the large-scale immigration into the hill country that we can now document archaeologically in the late thirteenth/twelfth century BCE. Certainly local pastoral nomads alone cannot account for the dramatic demographic increase or any more than a small part of it (above).

5. Foreign elements in addition to Sea Peoples in Canaan have recently been postulated by some scholars, at least in small numbers. Among them may have been groups of Anatolian, Hurrian, Neo-Hittite, Aramaean, and other extractions.[50] These largely marginalized classes were part of the large-scale displacement of peoples at the end of the Bronze Age that resulted in the eventual colonization of the hill-country frontier.

6. There were, no doubt, some of Finkelstein's (although few if any of Zertal's) hill-country and steppe-zone pastoralists in the cultural and ethnic mix that we are attempting to describe.

7. Finally, we should not discount the possibility that among these disparate elements there may have been other population increments. Specifically I refer to pastoralists from Transjordan who might indeed have traced their remote ancestry to Asiatic groups well-known in the Egyptian Delta from the Fifteenth Hyksos Dynasty onward. Positing a few such newcomers, or better latecomers, to Canaan in the early Iron Age would help to account for the Joseph and exodus-conquest stories in the literary tradition of the later Hebrew Bible. We archaeologists—who, after all, helped to precipitate the current crisis in the historiography of early Israel—cannot be aloof from the literary-historical and even theological issues raised by modern critical scholarship.[51]

---

50. Na'aman 1994; Beck 1994. On the possibilities of foreign elements in the archaeology of early Iron I Palestine, see Finkelstein 1994, 177; Na'aman 1989, 239–47; Beck 1994, 379–81. I doubt, however, whether these "foreign" elements in Iron I stem from anything more than long-assimilated minority groups and distant cultural influences, i.e., the diffusion of ideas rather than peoples.

51. To my knowledge, no archaeologists except Stager (1985) and myself (in many recent works) have attempted to resolve the theological dilemmas that the new archaeological data pose, but see also Halpern 1992. That may be because the major spokepersons in archaeological circles in Israel are generally isolated from biblical scholarship, and even more so from the religious community, a situation far different from that in America and even in Europe. The lack of dialogue is a pity. See further Dever 1989, 1993. In my view, the works of biblical scholars

6. Israelite Origins and the "Nomadic Ideal"

Finally, both questions matter: who the ancient Israelites thought they were and who we think they were. Perhaps we shall never know precisely about the former or agree on the latter. But I think that it is high time to stop saying so much about what we do not know and time to stress what we do know after two decades of textual reanalysis and intensive archaeological investigation. And there must be much more honest, searching dialogue between our several disciplines in the future, as well as much more detailed attention to the archaeological facts on the ground, for so they are. That dialogue, begun so well by this symposium, must continue.

6.5. Conclusion

In conclusion, I would characterize the early Iron I hill-country population and my Proto-Israelites as part of a diverse yet increasingly focused socio-economic and ideological movement born out of the collapse of the Late Bronze Age civilizations of Canaan and the Levant. This nascent ethnic entity, whose momentum led eventually to the formation of the Israelite state, was a largely rural and agrarian movement in the beginning, with a social, economic and political base, but it also had pronounced reformist tendencies.[52] Its tribal structure, the descriptions of which in the Hebrew

---

such as Ahlström 1986, Davies 1992, Thompson 1992a, Skjeggestad 1992, and Whitelam 1994—despite their tacit acknowledgement of the now-pivotal role of archaeology—are not attempts at dialogue but simply monologues.

52. By introducing the notion of reformist, I mean to take ideology, and religion specifically, into account as significant factors in cultural change. I am certainly neither a functionalist nor a determinist. But I do not espouse the views of Mendenhall 1973 or Gottwald 1979 that Yahwism was the driving force (even though Finkelstein [1992b, 63] and Zertal [1992, 77] have accused me of beating the drum for them). In recent writing I have stressed the severely limited role of archaeology in dealing with ideology and religion. Archaeology focuses first on material culture remains, second on individual and social behavior, and, lastly, if at all, on thought and motive. I have tried to show that the quest for the origins of both the Iron I highland villagers and "early Israel" are worthwhile goals for the archaeologist and biblical historian, even though they may, and often must, be separated. Whitelam's (1994) declaration that the latter is merely a "distraction" betrays his failure to understand the goals of archaeology, not to mention his desperation as a historian without a history.

Bible are not nomadic origins at all, is an ideal,[53] a solidarity, whether actually kin-based or not. It was the expression of powerful antistatist tendencies of those who survived, but never forgot, the crisis at the end of the Bronze Age. It was the crucible in which they were forged, as people, state, and nation.[54]

Works Cited

Ahlström, Gösta W. 1986. *Who Were the Israelites?* Eisenbrauns.

———. 1991. "The Role of Archaeological and Literary Remains in Reconstructing Israel's History." Pages 116–41 in *The Fabric of History: Text, Artifact and Israel's Past*. Edited by Diana V. Edelman. JSOTSup 127. JSOT Press.

———. 1993. *The History of Ancient Palestine from the Paleolithic Period to Alexander's Conquest*. JSOTSup 146. JSOT Press.

Banning, Edward B. 1993. "Where the Wild Stones Have Been Gathered Aside: Pastoral Campsites in Wadi Ziqlab, Jordan." *BA* 56:212–21.

Bar-Yosef, Ofer, and Anatoly M. Khazanov, eds. 1992. *Pastoralism in the Levant: Archaeological Materials in Anthropological Perspectives*. Prehistory Press.

Barth, Fredrick. 1973. "A General Perspective on Nomad-Sedentary Relations in the Middle East." Pages 11–27 in *The Desert and the Sown: Nomads in the Wider Society*. Edited by Cynthia Nelson. University of California Press.

---

53. Anyone wishing to compare the rise of Israel with other regional Iron I peoples and nation-states would do well to consult the brilliant treatment of the early Aramaeans in Sader 1992; the parallels with "nomadic Israel" are amazingly close. Finally, Finkelstein and Na'aman 1994, while one of the most innovative works in biblical and archaeological studies in a long time, should be compared now with Neu 1992, which attempts to cover the same trajectory toward a statehood from a very different perspective.

54. After this paper was completed, I learned of the recent discovery of a transitional Late Bronze II/early Iron I horizon at Tell el-'Umeiri in Jordan. This may in time modify my assertion that there is little if any archaeological background in Transjordan to supply a context in which a Proto-Israel could have originated in the late thirteenth century BCE. See Herr 1998, a manuscript of which he generously supplied in advance of the original publication of this chapter.

Bates, Daniel G., and Susan H. Lees. 1977. "The Role of Exchange in Productive Specialization." *AA* 79:824–41.
Beck, Pirhiya. 1994. "The Cult Stands from Taanach: Aspects of the Iconographic Tradition of Early Iron Age Cult Objects in Palestine." Pages 352–81 in *From Nomadism to Monarchy: Archaeological and Historical Aspects of Early Israel*. Edited by Israel Finkelstein and Nadav Na'aman. Biblical Archaeology Society.
Bimson, John J. 1989. *Redating the Exodus and Conquest*. 2nd ed. JSOTSup 5. Sheffield Academic.
———. 1991. "Merneptah's Israel and Recent Theories of Israelite Origins." *JSOT* 49:3–29.
Bunimovitz, Shlomo. 1994. "Socio-political Transformations in the Central Hill Country in the Late Bronze Iron I Transition. Pages 179–202 in *From Nomadism to Monarchy: Archaeological and Historical Aspects of Early Israel*. Edited by Israel Finkelstein and Nadav Na'aman. Biblical Archaeology Society.
———. 1995. "Philistine and Israelite Pottery: A Comparative Approach to the Question of Pots and People." Paper presented at the American Schools of Oriental Research Annual Meeting, November 1995.
Chaney, Marvin. 1983. "Ancient Palestinian Peasant Movements and the Formation of Premonarchic Israel." Pages 39–90 in *Palestine in Transition: The Emergence of Ancient Israel*. Edited by David Noel Freedman and David F. Graf. SWBA 2. Sheffield Academic.
Coote, Robert B. 1990. *Early Israel: A New Horizon*. Fortress.
———. 1991. "Early Israel." *SJOT* 5.2:35–46.
Coote, Robert B., and Keith W. Whitelam. 1987. *The Emergence of Early Israel in Historical Perspective*. SWBA 5. Almond.
Cribb, Roger. 1991. *Nomads in Archaeology*. Cambridge University Press.
Davies, Philip R. 1992. *In Search of "Ancient Israel."* JSOTSup 148. JSOT Press.
Dever, William G. 1977. "Palestine in the Second Millennium B.C.E.: The Archaeological Picture." Pages 70–120 in *Israelite and Judean History*. Edited by John H. Hayes and J. Maxwell Miller. Westminster.
———. 1989. "Yigael Yadin: Prototypical Biblical Archaeologist." *ErIsr* 20:44*–51*. Republished as chapter 1 in this volume.
———. 1990a. "Archaeology and Israelite Origins: A Review Article." *BASOR* 279:89–95.
———. 1990b. *Recent Archaeological Discoveries and Biblical Research*. University of Washington Press.

———. 1991. "Archaeological Data on the Israelite Settlement: A Review of Two Recent Works." *BASOR* 284:77–90.

———. 1992a. "How to Tell a Canaanite from an Israelite." Pages 26–56 in *The Rise of Ancient Israel*. Edited by Hershel Shanks. Biblical Archaeology Society.

———. 1992b. "The Late Bronze-Early Iron I Horizon in Syria-Palestine: Egyptians, Canaanites, 'Sea Peoples,' and 'Proto-Israelites.'" Pages 99–110 in *The Crisis Years: The Twelfth Century B.C.: From Beyond the Danube to the Tigris*. Edited by William A. Ward and Martha S. Joukowsky. Kendall/Hunt.

———. 1993. "Cultural Continuity, Ethnicity in the Archaeological Record, and the Question of Israelite Origins." *ErIsr* 24:22*–33*.

———. 1995a. "Archaeology and the Current Crisis in Israelite Historiography." *ErIs* 25:18*–27*.

———. 1995b. "'Will the Real Israel Please Stand Up?' Archaeology and Israelite Historiography: Part 1." *BASOR* 297:61–80.

———. 1995c. "'Will the Real Israel Please Stand Up?' Part II: Archaeology and the Religions of Israel." *BASOR* 298:37–58.

———. 2001. "Iron Age Kernoi and the Israelite Cult." Pages 119–33 in *Studies in the Archaeology of Israel and Neighboring Lands in Memory of Douglas L. Esse*. Edited by Samuel R. Wolff. ASOR Books 5. Oriental Institute of the University of Chicago; American Schools of Oriental Research.

Esse, Douglas L. 1989. Review of *The Archaeology of the Israelite Settlement*, by Israel Finkelstein. *BAR* 14.5:6–12.

Finkelstein, Israel. 1986. *'Izbet Ṣarṭah: An Early Iron Age Site Near Rosh Ha'ayin, Israel*. British Archaeological Reports.

———. 1988. *The Archaeology of the Israelite Settlement*. Israel Exploration Society.

———. 1989. "The Emergence of the Monarchy in Israel: The Environmental and Socio-economic Aspects." *JSOT* 44:43–74.

———. 1991. "The Emergence of Israel in Canaan: Consensus, Mainstream and Dispute." *SJOT* 2:47–59.

———. 1992a. "Pastoralism in the Highlands of Canaan in the Third and Second Millenia B.C.E." Pages 133–42 in *Pastoralism in the Levant: Archaeological Materials in Anthropological Perspectives*. Edited by Ofer Bar-Yosef and Anatoly Khazanov. Prehistory Press.

———. 1992b. "Response to William G. Dever." Pages 63–69 in *The Rise of Ancient Israel*. Edited by Hershel Shanks. Biblical Archaeology Society.

———. 1994. "The Emergence of Israel: A Phase in the Cyclic History of Canaan in the Third and Second Millennia BCE." Pages 150–78 in *From Nomadism to Monarchy: Archaeological and Historical Aspects of Early Israel*. Edited by Israel Finkelstein and Nadav Na'aman. Biblical Archaeology Society.

———. 1995. "The Great Transformation: The 'Conquest' of the Highland Frontiers and the Rise of the Territorial States." Pages 349–65 in *The Archaeology of Society in the Holy Land*. Edited by Thomas E. Levy. Facts on File.

Finkelstein, Israel, and Yitzhak Magen, eds. 1993. *Archaeological Survey of the Hill Country of Benjamin* [Hebrew]. Israel Antiquities Authority.

Finkelstein, Israel, and Nadav Na'aman, eds. 1994. *From Nomadism to Monarchy: Archaeological and Historical Aspects of Early Israel*. Biblical Archaeology Society.

Finkelstein, Israel, and Avi Perevolotsky. 1990. "Processes of Sedentarization and Nomadization in the History of the Sinai and the Negev." *BASOR* 279:67–88.

Flight, John. 1923. "The Nomadic Idea and Ideal in the OT." *JBL* 42:158–226.

Fritz, Volkmar. 1977. "Bestimmung und Herkunft des Pfeilerhauses in Israel." *ZDPV* 93:30–45.

———. 1980. "Die Kulturhistorische Bedeutung der Früheisenzeitlichen Siedlung auf dem Hirbet el-Masos und das Problem der Landnahme." *ZDPV* 96:121–35.

———. 1981. "The Israelite 'Conquest' in the Light of Recent Excavation at Khirbet el-Meshâsh." *BASOR* 241:61–73.

———. 1987. "Conquest and Settlement? The Early Iron Age in Palestine." *BA* 50:84–100.

Gal, Zvi. 1992. *Lower Galilee during the Iron Age*. Eisenbrauns.

———. 1994. "Iron I in Lower Galilee and the Margins of the Jezreel Valley." Pages 35–46 in *From Nomadism to Monarchy: Archaeological and Historical Aspects of Early Israel*. Edited by Israel Finkelstein and Nadav Na'aman. Biblical Archaeology Society.

Geus, C. H. J. de. 1975. "The Importance of Archaeological Research into the Palestinian Agricultural Terraces, with an Excursus on the Hebrew Word *gbî*." *PEQ* 107:65–74.

———. 1976. *The Tribes of Israel: An Investigation into Some of the Presuppositions of Martin Noth's Amphictyony Hypothesis*. Van Gorcum.

Gottwald, Norman K. 1974. "Were the Early Israelites Pastoral Nomads?" Pages 223–55 in *Rhetorical Criticism: Essays in Honor of James Muilenburg*. Edited by Jared J. Jackson and Martin Kessler. Pickwick.

———. 1978. "The Hypothesis of the Revolutionary Origins of Ancient Israel: A Response to A. J. Hauser and Thomas L. Thompson." *JSOT* 7:37–52.

———. 1979. *The Tribes of Yahweh: A Sociology of the Religion of Liberated Israel, 1250–1050 B.C.E.* Orbis Books.

———. 1992. "Sociology." *ABD* 6:79–89.

———. 1993a. "Recent Studies of the Social World of Premonarchic Israel." *CurBS* 1:163–89.

———. 1993b. "Method and Hypothesis in Reconstructing the Social History of Early Israel." *ErIsr* 24:77*–82*.

Halpern, Baruch. 1992. "Settlement in Canaan." *ABD* 5:1120–43.

Hauser, Alan J. 1978. "Israel's Conquest of Palestine: A Peasants' Rebellion?" *JSOT* 7:2–19.

Herr, Larry G. 1998. "Tell el-'Umayri and the Madaba Plains Region during the Late Bronze–Iron Age I Transition." Pages 251–64 in *Mediterranean Peoples in Transition: Thirteenth to Early Tenth Centuries BCE*. Edited by Seymour S. Gitin, Amihai Mazar, and Ephraim Stern. Israel Exploration Society.

Herzog, Ze'ev. 1984. *Beer-Sheba II: The Early Iron Age Settlements*. Tel Aviv University, Institute of Archaeology.

———. 1994. "The Beer-Sheba Valley: From Nomadism to Monarchy." Pages 122–49 in *From Nomadism to Monarchy: Archaeological and Historical Aspects of Early Israel*. Edited by Israel Finkelstein and Nadav Na'aman. Biblical Archaeology Society.

Hesse, Brian. 1990. "'Pig Lovers' and 'Pig Haters': Patterns of Palestinian Pork Production." *Journal of Ethnobiology* 10:105–205.

Hesse, Brian, and Paula Wapnish. 1997. "Can Pig Bones Be Used for Ethnic Diagnosis in the Ancient Near East?" Pages 238–70 in *The Archaeology of Israel: Constructing The Past, Interpreting the Present*. Edited by Neil Asher Silberman and David Small. JSOTSup 237. Sheffield Academic.

Hopkins, David C. 1985. *The Highlands of Canaan: Agricultural Life in the Early Iron Age*. SWBA 3. Almond.

———. 1987. "Life on the Land." *BA* 50:178–91.

———. 1993. "Pastoralists in Late Bronze Age Palestine: Which Way Did They Go?" *BA* 56:200–211.

Jamieson-Drake, David W. 1991. *Scribes and Schools in Monarchic Judah: A Socio-archaeological Approach.* SWBA 9. Sheffield Academic.
Kempinski, Aaron. 1978. "Tel Masos." *Expedition* 20.4:29–37.
———. 1985. "The Overlap of Cultures at the End of the Late Bronze Age and the Beginning of the Iron Age" [Hebrew]. *ErIsr* 18:399–407.
Khazanov, Anatoly M. 1984. *Nomads and the Outside World.* University of Wisconsin Press.
Khoury, Philip S., and Joseph Kostiner, eds. 1990. *Tribes and State Formation in the Middle East.* University of California Press.
Killebrew, Ann, and D. B. MacKay. 1995. "Pots and Peoples in Canaan during the Thirteenth–Twelfth Centuries BCE: The Ethnic Origin and Identity of Canaanites, Egyptians, Philistines, and Israelites." Paper presented at ASOR Annual Meeting, November 1994.
Knauf, Ernst Axel. 1991. "From History to Interpretation." Pages 26–64 in *The Fabric of History: Text, Artifact and Israel's Past.* Edited by Diana V. Edelman. JSOTSup 127. JSOT Press.
Lederman, Zvi. 1990. "Nomads They Never Were. A Reevaluation of Izbet Sarta." Page 238 in *Abstracts, American Academy of Religion/ Society of Biblical Literature.* Atlanta.
Lemche, Niels Peter. 1985. *Early Israel: Anthropological and Historical Studies on the Israelite Society before the Monarchy.* VTSup 37. Brill.
———. 1991. "Sociology, Text and Religion as Key Factors in Understanding the Emergence of Israel in Canaan." *SJOT* 5:7–18.
———. 1992. "Israel, History of (Premonarchic Period)." *ABD* 3:526–45.
London, Gloria. 1989. "A Comparison of Two Contemporaneous Lifestyles in the Late Second Millennium B.C." *BASOR* 273:37–55.
Luke, J. Tracy. 1965. *Pastoralism and Politics in the Mari Period: A Reexamination of the Character and Political Significance of the Major West Semitic Tribal Groups on the Middle Euphrates, ca 1827–1758 B.C.* University of Michigan Press.
Martin, J. D. 1989. "Israel as a Tribal Society." Pages 95–118 in *The World of Ancient Israel: Sociological, Anthropological and Political Perspectives.* Edited by R. E. Clements. Cambridge University Press.
Matthews, Victor H. 1978. *Pastoral Nomadism in the Mari Kingdom (ca. 1830–1760 B.C.).* ASOR Dissertation Series 3. American Schools of Oriental Research.
Mazar, Amihai. 1994. "Jerusalem and Its Vicinity in Iron I." Pages 70–91 in *From Nomadism to Monarchy: Archaeological and Historical Aspects of*

Early Israel. Edited by Israel Finkelstein and Nadav Na'aman. Biblical Archaeology Society.

McCarter, P. Kyle, Jr. 1992. "The Origins of Israelite Literature." Pages 118–41 in *The Rise of Ancient Israel*. Edited by Hershel Shanks. Biblical Archaeology Society.

Mendenhall, George E. 1973. *The Tenth Generation: The Origins of the Biblical Tradition*. Johns Hopkins University Press.

Miller, J. Maxwell. 1991. "Is it Possible to Write a History of Israel without Relying on the Hebrew Bible?" Pages 93–102 in *The Fabric of History: Text, Artifact and Israel's Past*. Edited by Diana V. Edelman. JSOTSup 127. JSOT Press.

Mueller, James W., ed. 1979. *Sampling in Archaeology*. University of Arizona Press.

Na'aman, Nadav. 1986. "Ḫabiru and Hebrews: The Transfer of a Social Term to the Later Literary Sphere." *JNES* 45:271–88.

———. 1994. "The 'Conquest of Canaan' in the Book of Joshua and in History." Pages 218–81 in *From Nomadism to Monarchy: Archaeological and Historical Aspects of Early Israel*. Edited by Israel Finkelstein and Nadav Na'aman. Biblical Archaeology Society.

Neu, Rainer. 1992. *Von der Anarchie zum Staat: Entwicklungsgeschichte Israels vom Nomadentum zur Monarchie im Spiegel der Ethnosoziologie*. Neukirchener Verlag.

Ofer, Avi. 1994. "'All the Hill Country of Judah': From a Settlement Fringe to a Prosperous Monarchy." Pages 92–121 in *From Nomadism to Monarchy: Archaeological and Historical Aspects of Early Israel*. Edited by Israel Finkelstein and Nadav Na'aman. Biblical Archaeology Society.

Rafferty, Janet E. 1985. "The Archaeological Record on Sedentariness: Recognition, Development and Implications." Pages 113–56 in vol. 8 of *Advances in Archaeological Method and Theory*. Edited by Michael B. Schiffer. Springer.

Rogerson, J. W. 1986. "Was Early Israel a Segmentary Society?" *JSOT* 36:17–26.

Rosen, Baruch. 1986. "Subsistence Economy of Stratum II." Pages 156–85 in *'Izbet Ṣarṭah: An Early Iron Age Site Near Rosh Ha'ayin, Israel*. By Israel Finkelstein. British Archaeological Reports.

Rosen, Steven A., and Gideon Avni. 1993. "The Edge of Empire: The Archaeology of Pastoral Nomads in the Southern Negev Highlands in Late Antiquity." *BA* 56:189–99.

Rowton, Michael B. 1977. "Dimorphic Structure and the Parasocial Element." *JNES* 36:181–98.

Sader, Hélène. 1992. "The Twelfth Century B.C. in Syria: The Problem of the Rise of the Aramaeans." Pages 137–63 in *The Twelfth Century B.C.: From beyond the Danube to the Tigris*. Edited by William A. Ward and Martha S. Joukowsky. Kendall/Hunt.

Salzman, Philip Carl, et al. 1980. *When Nomads Settle: Processes of Sedentarization as Adaption and Response*. Praeger.

Skjeggestad, Marit. 1992. "Ethnic Groups in Early Iron Age Palestine: Some Remarks on the Use of the Term 'Israelite' in Recent Research." *SJOT* 6:159–86.

Stager, Lawrence E. 1982. "The Archaeology of the East Slope of Jerusalem and the Terraces of the Kidron." *JNES* 41:111–21.

———. 1985. "The Archaeology of the Family in Ancient Israel." *BASOR* 260:1–35.

———. 1989. "The Song of Deborah: Why Some Tribes Answered the Call and Others Did Not." *BAR* 15.1:50–64.

Thompson, Thomas L. 1992a. *Early History of the Israelite People: From the Written and Archaeological Sources*. SHANE 4. Brill.

———. 1992b. "Palestinian Pastoralism and Israel's Origins." *SJOT* 6:1–13.

Weippert, Manfred. 1976. "Canaan, Conquest and Settlement of." *IDSup*, 125–30.

Weippert, Manfred, and Helga Weippert. 1991. "Die Vorgeschichte Israels in neuem Licht." *TRu* 56:341–90.

Whitelam, Keith W. 1991. "Between History and Literature: The Social Production of Israel's Traditions of Origin." *SJOT* 2:60–74.

———. 1994. "The Identity of Early Israel: The Realignment and Transformation of Late Bronze–Iron I Palestine." *JSOT* 63:57–87.

Wood, Bryant G. 1990. *The Sociology of Pottery in Ancient Palestine: The Ceramic Industry and the Diffusion of Ceramic Style in the Bronze and Iron Ages*. JSOTSup 103. JSOT Press.

Yurco, Frank J. 1986. "Merenptah's Canaanite Campaign." *JARCE* 23:189–215.

———. 1990. "3,200-Year-Old Picture of Israelites Found in Egypt." *BAR* 16.5:20–38.

Zertal, Adam. 1991. "Israel Enters Canaan—Following the Pottery Trail." *BAR* 17.5:28–49, 75.

———. 1992. "Response to William G. Dever." Pages 76–78 in *The Rise of Ancient Israel*. Edited by Hershel Shanks. Biblical Archaeology Society.

———. 1994. "'To the Land of the Perizzites and the Giants': On the Israelite Settlement in the Hill Country of Manasseh." Pages 47–69 in *From Nomadism to Monarchy: Archaeological and Historical Aspects of Early Israel*. Edited by Israel Finkelstein and Nadav Na'aman. Biblical Archaeology Society.

Updated Bibliography

Rainey, Anson F. 2007. "Whence Came the Israelites and Their Language?" *IEJ* 57:41–64.

Saidel, Benjamin, and Evaline J. van der Steen, eds. 2007. *On the Fringe of Society: Archeological and Ethnoarchaeological Perspectives on Pastoral and Agricultural Societies*. BAR International Series 1657. Archaeopress.

Barnard, Hans, and Willeke Wendrich, eds. 2008. *The Archaeology of Mobility: Old World and New World Nomadism*. University of California Press.

Rainey, Anson F. 2008. "Shasu or Habiru? Who Were the Early Israelites?" *BAR* 34.6:51–55.

Hiebert, Theodore. 2009. "Israel's Ancestors Were Not Nomads." Pages 199–205 in *Exploring the Longue Durée: Essays in Honor of Lawrence E. Stager*. Edited by J. David Schloen. Eisenbrauns.

Saidel, Benjamin. 2009. "Pitching Camp: Ethnological Investigations of Inhabited Tent Camps in the Wadi Hisma, Jordan." Pages 87–104 in *Nomads, Tribes, and the State in the Ancient Near East: Cross-Disciplinary Perspectives*. Edited by Jeffrey Szuchman. OIS 5. University of Chicago Press.

Szuchman, Jeffrey, ed. 2009. *Nomads, Tribes, and the State in the Ancient Near East: Cross-Disciplinary Perspectives*. OIS 5. University of Chicago Press.

Dever, William G. 2011. "Earliest Israel: God's Warriors, Revolting Peasants, or Nomadic Hordes?" *ErIsr* 30.4:4*–12*.

Porter, Ann. 2012. *Mobile Pastoralism and the Formation of Near Eastern Civilization: Weaving Together Society*. Cambridge University Press.

Steen, Evaline J. van der. 2013. *Near Eastern Tribal Societies during the Nineteenth Century: Economy, Society and Politics between Tent and Town*. Acumen.

Dever, William G. 2017. *Beyond the Texts: An Archaeological Portrait of Ancient Israel and Judah*. SBL Press. Pages 194–210, 249–53.

7

Merenptah's "Israel," the Bible's, and Ours

In previous publications on revisionism and the challenge of writing new histories of ancient Israel, and on the earliest phases of that history in the Iron Age, 1200–1000 BCE (e.g., Dever 2005, republished as chapter 5 in this volume), I faced more resolutely the question of *sources*, both textual and archaeology. That trajectory eventually led to *Beyond the Texts: An Archaeological Portrait of Ancient Israel and Judah* (2017), when I argued forcibly for taking the archaeological evidence as the primary data.

As is well known, our earliest textual and historical reference to Israel is in the Victory Stela of Pharaoh Merenptah, which is dated circa 1210 BCE. Yet despite having this indisputable reference to an actual Israel in Canaan circa 1200 BCE, the biblical revisionists have disputed or even rejected the evidence (see in this chapter references to Davies, Edelman, Lemche, Thompson, and Whitelam). Among archaeologists (who would know better if they were not intent on being contrarians), Finkelstein has expressed some doubts as to the relevance of the inscription. But Larry Stager had seen the value of the Merenptah inscription, so I decided to contribute this piece to his Festschrift.

So … back to sources, if an archaeologist aspires to be a real historian (what else would we be?). For me, that meant confronting extreme skeptics head on, trying to establish a critical middle ground—"a judgment beyond a reasonable doubt"—exactly as with any text. Thus I choose to republish this essay despite its recent date.

Relevant bibliography since about 2005 will be found in chapter 6 on nomadism, since several scholars connect the Merenptah Stela on Israel as a loosely affiliated ethnic group and thus pastoral nomads. (The Egyptian ethicon, of course, does not necessarily mean that.)

Originally published as pages 90–96 in *Exploring the Longue Durée: Essays in Honor of Lawrence E. Stager*. Edited by J. David Schloen. Eisenbrauns, 2009. Reprinted by permission.

One of current biblical scholarship's liveliest debates has to do with defining earliest Israel, that is, locating it historically (if at all) in both the textual and the archaeological records. Until recently, the most pertinent nonbiblical datum was the well-known inscription of the Egyptian Pharaoh Merenptah that mentions Israel, which is securely dated to circa 1210 BCE. Now, however, several studies have attempted to correlate Merenptah's Israel with the growing body of archaeological evidence from the thirteenth–twelfth centuries BCE that documents a complex of some three hundred hill-country settlements in central Canaan.

The discussion on early Israel is brought up to date and thoroughly documented in my book *Who Were the Early Israelites and Where Did They Come From?* (Dever 2003). But it was Lawrence Stager who initiated this discussion in a brilliant 1985 article entitled "The Archaeology of the Family in Ancient Israel," as well as in an article on Merenptah, our subject here, in the same year. Then in 1998 Stager offered an authoritative survey of the more current archaeological evidence in *The Oxford History of the Biblical World,* in an article entitled "Forging an Identity: The Emergence of Ancient Israel."[1] I am delighted to offer to Larry Stager, a longtime colleague and friend, this further investigation of the Merenptah datum in the light of its recent archaeological context.

7.1. Merenptah's "Israel"

Merenptah's hymn of victory celebrates the pharaoh's triumph over a series of enemies in Canaan, among them the peoples of places such as "Tehenu/Canaan" (both specified), "Hurru" (the Hurrian Empire in Syria), "Hatti" (the Neo-Hittite entity in northern Syria), and "Israel." It also mentions several specific Canaanite cities, such as Ashkelon, Gezer, and Yanoam. Egyptologists have long noted that the references to enemies that are countries or states are preceded in every case by the determinative sign for "foreign country" (the throw stick plus the three-hills sign). But the term "Israel," the sole exception, is preceded by the determinative sign for "people," or nonstate entity (the throw stick for foreigners plus the man-woman over plural strokes). Kenneth Kitchen, an acknowledged authority, describes this as:

---

1. Stager 1985a, 1985b, 1998.

the mark in numberless instances of a people-group, and not a settled state with an urban center. So far as Merenptah's soldiers, record-keepers and this stele's scribe were concerned, this "Israel" was a people-group in western Palestine, and neither a land nor a mini-state.... The logic of the situation leaves only the hill-country to which "Israel" may be assigned.[2]

A standard translation is that of John A. Wilson:

Desolation is for Tehenu; Hatti is pacified;
Plundered is the Canaan with every evil;
Carried off is Ashkelon; seized upon is Gezer;
Yanoam is made as that which does not exist;
Israel is laid waste, his seed is not;
Hurru is become a widow for Egypt!
All lands together, they are pacified.[3]

There have been innumerable analyses of the poetic structure of the Victory Stela, with consequent differences in the interpretation of its meaning and historical significance. Similarly, the phrase describing Israel's "seed" as having been wiped out has been subjected to exhaustive critical scrutiny.[4] None of this need concern us here, however, since the meaning of the key term "Israel" is unambiguous, as all Egyptologists have maintained since Flinders Petrie's discovery of the Victory Stela at Thebes over a century ago. Furthermore, as Kitchen and many others have pointed out, the term "Israel" not only is preceded by the determinative for "people" rather than "country/state" but is a gentilic. Thus, the only correct reading is "the Israelite people."[5]

That would seem to be the end of the discussion, but, unfortunately, it is not. Elsewhere I have characterized the biblical revisionists as naïve postmodernists who have unwittingly borrowed an epistemology according to which there is no knowledge. As Baruch Halpern has cogently observed, the revisionists are not simply minimalists; their intent is to erase Israel

---

2. Kitchen 2004, 271–72.
3. Wilson 1969, 378.
4. The literature is vast, but for convenient orientation and references, see McNutt 1999, 35–45; Hasel 1998; Noll 2001, 162–64; Stager 1985b. Fundamental Egyptological sources are Redford 1992, 247–57; Kitchen 1994, 71–76; 2004.
5. Kitchen 2004, 271–72.

from history altogether.[6] Of course, the revisionists must perforce begin their campaign right at the beginning, with Israel's supposed origin. There cannot have been an early Israel, or that would prove inconvenient for their agenda. Lest this charge seem too extreme, let me cite here some revisionist distortions of the Merenptah reference to Israel.

In his book *Prelude to Israel's Past: Background and Beginning of Israelite History and Identity,* Niels Peter Lemche acknowledges that for a hundred years the Merenptah Stela has been considered correctly as concrete proof of an Israel in Palestine around 1200 BCE. But in his more radical book, *The Israelites in History and Tradition,* Lemche declares that the traditional reading is irrelevant: "The victory stele of Merneptah, however, does not confirm the date of the Hebrew conquest of Palestine: in fact, it has no bearing on that topic." He argues that "the inscription's use of determinatives is inconsistent," quoting Gösta Ahlström (I presume).[7] Yet Kitchen has demonstrated that the Egyptian scribe was not careless or inconsistent, and the archaeological facts on the ground, discussed below, confirm that Egyptian intelligence was remarkably precise. The differences implied by the use of differing determinatives in the Merenptah Stela correspond exactly to what we now know of the several political entities listed in the inscription. Israel *was* different.

Thomas L. Thompson, always the most extreme of the revisionists, goes even further than Lemche. He simply disposes of the issue of ethnicity, stating that "ethnicity, however, is an interpretive historiographical fiction.... Ethnicity is hardly a common aspect of human existence at this very early period."[8]

Thompson elaborates by declaring that ethnicity is only a modern attempt to describe societal relationships and collective decisions. But "the physical effects [material culture remains—WGD] of such collective decisions are often arbitrary and are, indeed, always accidental."[9] Of the Merenptah inscription that mentions "Israelites," Thompson opines:

---

6. Halpern 1995. I have also leveled the charge of nihilism in my book *What Did the Biblical Writers Know and When Did They Know It? What Archaeology Can Tell Us about the Reality of Ancient Israel* (Dever 2001, 28–52 and passim).

7. See Lemche 1998b; 1998a, 36.

8. Thompson 1997, 175.

9. Thompson 1997, 175.

The sharp boundaries that the use of the terms "Canaanite" and "Israelite" makes possible are wholly unwarranted. "Canaan" appears on the Merenptah stele and has been shown to be paired with "Israel" as his spouse. They are the metaphorical parents of three towns destroyed by the Egyptian army.[10]

At an international symposium in 2000 in Copenhagen, where Thompson and I opposed each other, he went so far as to suggest that, while the Merenptah Stela does mention "Israelites," that is only a coincidence. The Egyptian scribe invented these peoples and their names and by accident came up with the same ethnic designation that we have in the Hebrew Bible. This line of argument is patently absurd and is readily refuted on both philological and archaeological grounds.[11]

Thompson subsequently collaborated with Ingrid Hjelm on an article entitled "The Victory Song of Merenptah: Israel and the People of Palestine."[12] In their treatment of the Merenptah inscription, Hjelm and Thompson advance four basic arguments.

1. The inscription is poetry, not history, so it is irrelevant for the historical question of Israelite origins. There was no Egyptian victory in Canaan, so nothing else in the inscription matters. Of course, one may ask how Hjelm and Thompson know this. In fact, there is some specific evidence for Egyptian destructions in Canaan in this horizon, and precisely at Ashkelon and Gezer, which are the sites singled out for mention in the inscription.[13]

---

10. Thompson 1997, 175.

11. If Thompson were correct that ethnicity is "often arbitrary ... always accidental," then none of the social-scientific disciplines would be viable, for they all depend upon our ability to discern patterns and purpose in culture. Archaeology, in particular, seeks the "material correlates of behavior," an impossible task if there is no patterning in culture and history. The topic of archaeology and ethnicity is especially timely, and the literature is vast. See, provisionally, Killebrew 2005. See also Dever 2007.

12. Hjelm and Thompson 2002. Here and elsewhere, Thompson avoids using "Israel" as an ethnic label, even for the period of the Israelite monarchy, when he refers to "the province of Samarina" (adopting the Neo-Assyrian usage) or more often "Syria's marginal southern fringe." See Thompson 1999, 9, 235, 252; 1997, 176–78, 183–84. See also Lemche 1998a, 51–54.

13. See Hjelm and Thompson 2002, 13–17. As I (and others) have argued, whether or not Merenptah actually defeated his enemies in Canaan, or even cam-

2. The term *ysr'el* in the inscription, universally translated by Egyptologists as "Israel," can just as easily refer to any number of other entities. Hjelm and Thompson offer as many as five alternatives: Sharon, Yeshurun, Asher, Asher'el, and Jezreel.[14]

3. In any case, *ysr'el* here refers to the whole population of Hurru (Canaan), not some putative Israel. Again, how do they know that?

4. In any case, "Israel" is only "an eponym ... a literary reality," not "a specific people in history."

Happily, Kitchen, with his formidable Egyptological expertise, has refuted all of Hjelm and Thompson's tortured arguments, particularly their notion that the term *ysr'el* can just as easily be translated in other ways. He also effectively disposes of their assertion that the poetic and metaphorical character of the hymn negates any historical significance. The presence of rhetoric and its ideology has no bearing on the historical element; to think otherwise is simply to miss the point of Egyptian usage. Finally, Kitchen demonstrates, with copious documentation from numerous other inscriptions, that the significance of the determinative sign for "people" that accompanies the term "Israel" cannot be explained away by the carelessness of Egyptian scribes.[15]

At least we have to acknowledge that Hjelm and Thompson's arguments here are consistent with Thompson's (and the other revisionists') ideological program in their other voluminous publications, in which they insist that there was no early Israel. The most notoriously anti-Israel of the revisionists, Keith W. Whitelam, insists that the attempt to write the history of this nonpeople is not only impossible but illegitimate. All along, it

---

paigned there, is irrelevant for our purposes, since the reference to Israel stands on its own. Nevertheless, in our excavations at Gezer, Stratum XV does show signs of major disruptions in the late thirteenth century BCE, which can hardly have been caused by Israelites or Philistines. This would provide a context for the pectoral of Merenptah found by Macalister (Dever 1986, 50–51). The evidence from Ashkelon is now published in Stager, Schloen, and Master 2008, 256. If Yurco and Stager are correct, the Egyptian relief showing the siege of Ashkelon, now redated from Ramesses II to Merenptah, may have some historical basis (see Stager 1985b).

14. For rebuttal, see Kitchen 2004, 270–71.

15. Kitchen 2004, 268–71.

is the history of the "Palestinian peoples" that biblical scholars and archaeologists should have been writing.[16]

One final revisionist scholar may be cited here. In a 1996 contribution to a volume of essays on ethnicity and the Bible, Diana V. Edelman, like some others who have adopted the postmodern notion that ethnicity equals racism, rejects the very category. As for the data often cited by archaeologists, Edelman, despite having gained considerable field experience herself, nevertheless insists that "there are no *artifactual* remains that can consistently be used to understand a group's ethnicity."[17] It is not surprising, then, that Edelman seeks to dispense with the textual data as well. She repeats the old canard that the term Israel in the Merenptah Stela may mean something else, in this case Jezreel, citing only Otto Eissfeldt's long-discredited reading. She also repeats the error, so well refuted by Kitchen and others, that the determinative sign for "people" may not mean anything because Egyptian scribes used these signs "loosely, mistakenly."[18] Thus, apparently, even texts do not help to determine ethnicity—and certainly not those of the Bible, in the opinion of Edelman and the other revisionists. So let us turn to that issue.

Virtually all the scholars who devalue the Merenptah reference to Israel are biblical scholars (although by no means do the majority of biblical scholars agree with them). One archaeologist, however, has joined the minimalists. Israel Finkelstein, who literally wrote the book on early Israel in his work *The Archaeology of the Israelite Settlement*, now insists that in the three hundred or so early Iron Age hill-country villages that he himself put on the map, there was no ethnic group that we can positively identify as Israelites.[19] When his book was first published, Finkelstein accepted the caution of reviewers such as myself concerning the use of the term *Israelite* in this period, then he adopted my term *Proto-Israelite*, and finally he rejected the term *Israelite* altogether. He argues that the distinctive Iron I material culture traits that we both recognize on the Late Bronze/Iron I horizon are more the result of environmental and socioeconomic factors

---

16. Whitelam 1996. Other reviewers also correct identify "the political agenda that dominates this book" (Sommer 1998) and conclude that it "comes close to being a political manifesto" (Levine and Malamat 1996, 288).
17. Edelman 1996, 26, emphasis original.
18. Edelman 1996, 35; cf. Kitchen 2004, 270–71.
19. Finkelstein 1988.

than they are reflective of any new ethnic self-consciousness. It is all about lifestyle, he concludes. But Finkelstein does not seem to understand that lifestyle *is* ethnicity; it is what makes *us* different from *them*. In any case, in his 2001 popular book with Neil Silberman, *The Bible Unearthed*, he reverts to the term *Israel*.[20]

7.2. The Hebrew Bible's "Israel"

One of the recurring motifs of the skepticism of the biblical revisionists concerning ethnicity is that Merenptah's Israel, as well as the early Israel of archaeologists, has nothing whatsoever to do with biblical Israel.[21] Of course not, but that is irrelevant. Israel of the settlement horizon in the thirteenth to eleventh centuries BCE is obviously different from the state of Israel and its population during the monarchy in the tenth to early sixth centuries. Even the biblical writers knew that.

In the Bible's prehistory—that is, in the narratives about the patriarchs and the exodus-conquest—the writers sometimes use the term *Hebrew* rather than *Israel*. Then, in describing the earliest phases of the settlement in Canaan, *Canaanite* peoples such as the inhabitants of Shechem and Gibeon are said to have joined the emergent Israelite confederation with few apparent barriers. The Israelite "tribes" are by no means unified in the stories in Joshua and Judges, and their lack of solidarity probably stems from an ethnic identity that was still fluid. Some even spoke different dialects, as the famous shibboleth/sibboleth incident of Judg 12:5–6 reveals. Even later, during the monarchy, Uriah, a Hittite, is a prominent career officer in David's army. There is much other evidence to show that, at least originally, the ethnic designation Israelite was neither self-evident in meaning nor exclusive and that it became so only much later. Early Israel, as many now maintain, was a motley crew.[22]

---

20. Finkelstein and Silberman 2001. For references, see Dever 2001, 40–41; 2003, 194–95.

21. This notion is ubiquitous; see, e.g., Davies 1992, 61–63; Thompson 1992, 310–11; Lemche 1998a, 36–38; Whitelam 1996, 209–10, 228; Edelman 1996, 35–42.

22. See Dever 2003, 181–82; Killebrew 2005, 149–96. Note that the fluidity in ethnic identity in Iron I and even into early Iron II does not contradict the conti-

To be sure, the later Deuteronomistic writers do speak of "all Israel," but they are assuming an ethnic homogeneity that even then may not have been factual. It is significant that 1 Sam 13:34 uses the gentilic "Hebrew" and the phrase "all Israel" in parallel. Moreover, the term "all Israel" is used so paradigmatically that it may be largely hyperbole, just as we speak in everyday parlance about "all Americans," despite our awareness of the enormous diversity of the U.S. population.

In light of the foregoing, the revisionist's insistent depreciation of the ethnic designation "Israelite" in the Merenptah Stela—our earliest, best-dated, and least-biased reference to Israel—appears to be more a reflection of ideology than honest, fair-minded scholarship. As for the reluctance on the part of some of these scholars to use the term Israel even for later periods, we need only point out that by the ninth century BCE, Israel is the designation used by Israel's neighbors and enemies—no hesitancy there about ethnic labels, much less a biblical bias. The Tel Dan inscription in Aramaic refers to a "king of Israel" (whether David or not). The Moabite Stone also speaks of a "king of Israel," in the case of Omri. Finally, the earliest of the cuneiform texts that describe the first encounter of the Assyrians with the petty states in the west, Shalmaneser III's account of the battle of Qarqar in 853 BCE, mentions "Ahab, king of Israel."[23]

7.3. Our "Israel"

That leaves us with the Israel of modern scholarship, in particular the Israel of the Iron Age (not a Persian or Hellenistic Israel) that is so well attested archaeologically. Elsewhere I have written extensively on the general question of the date and the historicity of the biblical sources, assessed on the basis of the context now supplied by archaeology, and in *Who Were the Early Israelites and Where Did They Come From?* I have discussed at length the specific question of Israelite origins, adducing virtually all the current archaeological evidence and interpretive theories.[24]

---

nuity in material culture during that time span (see below). The two overlap but are not necessarily identical.

23. For references, see Dever 2001, 29–30, 163–66.

24. Dever 2001, 2003. See also Noll 2001; Killebrew 2005; Faust 2006.

Having previously presented in full the empirical data for the existence of an early Israel (my Proto-Israelites), here I need only raise the question of how or indeed whether this Israel may correspond to that of the Merenptah Stela. To do that, we need first to summarize what we can actually know from the passage in the stela that describes Israel, whatever its literary structure and its historical veracity. The following are the salient points, all of which I believe are obvious to any dispassionate observer.

1. There was an ethnic group in Canaan sometime before circa 1210 BCE who called themselves "the Israelite people" and who were known as such to Egyptian intelligence.

2. These people were sufficiently numerous and well established that they were perceived as a threat to Egyptian hegemony in the region.

3. These peoples were not, however, organized into city-states, much less state-like entities, like the other peoples listed, a fact reflected in the unique determinative sign with the gentilic.

4. These Israelites were distinct socioeconomically and politically from the general Canaanite ("Hurru"/Hurrian) population and specifically from the population of city-states such as Ashkelon and Gezer along the coastal plain and Yanoam in Galilee. The central hill country is conspicuously empty on a map of Merenptah's campaigns in Canaan (regardless of whether these were real or imaginary).[25]

Skeptics such as the biblical scholars discussed above typically argue that there is not enough information in the Merenptah Stela to specify anything about who these "Israelites" actually were or to ascertain whether they have anything to do with later biblical Israel. These, however, are arguments of which we can easily dispose.

First, although the information derived from the Merenptah Stela is minimal, it tells us all that we need to know about the Israelites at this juncture, and, however cryptic, all the information conveyed by Egyptian intelligence is correct. Earliest Israel was a loosely organized "tribal" confederation somewhere in central Canaan at this time: a group of people contiguous with the indigenous population but already beginning to distinguish themselves as a separate ethnic group and on an evolutionary scale far short of state-level development.

---

25. We have noted Kitchen's recognition of this fact. See also Redford 1992, 275; Ahlström 1986, 40–42; Finkelstein 1988, 28–29. Even Lemche (1998a, 38) acknowledges this. See further Dever 2003, 201–8.

What is significant here is that all of this information about early Israel, derived independently from a source far removed from the nationalist biases of the biblical writers, is corroborated by the archaeological data that we have accumulated in the past two decades or so. Yet the revisionists, despite paying lip service to archaeology, have never responded to the vast body of data that I and many other archaeologists have presented. They only demonize archaeologists as "credulous" or worse.[26] Some have likened these revisionists to secular fundamentalists whose minds are made up and who do not wish to be confused by facts. Nevertheless, the Merenptah inscription's facts and the archaeological facts converge at all the salient points, and it is just such convergences that place us on firm historical ground.

The second answer to the revisionists' unwillingness to connect Merenptah's "Israel" to later biblical Israel obviously has to do with cultural and historical continuity and how these are perceived. To give skeptics the benefit of the doubt, there is indeed no textual continuity. The Merenptah text dates to the late thirteenth century BCE, while the earliest relevant biblical texts (the Pentateuch/Tetrateuch, the Deuteronomistic History, and the early prophetic writings) are from the late eighth century at best—a gap of some five centuries.[27] Even if the gap is partially bridged by presuming earlier oral tradition embedded within our canonical sources, that gap is considerable.

What few biblical scholars seem to realize is that it is archaeology that bridges the gap. We have a complete and continuous archaeological record from the late thirteenth through the early sixth century, with not even a generation missing. If from about the eighth century onward this continuous Iron II culture is Israelite (as even some of the revisionists must admit), then its immediate predecessor in Iron I was also Israelite—or, at the very least, as I have suggested, Proto-Israelite, to err on the side

---

26. See Dever 2001, 30–40. The rhetoric only escalates in Thompson 2001 and Lemche 2000. Lemche dismisses me as a "rustic," but he has much more difficulty refuting my charge of postmodernism, as extended and carefully documented by James Barr (2000, 102–78). See further Hagelia 2002.

27. Both biblical scholars and archaeologists have tended recently to lower the dates of J, E, and Dtr by as much as two to three centuries (see, conveniently, Schniedewind 2004). The Persian or Hellenistic date advocated by the revisionists is not justified, however.

of caution.[28] Merenptah's "Israelites" are the authentic progenitors of the biblical Israelites. Yet I can find few biblical scholars who are aware of the distinctive archaeological assemblage and its striking continuity through the Iron Age.

As Baruch Halpern has observed, we are still plagued by two monologues rather than the dialogue that some of us have advocated for years.[29] The revisionists seldom cite the numerous archaeological handbooks that are now available to any interested reader.[30] Their agenda becomes increasingly ideological—political rather than scholarly. And as the rhetoric escalates, the facts on the ground are obscured. The deconstruction of the Merenptah inscription, our earliest reference to the early Israelites, is just another sad example of the inroads that postmodernism has made into the field of biblical criticism, which was once a historical discipline. Fortunately, mainstream biblical scholarship, buttressed by old-fashioned positivists (shall we say empiricists) such as Lawrence Stager, help us to hold the middle ground.

7.4. Conclusion

I seem to have been the first to charge that the biblical revisionists are really thinly disguised postmodernists. Now, however, James Barr—arguably the dean of British Old Testament scholars—has agreed with me specifically

---

28. On my Proto-Israelites, see Dever 2003, 194–200 and passim. I am not the first to use the term, however. Both Norman Gottwald and P. Kyle McCarter preceded me with a sort of offhand use of the term, but it was I who first employed the term in a deliberate archaeological sense. Many of my archaeological colleagues in Israel urge me to drop it now that a consensus is emerging that there *was* an early Israel.

29. See Halpern 1997. My own calls for such a dialogue go back to 1974; see my *Archaeology and Biblical Studies: Retrospects and Prospects* (Dever 1974).

30. These include Weippert 1988; Mazar 1990; Ben-Tor 1992; Levy 1995. The most egregious example of this lack of attention to basic information is provided by Davies, who in his book *In Search of "Ancient Israel"* (Davies 1992) cites Mazar only once, in a footnote explaining that Mazar's handbook deals with the Iron Age and is thus irrelevant to Davies's "Persian-period Israel" (1992, 24 n. 4). Here, as too often, the presupposition trumps the evidence.

and has in fact gone well beyond my original critique.[31] I can only conclude that, in their deprecation of the Merenptah datum on early Israel, the revisionists are simply behaving like typical postmodernists. Otherwise, I am at a loss to explain their recalcitrance in the face of the overwhelming evidence, both textual and archaeological. Consider how similar the basic tenets of the two schools are:

1. A contrarian attitude. This is Jean-François Lyotard's much-touted "incredulity toward all metanarratives," in this case the grand metanarrative of the Western cultural tradition, the Bible.

2. A preference for novel, even exotic, "readings of all texts" (and, in this case, artifacts). The only legitimate technique is "deconstruction"; the text can mean anything—except, it seems, what it appears to mean.

3. "All readings are political," postmodernism's most typical mantra. Reading is not about truth at all, for there is none, but rather about race, class, gender, politics, and power.

4. In any case, "all claims to knowledge are simply social constructs." Therefore, following Foucault, "all history is fiction."

This is not the place to offer a full-scale refutation of postmodernism, even in its revisionist guise. There is, however, a growing literature that suggests that it is becoming passé in real intellectual circles.[32] If that is true, then devotees of Hayden White–style "metahistory" such as Davies, Thompson, Lemche, Whitelam, and the other revisionists will soon be as obsolete as their Merenptah.

Works Cited

Ahlström, Gösta W. 1986. *Who Were the Israelites?* Eisenbrauns.
Barr, James. 2000. *History and Ideology in the Old Testament: Biblical Studies at the End of a Millennium.* Oxford University Press.
Ben-Tor, Amnon, ed. 1992. *The Archaeology of Ancient Israel.* Yale University Press.

---

31. Barr 2000, 102–78.
32. See, for instance, the devastating critiques in Gress 1998 and especially Windschuttle 1996. Recently, however, John Collins (2005)—as much a modernist as I am—has conceded ground to the revisionists, arguing that they have had considerable influence on American biblical scholarship.

Collins, John J. 2005. *The Bible after Babel: Historical Criticism in a Postmodern Age.* Eerdmans.

Davies, Philip R. 1992. *In Search of "Ancient Israel."* JSOTSup 148. JSOT Press.

Dever, William G. 1974. *Archaeology and Biblical Studies: Retrospects and Prospects.* Seabury-Western Theological Seminary.

———, ed. 1986. *The 1969–71 Seasons in Field VI, the "Acropolis."* Vol. 4 of *Gezer.* Nelson Glueck School of Biblical Archaeology.

———. 2001. *What Did the Biblical Writers Know and When Did They Know It? What Archaeology Can Tell Us about the Reality of Ancient Israel.* Eerdmans.

———. 2003. *Who Were the Early Israelites and Where Did They Come From?* Eerdmans.

———. 2007. "Ethnicity and the Archaeological Record: The Case of Early Israel." Pages 49–66 in *The Archaeology of Difference: Gender, Ethnicity, Class and the "Other" in Antiquity; Studies in Honor of Eric M. Meyers.* Edited by Douglas R. Edwards and C. Thomas McCollough. American Schools of Oriental Research. Republished as chapter 8 in this volume.

Edelman, Diana V. 1996. "Ethnicity and Early Israel." Pages 25–55 in *Ethnicity and the Bible.* Edited by Mark G. Brett. BibInt 19. Brill.

Faust, Avraham. 2006. *Israel's Ethnogenesis: Settlement, Interaction, Expansion and Resistance.* Equinox.

Finkelstein, Israel. 1988. *The Archaeology of the Israelite Settlement.* Israel Exploration Society.

Finkelstein, Israel, and Silberman, Neil Asher. 2001. *The Bible Unearthed: Archaeology's New Vision of Ancient Israel and the Origin of Its Sacred Texts.* Free Press.

Gress, David. 1998. *From Plato to Nato: The Ideo of the West and Its Opponents.* Free Press.

Hagelia, Hallvard. 2002. "Review or Response? A Critical Evaluation of Thomas L. Thompson's Review of William G. Dever." *SJOT* 16:314–18.

Halpern, Baruch. 1995. "Erasing History: The Minimalist Assault on Ancient Israel." *BRev* 11.6:26–35, 47.

———. 1997. "Text and Artifact: Two Monologues." Pages 311–41 in *The Archaeology of Israel: Constructing the Past, Interpreting the Present.* Edited by Neil Asher Silberman and David Small. JSOTSup 237. Sheffield Academic.

Hasel, Michael G. 1998. *Domination and Resistance: Egyptian Military Activity in the Southern Levant, ca. 1300–1185 B.C.* PAe 11. Brill.

Hjelm, Ingrid, and Thomas L. Thompson. 2002. "The Victory Song of Merenptah: Israel and the People of Palestine." *JSOT* 27:3–18.

Killebrew, Ann E. 2005. *Biblical Peoples and Ethnicity: An Archaeological Study of Egyptians, Canaanites, Philistines, and Early Israel, 1300–1100 B.C.E.* ABS 9. Society of Biblical Literature.

Kitchen, Kenneth A. 1994. "The Physical Text of Merenptah's Victory Hymn (The 'Israel Stela')." *JSSEA* 24:71–76.

———. 2004. "The Victories of Merenptah, and the Nature of Their Record." *JSOT* 28:259–72.

Lemche, Niels Peter. 1998a. *The Israelites in History and Tradition*. LAI. Westminster John Knox.

———. 1998b. *Prelude to Israel's Past: Background and Beginnings of Israelite History and Identity*. Hendrickson.

———. 2000. "Ideology and the History of Ancient Israel." *SJOT* 14:165–93.

Levine, Baruch A., and Avraham Malamat. 1996. Review of *The Invention of Ancient Israel: The Silencing of Palestinian History*, by Keith W. Whitelam *IEJ* 46:284–88.

Levy, Thomas E., ed. 1995. *The Archaeology of Society in the Holy Land*. Facts on File.

Mazar, Amihai. 1990. *Archaeology of the Land of the Bible, 10,000–586 B.C.E.* Doubleday.

McNutt, Paula M. 1999. *Reconstructing the Society of Ancient Israel*. LAI. Westminster John Knox.

Noll, Kurt L. 2001. *Canaan and Israel in Antiquity: An Introduction*. BibSem 83. Sheffield Academic.

Redford, Donald B. 1992. *Egypt, Canaan, and Israel in Ancient Times*. Princeton University Press.

Schniedewind, William M. 2004. *How the Bible Became a Book: The Textualization of Ancient Israel*. Cambridge University Press.

Sommer, Benjamin D. 1998. Review of *The Invention of Ancient Israel: The Silencing of Palestinian History*, by Keith W. Whitelam. *Middle East Quarterly* 5. https://tinyurl.com/SBLPress9035d1.

Stager, Lawrence E. 1985a. "The Archaeology of the Family in Ancient Israel." *BASOR* 260:1–35.

———. 1985b. "Merenptah, Israel and Sea Peoples: New Light on an Old Relief." *ErIsr* 18: 56*–64*.

———. 1998. "Forging an Identity: The Emergence of Ancient Israel." Pages 123–75 in *The Oxford History of the Biblical World*. Edited by Michael D. Coogan. Oxford University Press.

Stager, Lawrence E., J. David Schloen, and Daniel M. Master, eds. 2008. *Introduction and Overview (1985–2006)*. Vol. 1 of *Ashkelon*. Eisenbrauns.

Thompson, Thomas L. 1992. *Early History of the Israelite People: From the Written and Archaeological Sources*. SHANE 4. Brill.

———. 1997. "Defining History and Ethnicity in the Southern Levant." Pages 166–87 in *Can a "History of Israel" Be Written?* Edited by Lester L. Grabbe. JSOTSup 245. Sheffield Academic.

———. 1999. *The Mythic Past: Biblical Archaeology and the Myth of Israel*. Basic Books.

———. 2001. "Methods and Results: A Review of Two Recent Publications." *SJOT* 15:306–25.

Weippert, Helga. 1988. *Palästina in vorhellenistischer Zeit*. Beck.

Whitelam, Keith W. 1996. *The Invention of Ancient Israel: The Silencing of Palestinian History*. Routledge.

Wilson, John A. 1969. "Hymn of Victory of Mer-ne-Ptah (The 'Israel Stela')." Pages 376–78 in Ancient Near Eastern Texts Relating to the Old Testament. Edited by James B. Pritchard. 3rd ed. Princeton University Press.

Windschuttle, Keith. 1996. *The Killing of History: How Literary Critics and Social Theorists Are Murdering Our Past*. Free Press.

8

Ethnicity and the Archaeological Record: The Case of Early Israel

Several previous chapters have dealt with scholarly discussions of origins of the people known as early Israelites. But how do we *know* that such an ethnic label is justified? Obviously, if we do not know who these people were, we cannot write *their* history.

When I wrote this piece in 2005, ethnicity and questions of identity were among the most controversial topics in archaeology worldwide, especially since Sian Jones's 1997 work *The Archaeology of Ethnicity: Constructing Identities in the Past and Present*. I recall discovering this work and speaking to my colleagues in a Jerusalem symposium about its postmodern underpinnings (note the term *constructing* in the title). Few seemed impressed at the time. But I soon tackled the topic in a 1995 article (see chapter 6 in this volume), and, of course, my 2003 *Who Were the Early Israelites and Where Did They Come From?* was essentially all about recognizing and addressing the archaeological correlates to ethnicity.

Many recent archaeological publications, however, have now taken up the topic of ethnicity, especially Israel Finkelstein, Raz Kletter, Avraham Faust, Ann E. Killebrew, and others (see Updated Bibliography, arranged chronologically, at the end of the Works Cited).

Can a specific ethnic identification of an ancient people be determined on the basis of material culture remains unearthed by archaeology? That

Originally published as pages 49–66 *The Archaeology of Difference: Gender, Ethnicity, Class and the "Other" in Antiquity; Studies in Honor of Eric M. Meyers*. Edited by Douglas R. Edwards and C. Thomas McCollough. American Schools of Oriental Research, 2007. Reprinted by permission.

question poses one of the most fundamental, most urgent, yet most difficult issues in archaeology. The author of the most recent book on the subject, *The Archaeology of Ethnicity*, begins with a statement of Laurent Olivier and Anick Coudart that "the crucial theoretical question of archaeology today is that of national identity, or more specifically that of the relationship archaeology enjoys with the construction (or the fabrication) of collective identities."[1]

This chapter will use the case of early Israel—or the question of Israelite origins—as a test case in addressing the issue of ethnicity in the archaeological record. It is offered as a tribute to Eric M. Meyers, a colleague and friend of more than thirty-five years, who has been a pioneer in confronting similar methodological concerns in his efforts to identify early Jewish and Christian ethnicity in the archaeology of the Galilee.[2]

8.1. Ethnicity and Israelite Origins In Recent Scholarship

In the wake of Israeli archaeological surveys in the West Bank in the 1980s, by Israel Finkelstein in *The Archaeology of the Israelite Settlement*, the discussion of Israelite origins in Canaan has burgeoned.[3] The basic archaeological evidence has been widely discussed and summarized by several archaeologists, including myself, and by now should be well known to most biblical scholars and historians.[4] This extensive complex of many

---

1. Jones 1997, 1; Olivier and Coudart 1995, 365.

2. This chapter was written in 2001 and was only slightly updated in 2003. Later literature cannot be surveyed but would include Dever 2003, as well as, specifically on the question of archaeology and ethnicity, Bloch-Smith 2003; Miller 2004; Killebrew 2005; Kletter 2006; Faust 2006. For representative works of Meyers on Jewish and early Christian ethnicity, see Meyers and Chancey 2000; Meyers 1993.

3. For the basic survey data, see the original report and brief synthesis in Finkelstein 1988; see also the final report in Finkelstein and Lederman 1997 and the review of the latter in Dever 1999b.

4. Full references to the literature will be found conveniently in Dever 1995a, 1995b, 1997b, 1998. The response from the biblical scholars other than those of the revisionist or minimalist school has been scant, but see Gottwald 1993; Stager 1998; McNutt 1999, 64–103; and Miller and Callaway 1999 for balanced, centrist interpretations of the data. For the revisionists, see n. 5, below.

types of diverse but related data constitutes what archaeologists call an assemblage, and such an assemblage is *always* assumed to have cultural, and therefore what I would call ethnic, significance. The aspects of this Iron I or twelfth- to eleventh-century BCE assemblage that are relevant for our discussion here will be discussed presently.

Prior to the availability of the recent archaeological data, scholars have had as their only source for the history of the formative era of early Israel (the biblical period of the judges) the narratives of the exodus and conquest in the Hebrew Bible. Yet there has been increasing skepticism in recent years among scholars of all schools, "maximalists" as well as "minimalists," as to whether much, if any, genuine historical information can be derived from the biblical texts.[5] These texts are all later literary compositions, highly selective in content, idealist and elitist in perspective, and, above all, theologically tendentious.

The current, pervasive historiographical crisis in biblical studies has brought us to the point where leading scholars can assert that there *was* no early Israel in the twelfth–eleventh centuries BCE, indeed not even an Israelite monarchy before the ninth century BCE, and no Judean (or southern) kingdom worthy of the name before the seventh century BCE.[6]

For adherents of the revisionist schools of Sheffield and Copenhagen—the most radical of the current schools of biblical criticism—the skepticism rests not only on a minimalist (if not nihilist) view of the biblical texts but upon two other *theoretical assumptions*. Unfortunately, these are rarely advanced as rigorous intellectual constructs, merely what I would call notions and, as I shall show, uninformed notions at that. These assumptions are: (1) that the Iron I hill-country archaeological assemblage that we now have, although well documented, cannot be confidently associated with any known ethnic group because of the limitations of all

---

5. See, for instance, Grabbe 1997. The basic literature and a summary of various schools of thought will be found in Dever 1999a. See also my own later treatments in Dever 2001a, 2001b, and add now Lemche 1998a, 1998b; Thompson 1999. For an authoritative survey of contemporary scholarship on the Hebrew Bible in general, with a critique of revisionist ideology similar to my own, see now Barr 2000 (and cf. Lemche's response in 2000).

6. See references in works cited in nn. 4–5 above, especially essays in Fritz and Davies 1996; and cf. Lemche 1998a, 1998b; Thompson 1999 for the latest revisionist treatments.

archaeological evidence; and (2) that, in any case, ethnicity is a modern social construct, so it is illegitimate to project it back upon the ancient textual or archaeological record. Thus the revisionists simply write early Israel out of history.[7]

Here are some typical revisionist statements. Niels Peter Lemche concludes his 1998 book, *The Israelites in History and Tradition*, with this statement:

> The Israel of the Iron Age proved to be most elusive, in historical documents as well as in material remains, where hardly anything carries an ethnic tag that helps the modern investigator to decide what is Israelite and what is not.[8]

Thomas L. Thompson simply disposes of the issue:

> Ethnicity, however is an interpretive historiographical fiction.... Ethnicity is hardly a common aspect of human existence at this very early period.... Ethnicity is only a modern attempt to describe societal relationship and collective decisions.... the physical effects of such collective decisions are often arbitrary and are, indeed, always accidental.[9]

It is no wonder, then, that in his 1999 book, *The Mythic Past: Biblical Archaeology and the Myth of Israel*, Thompson concludes that

> so much of the Bible deals with the origin traditions of a people that never existed as such. This metaphorical nation's land and language, this imagined people's history, moreover, is an origin tradition that belongs to the "new Israel" (i.e., much later Judaism: WGD), not the "old."[10]

Elsewhere, Thompson broadens his skepticism to include other ancient peoples. Thus, Philistines, Canaanites, and Israelites are all "peoples writ large in tradition for purposes fictional."[11]

---

7. Halpern 1995.
8. Lemche 1998a, 166.
9. Thompson 1997, 175.
10. Thompson 1999, 34.
11. Thompson 1997, 177. Thompson's entire chapter (in Grabbe 1997) consists of a vicious, often slanderous attack on my early, positivist views of "Israelite ethnicity," such as Dever 1993, 1995a, 1995b. Thompson's nihilism regarding any

Keith W. Whitelam's position in his 1996 *The Invention of Ancient Israel: The Silencing of Palestinian History* goes to the point of absurdity. The biblical Israel is a fiction concocted by ancient Judaism as a tortuous exercise in self-identity and perpetuated by all later Jewish and Christian scholars (especially Zionist Israelis). There was no ancient or Iron Age Israel in an ethnic sense. Yet the Palestinians as a people—a distinct *ethnos*—flourished already in the Bronze Age. Historians and archaeologists biased by the Judeo-Christian tradition have simply written them out of history.[12]

A recent collection of essays by biblical scholars, *Ethnicity and the Bible* (Brett 1996), does not deign to include any archaeologists, presumably because the editors did not consider their data relevant. Yet one of them, Diana V. Edelman (now with the Sheffield group), draws up a trait list of the sort that has been used by some archaeologists in the past to identify ethnicity. Nevertheless, she concludes that attempting to identify any of the Iron I-II peoples of Palestine ethnically, based on material culture remains, "is to wish upon a star." As she puts it in the very first sentence of her chapter: "Given the present state of textual and artifactual evidence, nothing definitive can be said about the ethnicity of premonarchical Israel."[13]

---

historical Canaanites is undoubtedly borrowed from Lemche 1991, but see the decisive refutation by Rainey 1996. Thompson's (1997, 173) similar skepticism regarding the archaeological identifications of Philistines reveals his complete ignorance of archaeological scholarship of the past fifteen years; see, e.g., Stager 1995, 1998 and references there. On archaeological data and the ethnicity of Canaanites, Philistines, and the peoples of Transjordan, see further Dever 1995a, 1998.

12. See Whitelam 1996, passim; and my critique of Whitelam's ideological biases and his distortion of the archaeological data in Dever 1998, 1999a. Even Whitelam's fellow revisionist Lemche (1997, 151) has pointed out the absurdity of his attempt to identify the *Iron Age* population of Palestine as "Palestinians"; see also Thompson 1997, 179. This is simply ideological cant. Lately Thompson has even refused to use the term *Israelite*, preferring to see the people (not an *ethnos*) in question as something like "the Iron Age population of southern Syria's marginal fringe"; see 1997, 176-77, 184; 1999, 168, 190, 235.

13. Edelman 1996, 25, 55. Edelman, to her credit, has done some archaeological fieldwork, and she is currently one of the staff of Mazar's excavation at Tel Rehov. Despite her recent affiliation with Davies, Whitelam, and other revisionists at Sheffield, she is not as radical as they are. Nevertheless, her basic minimalist

Most of the above statements scarcely need refutation. For Lemche, Thompson, and Whitelam, as well as Philip R. Davies, there cannot have been an ancient Israel because that would not suit their presuppositions (for that is what they are).[14] Further, Thompson's incredible notions that ethnic markers are all "arbitrary, accidental," if taken seriously, would put *all* the social sciences out of business, since these disciplines proceed on the essential principle that culture is patterned, that is, intentional, and thus diagnostic for describing culture and cultural change (below). As for Edelman, her survey of some of the archaeological data is typical of the selective, cavalier, and amateurish use of archaeology by most of the other revisionists.[15]

Unfortunately, the antipositivist bias of some biblical scholars—in my judgment largely a reflex of the naive, belated borrowing of postmodernist epistemology—has affected a few Palestinian archaeologists (below).[16] Most archaeologists until recently have been comfortable and confident in applying to typical Bronze or Iron Age assemblages in Palestine such ethnic labels as Canaanite, Egyptian, Philistine, Aramaean, Phoenician, and, of course, Israelite.

Now, however, it seems suddenly fashionable to call such ethnic identifications into question and even to impute to scholars still using them improper motives—in the case of the term Israelite, a theological or biblicist bias (as Whitelam 1996). Ironically, the most outspoken current opponent of the "Israelite" terminology, or even my cautious term Proto-

---

position is revealed in such statements as "there are no *artifactual* remains that can consistently be used to understand a group's ethnicity" (1996, 26; emphasis original).

14. See references in nn. 4–6 above, especially Dever 1998, 1999a, 2000, 2001b.

15. See Edelman 1996, 39–54. Despite some reference to the archaeological data and literature, this entire discussion lacks authority. It is typical of the monologues that result when most biblicists resort on their own to archaeology; see further Halpern 1997.

16. On the postmodernist background of much revisionist discourse, see Dever 1998, 2000, 2001b. Ironically, postmodernism's overriding emphasis on "multiculturalism" ought to have stimulated a renewed appreciation of the ethnic distinctiveness of many cultures. Archaeologists are the real multiculturalists, as the astute social critic Camille Paglia (1999) has pointed out. On Finkelstein's flirtation with the "post-Zionist" version of postmodernism, see below.

Israelite, is Israel Finkelstein. He had originally written the book on the subject, *The Archaeology of the Israelite Settlement* (1988). But since 1991, Finkelstein has denied that we can use the ethnic label Israelite for the Iron I hill-country assemblage that he did so much to put on the map. In 1996, specifically attacking my more optimistic treatments of early Israel (Dever 1992a, 1995a), Finkelstein argues that the distinctive material culture traits that we both acknowledge on the Late Bronze/Iron I horizon are more the result of environmental and socioeconomic factors than reflective of any new ethnic elements in the population. To support his views, Finkelstein minimizes the importance of a unique, new combination of agricultural technologies—terraces, silos, cisterns—even denying that they are innovative. Finally, he misrepresents my reconstruction as based either on Norman K. Gottwald's peasant-revolt model or on theories "too wedded to the Biblical story." He concludes that an ethnic identification based even on texts, such as those of the Hebrew Bible, is an "illusion." Yet in his most recent popular book, Finkelstein speaks throughout quite glibly about an "early Israel." All this, in my opinion, is *ideology*, not reasoned, well-documented, balanced scholarship.[17]

On the other hand, I have consistently maintained a more positive view, presumably one in line with mainstream archaeological scholarship, although I have not defended this view explicitly until now. Nor is there much other treatment of the subject of ethnicity in the literature of Palestinian archaeology.[18]

One of the few explicit treatments of archaeology and the problem of Israelite ethnicity, although focused on the Iron II rather than the more problematic Iron I period, is that of a young Tel Aviv archaeologist, Avraham Faust (2000a, 2000b), with excellent general bibliography. Faust concentrates on the rural areas of ninth- to eighth-century BCE northern Israel, where he persuasively identifies an "Israelite" as well as a regional

---

17. See Finkelstein 1996, passim; and his further attack on my views in Finkelstein 1997. These articles actually go back to an ideological shift in the early 1990s, which Finkelstein rarely acknowledges or cites. For his latest reversion to using the term Israel, see Finkelstein and Silberman 2001, e.g., throughout ch. 4, 97–122; see my review of this popular book in Dever 2001a.

18. See Dever 1998. In addition to Finkelstein 1996, 1997, discussed above; Dever 1995a, 1998; Kletter 1999; and Faust 2000a, I can cite only Bunimovitz and Yasur-Landau 1996; Bunimovitz and Faust 2001, 2003.

"Canaanite-Phoenician" archaeological assemblage, coinciding with both geographical and socioeconomic or cultural boundaries.

Of particular significance here is Faust's utilization of Randall H. McGuire's postulate that it is not the totality of cultural traits that identifies ethnic differences but rather "those traits that the groups utilized as symbols of their identity separate from other groups." These traits, McGuire holds, "may be behavioral or material in form." Furthermore, ethnic boundaries may be most readily recognized (1) when they are not connected with factors such as ecology, wealth, social status, or setting and (2) when the focus is on simpler, supposedly more monolithic rural groups. Faust's consequent look at rural areas in Iron II is closely comparable to our look at the overwhelmingly rural "Israel" in Iron I.[19]

A similar attempt to identify Judean ethnicity in Iron II has been made recently by another young Tel Aviv archaeologist, Raz Kletter. Kletter analyzes two distinctive classes of southern artifacts of the late eighth–seventh centuries BCE: (1) pillar-base (Asherah) figurines; and (2) stone shekel weights. Not surprisingly, Kletter's detailed distribution maps of both coincide almost exactly with the *political* boundaries of Judah as reflected in texts of the seventh-century BCE Deuternomistic History in 2 Kings. Thus a sense of Judean ethnicity must have actually prevailed in late Iron II and was not simply "invented" by the biblical writers and later editors, as the revisionists fatuously proclaim.[20]

8.2. General Theoretical Considerations of Ethnicity

None of the theoretical objections noted above to the use of the concept of ethnicity stands up to close scrutiny. Let us analyze them in order.

(1) Ethnicity is a modern social construct. This, of course, is simply one of the typical slogans of postmodernism, borrowed mindlessly here. The point is that *all* intellectual formulations are social constructs, as, indeed, culture itself is—unless one supposes that the phenomena are handed down from heaven. Religion is a social construct. Does that mean

---

19. Faust 2000a, 2000b; see also McGuire 1982, 160.

20. See Kletter 1999. Note the overweening use of the terms "invention" by Whitelam 1996 and "myth" by Thompson 1999. Whitelam and Thompson insist that the ancient Israelites and Judeans did not know who they were, but *they* know.

that it is not a significant factor in cultural change or that it is too elusive to be analyzed?

The question is only the degree to which such constructs reflect facts, that is, reality. In the case of ethnicity, the construct *is* the reality. Ethnicity means simply "a sense of peoplehood" (Greek *ethnos*, "a community of people"). If a certain group thinks itself a distinctive people, then they *are* by that very fact. Finally, such a sense of peoplehood is not a modern phenomenon, as claimed by the revisionists, but has characterized every known human community in every time and circumstance. A sense of unique *selfhood* is fundamental to human nature, not a mere epiphenomenon, an arbitrary and flimsy social construct.

(2) What may be called ethnic boundaries are flexible, constantly changing. No doubt, but again that does not mean that they do not exist in reality or cannot be subjected to rigorous scrutiny and systematic analysis. Here, too, the analogy with certain aspects of culture, such as religion, is appropriate.

(3) Specific markers, or ethnic traits, either cannot be adequately characterized or will turn out not to be reflected in material culture. If this were true, however, archaeology as a discipline would be impossible, since archaeology is widely acknowledged to be essentially the study of the *material correlates* of behavior, that is, of culture in all its dimensions, including a sense of ethnic identity. If there *are* no material correlates, then human thought, behavior, and culture are all arbitrary, inscrutable, and not susceptible to any systematic analysis. Yet that is not the case, as I shall show presently. Culture is patterned social behavior, or it is nothing, and archaeology seeks to comprehend those patterns, as they are inevitably reflected in material culture remains as well as in ideology.

(4) Finally, revisionists and other assert that, without texts, material culture is "mute" and thus cannot be said to reflect any specific ethnic identity. Yet if the arguments above are valid, it is evident that archaeology *can* characterize distinctive material culture assemblages and then can legitimately assume that they do reflect various ethnic groups. It is only the specific ethnic *label* that texts necessarily supply, and, in the case of ancient Israel, we have the requisite texts, both biblical and nonbiblical (below).

If one examines the currently faddish negative rhetoric about ethnicity, as in Sian Jones's *The Archaeology of Ethnicity* (1998; above), it soon becomes evident that much of the skepticism is due to the confusion of attempts to identify ethnicity with *racism*, which is and should be politically incorrect. Thus, Jones's principal case study in the abuse of the concept of ethnicity is the program of the Nazis to use archaeology to document the superiority of their Super Race. But that is surely a monstrous caricature. Such a distorted concept of race has long been repudiated by archaeologists and anthropologists everywhere. But that does not invalidate the category of ethnicity, which was never really based on supposed racial characteristics and still remains both valid and useful.

Ironically, the call of many postmodernist social scientists for "multicultural" approaches presupposes our ability to *identify* distinctive individual ethnic groups. And if we can do so in modern times, why not in antiquity, as long as we have adequate evidence? Instead of denying the existence of ethnic identity, archaeologists are engaged in recognizing and indeed celebrating it. *We* are the true multiculturalists, and instead of using archaeology as a tool of cultural imperialism, as sometimes charged, we archaeologists are the real champions of cultural diversity.[21]

8.3. Toward a Working Archaeological Model of Ethnicity

Much of the current frustration and apparent failure in recognizing ethnicity in the archaeological record is due, I believe, to (1) inadequate or unrealistic definitions of ethnicity and (2) the lack of an appropriate analytical methodology, especially in assessing ethnic traits in material culture remains.

Elsewhere I have drawn on the work of the eminent anthropologist and ethnographer Fredrik Barth in order to define an ethnic group as a population that is (1) biologically self-perpetuating; (2) shares a fundamental, recognizable, relatively uniform set of cultural values, including language; (3) constitutes a partly independent interaction sphere; (4) has a membership that defines itself, as well as being defined by others, as a category distinct from other categories of the same order; and (5) perpetuates its sense of separate identity by developing rules for maintaining ethnic boundaries, as well as for participating in interethnic social encounters.[22]

---

21. See n. 16 above.
22. See Barth 1969; see also Dever 1995a, 201.

However heuristically valuable the methodology of Barth and other ethnographers may be, it is best suited to the analysis of modern, not ancient, cultures. Our primary task here is to identify a list of distinctive and specifically *archaeological* ethnic traits that may realistically be expected to be preserved and capable of being identified in the archaeological record of typical sites. Yet few archaeologists, and none in the field of Palestinian or biblical archaeology, has developed such an archaeological trait list (table 8.1).[23] I offer the following as a tentative step in the right direction. After long reflection, it seems to me that we ought to be able to discern ethnic differences in comparing the following material culture traits in different assemblages and cultures, especially when they are contiguous or roughly contemporary:

1. environmental setting
2. settlement type and pattern
3. demography
4. technology, adaptation, and subsistence, especially food systems
5. house type
6. burial customs
7. dress
8. language
9. social organization
10. political structure
11. religion and cult
12. external relations

These are, of course, modern analytical categories that ancient peoples would not have comprehended in the same way that we do or of which

---

23. Oddly enough, only Edelman (1996)—a biblical scholar—has employed such a trait list, although superficially; see n. 15 above. The scant works of other biblicists, such as Sparks (1998), ignore the archaeological data completely and focus on texts, with predictably minimal and quite unrealistic results. On Finkelstein's fundamental skepticism regarding "ethnic traits," see, for instance, 1996, 202–6. He sees only diet—i.e., the statistically significant absence of pig bones in early Iron Age hill-country sites—as a valid ethnic marker; see Finkelstein 1996, 206; 1997, 227–30; and further below. Obviously, I think that there we have many other ethnic markers. On pottery, for instance, see Bunimovitz and Yasur-Landau 1996 ("Philistine ethnicity").

they may not even have been consciously aware. But nevertheless, I would argue, they did understand the differences that such traits reflect, especially when comparing themselves with other groups. In short, the ancient Israelites of the Iron Age in Palestine surely knew who they were, and it is up to us to find that out, even when they have not always candidly revealed themselves in the biblical texts. It is archaeology that may be our best clue.

8.4. The Archaeological Evidence for Early Israelite Ethnicity

In summarizing the archaeological data now available that might bear upon each of the above ethnic markers for identifying an early Israel, I must be brief, referring to more extensive documentation elsewhere.[24]

Table 8.1 Comparison of cultural traits exhibited in the Iron I archaeological record, by ethnic group; numbers refer to the list in the text. If these other Iron I groups in Palestine can be distinguished by an ethnic label, as they are in contemporary scholarship, so can our highland peoples.

Trait	Canaanite	Egyptian	Philistine	Proto-Israelite
1	Central	Strategic	Coastal	Marginal; hill country
2	Declining urban	Forts; garrisons	New urban foundations	Village/Rural
3	LB urban tradition	"Residencies"	Nonspecific	"Four room" / courtyard
4	Long-term decline	Penultimate collapse	Slow growth	Rapid growth

---

24. The fundamental evidence, on which all reconstructions necessarily rest are first the survey data, for which see Finkelstein 1988; Finkelstein and Na'aman 1994; Finkelstein and Lederman 1997. The few excavated sites would include 'Ai (Callaway 1993), Radanna (Callaway and Cooley 1971; Callaway 1983), 'Izbet Ṣarṭah (Finkelstein 1986), Shiloh (Finkelstein 1993a), and Giloh (Mazar 1981). One might add Tel Masos (Fritz and Kempinski 1983; see also Dever 1990), the Bull Site (Mazar 1982), and the Mount Ebal installation (Zertal 1986–1987). A convenient, semipopular summary of the evidence is Dever 1992b; see also Stager 1985, 1998.

5	Mixed, local	Subsidized	Mixed	Agrarian
6	NA	NA	NA	NA
7	Stagnant	Egyptian	Foreign, innovative	Local, innovative
8	Long-term Canaanite	Bilingual	Unknown	Canaanite dialect
9	Stratified	Hierarchal	Elitist	Egalitarian
10	Declining city-states	Imperial	City-state	Segmentary
11	LB Canaanite	Egyptian	Aegean	"Canaanite"
12	Egyptian	Egyptian	Aegean, Mycenaean	"Proto-Israelite"

1. Environmental Setting. The more than three hundred small Iron I or twelfth- to eleventh-century BCE villages, which constitute our best evidence for what I have designated a Proto-Israelite population, are all located in marginal areas. They are found in the heretofore sparsely occupied central hill country, principally in Samaria and Judea, but also extending into the northern Negev and probably on to lower Galilee. The environmental setting in these regions, with ample rainfall, is conducive to dry farming, stock breeding, and pastoralism, but only with the development of new technologies (below). The isolation and scarcity of resources, however, do not encourage larger-scale industry, much less trade or international connections. This is in sharp contrast to both the Late Bronze Age Canaanite city-states and the contemporary Philistine establishments along the coast and in the riverine valleys.

2. Settlement Type and Pattern. The basic features have been noted above. The essential point here is that the settlements and their distribution mark again a sharp and relatively sudden shift from the prevailing urban pattern of the Late Bronze Age Canaanite society, as well as a contrast to the coastal Philistine sites. None of the three hundred or so Proto-Israelite sites is larger than a few acres, has a population in excess of about three hundred, exhibits monumental architecture, or boasts city defenses. This is a decidedly *rural* culture, which, as we saw above, may provide our best test case.

3. Demography. The demographic data, based on recent surveys of the hill-country sites, show another radical change accompanying the transition from the Late Bronze Age Canaanite society into the early Iron Age.

The estimated population of the central hill country, for instance, grows dramatically from circa 12,000 in the thirteenth century BCE, to circa 50,000 in the twelfth century BCE, to circa 75,000 in the eleventh century BCE.[25] Such a population explosion cannot possibly be explained by natural increase alone but points to a large-scale in-migration of new peoples, whom it is not unreasonable to designate as an ethnic group, especially when other evidence points in the same direction. The only questions are who and from where.

4. Technology, Adaptation, and Subsistence. The evidence adduced above shows that the Iron I hill-country assemblage reflects a society and economy that are fundamentally village-based and agrarian. A major agricultural component is visible, of course, in the society and economy of every era in ancient Palestine, from the Neolithic onward. Yet in scarcely any other period does the rural aspect dominate so *exclusively* as it does in the Iron I hill-country assemblage. Nearly all the new technology is geared to adapting to the challenges of settling the hill-country frontier and opening it for agricultural development: extensive terracing of the hillsides; the hewing out of cisterns in the bedrock; stone-lined silos for grain storage; large collar-rim jars for storage of various foodstuffs; the introduction of heavy iron implements (although limited at first); and the proliferation of stereotyped courtyard houses especially well suited to farming families. Some aspects of these technologies go back to the Bronze Age, but the peculiar and standardized *combination* is new in Iron I and also peculiar to the hill-country settlements.[26]

---

25. For the figures, see Finkelstein 1988, 296–97, 330–35; 1994, 154. See also Stager 1985, 3, 21, 23, with slightly different results (ca. 17,000 in the Late Bronze; ca. 48,000 in early Iron I). Elsewhere, Stager (1998, 135) documents an increase in the number of individual sites from 36 in the Late Bronze to 319 in early Iron I, most of the latter newly founded in the twelfth century BCE.

26. On these aspects of technology, see Finkelstein 1988, 202–4, 264–69; Stager 1985, 5–10, with full references in both. I have argued strongly that it is not a single, innovative technology that characterizes the new hill-country archaeology assemblage in Iron I but rather the distinctive *combination* (Dever 1992a, 38, 79; 1995a, 207–8). Finkelstein's criticisms (1993b, 64–65; 1996, 201–2; 1997, 222–23) are a distortion of my views. Originally, he himself had emphasized the importance of such technologies as terracing, the hewing of cisterns, and the construction of silos—at least for the Iron I settlement west of the central ridge, i.e., the majority (1988, 202–4, 264–69). One aspect of technology—ceramics—has

One aspect of food production is now widely acknowledged to be significant, even by skeptics: the almost complete absence of pig bones in the presumed hill-country Proto-Israelite sites of Iron I, whereas they are common in other periods and areas. This phenomenon suggests that one of the most conspicuous ethnic markers of the later, well-documented Israelite (or biblical) culture—the prohibition of pork—was in fact an early distinction from Canaanite religion and culture.[27]

5. House Type. The typical Iron I hill-country village house has been mentioned above. These houses are very stereotyped in plan, with three banks of rooms surrounding a central courtyard (thus the common name, "four-room house") and usually a second story. The ground floor provides animal stables, ample storage facilities, and food-preparation areas. The second story, with its six to ten rooms, would accommodate a large, multigenerational family of perhaps as many as twenty to twenty-five people. These are obviously ideal farmhouses, and with rare exceptions they are unattested in the preceding Late Bronze Age. Despite the fact that this was formerly dubbed the Israelite type house, similar structures have recently been brought to light in Transjordan, which may or may not have been part of the Proto-Israelite territories. These distinctive houses do, however, characterize later and undisputedly Israelite sites in western Palestine in the tenth–sixth centuries BCE. If the house type provides one of the most instructive commentaries on ethnicity, as most archaeologists and anthropologists would maintain, then these unique courtyard houses of the Iron Age reflect a distinctive mentality—in this case, one that enshrines an agrarian, family-based lifestyle and its social and communal values.[28]

---

been omitted here, since the discussion is very technical, but see Dever 1995a and contrast Finkelstein 1996, 204.

27. See Finkelstein 1996, 206; 1997, 227–30; Hesse and Wapnish 1997. At least Finkelstein and I agree on the ethnic significant of this particular datum.

28. On the early Iron Age courtyard houses, see Stager 1985, 11–17; Finkelstein 1988, 254–59; 1996, 204–6. On its development and diffusion in Iron II, see the extensive treatment of Holladay 1992. Shlomo Bunimovitz, originally a skeptic regarding ethnicity in the archaeological record, has demonstrated convincingly in several publications that the ubiquitous courtyard or four-room house in the Iron II period reflects precisely an Israelite cultural ideal; see, e.g., Bunimovitz and Faust 2003.

6. Burial Customs. Unfortunately, thus far we have discovered no cemeteries associated with the hill-country settlements and only an occasional individual twelfth- to eleventh-century BCE burial elsewhere.[29]

7. Dress. Manner of dress is another well-recognized ethnic marker, but again our evidence is scant or nonexistent, due to the fact that textiles are well preserved in the archaeological record only under exceptional circumstances. Dress is sometimes indicated in tomb or wall paintings, where, for instance, in earlier periods we can clearly distinguish between Egyptians, Canaanites, Assyrians, and others. But we have no such evidence for the twelfth–eleventh centuries BCE and no surviving portraits of Israelites at all, until much later in the Iron Age.[30]

8. Language. Language is, without doubt, one of the most critical and sensitive indicators of ethnic affiliation and has been so regarded since Herodotus's discussion of the Greek *ethnos*. Currently we have only a handful of putative early Israelite inscriptions, including a Hebrew personal name on a jar handle from Khirbet Radanna and an abecedary (or list of alphabetic characters in order) from 'Izbet Ṣarṭah. The form of the letters is demonstrably Old Canaanite, and this plus other linguistic data from later periods demonstrates that Israelite Hebrew of the Iron Age derived directly from Late Bronze Age Canaanite. But by the tenth century BCE, Hebrew had diverged sufficiently in vocabulary, syntax, orthography, and script so as to constitute a separate, well-developed national language. By the Iron II period, Hebrew was distinguished as well from Aramaic, Phoenician, and such languages of Transjordan as Ammonite, Moabite, and Edomite, by both language and script.[31]

9. Social Organization. Social organization is not nearly as elusive as many nonarchaeologists suppose, and it can be inferred from several of the categories of material culture already discussed. In keeping with small-scale agrarian societies in general, the social structure of our hill-

---

29. See Bloch-Smith 1992, 60, 64. It has even been suggested that the Proto-Israelites typically cremated their dead, but that is extremely unlikely. On mortuary customs and ethnicity, see Brown 1971.

30. For perhaps the only real portraits we have on the famous Neo-Assyrian depictions of the fall of Lachish in 701 BCE, see Ussishkin 1982, 84, 88, 100, 113.

31. For the 'Izbet Ṣarṭah abecedary, see Demsky 1977; for the Radanna jar handle, see Callaway and Cooley 1971, 20–21. On the related Iron Age West Semitic languages and scripts in general, see Naveh 1982.

country assemblage may best be characterized as kin-based, centered on extended family and clan units, relatively unstratified, and with strong egalitarian tendencies. Lawrence Stager has shown that the typical clusters of courtyard houses reflect almost exactly the biblical ideal of the *mišpāḥâ* or "extended multigenerational family," of the books of Joshua, Judges, and Samuel (later compositions but set in the Iron I period). This correspondence can scarcely be fortuitous and suggests that later traditions of what I have called the "domestic mode of production" had ancient roots.[32]

10. Political Structure. Political organization has already been hinted at above. There can be little doubt that the twelfth- to eleventh-century BCE complex represents not only a preurban but a prestate level of political organization, probably even a prechiefdom level in the typical parlance of the literature on state-formation processes. Later biblical traditions recall the formative period nostalgically as tribal not entirely without reason, but perhaps *segmentary* best describes the early system of political organization.[33] In any case, it contrasts sharply with the Late Bronze Age Canaanite system of city-states and also with the contemporary Philistine feudal system.

11. Religion and Culture. Religion, like language, is one of the most fundamental indicators of ethnic identity. The archaeological data for religious belief and practice in the twelfth- to eleventh-century BCE highland village consists, on the one hand, of negative evidence: the complete absence of the temples and their impressive paraphernalia that characterized the previous Late Bronze Age Canaanite civilization. Nor is there any trace of the mythological and liturgical literature so well attested from Canaan in this period, much less the organized priesthood and cult personnel who could have produced such a literature.[34]

---

32. Stager 1985. See further Dever 1991b, 201; the model is adapted from Sahlins 1972. This is in some ways similar to Gottwald's "communitarian" model (1993).

33. The issue of whether Israel's "tribal" origins were historical or simply one aspect of the nationalist ideology of the later literary traditions is vexed. For my own view, with references to the wider literature, see Dever 1997c. See also the exhaustive but rather ideological discussion of Gottwald 1979, 224–28, 429–76.

34. For a general discussion of the archaeological evidence for early Israelite religion, see Dever 1997b and references there.

On the other hand, we do have at least one open cult place, Mazar's Bull Site in the tribal territory of Ephraim. It is a small hilltop shrine with a low enclosure wall, a standing stone reminiscent of the biblical *maṣṣēbâ*, and a few scraps of metal, and Iron I pottery. The only outstanding find is a fine bronze bull figurine, almost identical to a Late Bronze example from Hazor and best understood in the light of the iconography of Bull El, the principal male deity of the old Canaanite pantheon.[35]

Again, we have both elements of continuity and discontinuity with Late Bronze Age Canaan. It is noteworthy that the El cult continues into later Israelite society, the name itself and typical El epithets being common in the older strands of the biblical literature. Thus what little we can say of the religion of our hill-country settlements suggests that it grew out of the Late Bronze Age Canaanite cult, but it was more in keeping with the simple character of the new settlements, yet on its way toward becoming a new and unique religious syncretism, "Yahwism."[36]

12. External Relations. By external relations, I refer to those relationships of a community with outsiders, or *others*, that help to define who *we* are. The notions of us and them will always be, of course, partly subjective, but they are, nonetheless, real as perceptions and thus subject to analysis. In the case of the Iron I hill-country assemblage, it is the relative isolation of the peoples in question that strikes us. Part of this isolation was due to the natural setting of the dozens of small villages in a region that had long been on the somewhat remote frontier of Canaanite civilization, hitherto sparsely settled. It was not so much a matter of physical distance, since the hill country, at least the foothills, lies in fairly close proximity to the lowlands, but rather a matter of difficulty of access. The new settlements constituted a mountain redoubt, much like the small Christian enclaves in the mountains of Lebanon today. There is little evidence of outside trade of any kind. There are none of the Syrian, Egyptian, Cypriot, and Mycenaean imports so characteristic of the previous Late Bronze Age and scarcely any trace of even the contemporary Philistine Bichrome pottery. The overwhelming impression one has is that of an entirely self-sufficient economy

---

35. Mazar 1982.

36. For the latest treatments of the development of Yahwism, see Day 2000; most other standard treatments by biblical scholars are deficient because they fail to utilize the archaeological and art historical data. For my own synthesis, see Dever 1992a, 1997b.

and society, one, moreover, that is not interested in outside contacts, perhaps even hostile to them. The transitional Late Bronze Age/Iron I culture might be said to represent a new group of people in the marginal zones whose ethnic self-identification is based partly on its sense of being displaced, both geographically and ideologically.[37] This group's isolation was relatively short-lived, however, in the twelfth–eleventh centuries BCE, but it was nevertheless formative—indeed, if I am right, later mythologized in the Hebrew Bible as a golden age, the *ideal* Israel.

8.5. The Iron I Hill-Country Assemblage: Proto-Israelites?

It is time now to draw together the principal arguments in favor of labeling the Iron I hill-country archaeological assemblage as Israelite or—as I prefer, on the side of caution—Proto-Israelite. There are, in my opinion, two arguments that taken together are conclusive.

8.5.1. A Distinctive Iron I Archaeological Assemblage and Ethnos

The first argument is based on analyzing the cultural traits reflected in the archaeological record as outlined above, in order to compare and contrast a putative early Israel with *other* Iron I ethnic groups whose existence and identity is beyond reasonable doubt. The results of such an analysis are tabulated for brevity's sake in table 8.1. It will hardly be sufficient to dub these the "X-people," if for no other reason than the well-known reference to Israel on the Victory Stela of the Egyptian pharaoh Merenptah. Dated closely to 1207 BCE, this inscription refers to several ethnic groups in Palestine identified by Egyptian intelligence and sufficiently well known to be perceived as a threat, among them "Hurrians," the common Egyptian term for the Canaanite population in New Kingdom times (the texts also mentions "Canaanites" directly), and "Israelites," the term followed by the determinative sign for "people," rather than nation-state, the whole phrase being a plural gentilic, thus designating "the Israelite peoples."[38]

---

37. The term *displaced* owes much to Norman Gottwald's study on the *ideological* aspects, simply because the archaeological evidence is scant and ambiguous.

38. The latest, exhaustive treatment is that of my student Michael Hasel (1998).

The reading "Israel" has never been seriously questioned, and the date of circa 1207 BCE is fixed within the margin of a very few years. Furthermore, the location of the Egyptian strongholds, of sites such as Ashkelon and Gezer, of the Hurrian or Canaanite population, and of the Shasu or nomadic populations of other Egyptian texts can easily be charted on a map of Palestine, and the only area *left* for Merenptah's Israelites is in the central hill country north and south.[39] Thus, we have in the Merenptah inscription a firm extrabiblical reference to Israelite peoples in Palestine, precisely *when* and *where* the recently discovered late thirteenth- to early twelfth-century BCE settlements are located—and, furthermore, in what was the heartland of later biblical Israel, which is even better textually documented (below).

The Merenptah datum *alone* would seem to be sufficient textual warrant for designating the Iron I settlements Israelite. How do the revisionists, who as we have seen are skeptical of the very concept of Israelite ethnicity, confront this inconvenient datum? Lemche is the most sanguine, although he refers to the inscription as the "so-called Israel-stele." He does concede that the entity in question is to be located somewhere in the central highlands, but he concludes that this evidence has little to do with later, *biblical* Israel.[40]

Whitelam concedes that the Merenptah Stela mentions an entity called Israel, but he argues that "the term 'Israelite' when applied to these (Iron I) settlements is meaningless."[41] Apparently that is to be understood as meaningless to Whitelam, since it does not meet *his* expectations of significant information. Yet the Merenptah datum tells us all that we *need* to know at this point, that a late thirteenth-century BCE Israelite ethnic group existed in the highlands. The archaeological data, which the revisionists all refuse to connect with this Israel and scarcely appreciate anyway, reveal much of

---

39. For the best map locating the peoples referred to on the Merenptah Stela, see Yurco 1990, 34; note the obvious lacuna in the central hill country, where I would place the "Proto-Israelites."

40. See Lemche 1998b, 75; 1998a, 35–38, 42, 57. Lemche concedes that the stela does refer to "some sort of ethnic [*sic*] unity, which was identifiable as far as it has its own name, Israel" (1998a, 36). But he thinks that what this is not "easy to ascertain" (1998a, 36). Perhaps not easy—but possible.

41. Whitelam 1996, 228.

the rest, such as socioeconomic structure and political organization and even origins, if I am correct.

Thompson, as usual, is the most radical. He simply dismisses the reference to Israel, declaring that "it does not correspond with the highland Israel or any biblical Israel." Elsewhere, he contends that the Egyptian term Israel is to be paired with the term Canaan as a spouse and that the two are "metaphorical parents of three towns destroyed by the Egyptian army."[42] What is a sensible person to make of such scholarship?

Edelman's treatment of the Merenptah Stela is equally tortured. Not only does it yield "almost no firm data about this unit or entity," but the reading "Israel" is suspect and "could just as well be Jezreel," that is, the Jezreel Valley.[43]

Finkelstein, an archaeologist now virtually in the revisionist camp, does somewhat better. In his latest work, he acknowledges that the reference to Israel does indicate that some group by that name was in Canaan at the time and that this group is probably to be linked with the highland settlements of the period. Finkelstein continues to deny that any of the textual or archaeological data distinguishes an *ethnic* group. Thus he declares that the evidence gives "no sign ... of a clearly defined ethnic group. Instead, it seems to be a revolution in lifestyle."[44] Finkelstein does not seem to understand that ethnicity *is* lifestyle! The fact that we moderns do not know all we wish to know about the Israelites' lifestyle or perceptions of themselves in Iron I does not mean that they had no such perceptions. Finkelstein's reluctance to use specific ethnic terms is reminiscent of Lemche's dictum that "the Canaanites of the ancient Near East did not know that they were themselves Canaanites." Yet somehow Lemche knows that they were *not*. This elevates creeping skepticism from simply a proper critical attitude to an overarching scholarly method.[45]

---

42. In a session of the Second International Congress on Ancient Near Eastern Archaeology in Copenhagen in May 2000, where Thompson and I presented papers opposite each other, he went so far as to suggest that the Egyptian scribe may have simply invented the name "Israel" and that its being identical with the biblical Israel is coincidental. Leading Egyptologists with whom I have consulted consider all of Thompson's opinions absurd.

43. Edelman 1996, 36.

44. Finkelstein and Silberman 2001, 107.

45. Lemche 1991, 152. On "creeping skepticism," see Hallo 1990; see also my

8.5.2. The Continuity of Early Israel and Biblical Israel

Even the most doctrinaire of the revisionists are forced to concede that there was an Israel in Palestine by the mid-ninth century BCE—but *only* because a series of Neo-Assyrian records dealing with military campaign in the west now mentions such an entity. (The biblical narratives, of course, are all dismissed as late and unhistorical.) For instance, in the Neo-Assyrian annals describing their very first encounter with a coalition of western kings following the battle of Shalmaneser III at Qarqar in central Syria in 853 BCE, the texts refers to one of the kings as "Ahab of Israel."[46]

Even this explicit reference to Israel, however, is not sufficient to dispel the revisionists' doubts (or predilections?). They consistently prefer the later Neo-Assyrian term "house (dynasty) of Omri," or the still later usage "province of Samarina." As Lemche puts it, "there can be no doubt that in the eyes of the Assyrians, after they obtained a firsthand knowledge of the territories of Palestine, Israel was not the name of the Northern Kingdom."[47] The extraordinary lengths to which the revisionists go to delegitimize even the *name* Israel suggests to me that it is ideology, not scholarship, that is at work here. There cannot have *been* an ancient Israel because that is a biblical concept (read "social construct" or "fiction").

Despite rather desperate recent attempts to erase ancient Israel from history, it should be obvious to any honest and well-informed person that an Israelite state (or biblical divided monarchy) did exist in Palestine throughout the era that archaeologists designate the Iron II period, circa 900–600 BCE.[48] The point here is that, if it can be shown that the fundamental material culture of this Iron II Israel is in direct continuity with and derives from that of the Iron I assemblage, then the latter may be

---

expansion of this as part of my critique of the revisionists in the conclusion of Dever 2001b.

46. See, for example, the reference in Lemche 1998a, 52. Nevertheless, Lemche and Thompson both regularly ignore this clear extrabiblical reference to a ninth-century BCE "Israel"; see below.

47. Lemche 1998a, 53.

48. Note that standard recent archaeological handbooks devote hundreds of pages to this Iron Age Israel, never once supposing that it is not consonant in many or even most ways with biblical Israel; see Weippert 1988 (264 pages); Mazar 1990 (127 pages); and Ben-Tor 1992 (71 pages). Why is this evidence never cited by the revisionists?

legitimately known as Israelite or, better, Proto-Israelite, as well. Yet virtually no scholar seems to have seen the force of such an argument, which I would regard as impeccable in principle and certainly founded now on ample archaeological evidence.[49] Again, in the interest of brevity, a chart will be used to summarize a mass of data (table 8.2).

Table 8.2 Elements of continuity/discontinuity in cultural traits in the archaeological sequence from Iron I to Iron II.

Cultural Trait	Mostly Continuous	Discontinuous
1. Settlement Type or Pattern		X
2. House Type	X	
3. Demography	X	
4. Subsistence, Economy	X	
5. Technology	X	
6. Pottery	X	
7. Social Structure	X	
8. Political Organization		X
9. Ideology, Art, Religion	X	
10. Language, Literature	X	
11. External Relations		X

Note that the only elements of discontinuity in the entire Iron I–II sequence of central Palestine of the span of some six hundred years are those three (nos. 1, 8, 11) that have to do with *urbanization* and *centralization*—precisely those traits that in the comparative and cross-cultural literature define statehood.[50] And the emergence of the state, whether in

---

49. Even Finkelstein, who has reservations about my term *Proto*-Israelite (see n. 52 below), agrees unequivocally with the argument based on Iron I–II continuity, which he says "is doubtless correct" (1996, 200). For details, see Dever 1995a, 207–10.

50. See the full exposition in Dever 1997a. The revisionists, while vociferously denying that there was an early Israelite state, never really define "statehood," nor

the conventional tenth century BCE or in the minimalist ninth century BCE, is not only well attested by extensive archaeological evidence, but it also fits remarkably well with the biblical scheme of "tribe to nation," however artificial that may seem to some. Elsewhere I have argued that, when the core history of the biblical narratives is isolated, stripped of its mythical and propagandistic elements, it coincides closely with archaeological facts on the ground, then historians are on reasonably solid ground.[51]

Why, then, do I continue to favor the term Proto-Israelite for the Iron I assemblage? I do so principally to err on the side of caution—both because ethnicity *is* difficult to define archaeologically and also because the objection of some that this Israel is not the *same* as the later, biblical Israel is sound (as far as it goes). Thus in my view, the conglomerate of peoples of the Iron I highland settlements, although they were neither homogeneous nor constituted anything like a modern nation-state, nor were even conscious of all the implications of the ethnic term Israelite, were nevertheless the *authentic progenitors* of later biblical Israel and the Iron II period.

Several other scholars, even Finkelstein at times, have adopted the term Proto-Israelite, while others have objected to it as too cautious or even arbitrary.[52] But archaeologists are familiar and comfortable with various "proto" terminologies, especially in attempting to define transitional periods such as the Late Bronze II–Iron I horizon, where cultural changes are gradual and complex. The Israelite peoples and states did exist, but they did not spring into existence overnight: they had a long prehistory. Much later biblical writers and editors knew that.

---

do they show familiarity with any of the extensive anthropological and archaeological literature on what are called state-formation processes.

51. Dever 2000b.

52. For the introduction and rationale of the term Proto-Israelite, see Dever 1991a, 87 and subsequently 1992b; 1993; 1995a, 208–10; 1997b, 42–45. Finkelstein initially accepted the term, then rejected it, and he now (1996) uses it without comment. Mazar (2003), on the other hand, argues that it should be abandoned as needlessly hesitant. Similarly, Stager (1998) speaks without qualification of an early "Israel" in the twelfth–eleventh century BCE.

8.6. Conclusion

The current ideologically driven trend to deny the earliest Israelites their ethnic identity is ominous—the first step in an agenda that would erase ancient and biblical Israel from history, from memory, and from any claim to moral authority. Fortunately, there is ample empirical evidence from archaeology to frustrate this scheme and to discredit its perpetrators.

Works Cited

Barr, James. 2000. *History and Ideology in the Old Testament: Biblical Studies at the End of a Millennium.* Oxford University Press.
Barth, Fredrik, ed. 1969. *Ethnic Groups and Boundaries: The Social Organization of Culture Difference.* Little, Brown.
Ben-Tor, Amnon, ed. 1992. *The Archaeology of Ancient Israel.* Yale University Press.
Bloch-Smith, Elizabeth. 1992. *Judahite Burial Practices and Beliefs about the Dead.* JSOTSup 123. JSOT Press.
———. 2003. "Israelite Ethnicity in Iron I: Archaeology Preserves What Is Remembered and What Is Forgotten in Israel's History." *JBL* 122:401–25.
Brett, Mark G., ed. 1996. *Ethnicity and the Bible.* BibInt 19. Brill.
Brown, James Allison, ed. 1971. *Approaches to the Social Dimensions of Mortuary Practices.* Society of American Archaeology.
Bunimovitz, Shlomo, and Avraham Faust. 2001. "Chronological Separation, Geographical Segregation or Ethnic Demarcation? Ethnography and the Iron Age Low Chronology." *BASOR* 322:1–10.
———. 2003. "Building Identity: The Four Room House and the Israelite Mind." Pages 411–23 in *Symbiosis, Symbolism and the Power of the Past: Canaan Ancient Israel and Their Neighbors.* Edited by William G. Dever and Seymour Gitin. Eisenbrauns.
Bunimovitz, Shlomo, and Asaf Yasur-Landau. 1996. "Philistine and Israelite Pottery: A Comparative Approach to the Question of Pots and People." *TA* 23:88–102.
Callaway, Joseph A. 1983. "A Visit With Ahilud." *BAR* 9.5:42–53.
———. 1993. "Ai." *NEAEHL* 1:39–45.

Callaway, Joseph A., and Robert Cooley. 1971. "A Salvage Excavation at Radanah, in Bireh." *BASOR* 201:9–19.

Day, John. 2000. *Yahweh and the Gods and Goddesses of Canaan.* JSOTSup 265. Sheffield Academic.

Demsky, Aharon. 1977. "A Proto-Canaanite Abecedary Dating from the Period of the Judges and Its Implications for the History of the Alphabet." *TA* 4:1–13.

Dever, William G. 1990. "Archaeology and Israelite Origins: A Review Article." *BASOR* 279:89–95.

———. 1991a. "Archaeological Data on the Israelite Settlement: A Review of Two Recent Works." *BASOR* 284:77–90.

———. 1991b. "Unresolved Issues in the Early History of Israel: Toward a Synthesis of Archaeological and Textual Reconstructions." Pages 195–208 in *The Bible and the Politics of Exegesis: Essays in Honor of Norman K. Gottwald on His Sixty-Fifth Birthday.* Edited by David Jobling, Peggy L. Day, and Gerald T. Sheppard. Pilgrim.

———. 1992a. "How to Tell a Canaanite from an Israelite." Pages 26–56 and 79–85 in *The Rise of Ancient Israel.* Edited by Hershel Shanks. Biblical Archaeology Society.

———. 1992b. "Israel, History of (Archaeology and the Israelite 'Conquest')." *ABD* 3:545–58.

———. 1993. "Cultural Continuity, Ethnicity in the Archaeological Record, and the Question of Israelite Origins." *ErIsr* 24:22*–33*.

———. 1995a. "Ceramics, Ethnicity, and the Question of Israel's Origins." *BA* 58:200–213.

———. 1995b. "'Will the Real Israel Please Stand Up?' Archaeology and Israelite Historiography: Part 1." *BASOR* 297:61–80.

———. 1997a. "Archaeology and the 'Age of Solomon': A Case Study in Archaeology and Historiography." Pages 217–51 in *The Age of Solomon: The Scholarship at the Turn of the Millennium.* Edited by Lowell K. Handy. SHANE 11. Brill.

———. 1997b. "Archaeology and the Emergence of Early Israel." Pages 20–50 in *Archaeology and Biblical Interpretation.* Edited by John Bartlett. Routledge.

———. 1997c. "Philology, Theology, and Archaeology: What Kind of History of Israel Do We Want, and What Is Possible?" Pages 290–310 in *The Archaeology of Israel: Constructing the Past, Interpreting the Present.* Edited by Neil Asher Silberman and David Small. JSOTSup 237. Sheffield Academic. Republished as chapter 3 in this volume.

———. 1998. "Archaeology, Ideology, and the Quest for 'Ancient' or 'Biblical Israel.'" *NEA* 61:39–52.

———. 1999a. "Histories and Nonhistories of Ancient Israel." *BASOR* 316:89–195.

———. 1999b. Review of *Highlands of Many Cultures: The Southern Samaria Survey, The Sites*, ed. Israel Finkelstein and Zvi Lederman. *BASOR* 313:87–88.

———. 2000. "Save Us from Postmodern Malarkey." *BAR* 26.2:28–35, 68.

———. 2001a. "Excavating the Hebrew Bible, Or Burying It Again?" *BASOR* 322:67–77.

———. 2001b. *What Did the Biblical Writers Know and When Did They Know It? What Archaeology Can Tell Us about the Reality of Ancient Israel*. Eerdmans.

———. 2003. *Who Were the Early Israelites and Where Did They Come From?* Eerdmans.

Edelman, Diana V. 1996. "Ethnicity and Early Israel." Pages 25–55 in *Ethnicity and the Bible*. Edited by Mark G. Brett. BibInt 19. Brill.

Faust, Avraham. 2000a. "Ethnic Complexity in Northern Israel During Iron Age II." *PEQ* 132:2–27.

———. 2000b. "The Rural Community in Ancient Israel during Iron Age II." *BASOR* 317:17–39.

———. 2006. *Israel's Ethnogenesis: Settlement, Interaction, Expansion and Resistance*. Equinox.

Finkelstein, Israel. 1986. *'Izbet Ṣarṭah: An Early Iron Age Site Near Rosh Ha'ayin, Israel*. British Archaeological Reports.

———. 1988. *The Archaeology of the Israelite Settlement*. Israel Exploration Society.

———. 1993a. "Response." Pages 63–69 in *The Rise of Israel*. Edited by Hershel Shanks. Biblical Archaeological Society.

———. 1993b. *Shiloh: The Archaeology of a Biblical Site*. Institute of Archaeology, Tel Aviv University.

———. 1994. "The Emergence of Israel: A Phase in the Cyclic History of Canaan in the Third and Second Millennia BCE." Pages 150–78 in *From Nomadism to Monarchy: Archaeological and Historical Aspects of Early Israel*. Edited by Israel Finkelstein and Nadav Na'aman. Biblical Archaeology Society.

———. 1996. "Ethnicity and Origin of the Iron I Settlers in the Highlands of Canaan: Can the Real Israel Stand Up?" *BA* 59:198–212.

———. 1997. "Pots and Peoples Revisited: Ethnic Boundaries in the Iron Age." Pages 216–37 in *The Archaeology of Israel: Constructing the Past, Interpreting the Present*. Edited by Neil Asher Silberman and David Small. JSOTSup 237. Sheffield Academic.

Finkelstein, Israel, and Zvi Lederman, eds. 1997. *Highlands of Many Cultures: The Southern Samaria Survey, The Sites*. Monographs of the Institute of Archaeology, Tel Aviv University 14. Institute of Archaeology, Tel Aviv University.

Finkelstein, Israel, and Nadav Na'aman, eds. 1994. *From Nomadism to Monarchy: Archaeological and Historical Aspects of Early Israel*. Biblical Archaeological Society.

Finkelstein, Israel, and Silberman, Neil Asher. 2001. *The Bible Unearthed: Archaeology's New Vision of Ancient Israel and the Origin of Its Sacred Texts*. Free Press.

Fritz, Volkmar, and Philip R. Davies, eds. 1996. *The Origins of the Ancient Israelite States*. JSOTSup 228. Sheffield Academic.

Fritz, Volkmar, and Aharon Kempinski, eds. 1983. *Ergebnisse der Ausgrabungen auf der Hirbet el-Mšāš (Tel Māśōś) 1972–1975*. Harrassowitz.

Gottwald, Norman K. 1979. *The Tribes of Yahweh: A Sociology of the Religion of Liberated Israel, 1250–1050 B.C.E.* Orbis Books.

———. 1993. "Method and Hypothesis in Reconstructing the Social History of Early Israel." *ErIsr* 24:77*–82*.

Grabbe, Lester L., ed. 1997. *Can a "History of Israel" Be Written?* JSOTSup 245. Sheffield Academic.

Hallo, William W. 1990. "The Limits of Skepticism." *JAOS* 110:187–99.

Halpern, Baruch. 1995. "Erasing History: The Minimalist Assault on Ancient Israel." *BRev* 11.6:26–35, 47.

———. 1997. "Text and Artifact: Two Monologues." Pages 311–41 in *The Archaeology of Israel: Constructing the Past, Interpreting the Present*. Edited by Neil Asher Silberman and David Small. JSOTSup 237. Sheffield Academic.

Hasel, Michael G. 1998. *Domination and Resistance: Egyptian Military Activity in the Southern Levant, ca. 1300–1185 B.C.* PAe 11. Brill.

Hesse, Brian, and Paula Wapnish. 1997. "Can Pig Bones Be Used for Ethnic Diagnosis in the Ancient Near East?" Pages 238–70 in *The Archaeology of Israel: Constructing The Past, Interpreting the Present*. Edited by Neil Asher Silberman and David Small. JSOTSup 237. Sheffield Academic.

Holladay, John S., Jr. 1992. "House, Israelite." *ABD* 3:308–18.

Jones, Sian. 1997. *The Archaeology of Ethnicity: Constructing Identities in the Past and Present*. Routledge.

Killebrew, Ann. 2005. *Biblical Peoples and Ethnicity: An Archaeological Study of Egyptians, Canaanites, Philistines, and Early Israel, 1300–1100 B.C.E.* ABS 9. Society of Biblical Literature.

Kletter, Raz. 1999. "Pots and Polities: Material Remains of Late Iron Age Judah in Relation to Its Political Borders." *BASOR* 314:19–54.

———. 2006. "Can a Proto-Israelite Please Stand Up?" Pages 573–86 in *"I Will Speak the Riddles of Ancient Times": Archaeological and Historical Studies in Honor of Amihai Mazar on the Occasion of His Sixtieth Birthday*. Edited by Aren M. Maeir and Pierre de Miroschedji. Eisenbrauns.

Lemche, Niels Peter. 1991. *The Canaanites and Their Land: The Tradition of the Canaanites*. JSOTSup 110. JSOT Press.

———. 1997. "Clio Is Also among the Muses! Keith W. Whitelam and the History of Palestine: A Review and Commentary." Pages 123–55 In *Can a History of Israel Be Written?* Edited by Lester L. Grabbe. JSOTSup 245. Sheffield Academic.

———. 1998a. *The Israelites in History and Tradition*. LAI. Westminster John Knox.

———. 1998b. *Prelude to Israel's Past: Background and Beginnings of Israelite History and Identity*. Hendrickson.

———. 2000. "Ideology and the History of Ancient Israel." *SJOT* 14:165–93.

Mazar, Amihai. 1981. "Giloh: An Early Israelite Settlement Site Near Jerusalem." *IEJ* 31:1–36.

———. 1982. "The 'Bull Site'—An Iron Age I Open Cult Place." *BASOR* 247:27–42.

———. 1990. *Archaeology of the Land of the Bible, 10,000–586 B.C.E.* Doubleday.

———. 2003. "Remarks of Biblical Traditions and Archaeological Evidence Concerning Early Israel." Pages 85–98 in in *Symbiosis, Symbolism and the Power of the Past: Canaan Ancient Israel and Their Neighbors*. Edited by William G. Dever and Seymour Gitin. Eisenbrauns.

McNutt, Paula M. 1999. *Reconstructing the Society of Ancient Israel*. LAI. Westminster John Knox.

McGuire, Randall H. 1982. "The Study of Ethnicity in Historical Archaeology." *Journal of Anthropological Archaeology* 1:159–78.

Meyers, Eric M. 1993. "Identifying Religious and Ethnic Groups through Archaeology." Pages 738–46 in *Biblical Archaeology Today, 1990: Proceedings of the Second International Congress on Biblical Jerusalem,*

June 1990. Edited by Joseph Aviram and Avraham Biran. Israel Exploration Society.

Meyers, Eric M., and Mark Chancey. 2000. "How Jewish Was Sepphoris in Jesus' Time?" *BAR* 26.1:18–33, 61.

Miller, J. Maxwell, and Joseph A. Callaway. 1999. "The Settlement in Canaan: The Period of the Judges." Pages 55–89 in *Ancient Israel: From Abraham to the Roman Destruction of the Temple*. Rev. and exp. edition. Edited by Hershel Shanks. Biblical Archaeological Society.

Miller, Robert D., II. 2004. "Identifying Earliest Israel." *BASOR* 333:55–68.

Naveh, Joseph. 1982. *Early History of the Alphabet: An Introduction to West Semitic Epigraphy and Paleography*. Magnes; Brill.

Olivier, Laurent, and Anick Coudart. 1995. "French Tradition and the Central Place of History in the Human Sciences: Preamble to a Dialogue between Robinson Crusoe and His Man Friday." Pages 363–81 in *Theory in Archaeology: A World Perspective*. Edited by Peter J. Ucko. Routledge.

Paglia, Camille. 1999. "The Right Kind of Multiculturalism." *The Wall Street Journal*, September 30:2.

Rainey, Aanson. 1996. "Who is a Canaanite? A Review of the Textual Evidence." *BASOR* 304:1–15.

Sahlins, Marshall D. 1972. *Stone Age Economics*. Aldine.

Sparks, Kenton L. 1998. *Ethnicity and Identity in Ancient Israel: Prolegomena to the Study of Ethnic Sentiments and Their Expression in the Hebrew Bible*. Eisenbrauns.

Stager, Lawrence E. 1985. "The Archaeology of the Family in Ancient Israel." *BASOR* 260:1–35.

———. 1995. "The Impact of the Sea Peoples (1185–1050 BCE)." Pages 332–48 in *The Archaeology of Society in the Holy Land*. Edited by Thomas E. Levy. Facts on File.

———. 1998. "Forging an Identity: The Emergence of Ancient Israel." Pages 123–75 in *The Oxford History of the Biblical World*. Edited by Michael D. Coogan. Oxford University Press.

Thompson, Thomas L. 1997. "Defining History and Ethnicity in the Southern Levant." Pages 166–87 in *Can a "History of Israel" Be Written?* Edited by Lester L. Grabbe. JSOTSup 245. Sheffield Academic.

———. 1999. *The Mythic Past: Biblical Archaeology and the Myth of Israel*. Basic Books.

Ussishkin, David. 1982. *The Conquest of Lachish by Sennacherib*. Institute of Archaeology, Tel-Aviv University.

Weippert, Helga. 1988. *Palästina in vorhellenistischer Zeit.* Beck.
Whitelam, Keith W. 1996. *The Invention of Ancient Israel: The Silencing of Palestinian History.* Routledge.
Yurco, Frank J. 1990. "3,200-Year-Old Picture of Israelites Found in Egypt." *BAR* 16.5:20–38.
Zertal, Adam. 1986-1987. "An Early Iron Age Cultic Site on Mount Ebal: Excavation Seasons 1982–1987." *TA* 13–14:105–65.

Updated Bibliography

Killebrew, Ann E. 2005. *Biblical Peoples and Ethnicity: An Archaeological Study of Egyptians, Canaanites, Philistines, and Early Israel, 1300–1100 B.C.E.* ABS 9. Society of Biblical Literature.
Faust, Avraham. 2006. *Israel's Ethnogenesis: Settlement, Interaction, Expansion and Resistance.* Equinox.
Rainey, Anson F. 2007. "Whence Came the Israelites and Their Language?" *IEJ* 57:41–64.
Saidel, Benjamin, and Evaline J. van der Steen, eds. 2007. *On the Fringe of Society: Archeological and Ethnoarchaeological Perspectives on Pastoral and Agricultural Societies.* BAR International Series 1657. Archaeopress.
Barnard, Hans, and Willeke Wendrich, eds. 2008. *The Archaeology of Mobility: Old World and New World Nomadism.* University of California Press.
Rainey, Anson F. 2008. "Shasu or Habiru? Who Were the Early Israelites?" *BAR* 34.6:51–55.
Hiebert, Theodore. 2009. "Israel's Ancestors Were Not Nomads." Pages 199–205 in *Exploring the Longue Durée: Essays in Honor of Lawrence E. Stager.* Edited by J. David Schloen. Eisenbrauns.
Saidel, Benjamin. 2009. "Pitching Camp: Ethnological Investigations of Inhabited Tent Camps in the Wadi Hisma, Jordan." Pages 87–104 in *Nomads, Tribes, and the State in the Ancient Near East: Cross-Disciplinary Perspectives.* Edited by Jeffrey Szuchman. OIS 5. University of Chicago Press.
Ebeling, Jennie R. 2010. *Women's Lives in Biblical Times.* T&T Clark.
Gitin, Seymour. 2010. "Philistines in the Book of Kings." Pages 301–64 in *The Book of Kings: Sources, Composition, Historiography and Reception.* Edited by Baruch Halpern and André Lemaire. VTSup 129. Brill.

Bunimovitz, Shmuel, and Zvi Lederman. 2011. "Close Yet Apart: Diverse Cultural Dynamics at Iron Age Beth-Shemesh and Lachish." Pages 33–53 in *The Fire Signals of Lachish: Studies in the Archaeology of Israel in the Late Bronze Age, Iron Age, and Persian Period in Honor of David Ussishkin*. Edited by Israel Finkelstein and Nadav Na'aman. Eisenbrauns.

Faust, Avraham, and Justin Lev-Tov. 2011. "The Constitution of Philistine Identity: Ethnic Dynamics in Twelfth to Tenth Century Philistia." *OJA* 30:13–31.

Dever, William G. 2012. *The Lives of Ordinary People in Ancient Israel: Where Archaeology and the Bible Intersect*. Eerdmans.

Porter, Ann. 2012. *Mobile Pastoralism and the Formation of Near Eastern Civilization: Weaving Together Society*. Cambridge University Press.

Killebrew, Ann E., and Gunnar Lehmann, eds. 2013. *The Philistines and Other "Sea Peoples" in Text and Archaeology*. ABS 15. Society of Biblical Literature.

Maeir, Aren M., Louse A. Hitchcock, and Liora K. Horowitz. 2013. "On the Constitution and Transformation of Philistine Identity." *OJA* 32:1–38.

Faust, Avraham, and Shlomo Bunimovitz. 2014. "The House and the World: The Israelite House as a Microcosm." Pages 143–64 in *Family and Household Religion: Toward a Synthesis of Old Testament Studies, Archaeology, Epigraphy, and Cultural Studies*. Edited by Rainer Albertz, Beth Alpert Nakhai, Saul M. Olyan, and Rüdiger Schmitt. Eisenbrauns.

Levy, Thomas E., Thomas Schneider, and William C. Propp, eds. 2015. *Israel's Exodus in Transdisciplinary Perspectives: Text, Archaeology, Culture, and Geoscience*. Springer.

Dever, William G. 2017. *Beyond the Texts: An Archaeological Portrait of Ancient Israel and Judah*. SBL Press. Pages 194–210, 249–53.

Faust, Avraham. 2018. "Pigs in Space (and Time): Pork Consumption and Identity Negotiation." *NEA* 81:276–99.

Sapir-Hen, Lidar. 2019. "Food, Pork Consumption, and Identity in Ancient Israel." *NEA* 82:52–59.

Faust, Avraham. 2020. "An All-Israelite Identity: Historical Reality or Biblical Myth?" Pages 169–92 in *The Wide Lens in Archaeology: Honoring Brian Hesse's Contributions to Anthropological Archaeology*. Edited by Justin Lev-Tov, Paula Wapnish, and Allan Gilbert. Lockwood.

Ben-Yosef, Erez. 2021. "Rethinking Social Complexity of Early Iron Age Nomads." *Jerusalem Journal of Archaeology.* 1:155–79.

Faust, Avraham. 2023. "The Problem of P: Israelite Society, Israel's Egalitarian Ethos, and the Raison D'être of the Priestly History." *BN* 197:3–36.

Maeir, Aren M. 2023. On Defining Israel: Or, Let's do the *Kulturkreslehre* Again! *Hebrew Bible and Ancient Israel* 10:106–47.

9
Archaeology, Urbanism, and the Rise of the Israelite State

Already in some of their earliest publications, revisionists had made the attack on the united monarchy one of their key points in what Baruch Halpern called the attempt to "erase ancient Israel from history" (see Halpern 1995 and bibliography for chapter 3, especially Davies 1992; Whitelam 1996; Lemche 1998; and Thompson 1999, cited there). By the mid- to late 1990s all the revisionists were united in denying that there ever had *been* a so-called united monarchy; kings such as Saul, David, and Solomon were "no more historical than King Arthur," Niels Peter Lemche and Thomas L. Thompson declared. Jerusalem was not the capital of any political entity before the ninth century BCE, and then only as the house of Omri, or province of Samarina (and Thompson hinted that Jerusalem was not a real capital until the Hasmonean era in the second century BCE). The revisionists were soon co-opting Israel Finkelstein's idiosyncratic 1996 low chronology in order to move all the archaeological evidence for statehood, that is, for urbanization and centralization, from the tenth to the ninth century BCE. Nevertheless, it was clear that the revisionists had no understanding of any of the complex stratigraphic and ceramic arguments, nor, for that matter, did they ever define what they meant by a state.

It became obvious to me that someone who knew the archaeological data, as well as the pivotal anthropological theory on state-formation processes, needed to intervene in this increasingly acrimonious and futile controversy. (I had published a preliminary analysis in 1994b, but few colleagues ever saw the proceedings of the congress on "Nouve fondazione" in Pisa.) When Wally Aufrecht convened an international symposium on "Urbanism in Antiquity" at Lethbridge University in the spring of 1995, I came from sabbatical on Cyprus to accept his invitation. Naturally, I chose to address the

---

Originally published as pages 172–93 in *Urbanism in Antiquity: From Mesopotamia to Crete*. Edited by Walter E. Aufrecht, Neil A. Mirau, and Steven W. Gauley. JSOTSup 244. Sheffield Academic, 1997. Reprinted by permission.

issue of Israelite urbanization in the tenth century BCE as one aspect of the rise of the state, the result being the paper published here.

Bibliography since this essay was written will be found in the Updated Bibliography (arranged chronologically) at the end of the Works Cited.

In the English-speaking world, scholarly interest has been focused on state-formation processes since Morton Fried's *The Evolution of Political Society: An Essay in Political Anthropology* (1967) and Elman R. Service's *Origins of the State and Civilization: The Process of Cultural Evolution* (1975). Service proposed an evolutionary sequence that envisioned all social organizations as moving inevitably through progressive stages, from band to tribe to chiefdom to state. Since then, more than twenty other major analyses have been published, many advancing rival theories of the state and state formation.[1]

Meanwhile, biblical scholars in the last two decades began to borrow socioanthropological models for elucidating biblical texts, in this case specifically the notions of (1) tribe, (2) chiefdom, and (3) state. These models were used to explain, in modern terms, the evolution of early Israel from a supposed tribal confederation in the twelfth–eleventh centuries BCE, to a chiefdom under Saul in the late eleventh century BCE, and, finally, to a fully developed nation-state under David and Solomon during the united monarchy in the tenth century BCE. Representative works in this genre would include those of de Geus 1976; Gottwald 1979; Frick 1985; Lemche 1985; and Flanagan 1988. There were also published in the 1970s and 1980s a dozen or more other major works on the emergence of early Israel, using more traditional literary-critical methods. In this paper, only the latter period, the tenth century BCE, which sees the formation of the Israelite state, will be discussed.

9.1. Recent Discussions on the Rise of the Israelite State

Some of the models suggested in the recent proliferation of theoretical literature on state-formation processes have been borrowed by a few

---

[1]. See the following major works: Renfrew 1972; Flannery 1972; Carneiro 1970; Friedman and Rowlands 1977; Cohen and Service 1978; Haas 1982; Tainter 1988.

historians of early Israel (e.g., Frick 1985; Coote and Whitelam 1987; Flanagan 1988; Fritz 1995). In all these works, definitions of the state vary widely, but there is a common denominator in the stress on centralization of decision-making and administration that denotes, practically speaking, kingship. Thus, the state is "bureaucratic governance by legal force." Or, "the State is a society in which there is a set of offices of the society at large, conferring governance over the society at large." A further distinction is often made between (1) pristine states that developed independently, of which only six are known (Service's "precocious" states): Egypt; Mesopotamia; the Indus Valley; the Han Dynasty in China; the Mesoamerican Maya-Aztec; and the Inca in Peru; and (2) secondary states, which are usually imposed by force on neighboring peoples, of which there are many examples. In addition, other scholars have sought to identify primitive states by the terms "inchoate early state" or "conditional state." More recent works, focusing specifically on the Near/Middle East, develop the model of tribal state, which refers specifically to indigenous Levantine societies that have remained tribal, or "segmentary," and characteristically nonurban, yet have developed sufficient centralized authority to qualify them as states, as, for example, in Transjordan. Despite this typology of early states, Richard Tapper has cautioned that such categories may be too rigid, that most early states are in fact hybrids.[2]

But why did states form at all? In his seminal work *The Collapse of Societies* (1988), Joseph Tainter, following Henry T. Wright (1977), has arranged the various hypotheses into four general categories: (1) managerial; (2) internal conflict; (3) external conflict; and (4) synthetic. These can be further reduced to just two main schools of thought, that is, conflict and integration. Here, only Tainter's managerial and synthetic scenarios will be examined, with reference to the case of ancient Israel.[3]

The managerial model holds that, as populations increase and societies come under socioeconomic stress, managerial hierarchies inevitably emerge to meet the challenge. This model is perhaps most useful in

---

2. See Service 1962, 175; Sahlins 1968, 6; Claessen and Skalnik 1978; Webb 1975. For further discussion, see the convenient summary and bibliography in Tainter 1988, 26–38; Koury and Kostiner 1990; and especially Tapper 1990.

3. See Tainter 1988. Marxist class-conflict theories such as Fried 1967 have too much excess Hegelian baggage, and external conflict theories such as Carneiro's 1970 circumscription model are not wholly applicable to early Israel.

explaining pristine states, but there is no inherent reason why it cannot also be applied to what one could call peripheral states such as ancient Israel. But how well does such a model fit, either with the textual or the archaeological data?

The biblical texts are not unanimous in their explanation of the rise of kingship. The Deuteronomistic writers and editors of Samuel–Kings belonged to ultra-orthodox theocratic parties and were thus quite naturally antistatist in outlook. Indeed, in the annalistic accounts in Kings, the writers really approve of only three kings in the four-hundred-year history of Israel and Judah: David, always the ideal (and idealized) prototype; and Hezekiah and Josiah, late reform kings of Judah who had obviously been co-opted by the extremist religious parties. Thus, in the final redaction of the biblical tradition, the prophet Samuel, who represents the antimonarchic ideal par excellence, is confronted by the people's demands for a king "like all the nations," presumably to meet the growing Philistine military threat (1 Sam 8:5). Samuel warns them of the dire consequences of setting up any sovereign but Yahweh, but nonetheless he is forced to acquiesce. Samuel thus anoints Saul, who is then acclaimed king by a sort of popular election, that is, a widespread recognition of his charismatic powers, which are seen as signs of divine approval. In other strands of the literary tradition, however, Saul's rise to kingship is looked upon in a more favorable light, as a beneficial and even necessary adaptation to the changing needs of an increasingly complex society. This biblical explanation would conform to elements of both Tainter's managerial and synthetic models.

Although all the literary materials have been later woven into the fabric of Deuteronomistic antiroyalist propaganda in the Bible, it is striking that the contradictions have not been edited out. This fact suggests an ambivalence about kingship that was genuine, indeed native, to early and even to later Israel. In any case, however, the textual tradition in the Hebrew Bible cannot yield for us today a satisfactory historical explanation of the state when taken at face value, for these texts are late, tendentious, and elitist. Several recent studies by biblical scholars, however, outline a more radical approach, and it is interesting that all agree in suggesting that archaeological data may provide a corrective to the texts.[4]

---

4. For orientation to the burgeoning literature, see Davies 1992, 1995; Lemche and Thompson 1994; Finkelstein and Na'aman 1994; Lemche 1996; Thompson

For example, Frank S. Frick's (1985) study on the rise of the Israelite state begins with the evolutionary sequence of tribe to chiefdom to state, following Fried, Service, and others. Rather than invoking any sort of determinism, however, Frick stresses the many factors that led to statehood, using a General Systems Theory approach. He attempts a survey of the archaeological and especially the ecological data in portraying earliest Israel as a highland agricultural society. He sees growth toward centralization, and ultimately the monarchy, largely as an overall "adaptive transformation," although the Philistine threat may have been one factor. Frick's approach is refreshing, but his use of the strictly archaeological data, mostly of the twelfth–eleventh centuries BCE, is much too limited to achieve his stated goal of socioanthropological explanation.

Robert B. Coote and Keith W. Whitelam's 1987 attempt to explain the rise of Israel as a natural development within the context of the long settlement history of the southern Levant is a laudable departure, and they make much more (though not always expert) use of archaeological evidence. For them, the rise of the monarchy is part of a cultural continuum, a matter of internal dynamics rather than either external threat or dialectical conflict. The monarchy was thus, in contrast to the later biblical tradition, not an alien and hostile institution at all. As for further explanation, Coote and Whitelam are inclined toward Robert L. Carneiro's conscription theory, though interpreted somewhat more broadly. Thus, "It is the combination of environmental and social circumscription with other internal and external factors that provide the impetus to the formation of the Israelite state."[5]

The most ambitious recent attempt to apply socioanthropological models to early Israel is that of James W. Flanagan (1988). Unfortunately, sociological jargon tends to obscure any value his novel "hologram" of early Israel might have. Take this quotation, for example:

> If we follow the biblical precedent and read the information sources together but without the restraints of the narrative sequence and rigid archaeological space-time systemics, the archaeological and literary models suggest simultaneous processes of devolution and evolution

---

1995; Provan 1995; cf. Dever 1991a, 1991b, 1994a, 1995, 1996a, 1996b, 1997a, 1997b.

5. Coote and Whitelam 1987, 147.

similar to the symbioses among sedentary, semi-nomadic and nomadic peoples documented in comparative sociology.⁶

Apparently this means that (1) societies are complex and (2) things change. To his credit, however, Flanagan does attempt to use archaeological, ecological, and even ethnographic data, as well as various systemic and holistic approaches. Nevertheless, in the end, all Flanagan really seems to say is that the rise of the Israelite state was due to a process of centralization and adaptation. The major weakness is the book's pretentious, but amateur and idiosyncratic, archaeological reconstruction of the Iron I period.

9.2. The Revisionist Paradigm and Early Israel

Subsequent to an earlier survey of the literature on the rise of the Israelite state, the discussion has mushroomed, largely because the question of statehood has now become part of the issue of whether it is possible to write a history of biblical (i.e., monarchical or Iron Age) Israel at all.⁷

These revisionist historians, as they call themselves, might well be called the new nihilists, recalling, of course, the clash in the 1950s between the American school W. F. Albright, G. Ernest Wright, and John Bright and the German school of Albrecht Alt, Martin Noth, Gerhard von Rad

---

6. Flanagan 1988, 288. The hologram is on the cover; it also waves.

7. Several recent papers (Dever 1996a, 1996b, 1997a, 1997b, 1998) have included comments on the historiographical crisis that many biblical scholars now acknowledge because of the nature of the texts. Archaeologists must be involved in this crisis because most participants are oblivious to or deliberately ignore the proliferating archaeological data that could prove decisive or, worse, misrepresent the proper relationship between archaeology and biblical studies (e.g., Whitelam 1994). Furthermore, in the last two years or so, historiographic views aired by biblical scholars in the annual meetings, in journals, in popular magazines, even on the internet, have become increasingly dogmatic, raucous, and even vindictive (Lemche and Thompson 1994, 3–4; Thompson 1995; Davies 1995, 700; Whitelam 1994). The few who have attempted to introduce archaeological data into the discussion are dismissed as "positivist," "maximalists," old-fashioned "biblical archaeologists," or even, astonishingly (in the case of the writer), as "fundamentalists," despite the twenty-five-year long battle against traditional-style "biblical archaeology" (Dever 1985 and references; 1993).

9. Archaeology, Urbanism, and the Rise of the Israelite State

and others over the historicity of the patriarchs. The principal full-scale works of the new nihilists are by David W. Jamieson-Drake (1991), Philip R. Davies (1992), Thomas L. Thompson (1992), and Keith W. Whitelam (1994, 1996). A review of the historiographical and methodological issues will be found in Diana V. Edelman (1991), which is already dated. All these discussions imply certain notions of urbanism and statehood, so they need to be analyzed here.[8]

The most recent, and most extreme, pronouncement of the revisionists is that of Lemche and Thompson:

> That is the issue we have today: namely, the question of whether the Bible in its stories is talking about history and the past at all. Our argument is not that the Bible exaggerates the exploits of David, nor is it that Solomon was never as rich as the Bible makes him out to be. We are not dealing with issues of skepticism here. Rather, we are trying to argue that the Bible's stories of Saul, David and Solomon are not about history at all. History writing is a very different thing from what the Bible's authors were doing.... To compare the Bible's tales about David with early Iron Age Palestine is like comparing the story of Gilgamesh with Bronze Age Uruk, Homer with ancient Mycenae, or, indeed, Arthur with early mediaeval England, or even Wagner's Siegfried with a Germany of the early Middle Ages.[9]

They go on to say:

> In the history of Palestine that we have presented, there is no room for a historical United Monarchy, or for such kings as those presented in the biblical stories of Saul, David or Solomon. The early period in which the traditions have set their narratives is an imaginary world of long ago that never existed as such. In the real world of that time, for instance, only a few dozen villagers lived as farmers in all of the Judaean highlands. Timber, grazing lands and steppe were all marginal possibilities. There could not have been a kingdom for any Saul or David to be king of, simply because there were not enough people. Not only did a state of Judah not yet exist, but we have no evidence of there having been any political force anywhere in Palestine that was large enough or developed enough to have been even conceivably capable of unifying the many different economies and regions of this land, given the near political

---

8. See n. 7 above.
9. Lemche and Thompson 1994, 18–20.

vacuum of the tenth century BCE. Rather, at this time, Palestine was far less unified than it had been for more than a thousand years. Jerusalem at this time can hardly be spoken of as a city.... Its relationship to Judah was marginal. It first took on the form and acquired the status of a city, capable of being understood as a state capital, sometime in the middle of the seventh century.[10]

Such *obiter dicta* of these revisionist historians reveal how oblivious they are to the mass of archaeological data now known. The latest absurdity is the unanimous rejection by the revisionists of the Tel Dan inscription found in 1993, a monumental Aramaic victory stela mentioning kings of Israel and specifically the "house of David." Additional fragments found in 1994 enable us to reconstruct the name of Jehoram (or Joram), who ruled 849–842 BCE, making the Aramaean king in question Hazael of Damascus. Now for many years biblicists have been chiding archaeologists for failure to turn up more written evidence. But when by chance a stunning early monumental inscription does turn up, and it can be dated almost precisely to the year, what do they do? They explain it away as being out of context and a century and a half later, torturing the paleographic arguments; or they read the crux, the phrase *btdwd*, as a place name rather than a personal name, on the pretext that a word divider is missing; and they even imply that the inscription may be a forgery, planted on the excavator, the venerable Avraham Biran. The careful and unbiased observer, however, who knows archaeology, epigraphy, and a bit of biblical criticism cannot escape the suspicion that Lemche, Thompson, and Whitelam (especially) cannot admit any evidence for an early Israel, much less a state, because they have gone too far out on a limb previously, declaring that on principle there cannot have been a real biblical Israel in the Iron Age; it is all a literary construct, a Persian-Hellenistic phantasmagoria. Yet the dogmatism of the revisionists is rather like that of the fundamentalists whom they decry so furiously. Their mind is made up; do not confuse them with facts.[11]

---

10. Lemche and Thompson 1994, 18–20.

11. The European School would no doubt charge in return that those who have the "biblical archaeological-harmonistic presuppositions common to much American reading" (Thompson 1995, 696) presume that there *must* have been an Iron Age Israel. That, however, is not true: most simply presume that sound historical method must allow for the possibility that there *can* have been such an Israel and that one must sift carefully through both biblical texts and archaeological evidence

9. Archaeology, Urbanism, and the Rise of the Israelite State

The revisionists' flawed historiographical (and theological?) presuppositions, as well as their neglect or abuse of the rich archaeological data that are now available, have been dealt with elsewhere.[12] Here one can only take up the challenge that they pose for the theme of this volume, namely, their assertion that there was no early Israelite state. It would be tempting, of course, to ignore the revisionists because they have so discredited themselves. But, since many biblicists have ceased to be interested in history and are pursuing ever more exotic literary theories, we undeconstructed archaeologists (who have always been historians) must come forward in the defense of ancient Israel. It really did exist, in spite of all the postmodernist piffle that one reads today. It is archaeology that resurrects those who, in the Bible's words, "sleep in the dust," that gives back to the people of the past their own long-lost voice. To argue that this Israel is not the ideal Israel of the reactionary orthodox writers of the Bible, is completely irrelevant. Of course, one must reject *Heilsgeschichte* as history, but there is another, "secular" history of Israel, a socioeconomic rather than political history, waiting to be written. And it will be written largely by Syro-Palestinian archaeologists, who now master a mature, independent discipline and who in today's climate of postprocessual archaeology will find history writing once again a respectable profession.[13]

---

to sort out reliable data, willing to recognize that when they do happen to converge (as often) it is the best witness to the reality of ancient Israel. One might recall the wise caution of a now-dismissed "positivist" biblical historian, John Bright, who reminded us that the historian *always* works with "the balance of probability." Both fundamentalism and liberal revisionism transgress that rule when they take dogmatic, extremist positions.

12. See Halpern 1995; Dever 1995, 1996a, 1996b, 1997a; and the mass of Iron Age archaeological data summarized in such standard reference works as Weippert 1988; Mazar 1990; and Ben-Tor 1992, to name only a few. Davies (1992, 24) dismisses Mazar's 160 pages on the Iron Age in a single footnote, as "irrelevant" for a reconstruction of ancient Israel, because Davies's own "Israel" is only a literary construct of the Persian period. This alone would illustrate why many of the revisionist statements are *presuppositions*, not conclusions. The point is that the revisionists assay to do archaeology but appear not to have even a minimal grasp of the methods and aim of today's archaeology or its potential for history writing.

13. See Hodder 1986; Dever 1995, 1997b.

9.3. On Defining the Terms of the Discussion

From its beginning, the present discussion on urbanization and statehood has been plagued by a general lack of definition of the basic terms, reflecting the unfamiliarity of most biblicists and Syro-Palestinian archaeologists with what is a considerable and sophisticated ethnographic and anthropological literature.

The older term *civilization*, which implied but rarely defined urbanization, has largely been replaced by the term *complex society*. By this latter term most socioanthropologists and other commentators refer to social configurations that are not only large, multifaceted, and often independent but are also marked by inequalities, that is, are hierarchically ordered, with individuals having differential access to goods and services based on inherited or acquired rank. Such differentiation is, indeed, more likely to take place in large urban settings, where administration is centralized. The term *complex society* is perhaps less ambiguous and thus better than *civilization*.

The term *urban* had been notoriously ambiguous, often among archaeologists denoting little more than a large or walled town. V. Gordon Childe (1950), who like Robert McCormick Adams (1966) virtually assumed that urban was synonymous with civilization, developed a trait list that today is often forgotten. Among Childe's criteria were such variables as size, socioeconomic stratification, institutionalized political administration, ability to produce surplus and sustain long-distance trade, monumental art and architecture, and the use of writing. The frustration with such trait lists, however, is that many of the variables in urbanization (such as the term *chiefdoms* mentioned above) are difficult or impossible to measure archaeologically; furthermore, any such list is bound to be somewhat subjective, even arbitrary.

A more objective, quantifiable model of urbanism for the southern Levant has been developed by Steven Falconer in his 1987 Arizona dissertation entitled "Heartland of Villages: Reconsidering Early Urbanism in the Southern Levant," obviously a takeoff from Adams's classic work on settlement patterns. Falconer basically argues that a population agglomerate may be defined as urban when it outgrows its capacity to feed and sustain itself on immediately available resources and so must organize and control the surrounding agricultural hinterland, that is, must become essentially a market town in central-place theory terminology. On the rich alluvial plains of southern Mesopotamia, agricultural yields can easily be calculated. The threshold at which the transition to an urban center took place can be fixed at about 85 acres, or a population of some 8,000–9,000. Of course, the southern Levant is characterized by a much smaller-scale landscape, not only fragmented but much less productive, because of poor soil and water sources. Thus, in the southern Levant, the threshold for truly urban configurations must be placed at about 15 acres and some 1,500 population. Frank Kolb (1984) proposed an even smaller criterion, 25 acres and 1,000 population (although if his 100 persons per hectare is raised to the more typical figure of 250, one arrives at a population estimate of 2,500). These widely accepted rules of thumb will be returned to when asking whether or not Israel in the Iron Age constituted an urban society.[14]

9.4. On the Relations between State, Civilization, and Urbanization: Toward a Working Methodology

A working model for identifying any state-formation process in early Israel may stem more from analysis of the relations between the concepts and terms defined above than from the definition themselves. For most earlier scholars, civilization was usually synonymous with state, and that may still be presumed. The more difficult question is the relation of urbanization to both. That is to say, can one have a true state without a high degree of urbanization? Or, to put it another way, is urbanization a prerequisite of the state, even the cause of state-formation processes? As noted above, two distinguished scholars, Adams (1966) and Childe (1950), have argued that urbanization does not cause the state but that it is the other way around: urbanization presumes the prior existence of the state. Service, however, disagrees, and one is inclined to side with him.[15] For example, all authorities would agree that the southern Levant in the Early and Middle Bronze Ages was highly urbanized, but no one supposes that a state yet existed, only the characteristic pattern of south Levantine city-states.

However the problem is approached, two things seem clear. On the one hand, there are early states that are predominantly nonurban, such

---

14. See Adams 1981; Kolb 1984.
15. See Service 1975, 280–82.

as Han Dynasty China and several of the Mesoamerican states. On the other hand, urbanization does ordinarily precede the development of the state, and although the development of cities does not necessarily cause the emergence of state-level organization, often it is a contributing factor. Thus, for methodological purposes, it may be assumed that a high degree of urbanization is the best criterion for recognizing at least incipient or peripheral states. Such an assumption underlies the following argument vis-à-vis early Israel. The justification for the argument is simply that both urbanization and the formation of states require and presuppose centralization of authority, and it is that phenomenon that archaeology, not texts, is often in the best position to analyze.

9.5. Archaeological Evidence for Centralization and Urbanization in Tenth-Century BCE Israel

9.5.1. Demography

Earlier scholars such as Albright had estimated the population of Iron II Israel (i.e., the period of the divided monarchy) to be as high as 900,000. Much more sophisticated recent demographic estimates, based on ethnoarchaeology, extensive surface surveys, and settlement-pattern studies, yield more realistic figures, broken down by subphases. Thus Finkelstein and others arrive at a population of some 50,000–65,000 for the Proto-Israelite period of the twelfth–eleventh centuries BCE. By the ninth–eighth centuries BCE, Yigael Shiloh estimates growth to about 150,000. Thus the population in the tenth century BCE may have been about 100,000.[16]

Compare these carefully researched figures of archaeologists with Lemche and Thompson's absurd "few dozen villages … in all the Judaean highlands" in the tenth century BCE.[17] For better comparisons, note that the lowland Maya state of Tikal had only perhaps 25,000—40,000 people, and several of the multivalley Andean states had populations of only 75,000–160,000.[18] Thus, on the basis of gross population size alone, Lemche and Thompson's attempt to deny early Israel state status can easily

---

16. See Dever 1996b, with references.
17. Lemche and Thompson 1994, 19.
18. Service 1975, 186–202.

be dismissed. Of course, even dramatic population increases from the twelfth to the tenth century BCE do not in themselves give evidence of urbanization or statehood, but there are other data to examine.

9.5.2. Settlement Type and Distribution

A better indication is the phenomenon of the concentration of the population in a relatively few large central cities, with the shrinkage or abandonment of many smaller rural sites, or what archaeologists call a classic three-tiered, hierarchically ordered settlement pattern. The southern Levant certainly reflects such a shift from the twelfth to the tenth century BCE. Most of the three hundred or so twelfth- to eleventh-century BCE "Proto-Israelite villages" that are known are abandoned by the mid to late tenth century BCE, with relatively few developing continuously into major Iron II tells. On the other hand, several sites, perhaps as many as eleven, do develop into what may legitimately be called cities by the above criteria (i.e., roughly one hundred persons per acre of built-up area).

These are (table 9.1): Dan, Hazor, Megiddo, Taʿanach, Beth-shan, Tell el-Farʿah (N), Shechem, Aphek, Gezer, Jerusalem, and Lachish.

Table 9.1 Three-tier hierarchy of major tenth-century BCE sites in Iron II Israel with population estimates.[19] Tier 1 includes cities whose population totaled circa 20,000; tier 2 includes towns; tier 3 includes villages, hamlets, camps, and the like.

Rank	Site and stratum	Size in acres	Population	Ninth century BCE	Source
Tier 1	Dan IVB–A	25.0	2,500	III	
	Hazor IX	15.0	1,500	VIII–VII	
	Megiddo VA/IVB	13.5 (15–25)	1,300 (500)	IVA	YS, H
	Taʿanach IIA–B	16.0	1,600	III	
	Beth-shean Upper	10.0	1,000	IV	
	Tell el-Farʿah (N) VIIb	15.01 (?)	1,500	VIIc–d	
	Shechem X	13.0	1,300	IX	

---

19. Some coastal and Jordan Valley sites are eliminated, since they are probably not ethnically Israelite. YS = Shiloh 1980; H = Herzog 1992a, 1992b.

Rank	Sites/stratum	Size (acres)	Population	Ninth century BCE	Source
	Aphek X₆	15.0	1,500	X₇	
	Gezer IX–VIII	33.0	3,300	VII	
	Jerusalem 14	32.0	2,500	13	YS
	Lachish V	18.01 (38)	1,800 (500)	IV	YS, H
Tier 2	Tel Kinrot V–IV	1.25	1,250	III	
	Tel Amal III	0.75	75		
	Yoqneam XVI–XIV	10.0	1,000	XIII	
	Tel Qiri VIIA	2.5	250	VIIB–C	
	Dothan 4 (?)	10.0 (15)	1,000		YS
	Tel Mevorakh VIII–VII	1.5	150		
	Tell Michal XIV–XIII	0.3	30		
	Tell Qasile IX–VIII	4.0	400	VII	
	Azekah	14 (?)	1,400 (?)		
	Tel Batash IV	6.5	650	III	
	Beth-shemesh IIa	10.0	1,000	IIb	
	Tell el-Ful II	?	?		
	Tell Hama	1.0	100		
	Tell Mazar XII	?	?		
	Tell Beit Mirsim B₃	7.5	750 (1,300)	A₂	H
	Tel Halif VII	3.0	300	VIA	
	Tel Ser'a VII	5.0	500	VI	
	Beersheba VI (V?)	2.5	250 (600)	(V) IV	H
	Arad XII	?	?	XI–X	
Tier 3	Tell el-Kheleifeh I			II?	
	Qadesh-barnea I			2	
	Negev forts				

Together these eleven Tier 1 cities may have had a total population of 20,000 or more, about 20 percent of the total population of some 100,000 that can be projected for the tenth century BCE. The relatively larger number of middle-tier sites required by the three-tier model of urbanization adopted by nearly all archaeologists would number at least twenty other towns, as Amahai Mazar and Volkmar Fritz have shown, most in the 300–1,000 range. The remaining two-thirds of the population would then have lived in dozens of smaller towns and villages in the rural areas and in hamlets, farmsteads and pastoral encampments in the hinterland.[20]

9.5.3. Regional Administrative Centers

Not only is the emergent pattern of urbanism clear in tenth-century BCE Israel, but it is precisely the few larger central places or market towns and administrative centers—such as Hazor, Megiddo, and Gezer—that exhibit nearly identical casemate city walls and four-entryway gates, as well as palaces or citadels adjacent to the fortifications (perhaps Lachish as well). As Yigael Yadin long ago pointed out, these similarities in design and engineering can hardly be coincidence.[21] They are obviously the result of centralized planning, not simply at one site, but countrywide, or, we may say, nationwide. Another indication of centralized planning is the construction of as many as fifty fortresses or enclosed settlements in the southern Negev Desert (rarely heavily populated in any period), most of them dated to the tenth century BCE.[22] What do these fortify, unless the borders of a self-conscious, independent state? The crucial data for attributing the above sites, together with a considerable archaeological assemblage, to the mid- to late tenth century BCE (i.e., to the time of Solomon) is (1) the distinctive red-slipped and hand-burnished (i.e., not yet wheel-burnished) ceramics, dated since the 1930s to the tenth century BCE; and (2) the fact that a terminal date for these diagnostic wares can apparently be historically fixed by destruction layers at several sites, probably related to Egyptian texts describing a Palestinian raid by Pharaoh Shoshenq circa 930 BCE (i.e., the biblical Shishak), which is said in 2 Kgs 14:25 to have taken place five years after Solomon's death. That correlation

---

20. For more detailed surveys of the data, see Weippert 1988, 471–781; Mazar 1990, 368–402; Fritz 1995, 76–120; Barkay 1992, 305–27; Holladay 1995; and Dever 1997a. On demography, see Shiloh 1980; Finkelstein 1988, 330–35; and Broshi and Finkelstein 1992. On rank-size and three-tier hierarchy models, see Hodder and Orton 1976, 55–73.
21. Yadin 1958.
22. Mazar 1990, 390–97.

yields a late tenth-century BCE date for the archaeological materials in question.[23]

Of course, a number of archaeologists of the Tel Aviv school now attempt to date some of the fortifications at Hazor, Megiddo, and elsewhere down into the ninth century BCE. But their arguments are based on faulty stratigraphy and ceramic typology.[24] Even if a ninth-century BCE date were conceded, however, one would still have to posit statelevel organization at that time, which the revisionists deny for Judah until the late seventh century BCE. The revisionists simply do not understand that a state, like an urban settlement plan, is defined not by the absolute size of the population aggregate but rather by settlement hierarchy and above all by centralization.

One useful model for understanding the emergence of urban centers is that of disembedded capitals. These are administrative centers that develop as relatively compact sites, often established *de novo*, or are refounded deliberately, and are built up of largely public buildings and facilities but contain relatively few domestic structures. From what we know of tenth-century BCE (or "Solomonic") Jerusalem, it is a classic example of a disembedded capital (which, it happens, fits the biblical description almost precisely), as is Samaria in the ninth–eighth centuries BCE. In the comparative literature, these Israelite and Judean cities would certainly be considered capitals of states.

9.5.4. Socioeconomic Structure

By the late tenth century BCE, Israelite society and economy were stratified and highly specialized. The gradual shift from a simple village-based, agrarian, acephalous kinship structure to an urban industrialized and entrepreneurial society is complete. A class of elites is clear in the archeological record, although luxury goods are still relatively rare. On the

---

23. On the hand-burnished pottery and the *terminus ante quem* that the Shishak raid supplies, see Holladay 1995, 372, 377–86. See also below and n. 24.

24. See Dever 1986 and full references there. The issues were aired in 1990 in an entire issue (no. 277/278) of *BASOR*, with arguments on the maximalist side by Holladay, Stager, and Dever and on the minimalist side by Finkelstein, Ussishkin, and Wightman. For the next round, see Holladay 1995 and especially Dever 1997a (in reply to Herzog).

basis of our present evidence, it appears that literacy was probably not very widespread: the twelfth-century BCE 'Izbet Ṣarṭah abecedary and the tenth-century BCE Gezer schoolboy's exercise tablet indicate at least functional literacy.

9.5.5. Material Culture

It is the overall material culture—domestic architecture, burial customs, and especially ceramics—that attests to a changeover from the formative period of the twelfth–eleventh centuries BCE to the florescent period that begins in the tenth century BCE and lasts until the early sixth century BCE, that is, the monarchical period. The pottery repertoire in particular exhibits a high degree of standardization of cultural norms, but the dominance of the so-called four-room house is no less indicative of cultural homogeneity. The emergence of a generic Iron II Israelite material culture is not fortuitous but reflects now a much more unified "national" ideology and ethnic solidarity. Even if the biblical label "Israelite-Judean" were unknown, one would recognize in the archaeological remains alone a national culture, that is, a true state.[25]

9.5.6. Internationalism

Finally, this growing sense of national identity expresses itself in Israel's emergence from relative isolation in the twelfth–eleventh centuries BCE into international trade and competition by the tenth century BCE. On the one hand, Phoenician and Cypriot arts and crafts are imported. On the other hand, decisive battles with the local Philistines take place, and the first sharp rivalries occur with other regional states, such as Ammon, Moab, and Edom in Transjordan and (before long) with the incipient Aramaean and Syro-Hittite states to the north.

Not only are these typical state-level processes of development clear in the archaeological record; they also accord quite well with detailed reports in the Bible in Samuel–Kings of the reigns of David and Solomon. Some biblical scholars are inclined to doubt the historical trustworthiness of the biblical version (above). Others, however, rightly regard the literary tradi-

---

25. See the material cited in n. 24. On the *continuity* of material culture from Iron I through Iron II, see Dever 1998.

tion as based, at least in part, on eyewitness accounts, archival records, and other quite reliable sources (although, of course, somewhat exaggerated in the final interpretation given in the Hebrew Bible). Indeed, few scholars until recently have ever questioned that by the tenth-century BCE ancient Israel did constitute a national state; it is largely the question of causation that is of concern here.

9.5.7. Centralization, Urbanization, and Statehood

Childe's trait lists of the characteristics of an urbanized, state-level society were noted above. It may be pertinent that, of his ten characteristics, tenth-century BCE Israel exhibits at least eight, and the other two are plausible, although in the nature of the case there is scant archaeological evidence (i.e., the beginnings of science and sophisticated art). Other authorities identify a site as urban if it (1) is a topographical unit with a fortification wall; (2) is densely occupied; (3) reflects social differentiation and centralized administration; (4) gives evidence of economic accumulation (surpluses) and distribution; (5) and constitutes a central place. By these criteria, some twenty sites in tenthcentury BCE Israel would qualify as urban. The point of the foregoing analysis is that, if we follow Adams's view that, in the typical evolutionary trajectory toward complex society, urbanization proceeds and presumes the development of social stratification and the state, then clearly urban Israel in the tenth century BCE was a state.[26] The archaeological data, even when surveyed minimally, are decisive. If the name "Israel" were not attested in the biblical or other texts, we should have to invent another term for this state, if not Solomon, then Solomon by another name. That our archaeologically attested Israel is not the exact equivalent of the idealistic biblical Israel is again evident but irrelevant.

Why do many biblicists like the revisionists not see this point? Why do they dismiss the biblical texts as unhistorical but then fail to grasp the obvious implication that it is the archaeological data that are now primary? Davies, Thompson, Lemche, and Whitelam have all made remarks in passing that reveal that they sense the importance of archaeology, but they continue to make declarations that fly in the face of all the archaeo-

---

26. Adams 1972.

logical evidence now available. Indeed, they appear to *ignore* the recent literature and data. For this, they cannot be forgiven, being scholars and historians, obligated to utilize all the rich data now available. Not only is early Israel now being recognized as a state, even if of the early inchoate or peripheral variety, but even the Transjordanian entities of Ammon, Moab, and Edom are seen in the proliferating recent literature as moving toward statehood (perhaps of the tribal variety) by the tenth century BCE.[27] Revisionist historians who are oblivious to these currents in scholarship are as reactionary as those theologians they so readily castigate. Neither can they any longer write a comprehensive, balanced, satisfying history of ancient Israel in the Iron Age, as Thompson attempts. Only archaeologists, and those working in dialogue with them, can. The fundamental question, long tacitly recognized, is: What kind of history of ancient Israel do we want, and what do we think is possible?

9.6. Conclusion

Presently, one can say of the development from village to state in ancient Israel only that this was a typical archaeological-cultural evolutionary phase. It is but a single episode in the long settlement history of the southern Levant, which looms larger in Western consciousness only because of the Jewish and Christian traditions. We must recall that throughout the history of this area (and indeed of the whole Middle East, whether ancient and modern) there have always been these recurring cycles of advance and abatement, specialization and despecialization, complexity and collapse. For the most part, the basic phenomenon has been the oscillation between rural and urban styles of life. The Israelite monarchy represents but a brief, illusory triumph of the sown over the desert.[28]

---

27. See Daviau 1997, Herr 1997, and Routledge 1997.

28. After this chapter was submitted, Finkelstein 1996 argued that there is at least as much evidence for dating the "Solomonic" complex discussed here to the ninth century BCE as there is for dating it to the tenth century BCE. Since, however, he had previously argued that there was *no* evidence for a tenth-century BCE date, that would seem to leave him with no ground on which to stand. Such pure speculation does not advance the discussion.

Works Cited

Adams, Robert McCormick. 1966. *The Evolution of Urban Society*. Aldine.
———. 1972. "Patterns of Urbanization in Early Southern Mesopotamia." Pages 735–49 in *Man, Settlement and Urbanism: Proceedings of a Meeting of the Research Seminar in Archaeology and Related Subjects Held at the Institute of Archaeology, London University*. Edited by Peter J. Ucko, Ruth Tringham, and G. W. Dimbleby. Duckworth.
———. 1981. *Heartland of Cities: Surveys of Ancient Settlement and Land Use on the Central Floodplain of the Eurphrates*. University of Chicago Press.
Barkay, Gabriel. 1992. "The Iron Age II–III." Pages 302–73 in *The Archaeology of Ancient Israel*. Edited by Amnon Ben-Tor. Yale University Press.
Ben-Tor, Amnon, ed. 1992. *The Archaeology of Ancient Israel*. Yale University Press.
Broshi, Magon, and Israel Finkelstein. 1992. "The Population of Palestine in Iron Age II." *BASOR* 287:47–60.
Carneiro, Robert L. 1970. "A Theory of the Origin of the State." *Science* 109:733–38.
Childe, V. Gordon. 1950. "The Urban Revolution." *Town Planning Review* 21:3–17.
Claessen, Henri J. M., and Peter Skalnik. 1978. "The Early State: Theories and Hypotheses." Pages 3–29 in *The Early State: Models and Reality*. Edited by Henri J. M. Claessen and Peter Skalnik. Mouton.
Cohen, Ronald, and Elman R. Service, eds. 1978. *Origins of the State: The Anthropology of Political Evolution*. Institute for the Study of Human Issues.
Coote, Robert B., and Keith W. Whitelam. 1987. *The Emergence of Early Israel in Historical Perspective*. SWBA 5. Almond.
Daviau, P. M. Michèle. 1997. "Tell Jawa: A Case Study of Ammonite Urbanism during Iron Age II." Pages 156–71 in *Urbanism in Antiquity: From Mesopotamia to Crete*. Edited by Walter E. Aufrecht, Neil A. Mirau, and Steven W. Gauley. JSOTSup 244. Sheffield Academic.
Davies, Philip R. 1992. *In Search of "Ancient Israel."* JSOTSup 148. JSOT Press.
———. 1995. "Method and Madness: Some Remarks on Doing History with the Bible." *JBL* 114:669–705.

Dever, William G. 1985. "Syro-Palestinian and Biblical Archaeology." Pages 31–74 in *The Hebrew Bible and Its Modern Interpreters*. Edited by Douglas A. Knight and Gene M. Tucker. Fortress; Scholars Press.

———. 1986. "Late Bronze Age and Solomonic Defenses at Gezer: New Evidence." *BASOR* 262:9–34.

———. 1991a. "Archaeology, Material Culture and the Early Monarchial Period in Israel." Pages 103–15 in *Fabric of History: Text, Artifact and Israel's Past*. Edited by Diana Vikander Edelman. JSOTSup 127. JSOT Press.

———. 1991b. "Unresolved Issues in the Early History of Israel: Toward a Synthesis of Archaeological and Textual Reconstructions." Pages 195–208 in *The Bible and the Politics of Exegesis: Essays in Honor of Norman K. Gottwald on His Sixty-Fifth Birthday*. Edited by David Jobling. Pilgrim.

———. 1993. "Biblical Archaeology—Death and Rebirth?" Pages 706–22 in *Biblical Archaeology Today, 1990: Proceedings of the Second International Congress on Biblical Archaeology, Jerusalem, June 1990*. Edited by Avraham Biran and Joseph Aviram. Israel Exploration Society. Republished as chapter 2 in this volume.

———. 1994a. "Archaeology, Texts, and History-Writing: Toward an Epistemology." Pages 105–17 in *Uncovering Ancient Stones: Essays in Memory of H. Neil Richardson*. Edited by Lewis M. Hopfe. Eisenbrauns.

———. 1994b. "From Tribe to Nation: A Critique of State Formation Processes in Ancient Israel." Pages 213–38 in *Nuove fondazioni nel Vicino Oriente antico: Realtà e ideologia*. Edited by Stefania Mazzoni. University of Pisa.

———. 1995. "'Will the Real Israel Please Stand Up?' Archaeology and Israelite Historiography: Part 1." *BASOR* 297:61–80.

———. 1996a. "The Identity of Early Israel: A Rejoinder to Keith W. Whitelam." *JSOT* 72:3–24.

———. 1996b. "Revisionist Israel Revisited: A Rejoinder to Niels Peter Lemche." *CurBS* 4:35–50.

———. 1997a. "Archaeology and the 'Age of Solomon': A Case Study in Archaeology and Historiography." Pages 217–51 in *The Age of Solomon: The Scholarship at the Turn of the Millennium*. Edited by Lowell K. Handy. SHANE 11. Brill.

———. 1997b. "On Listening to the Texts—and the Artifacts." Pages 1–23 in *The Echoes of Many Texts: Reflections on Jewish and Christian Tra-*

ditions. Edited by William G. Dever and J. Edward Wright. Scholars Press. Republished as chapter 4 in this volume.

———. 1998. "Israelite Origins and the 'Nomadic Ideal': Can Archaeology Separate Fact from Fiction?" Pages 220–37 in *Mediterranean Peoples in Transition: Thirteenth to Tenth Centuries BCE*. Edited by Seymour Gitin, Amihai Mazar, and Ephraim Stern. Israel Exploration Society. Republished as chapter 6 in this volume.

Edelman, Diana V., ed. 1991. *The Fabric of History: Text, Artifact and Israel's Past*. JSOTSup 127. JSOT Press.

Falconer, Steven E. 1987. "Heartland of Villages: Reconsidering Early Urbanism in the Southern Levant." PhD diss., University of Arizona.

Finkelstein, Israel. 1988. *The Archaeology of the Israelite Settlement*. Israel Exploration Society.

———. 1996. "The Archaeology of the United Monarchy: An Alternative View." *Levant* 28:177–87.

Finkelstein, Israel, and Nadav Na'aman eds. 1994. *From Nomadism to Monarchy: Archaeological and Historical Aspects of Early Israel*. Biblical Archaeology Society.

Flanagan, James W. 1988. *David's Social Drama: A Hologram of Israel's Early Iron Age*. SWBA 7. JSOT Press.

Flannery, Kent V. 1972. "The Cultural Evolution of Civilization." *Annual Review of Ecology and Systematics* 3:399–426.

Frick, Frank S. 1985. *The Formation of the State in Ancient Israel: A Survey of Models and Theories*. SWBA 4. Almond.

Fried, Martin H. 1967. *The Evolution of Political Society: An Essay in Political Anthropology*. Random House.

Friedman, J., and M. J. Rowlands, eds. 1977. *The Evolution of Social Systems: Proceedings of a Meeting of the Research Seminar in Archaeology and Related Subjects, Held at the Institute of Archaeology, London University*. Duckworth.

Fritz, Volkmar. 1995. *The City in Ancient Israel*. BibSem 29. JSOT Press.

Geus, C. H. J. de. 1976. *The Tribes of Israel: An Investigation into Some of the Presuppositions of Martin Noth's Amphictyony Hypothesis*. Van Gorcum.

Gottwald, Norman K. 1979. *The Tribes of Yahweh: A Sociology of the Religion of Liberated Israel, 1250–1050 B.C.E.* Orbis Books.

Haas, Jonathan. 1982. *The Evolution of the Prehistoric State*. Columbia University Press.

Halpern, Baruch. 1995. "Erasing History: The Minimalist Assault on Ancient Israel." *BRev* 11.6:26–35, 47.
Herr, Larry G. 1997. "Urbanism at Tell el-ʿUmeiri during the Late Bronze IIB–Iron IA Transition." Pages 145–55 in *Urbanism in Antiquity: From Mesopotamia to Crete.* Edited by Walter E. Aufrecht, Neil A. Mirau, and Steven W. Gauley. JSOTSup 244. Sheffield Academic.
Herzog, Zeev. 1992a. "Administrative Structures in the Iron Age. Pages 223–30 in *The Architecture of Ancient Israel from the Prehistoric to the Persian Periods.* Edited by Aharon Kempinski and Ronny Reich. Israel Exploration Society.
———. 1992b. "Settlement and Fortification in the Iron Age. Pages 231–74 in *The Architecture of Ancient Israel from the Prehistoric to the Persian Periods.* Edited by Aharon Kempinski and Ronny Reich. Israel Exploration Society.
Hodder, Ian. 1986. *Reading the Past: Current Approaches to Interpretation in Archaeology.* Cambridge University Press.
Hodder, Ian, and Clive Orton. 1976. *Spatial Analysis in Archaeology.* Cambridge University Press.
Holladay, John S. 1995. "The Kingdoms of Israel and Judah: Political and Economic Centralization in the Iron IIA-B (ca. 1000–750 BCE)." Pages 368–98 in *The Archaeology of Society in the Holy Land.* Edited by Thomas E. Levy. Facts on File.
Jamieson-Drake, David W. 1991. *Scribes and Schools in Monarchic Judah: A Socio-archaeological Approach.* SWBA 9. Almond.
Khoury, Philip S., and Joseph Kostiner, eds. 1990. *Tribes and State Formation in the Middle East.* University of California Press.
Kolb, Frank. 1984. *Die Stadt im Altertum.* Beck.
Lemche, Niels Peter. 1985. *Early Israel: Anthropological and Historical Studies on the Israelite Society before the Monarchy.* VTSup 37. Brill.
———. 1996. "Early Israel Revisited." *CurBS* 4:9–34.
Lemche, Niels Peter, and Thomas L. Thompson. 1994. "Did Biran Kill David? The Bible in the Light of Archaeology." *JSOT* 64:3–22.
Mazar, Amihai. 1990. *Archaeology of the Land of the Bible, 10,000–586 B.C.E.* Doubleday.
Provan, Ian W. 1995. "Ideologies, Literary and Critical: Reflections of Recent Writing on the History of Israel." *JBL* 114:585–606.
Renfrew, Colin. 1972. "Beyond a Subsistence Economy: The Evolution of Social Organization in Prehistoric Europe." Pages 69–85 in *Recon-*

structing Complex Societies. Edited by Charlotte B. Moore. American Schools of Oriental Research.

Routledge, Bruce. 1997. "Learning to Love the King: Urbanism and the State in Iron Age Moab." Pages 130–44 in *Urbanism in Antiquity: From Mesopotamia to Crete*. Edited by Walter E. Aufrecht, Neil A. Mirau, and Steven W. Gauley. JSOTSup 244. Sheffield Academic.

Sahlins, Marshall D. 1968. *Tribesmen*. Prentice-Hall.

Service, Elman R. 1962. *Primitive Social Organization: An Evolutionary Perspective*. Random House.

———. 1975. *Origins of the State and Civilization: The Process of Cultural Evolution*. Norton.

Shiloh, Yigal. 1980. *The Proto-Aeolic Capital and Israelite Ashlar Masonry*. Hebrew University Press.

Tainter, Joseph A. 1988. *The Collapse of Complex Societies*. Cambridge University Press.

Tapper, Richard. 1990. "Anthropologists, Historians, and Tribespeople on Tribe and State Formation in the Middle Easy." Pages 48–73 in *Tribes and State Formation in the Middle East*. Edited by Philip S. Khoury and Joseph Kostiner. University of California Press.

Thompson, Thomas L. 1992. *Early History of the Israelite People: From the Written and Archaeological Sources*. SHANE 4. Brill.

———. 1995. "A Neo-Albrighteam School in History and Biblical Scholarship?" *JBL* 114:683–705.

Webb, Malcolm C. 1975. "The Flag Follows Trade: An Essay on the Necessary Interaction of Military and Commercial Factors in State Formation." Pages 155–209 in *Ancient Civilizations and Trade*. Edited by Jeremy A. Sabloff and Carl C. Lamberg-Karlovsky. University of New Mexico Press.

Weippert, Helga. 1988. *Palästina in vorhellenistischer Zeit*. Beck.

Whitelam, Keith W. 1994. "The Identity of Early Israel: The Realignment and Transformation of Late Bronze-Iron Age Palestine." *JSOT* 63:57–87.

———. 1996. *The Invention of Ancient Israel: The Silencing of Palestinian History*. Routledge.

Wright, Henry T. 1977. "Recent Research on the Origin of the State." *Annual Review of Anthropology* 6:379–97.

Yadin, Yigael. 1958. "Solomon's City Wall and Gate at Gezer." *IEJ* 8:80–86.

Updated Bibliography

Dever, William G. 1994. "From Tribe to Nation: A Critique of State Formation Processes in Ancient Israel." Pages 213–38 in *Nuove fondazioni nel Vicino Oriente antico: Realtà e ideologia*. Edited by Stefania Mazzoni. University of Pisa.

Holladay, John S. 1995. "The Kingdoms of Israel and Judah: Political and Economic Centralization in the Iron IIA-B (ca. 1000–750 BCE)." Pages 368–98 in *The Archaeology of Society in the Holy Land*. Edited by Thomas E. Levy. Facts on File.

Finkelstein, Israel. 1996. "The Archaeology of the United Monarchy: An Alternative View." *Levant* 28:177–87.

Fritz, Volkmar, and Philip R. Davies, eds. 1996. *The Origins of the Ancient Israelite States*. JSOTSup 228. Sheffield Academic. (includes essays attacking my views, barely formulated).

Fritz, Volkmar. 1995. *The City in Ancient Israel*. BibSem 29. JSOT Press.

Dever, William G. 1997. "Archaeology and the 'Age of Solomon': A Case Study in Archaeology and Historiography." Pages 217–51 in *The Age of Solomon: The Scholarship at the Turn of the Millennium*. Edited by Lowell K. Handy. SHANE 11. Brill.

Grabbe, Lester L., ed. 1997. *Can a "History of Israel" Be Written?* JSOTSup 245. Sheffield Academic.

Handy, Lowell K., ed. 1997. *The Age of Solomon: Scholarship at the Turn of the Millennium*. SHANE 11. Brill.

Herzog, Zeev. 1997. *Archaeology of the City: Urban Planning in Ancient Israel and Its Social Implications*. Emery and Claire Yass Archaeology Press.

Knoppers Gary N. 1997. "The Vanishing Solomon: The Disappearance of the United Monarchy from Recent Histories of Ancient Israel." *JBL* 116:19–44.

Meyers, Carol. 1998. "Kinship and Kingship: The Early Monarchy." Pages 165–205 in *The Oxford History of the Biblical World*. Edited by Michael D. Coogan. Oxford University Press.

Lemche, Niels Peter. 1998. "The Origin of the Israelite State: A Copenhagen Perspective on the Emergence of Critical Historical Studies of Ancient Israel in Recent Times." *SJOT* 12:44–63.

Ash, Paul S. 1999. *David, Solomon, and Egypt: A Reassessment*. JSOTSup 297. Sheffield Academic.

Ben-Tor, Amnon. 1999. "Solomon's City Rises from the Ashes." *BAR* 5.2:26–37, 60.

Finkelstein, Israel. 1999. "State Formation in Israel and Judah: A Contrast in Context, a Contrast in Trajectory." *NEA* 62:35–52.

Ofer, Avi. 2001. "The Monarchic Period in the Judean Highlands: A Spatial Overview." Pages 14–37 in *Studies in the Archaeology of the Iron Age in Israel and Jordan*. Edited by Amiha Mazar. JSOTSup 331. Sheffield Academic.

Master, Daniel M. 2001. "State Formation Theory and the Kingdom of Ancient Israel." *JNES* 60:117–31.

Joffee, Alex H. 2002. "The Rise of Secondary States in the Iron I Levant." *JESHO* 45:425–67.

Finkelstein, Israel. 2003. "City-States to States: Polity Dynamics in the Tenth–Ninth Centuries B.C.E." Pages 75–83 in *Symbiosis, Symbolism and the Power of the Past: Canaan Ancient Israel and Their Neighbors*. Edited by William G. Dever and Seymour Gitin. Eisenbrauns.

Lehmann, Gunnar. 2003. "The United Monarchy in the Countryside: Jerusalem, Judah, and the Shepelah during the Tenth Century B.C.E." Pages 117–62 in *Jerusalem in Bible and Archaeology: The First Temple Period*. Edited by Andrew G. Vaughn and Ann E. Killebrew. SymS 18. Society of Biblical Literature.

Stager, Lawrence E. "The Patrimonial Kingdom of Solomon." 2003. Pages 63–74 in *Symbiosis, Symbolism, and the Power of the Past: Canaan, Ancient Israel, and Their Neighbors from the Late Bronze Age through Roman Palestina*. Edited by William G. Dever and Seymour Gitin. Eisenbrauns.

Vaughn, Andrew G., and Ann E. Killebrew, eds. 2003. *Jerusalem in Bible and Archaeology: The First Temple Period*. SymS 18. Society of Biblical Literature.

Dever, William G. 2004. "Histories and Non-histories of Ancient Israel: The Question of the United Monarchy." Pages 65–94 in *In Search of Pre-exilic Israel: Proceedings of the Oxford Old Testament Seminar*. Edited by John Day. JSOTSup 406. T&T Clark.

Kletter, Raz. 2004. "Chronology and United Monarchy: A Methodological Review." *ZDPV* 120:13–54.

Levy, Thomas E., and Thomas Highman, eds. 2005. *The Bible and Radiocarbon Dating: Archaeology, Texts, and Science*. Equinox.

Finkelstein, Israel, and Neil Asher Silberman. 2006. *David and Solomon: In Search of the Bible's Sacred Kings and the Roots of the Western Tradition*. Free Press.

Mazar, Amihai. 2007. "The Spade and the Text: The Interaction between Archaeology and Israelite History Relating to the Tenth–Ninth Centuries." Pages 143–72 in *Understanding the History of Ancient Israel*. Edited by H. G. M. Williamson. Proceedings of the British Academy 143. Oxford University Press.

Knauf, Ernst Axel. 2008. "From Archaeology to History: Bronze and Iron Ages with Special Regard to the Year 1200 B.C.E., and the Tenth Century." Pages 72–85 in *The Archaeology*, vol. 1 of *Israel in Transition: From Late Bronze II to Iron IIa (c. 1250–850 B.C.E.)*. Edited by Lester L. Grabbe. LHBOTS 191. T&T Clark.

Zevit, Ziony. 2008. "The Davidic-Solomonic Empire from the Perspective of Archaeological Bibliology. Pages 201–24 in *Birkat Shalom: Studies in the Bible, Ancient Near Eastern Literature, and Postbiblical Literature Presented to Shalom M. Paul on the Occasion of His Seventieth Birthday*. Edited by Chaim Cohen et al. Eisenbrauns.

Mazar, Eilat. 2009. *The Palace of King David: Excavations at the Summit of the City of David; Preliminary Report of Seasons 2005–2007*. Shoham Academic Research and Publication.

Garfinkel, Yosef, and Saar Ganor. 2009. *Excavation Report 2007–2008*. Vol. 1 of *Khirbet Qeiyafa*. Institute of Archaeology, Hebrew University of Jerusalem.

Mazar, Amihai. 2010a. "Archaeology and the Biblical Narrative: The Case of the United Monarchy." Pages 29–58 in *One God—One Cult—One Nation: Archaeological Perspectives*. Edited by Reinhard G. Kratz and Hermann Spieckermann. De Gruyter.

———. 2010b. "The Iron age Chronology Debate: Is the Gap Narrowing?" *NEA* 74:50–54.

Levy, Thomas E., and Daniel A. Frese. 2010. "The Four Pillars of the 'Low Chronology.'" Pages 187–202 in *Historical Biblical Archaeology and the Future: The New Pragmatism*. Edited by Thomas E. Levy. Equinox.

Finkelstein, Israel. 2011. "The Iron Age Chronology Debate: Is the Gap Narrowing?" *NEA* 77:50–54.

Lemaire, André. 2011. "The United Monarchy: Saul, David and Solomon." Pages 85–128 in *Ancient Israel: From Abraham to the Destruction of the Temple*. 3rd ed. Edited by Hershel Shanks. Biblical Archaeology Society.

Mazar, Amihai. 2011. "The Iron Age Chronology Debate: Is the Gap Narrowing? Another Viewpoint." *NEA* 74:105–11.

Garfinkel, Yosef, Katharina Streit, Saar Ganor, and Michael G. Hasel 2012. "State Formation in Judah: Biblical Tradition, Modern Historical Theories, and Radiometric Dates at Khirbet Qeiyafa." *Radiocarbon* 54:359–69.

Millard, Alan R. 2012. "The Archaeology of David and Solomon: Navigating the New Methods and Madness." Pages 497–516 in *Do Historical Matters Matter to Faith? A Critical Appraisal of Modern and Postmodern Approaches to Scripture*. Edited by James K. Hoffmeier and Denni R. Magary. Crossway.

Finkelstein, Israel. 2013. *The Forgotten Kingdom: The Archaeology and History of Northern Israel*. ANEM 5. SBL Press.

Ortiz, Steven. 2014. "United Monarchy: Archaeology and Literary Sources." Pages 227–61 in *Ancient Israel's History: An Introduction to Issues and Sources*. Edited by Bill T. Arnold and Richard S. Hess. Baker Academic.

Garfinkel, Yosef, Saar Ganor, and Michael G. Hasel. 2014. *Excavation Report 2009–2013: Stratigraphy and Architecture (Areas B, C, D, E)*. Vol. 2 of *Khirbet Qeiyafa*. Institute of Archaeology, Hebrew University of Jerusalem.

Garfinkel, Yosef, Mitka R. Golub, Haggai Misgav, and Saar Ganor. 2015. "The 'Ishba'al Inscription from Khirbet Qeiyafa." *BASOR* 373:217–33.

Kessler, Rainer, Walter Sommerfeld, and Leslie Tramontini, eds. 2016. *State Formation and State Decline in the Near and Middle East*. Harrassowitz.

Na'aman, Nadav. 2016. "Tel Dor and Iron Age II Chronology." *BASOR* 376:1–5.

Garfinkel, Yosef, Saar Ganor, and Michael G. Hasel. 2018. *In the Footsteps of King David: Revelations from an Ancient Biblical City*. Thames & Hudson.

Garfinkel, Yosef, and Madeleine Mumcouglu. 2018. *Solomon's Temple and Palace: New Archaeological Discoveries*. Bible Lands Museum and Biblical Archaeological Society.

Faust, Avraham. 2020. "Between the Highland Polity and Philistia: The United Monarchy and the Resettlement of the Shephelah in the Iron Age IIA, with a Special Focus on Tel Eton and Khirbet Qeiyafa." *BASOR* 383:115–36.

Dever, William G. 2021. "Solomon, Science, and Scripture: The Rise of the Judahite State in the Tenth Century BCE." *Jerusalem Journal of Archaeology* 1:1–15.

Keimer, Kyle H., and Zachary Thomas. 2020–2021. "Etic and Emic Expressions of Power in Ancient Israel: Recalibrating a Discussion." *JEOL* 48:71–92.

Faust, Avraham. 2021. "The 'United Monarchy' on the Ground: The Disruptive Character of the Iron I–II Transition and the Nature of Political Transformations." *Jerusalem Journal of Archaeology* 1:15–67.

Ben-Yosef, Erez, and Zachary Thomas. 2023. "Theoretical and Methodological Comments on Social Complexity and State Formation in Biblical Archaeology." Pages 472–533 in *"And in Length of Days Understanding"(Job 12:12): Essays on Archaeology in the Eastern Mediterranean and Beyond in Honor of Thomas E Levy*. Edited by Erez Ben-Yosef and I. W. N. Jones. Springer.

Webster, Lyndelle C., Samuel R. Wolff, Steven M. Ortiz, Marcella Barbosa, Cameron Coyle, Gary P. Arbino, Michael W. Dee, Quan Hua, and Geraldine E. Jacobsen. 2023. "The Chronology of Gezer from the End of the Late Bronze Age to Iron Age II: A Meeting Point for Radiocarbon, Archaeology, Egyptology, and the Bible." PLOS One. https://doi.org/10.1371/journal.pone.0293119.

10

Material Remains and the Cult in Ancient Israel: An Essay in Archaeological Systematics

Having a clerical and seminary background and having done an M.A. thesis on the revival of biblical theology even before I studied with Ernest Wright and Frank Cross, I eventually came to the perennial topic of archaeology and the religion of Israel quite naturally. In addition, my discovery and publication of the now-crucial Khirbet el-Qom inscription mentioning "a/Asherah" in 1968–1970 (Dever 1969–1970) had remained tucked away somewhere in my mind, waiting to resurface. Then in 1981–1982 I was a visiting professor at the Hebrew University of Jerusalem on a Guggenheim Fellowship. David Noel Freedman came to Jerusalem for a short stay, and in the fall I went to visit the Israel Museum with him, where we saw Ze'ev's Meshel's newly discovered Kuntillet ʿAjrud material. We read the Hebrew inscription on a large storejar—"Yahweh of Samaria and his Asherah"—and looked at each other in astonishment. That is how my contemporary Khirbet el-Qom inscription read! I thought: this will be a *bombshell*. But it didn't drop for years.

When the storejar with the Asherah inscription was published in the Hebrew magazine *Qadmoniot*, the inscription was blurred (Israelis can read Paleo-Hebrew), and when the storejar was displayed in the Israel Museum, it was turned around so the inscription was invisible. The full publication appeared only in 2012 (thirty-four years after the discovery) by Meshel, as *Kuntillet ʿAjrud (Ḥorvat Teiman): An Iron Age II Religious Site on the Judah-Sinai Border* (the name Hebraized).

That spring I wrote this article, the oldest in this collection, for the Freedman Festschrift. At the time, there was no literature on archaeology

---

Originally published as pages 571–87 in *The Word of the Lord Shall Go Forth: Essays in Honor of David Noel Freedman in Celebration of His Sixtieth Birthday*. Edited by Carol L. Meyers and M. O'Connor. Eisenbrauns, 1983. Reprinted by permission.

and cult apart from Meshel's preliminary reports in 1976 (with Carol Meyers) and 1978. This was a "programmatic" piece, a first foray into uncharted territory, speaking as an archaeologist and anticipating what *might* be found that could illuminate what came to be called folk religion, although I did not use this term. I soon followed up this piece with a detailed interpretation of the ʿAjrud texts, "Asherah, Consort of Yahweh? New Evidence from Kuntillet 'Ajrûd" (1984; a Hebrew version appeared later, in 1985). The argument that a cult of the old Canaanite mother goddess Asherah flourished in ancient Israel, at least in some circles, was heretical at the time. I had not yet seen Lemaire's rediscovery of my obscure publication of the el-Qom Asherah inscription (1984). But in 1988 Saul Olyan demonstrated on the basis of the biblical texts that Asherah was widely venerated, even in court and temple worship.

This first effort, written nearly forty years ago, introduced themes that would appear frequently in my writing: the inadequacies of the biblical texts, especially standing alone; the need for dialogue; the heuristic value of separating belief (theology) and practice (the religion of ordinary people). It is that thoughtful "positivism"—not the search for novelty—that I hope has guided all my work these past fifty-five years.

Between 1981 and 2005, I published ten more works on archaeology and ancient Israelite religion, followed finally by a full-scale work, *Did God Have a Wife? Archaeology and Folk Religion in Ancient Israel* (2005). The momentum in those years also resulted in Ziony Zevit's magisterial *The Religions of Ancient Israel: A Synthesis of Parallactic Approaches* (2001), in which he credited my 1984 piece as an inspiration.

Today there is a vast literature on archaeology and the Israelite cult, and it has developed along many of the lines that I laid out intuitively nearly forty years ago. That there was a widespread cult of Asherah is now taken for granted, especially in the burgeoning literature on household and family religion, where women's roles were often dominant. I am proud that scholars such as Beth Alpert-Nakhai, Jennie Ebeling, and Laura Mazow, now in the lead in studies on women's religion, were my students. To see how far we have come, one only needs to compare my 1970 discussion of the eighth-century BCE Khirbet el-Qom and Kuntillet ʿAjrud a/Asherah inscriptions, then virtually ignored by biblical historians, with the growing use of such materials in current discussions. I would like to think that my modest exercise in "archaeological systematics" helped to get things going. Indeed, a number of biblical scholars have quoted this piece favorably, and my colleague Ziony Zevit credits it with inspiring, in part, his recent work on Israelite religion, featuring a parallactic approach (i.e., using archaeology and texts as complementary data; Zevit 2001).

The most significant works since 1984, particularly those with reference to the wider literature, are listed in the Updated Bibliography (arranged chronologically) at the end of the Works Cited.

Although David Noel Freedman would insist that he is a biblical scholar rather than an archaeologist, as author and editor he has consistently drawn attention to the unique value of archaeology in reconstructing all aspects of the phenomenon of ancient Israel, not least its religious life and institutions.[1] It may therefore be appropriate for me as an archaeologist, in this Festschrift honoring a friend and colleague in biblical studies, to offer a brief essay on the problems of correlating literary and nonliterary remains with specific reference to the Israelite cult. For the purposes of this discussion, we shall confine ourselves to the period of the judges and the monarchy.

We may focus on the central problem by observing that much of Syro-Palestinian archaeology has been dominated until recently by biblical scholarship—particularly under the influence of the Albright school (of which Freedman is a prominent member). Yet despite several generations of intensive excavation and research, and what has sometimes amounted to an obsession with cultic interpretation, archaeology in the Holy Land appears to have produced surprisingly little direct illumination of ancient Israelite religious practice per se. It has recovered a great deal of the historical and cultural milieu from which the Hebrew Bible emerged, and in that sense archaeology has helped to correct the false presuppositions on which certain schools of *Religionsgeschichte* sought to base their reconstruction of Israelite religion.[2] But as I shall attempt to show, archaeology

---

1. One may cite Freedman's seminal essay (1965) and his more recent (if somewhat premature) focus on Ebla and patriarchal backgrounds in recent issues of the *Biblical Archaeologist*. As an editor, Freedman's contribution to archaeology is seen in his 1969 work (with coeditor Jonas Greenfield) and as editor of the popular but authoritative quarterly *The Biblical Archaeologist* from 1976 to 1982.

2. Albright has correctly pointed out that much of the study of the history of the religion of Israel from the time of Wellhausen on was, in effect, the analysis of literary tradition; as such, it tended to ignore the revolutionary results of historical-archaeological research. However, my point here is that, while the external evidence of archaeology may have enhanced our appreciation of the value of the biblical sources for understanding both Israelite history and theology, it has not proportionately given us an independent and direct witness to the ancient *cult*.

of either the biblical or the secular persuasion has scarcely augmented our understanding of the actual *cult* in ancient Israel in any specific and fundamental way.[3] Is the silence significant? Or is this curious failure due to the inherent limitations of archaeology itself? If not, how might we proceed in the future in a manner more beneficial to both archaeology and biblical criticism? In order to answer these questions, let us look first at the theoretical value of archaeology to the study of the cultic aspects of Israelite religion, against which we shall then measure the actual contribution.

10.1. The Unfulfilled Potential of Archaeology for Illuminating the Cult

10.1.1. What Might Be Found to Illumine the Cult

To speculate on the potential of archaeology for interpreting Israelite religious institutions and practice, we must isolate those aspects of the cult that may be expected to leave tangible traces in the archaeological record, that is, the material correlates of specifically religious behavior. For this purpose we shall distinguish religion as a set of beliefs concerning the supernatural nature of the universe and the moral nature of humans, usually institutionalized and expressed in ritual observance, and cult as a particular system of religious worship, especially with reference to its rites and ceremonies. Extrapolating from these definitions, we may then consult three basic sources: (1) what we know of Near Eastern religion in general; (2) the descriptions of religious life in ancient Israel in the Hebrew Bible (although the value of the texts is obviously limited); and (3) the artifactual discoveries made thus far in excavations in Palestine. From these sources we may thus derive a rough outline of the material remains of

---

3. The best recent survey of the archaeological material is Shiloh 1979, although this is confined to a brief description of Iron Age temples/shrines and their furnishings in general. The latest analysis from a literary point of view is Haran 1978, on which see below. My indictment, incidentally, would be even more applicable to the archaeology of early Judaism and Christianity, although a discussion of that would be beyond both out scope here and my competence. The Galilee synagogue project of Eric Meyers, Carol Meyers, James F. Strange, and others is, however, most promising.

the Israelite cult that might be amenable to archaeological investigation, somewhat as follows.

Architecture. This would include both (1) monumental structures and local shrines that served as public temples and (2) private household shrines. Here the significant features that might reveal belief and practice are likely to be the orientation of the building, its essential plan, and in particular the arrangement and presumed function of such features as forecourt, vestibule, vestry, cella, and any attached service or residential areas. The location, size, manner of construction, and degree of sumptuousness could also yield indirect information on the relative place of the cult in society.

Art. This might include: (1) monumental art, both architectural decor (reliefs, paintings) and .mobile works such as statuary; and (2) the minor arts, especially pottery and other ceramics (figurines, plaques, terra-cotta stands, temple models, censers, etc.), ivory carvings, seals, and possibly textiles. In theory at least, no other category of material culture should be so readily accessible or so potentially revealing in explicating the cult as works of art.

Artifacts. The first category would include: (1) architectural furnishings, generally fixed, such as benches, altars, *favissae*, various types of stands, lavers, braziers, censers, and other obviously cultic paraphernalia; and (2) smaller, more mobile objects, whether found in temple/shrine contexts or used in everyday life, such as votives of all kinds (including foundation deposits and funeral offerings), human or animal figurines, any "magical" items (such as masks or aids in divination and incantation), and also some of the objects considered above under Art (particularly the iconographic ivories and seals). Finally, although they are more ecofacts than artifacts, paleozoological and paleobotanical remains in possible cultic deposits do reflect human alteration and usage and constitute invaluable evidence for sacrificial customs.

Texts. The evidence provided by epigraphic remains (usually considered literary and thus nonartifactual) is rare in ancient Palestine but obviously of the greatest potential importance. Types of written data applicable to the cult might include monumental or dedicatory inscriptions, incantations and other magical texts, liturgical and mythological texts, votives, funeral inscriptions, ostraca, seals, and even graffiti.

Burials. A final category of material remains, often overlooked, includes all aspects of mortuary practice that may leave unique physical evidence for interpreting such matters as popular piety, ancestral worship, and belief in life after death.

10.1.2. What Is Currently Known Archaeologically of the Israelite Cult

In the light of the above outline—a brief compendium of the varieties of cultic material we could reasonably expect Syro-Palestinian archaeology to have produced—it is instructive to note how *scant* the actual usable data are, even after a century of exploration and discovery.

Architecture. Here the most striking fact is that no full-scale, monumental temple from ancient Israel has been found. Of the Solomonic temple in tenth-century Jerusalem, no actual trace has been (or is likely to be) found. We may, of course, combine the biblical descriptions (1 Kgs 6:2–36; 7:13–51; 2 Chr 3:3–5:1; Ezek 40–47) and archaeological finds from such sites as Ebla and Tell Tayinat in Syria and Shechem and Hazor in Palestine to elucidate the tripartite architectural plan. Further, the small finds from a number of sites in Syria and Palestine illustrate details described in the texts: furnishings such as altars, lavers, braziers, flesh hooks, and shovels, as well as the Phoenician-style construction and decoration of the Jerusalem temple.[4] The shrine of Stratum XI at Arad has been understood by the excavator as a tenth-century temple ultimately going back to the tabernacle as a prototype and functioning as a rival of the Jerusalem temple, but the structure is more likely to be ninth century in date and seems to be little more than a local shrine.[5]

Elsewhere, we have only the Dan sanctuary, apparently of the tenth-eighth century and modeled after the Canaanite outdoor *bāmôt*, or high

---

4. On the archaeological evidence for the Solomonic temple and its background, see Dever 1974b and references there and my chapter on the art and architecture of the Solomonic era (1982b). As a prime example of the ignoring of archaeology that I shall document below, note the exhaustive work of Th. A. Busink, *Der Tempel von Jerusalem, von Salamo bis Herodes* (1970), which uses *no* archaeological data.

5. See Aharoni 1968, 1969, 1973b. The confused stratigraphy and dating of Iron Age Arad are well known; for a drastic lowering of the date, for instance, of the two inscribed platters found near the cella of the sanctuary and ascribed variously by the excavator to Stratum X or VIII, see Dever 1969–1970, 173 (eighth century); and Cross 1979 (seventh century). On the *significance* of the sanctuary, however, see below and n. 36.

places; small household shrines at tenth-century Megiddo, Ta'anach, and Lachish; an eighth-century sanctuary (?), although preserved only in negative evidence, at Beersheba; and the ninth- to eighth-century caravan-serai shrine at Kuntillet 'Ajrud in eastern Sinai.[6] None of these structures in orientation, layout, scale, or contents has shed much light on cultic practice—at least as they have been interpreted thus far (but see below). Although they may be presumed to be Yahwistic, they give no direct evidence and indicate only that they were probably designed for the presentation of food and incense offerings and simple votives of terra-cotta and stone.

Art and artifactual evidence. There is so little evidence that these categories may be combined. No monumental Israelite art survives. No Israelite statuary or sculpture, large-scale iconographic representations, or paintings are known to us, save two tenth-century cultic stands from Ta'anach, with fantastic representations of what appears to be Asherah as the "Lion Lady."[7] Furnishings in the few attested shrines consist simply of niches and benches, presumably for placement of food or incense offerings; large platforms and several smaller "horned" altars, serving probably the same purpose; and a number of terra-cotta stands that have been interpreted as censers or combination censer-libation stands.[8] (Unfortu-

---

6. On the high place at Dan, see Biran 1974a; 1974b; 1980, 175–79; Stager and Wolff 1981; on Building 2081 of Stratum VA at Megiddo, see Loud 1948, 45–46; on the cultic structure at Ta'anach, see Lapp 1964, 26–32; 1969, 42–44; Glock 1978, 1142–44; Stager and Wolff 1981; on Cult Room 49 of Stratum V at Lachish, see Aharoni 1975b, 26–32, figs. 5–8, pls. 41–43; on the supposed Stratum III temple replaced by the Basement Building of Stratum II at Beersheba, see Aharoni 1973a, 16–17; 1975a, 158–63; and cf. the critique of Yadin 1976, together with the defense of Herzog, Rainey, and Moshkovitz 1977; on Kuntillet 'Ajrud, see Meshel 1978a, 1978b, 1979; Meshel and Meyers 1976. To this list one might add a Level III shrine (ninth century) at Tell el-Far'ah North, though this is debatable; cf. de Vaux 1951, 428; Stager and Wolff 1981. The two so-called *maṣṣēbôt* found by Kenyon in Jerusalem do not imply an eighth- to seventh-century cultic structure but a common house; see Graesser 1972, 54–55; Shiloh 1979, 147. I do not regard the Stratum XI installation at Hazor as necessarily an Israelite shrine; see n. 12 below.

7. Lapp 1969, 42–44; Glock 1978, 1142–44. These fascinating stands, which abound in evidence for Israelite syncretistic iconography, deserve *much* more attention.

8. See the references in nn. 5 and 6. Stands that may be censers or libartion

nately, no flotation analysis of paleozoological or paleobotanical remains has been done to determine the nature of possible animal sacrifices or other food offerings.[9]) The tenth- to eighth/seventh-century pottery occasionally found in the context of these shrines is all utilitarian rather than specifically manufactured for cultic use[10] (although that does not rule out secondary cultic use). Hundreds of female terra-cottas of the so-called Astarte (more accurately Asherah) type have been found, mostly Judean pillar-base figurines of the eighth–seventh century BCE. Obvious fertility aspects, usually exaggerated sexual characteristics, connect these figurines with the ancient Near Eastern cult of the mother goddess, but they do not specify the deity further.[11] Since these figurines are found almost without exception in domestic or tomb contexts, they are undoubtedly talismans to aid in conception and childbirth rather than idols in the true sense, that is, designed for sanctuary usage. It may be significant that no representations of a *male* deity in terra-cotta, metal, or stone have ever been found in clear Iron Age contexts, except possibly for an El statuette in bronze from twelfth-century Hazor and a depiction of an El-like stick figure on a miniature chalk altar from tenth-century Gezer; neither is necessarily Israelite.[12]

---

holders have been studied in C. Meyers 1976, 73–77. See also n. 7 above and n. 12 below.

9. Lapp (1969, 45–46) recovered 140 astragali (not pig but probably sheep/goat: Stager and Wolff 1981) from the Taʿanach cultic structure. Aharoni (1968, 19) noted the headless skeleton of a young lamb and pits with other bones near the large courtyard altar of the Arad sanctuary. Sheep, goat, and gazelle bones are also reported to have been found in an offering bowl of the earliest phase (A) of the Dan sanctuary (Biran 1980, 175–79). But to my knowledge no flotation or wet-sieving, of the sort used to recover quantities of animal bones from the MB IIC Gezer high place, has yet been employed on Iron Age cultic installations.

10. See, for instance, the large collection from the Lachish sanctuary (Aharoni 1975b, pls. 41–42), all common jugs, bowls, kraters, lamps, and chalices.

11. We desperately need a current and synthetic treatment of all the data on the Late Bronze and Iron Age figurines.

12. Yadin et al. 1961, pls. 38, 204–5; Yadin 1972, 132–34, pl. 24:c (Stratum XI); Dever et al. 1975, 67–68, pls. 41: 2, 75A (Stratum VI). Shiloh (1979, 150), following Yadin (1972, 132–34), considers the Hazor XI statuette evidence for an Israelite cult installation, but it is clearly part of a hoard in a votive jar, and since it is classic Late Bronze in type, it is probably a holdover—even if Stratum XI is regarded as Israelite. A broken head of a male figure from near the Dan sanctuary

The few specific votives we know (apart from use of the common pottery forms noted above) consist of several ninth- to eighth-century inscribed ceramic vessels from Hazor, el-Qom, Arad, Beersheba, and ʿAjrud and the inscribed stone bowls from ninth- to eighth-century ʿAjrud.[13] Conspicuously absent are pottery workshops for the production of votives, such as those found in connection with the sacred precincts of Late Bronze Canaanite temples at Hazor and elsewhere.[14]

The well-known ninth- to eighth-century seals and ivory plaques give us relatively abundant evidence for art and iconography in Palestine, but most of the motifs are of Phoenician derivation, and in any case they are too clearly decorative in nature to shed much light on theological conceptions, much less cultic practice.[15]

Finally, it is noteworthy that no identifiable foundation deposits or ritualmagical objects whatsoever have been found in undisputed Israelite contexts.[16]

Texts. As is well known, we have relatively little ancient Israelite epigraphic evidence in general. The ostraca witness personal names

---

has recently been reported (Biran 1980, 178–79), together with a painted stand of which it is probably a part (seen through the courtesy of Prof. Biran and his staff).

13. For Hazor, see Yadin et al. 1961, pl. 357: 4–6; 358: 4–5 (Stratum V bowl reading "Qodesh," ninth century); for Khirbet el-Qom, Dever 1969–1970, 172–73 (eighth-century bowl reading "El"); for Arad, Aharoni 1968, 20 (Stratum X platters inscribed with *qof, shin*, for "Qodesh"; see Dever 1969–1970; 173; for redating to the early seventh century, see Cross 1979); for Beersheba, Aharoni 1973a, pls. 42: 4 and 69: 2 (a Stratum II krater reading "Qodesh"); for Kuntillet ʿAjrud, Meshel 1979, 30–32 (ninth/eighth-century pithoi and two stone bowls with Yahwistic personal names and a plea for blessing; see below and n. 17).

14. See the evidence for Middle–Late Bronze Age pottery workshops cited in Dever 1974b, 43 nn. 29–30. Aharoni (1968, 21) mentions two pottery kilns and vessels near the entrance of the Arad Strata VIII–VII sanctuary, but no details are given. The only comparable Iron Age ceramic production in a cultic context is reflected in the Asherah figurine-mould from the cultic structure at Taʿanach (Lapp 1967, 26).

15. Again, no comprehensive, up-to-date study of the seals and ivories—especially with regard to iconography—can be cited. See provisionally the references in Dever 1982b, n. 61.

16. Several Iron I (twelfth-century} ceramic foundation deposits are known from Gezer, but these are almost certainly Philistine; see Dever, Lance, and Wright 1970, 23.

compounded with Baal or El. Apart from that, only a few eighth- to seventh-century tomb inscriptions from Jerusalem, Khirbet Beit Lei, Khirbet el-Qom, and elsewhere are of obvious religious import.[17] More significant are the several recently found graffiti and votive inscriptions on stone bowls and storejars from the Kuntillet ʿAjrud sanctuary in the Sinai.[18] Conspicuously absent are dedicatory or incantation texts or mythological and liturgical texts such as those from Canaanite Ugarit—except for parts of the Hebrew Bible, still almost our sole literary source for the Israelite cult (but hardly to be classed as an archaeological artifact).

Burials. Tomb offerings of the Israelite and Judean period are relatively abundant, but apart from an occasional human or zoomorphic figurine they consist overwhelmingly of quantities of common pottery, with a few items of personal adornment or utilitarian objects. Lamps, the occasional figurine, and small terra-cotta rattles from ninth- to seventh-century tombs have been interpreted as cultic in nature, but there is little evidence to support this view. The basic chamber-and-bench tomb type of the tenth–seventh century has not been studied in terms of the Israelite cult, but any analysis would have to begin with the observation that this tomb type seems to have been borrowed early in the Iron Age from the Aegean area via the Philistines.[19] In the disposal of the dead themselves, the normal Israelite primary extended burial—the body often deposited on a bench and subsequently removed to an adjacent repository to make

---

17. For Jerusalem, see Avigad 1953; for Khirbet Beit Lei, Naveh 1963 (funereal?); for Khirbet el-Qom, Dever 1969–1970, 169–74; and for a cave near ʿEin-gedi, Bar-Adon 1975. These sepulchral inscriptions have not usually been taken into account when considering the cult, but any anthropologist would quickly point out that funeral customs—particularly when combined with epigraphic evidence—may constitute prime data for the cult. Further, note that Lemaire (1977, 599–603) and Naveh (1979, 28) both now read "Asherah" in the el-Qom Inscription 3, which, when taken with the Kuntillet ʿAjrud readings of "Asherah," throws dramatic light on syncretism in the Israelite cult (below).

18. Meshel 1978a; 1979, 30–32; Meshel and Meyers 1976, 6–10; see also below on ʿKuntillet ʿAjrud.

19. I have not yet published the evidence for this view, but it derives from comparing the Aegean-style thirteenth- to twelfth-century Philistine tombs at Tell el-Farʿah South and Eitun with tenth-century and later bench tombs from many Israelite sites; see, provisionally, Dever 1969–1970, 150–51.

room for later burials—does not seem indicative of any distinctive religious conception or practice.

10.2. A Comparison and Critique

10.2.1. Comparison

A comparison of the theoretical agenda and actual achievement sketched above will suggest that archaeology's contribution to the study of the Israelite cult has been minimal. A brief examination of recent literature (since Shiloh 1979, written in 1975) confirms the suspicion.

Archaeology. On the side of archaeology, I note a symposium in 1977 in Jerusalem, sponsored by the Nelson Glueck School of Biblical Archaeology, that was devoted precisely to this theme. Published now as *Temples and High Places in Biblical Times*, the title is promising, but the results for our inquiry are disappointing. The majority of the essays have little to do with Palestine in the Iron Age, much less with the Israelite cult in particular. Those papers that might be relevant—on Dan, Arad, Beersheba, and ʿAjrud, for instance—offer no new data to supplement the little published evidence. Furthermore, they do not use the current archaeological material to confront recent textual treatments of the central topic of the symposium, *bāmôt*, or high places, such as those of Patrick H. Vaughan and Wilber B. Barrick. Finally, even a casual reading of the papers together with the published responses reveals that the biblical scholars and the archaeologists participating in this potentially significant symposium were for the most part simply talking past each other.[20]

Biblical studies. It is also instructive to examine the most exhaustive recent work of biblical scholarship on the subject, Menahem Haran's *Temples and Temple-Service in Ancient Israel* (1978). Haran's concern is almost solely with the literary tradition, for reasons he states with admirable clarity in his prologue: "The priestly source ... rests on historical conditions that prevailed not in the post-exilic but the pre-exilic period.... Data available from this source ... can properly serve as direct, substantial testimony to the cultic mannerisms, temple procedures and priestly

---

20. See Biran 1981; Vaughan 1974; Barrick 1975.

concepts that obtained in and around the First Temple during the last third of its existence."[21] Given this presupposition, it is not surprising that Haran makes almost no use of artifactual or even textual data supplied by archaeology. In discussing Israelite temples he derives a hypothetical list of twelve or thirteen solely from biblical accounts. He cites the Arad sanctuary but denies that it was a temple. No Israelite high places have been found, since the Dan installation is neither temple nor *bāmâ* (in Haran's opinion, these are always distinct) but simply an open-air sanctuary. Thus Iron Age cultic installations at Megiddo, Taʿanach, Tell el-Farʿah North, Lachish, and ʿAjrud are not mentioned, nor are any of the many cultic stands, censers, votives, or funeral inscriptions cited. In the case of the one category where Haran discusses the correlation of artifacts with texts, the several tenth-century and later miniature horned incense altars, it is argued that these are irrelevant, since textual evidence shows that incense was not used before the seventh century in Israel. Haran concludes, "The truth of the matter is that archaeological evidence will remain somewhat irrelevant to the question of the place of incense in the Israelite cult until actual remains of Israelite temples eventually come to light."[22] Haran has already ruled out Arad as an Israelite temple; even so, he asserts that no incense altar was found there—ignoring the fact of the two small altars found flanking the entrance to the cella, with remains of burnt organic substance still in situ.[23]

Case studies. To support our indictment further, let us look at some case studies. Arad is especially instructive. The discovery of the ninth- to eighth-century sanctuary by Aharoni in 1963—the first Israelite temple outside the Bible—was first hailed with excitement (and not a little envy). But faulty excavation, initial overinterpretation, and pointless polemics, as well as publication that never got beyond sketchy preliminary reports, resulted in neglect by archaeologists and almost all other scholars, leaving this unique find in limbo. The neglect of Arad may be rationalized by assuming that the archaeological data in this case are not clear. However, more is certain than some scholars seem willing to admit: the Arad structure is a cultic installation, whether temple or *bāmâ*; its chronological range, although not precise, is ninth–eighth century at *minimum* and

---

21. Haran 1978, 3.
22. Haran 1978, 237.
23. See Haran 1978, 237; Aharoni 1968.

thus contemporary with the supposedly centralized cultus in Jerusalem; its context is indisputably Israelite; and its plan and furnishings give *tangible evidence* of at least burnt animal and food (if not incense) offerings.

The high place discovered by Biran at Tell Dan has generated even more controversy. Here again, arguments over stratigraphic detail and semantic differences between temple and high place in the Bible and whether it is legitimate to connect the structure with either—important, to be sure—should not be allowed to obscure certain fundamental facts. A consensus already exists that this impressive structure and its precincts are cultic in nature and that it was in public use at least in the ninth–eighth century at a site that was one of Israel's most prominent provincial centers.

Similarly, polemics about the date, location, and even the existence of Yohanan Aharoni's reconstructed temple at Beersheba (supposedly destroyed by Josiah's reform) should not detract from the significance of at least one discovery. The dismantled monumental altar (the first yet found) constitutes incontrovertible evidence of a local Israelite sanctuary of some sort, destroyed sometime in the eighth or the seventh century BCE (i.e., possibly by either Hezekiah or Josiah).

Perhaps more significant than the controversy and the neglect surrounding the above is the hesitancy to deal with the sanctuary discovered most recently, one that has not yet even generated the expected dispute. The Kuntillet ʿAjrud sanctuary, excavated in 1975–1976 by Zeʾev Meshel, is one of the most astonishing finds yet made in the biblical world. Here is a full-fledged cultic installation in the context of a desert fort, with inscribed votives and graffiti, the texts indicating beyond doubt that offerings were made both to "Yahweh and to his Asherah." Yet despite an Israel Museum exhibition and catalog and several adequate preliminary reports, scholars have seemed reluctant to seize upon the revolutionary implications of this material for the history of the Israelite cult.[24] The site is certainly ninth to eighth century, the language is Hebrew, and the material context of the inscriptions is Israelite-Judean. Whether one understands *yhwh wʾšrth* (the reading is indisputable) as "Yahweh and his (consort) Asherah" or "Yahweh and his Asherah-shrine," the conclusion that one is dealing with a highly syncretistic Israelite cult in the wilderness is inescapable. Further,

---

24. Meshel and Meyers 1976.

the painted scenes and figures on the pithoi, however interpreted, point unmistakably in the same direction (see also below).

A word of caution is appropriate at this point. The foregoing attempt to clarify matters by emphasizing the positive aspects of the archaeological record is not meant to oversimplify. However palpable and apparently self-evident archaeological data may appear, one must never underestimate the necessity or the difficulty of interpreting the facts—whether artifacts or textual facts. This leads us to the next point.

10.2.2. A Hopeful Critique

Any critique of the failure to relate archaeology creatively to the study of the Israelite cult obviously must be two-sided.

Archaeology can certainly be faulted for its failure to produce reliable and accessible data, that is, properly excavated, adequately interpreted, published evidence. The sad fact is that the bulk of the excavated material from ancient Palestine has been largely useless to the historian or nonspecialist, and, until recently, even to many archaeologists. The material was poorly dug, sketchily recorded, naively interpreted, and rarely integrated in an overall historical-cultural explanatory framework; frequently the basic data were not even published in catalog fashion. The long tradition of amateurism in biblical and Syro-Palestinian archaeology has resulted in a field that is characterized by arguments based on supposed facts that turned out to be hearsay rather than evidence. It is no wonder, then, that reconstructions based on archaeology are greeted today with about as much skepticism as are the past generation's "assured results of biblical criticism." Nevertheless, as I insisted above, even archaeology of this sort has produced *some* hard data, which all too often have been ignored. Above all it must be emphasized that our branch of archaeology has become much more professional in the last decade or so and, in coming of age, is now more sophisticated in both field and analytical techniques.[25] Presently we shall see the promising implications of this development.

On the other hand, biblical studies cannot escape blame entirely. The failure to engage archaeology in a serious dialogue in studies of the Israelite cult may be due to several factors. First, there has been the gen-

---

25. See Dever 1971, 1974a, 1976, 1980, 1982a, 1985.

eral tendency of biblical scholars since Wellhausen to be preoccupied with internal analysis of the literary sources in the Hebrew Bible. This tendency certainly marked early literary criticism, but it is scarcely less visible in later form criticism and redaction history, as well as in much of liberal and conservative biblical scholarship in Europe and America in general (the chief exception being fundamentalism, which rejected the Documentary Hypothesis outright—often appealing to archaeology for support). My dissatisfaction with the treatment of Haran lies precisely in his exclusive concentration on the literary sources in the Hebrew Bible; it shows how little has changed methodologically in many circles of biblical studies.[26]

W. F. Albright's well-known reaction, based on an "archaeological revolution" that gave promise of external data, was correct in pointing out that the literary-critical approach, even if successful, resulted merely in a history of the *literature*, not necessarily of the religion, of ancient Israel. But that Albright's own approach was also literary may be seen from the fact that much of what he and his students called archaeology was really the comparative study of the extrabiblical texts brought to light in excavation throughout the ancient Near East.[27] Further, the biblical archaeology movement has tended to focus even more specifically on the biblical literature. Two well-intended assumptions of this school, in my opinion, were naive and actually diminished the value of archaeology for our inquiry: (1) the notion that religion may be defined essentially in terms of thought, that is, *theology* rather than cult; and (2) the assumption that theological inferences drawn from the Hebrew Bible/Christian Old Testament are *historically* (in this case, archaeologically) verifiable.[28]

---

26. The same criticism could be leveled at much of conservative Jewish scholarship in past, as in Yehezkiel Kaufmann's great *The Religion of Israel* (1960, 1970, 1976; see also 1953). Further, the Israeli school today, despite its special access to archaeological data, carries on biblical studies largely in isolation from archaeology, both institutionally and ideologically. The best-balanced blend of archaeology, history, and devout biblical criticism, in my opinion, is still seen in de Vaux's work; note his exemplary treatment of Israelite religion in 1961, 274–517 (although now dated archaeologically).

27. See, for instance, Albright 1969, 1–3; and Wright 1969.

28. On the latter, see my critique of Wright and Biblical archaeology in Dever 1980, 2–12.

A second influence in the neglect of the study of archaeology and the Israelite cult stemmed from preconceived notions of Yahwism. This bias took several forms. Liberal scholars such as Herbert G. May made pioneering use of archaeology for cultic studies, but the evolutionary framework into which the data were forced obscured the actual development of Israelite religion.[29] Both the *Religionsgeschichte* and myth and ritual schools focused specifically on the cult, but the basic conception of Israelite religion rested on philosophical presuppositions that went unchallenged by the empirical evidence of archaeology. (Folklore and ethnography were adduced a posteriori but in an eclectic and uncritical fashion that modern ethno-archaeology would certainly reject.) Conservative biblical scholarship generally accepted the highly idealized version of Yahwism centralized in the Jerusalem cult presented in the Deuteronomic and Priestly works, so it paid little attention to the occasional disturbing discoveries of archaeology. The conservative Protestant character of much American biblical scholarship (including biblical archaeology), despite the appeal made to archaeology, tended to approach Israelite religion more in terms of theology than religious practice—almost as though the cult were something of an embarrassment.[30] Evangelical scholarship has produced a number of amateur archaeologists, some of whom have been almost obsessed with cultic explanations, but this approach was always confined to the comparative study of the pre- or non-Israelite cult, so as to enhance the notion of Yahwism as pure monotheism.[31] Finally, to orthodoxy of all forms, the mere suggestion of syncretism (below) was so anathema that archaeology has always been regarded with great suspicion.[32]

---

29. Thus May's work on Megiddo (1935) was the first on precisely our topic and is still usable today. He later collaborated with Walter C. Graham on a classic of Protestant liberal scholarship in the evolutionary vein, now simply a historical curiosity: Graham and May 1936.

30. See, for instance, Wright 1962.

31. James L. Kelso's (1968) publication of the excavation of Bethel is a case in point; for the refutation of his supposed Middle Bronze I "shrine of the patriarchs," see my review in Dever 1971. I have collected a vast literature on such cultic explanations among early amateur "biblical archaeologists," most of them American fundamentalists like Albright's codirector at Tell Beit Mirsim, M. G. Kyle (one of the authors of the classic series *The Fundamentals*; see Dixon et al. 1910–1915). See also n. 36 below.

32. The opposition of orthodoxy to archaeology is nowhere more determined

A partial explanation for the minimal impact of archaeology on the study of cult is, of course, simply that biblical scholarship in recent years has been unable to cope with the veritable flood of new discoveries, not to mention the necessary specialization of the field of archaeology itself. That deficiency, however, is not due to methodological differences and should gradually be rectified with the progress of both disciplines. To show how archaeology may contribute, I turn now to my final point.

10.3. A Theory and Strategy for Archaeological Elucidation of the Israelite Cult

10.3.1. An Alternate Theory

In light of the impasse just described, it may be timely to advance a bold new agenda. I suggest an alternate theory to what seems to have been for too long the prevailing view: (1) the notion that Israelite "ethical monotheism" in the monarchy was too austerely intellectual or too spiritually rarified to have developed an elaborate cultic apparatus; and (2) the contention, following the Deuteronomic and Priestly works, that Israelite worship was always centralized in Jerusalem and that the local shrines were suppressed or totally destroyed. Whatever the archaeological evidence or its interpretation, neither of these views of the religion of ancient Israel can now be defended on literary or form-critical, theological, or historical grounds.

Instead, I propose, as a working hypothesis, that early Israelite religion developed gradually out of the Late Bronze and early Iron Age fertility cults of greater Canaan and that, despite the growth of a royal/priestly cultus and its theology in Jerusalem, local cults continued to flourish, and some of them reflected a highly syncretistic blend of Yahwism and foreign practice until the end of the monarchy. Normative Judaism, as portrayed in the Deuteronomic and Priestly literature, is a construct of the late Judean monarchy and in particular of the exilic period. Thus our only resource for religious practice in the early formative period lies in correlating the minority view reflected in scattered indirect references in the Pentateuch

---

and outspoken than in Israel, where excavations can and have been closed down. Elsewhere, where perhaps it is less visible, archaeology is simply ignored by orthodox religionists.

and the Former Prophets with actual material remains of local cults unearthed by archaeology. In the investigation, biblical scholars should reassess the early, relatively casual, statements mentioning high places in Joshua–Judges (often associated with the enigmatic Asherah), compared with the numerous denunciations of foreign cults in the prophets. However, in the reinterpretation of the texts, archaeology may take priority, since the texts are isolated and ambiguous. These will have to be amplified and interpreted by archaeology (rather than the other way around), which has only begun to sense its full explanatory potential.

The starting point for the testing of the above theory lies in the acceptance of the ever-increasing body of unambiguous archaeological evidence for the existence of local shrines, such as those discussed above, in particular, Dan, Arad, and ʿAjrud. The actual archaeological illustration of cult paraphernalia and practice of every sort—embracing, perhaps, dimensions of the cult not mentioned in the Hebrew Bible—must be taken seriously.[33] The parade example thus far of archaeology's revolutionary potential is the recent, dramatic confirmation of the persistence of the cult of Asherah (= Anath/Astarte), the Canaanite goddess of love and war. Here some of the longenigmatic references in the biblical texts may finally be illuminated by the discovery of Israelite Asherah cult stands from tenth-century Taʿanach and by the reinterpreted eighth-century Khirbet el-Qom funerary inscriptions, which may refer to Asherah in connection with Yahweh. All this is thrown into sharp relief by the ninth- to eighth-century sanctuary at Kuntillet ʿAjrud, with its shrine, new classes of votives, Hebrew dedicatory inscriptions, and texts mentioning both "Yahweh and his Asherah" and Baal and El in parallelism.[34] Now it remains to see how this alternate theory—and it is only a theory—may be tested.

---

33. Stager and Wolff's brilliant reconstruction (1981) of a hitherto-unrecognized oil-pressing complex associated with the Dan sanctuary (there were probably also similar complexes at Taʿanach and Tell el-Farʿah North) is a prime example of both the surprises archaeology can produce and the new multidisciplinary approach that I am advocating here. For the best illustration of the Dan installation (although the text still interprets it as a "libation area"), see Laughlin 1981.

34. See the references in n. 6 above on Kuntillet ʿAjrud; for the new reading of Khirbet el-Qom, see n. 17 above; on the Taʿanach stand, see n. 7 above.

10.3.2. A Deliberate Strategy

The somewhat optimistic program I shall outline assumes an awareness that archaeology, particularly in the last decade, has become much more sophisticated in theory and method and that this orientation of the New Archaeology has now begun to transform the outlook of much traditional-style biblical or Syro-Palestinian archaeology. Elsewhere I have sketched this development and called attention to both the opportunities and the dangers it presents.[35] Here I wish only to suggest, without being exhaustive, how the fundamental insights of the newer archaeology may be applied specifically to the elucidation of the Israelite cult.

Much of the new look in Syro-Palestinian archaeology can be traced to a shift, for reasons beyond consideration here, away from a narrowly chronological and historical orientation, that is, from the kind of political history that initially seemed best suited to solving certain problems in biblical studies. The altered perspective derived first from the natural sciences and secondarily from cultural anthropology. Some of the watchwords of the New Archaeology of particular interest to the present inquiry are as follows: (1) systemic: the insistence that archaeology is a specialized branch of anthropology that examines the material evidence for extinct societies in total cultural and environmental *context*, which entails the use of extensive multidisciplinary and comparative (or cross-cultural) methods; (2) processual: the view that archaeology is concerned primarily with the variability of human behavior and thus seeks laws or patterns of cultural *adaptations and change*; (3) scientific: the assumption that archaeology not only must adopt quantative-statistical and analytical techniques from the natural sciences but must increasingly devote itself in both excavation and interpretation to the formulation and testing of hypotheses, that is, to specific *problem-solving*.

The *systemic* concept of archaeology as applied to the study of the Israelite cult would call first for the much broader examination of potential sites, areas, and installations in their *total* setting. The chronological-historical framework derived from stratigraphy and comparative typology is fundamental. But it is now clear that the comprehension of patterns of human behavior behind the archaeological record requires, first, the use

---

35. See the references in n. 25 above, especially Dever 1982a.

of data from all sources—artifactual, literary, paleo-environmental—and, second, the attempt to reconstruct the place and function of individual features in the larger cultural context. This is particularly crucial in using archaeology to investigate the role of religion in primitive societies. Thus our strategy in Syro Palestinian archaeology must be deliberately to seek to locate potential cultic sites and areas in Israel, Jordan, Egypt, and Syria and to complete large-scale exposure of appropriate Late Bronze and Iron Age levels, using the most sophisticated methods of data retrieval. From project design to final publication, the mass of varied and complex data must be analyzed by a truly multidisciplinary staff, so that the insights of archaeology, history, philology, ethnography, cultural anthropology, comparative religion and literature, theology, aesthetics, the history of art and technology, not to mention a number of branches of the natural sciences, can all be brought to bear on the elusive phenomenon of ancient religion and cult. Obviously, this agenda is ambitious and perhaps idealistic, but the alternative is to continue to distort and even to destroy the little archaeological evidence that may remain.

Processual for our purposes implies that archaeology is capable of discerning in material remains evidence of how religion may have functioned in the adaptation of an ancient society to its natural and cultural environment, how cultic practice expressed and validated the belief systems of that society, and how both evolved through time and circumstance. This goal of the newer archaeology is even more ambitious than the above (and still hotly debated), but its application to SyroPalestinian archaeology and cultic studies should at least be tested. For instance, can we compare the archaeological remains of Canaanite-Philistine and Israelite temples/shrines in number, distribution, size, artistic embellishment, or economic investment in relation to site and society, in order to determine how ancient Israel differed? (Here the silence of the archaeological record may indeed be significant.) Through chemical and physical means of testing, or by high-magnification use-wear analysis, can we ascertain how implements such as Israelite altars, censers, and votives were actually employed and to what degree they may reflect the fertility cult of greater Canaan rather than the Yahwistic theology of Priestly literature? On the basis of the artifactual evidence, can we trace religious syncretism in Israel through chronological and cultural *stages*, so as to offer a critique of the older evolutionary hypothesis that based itself solely on literary criticism and posited a simple evolution from polydemonism to ethical monotheism? These are relevant questions; since they cannot be answered satisfactorily by the literary sources alone, it is surely worthwhile to pursue archaeology to its limit in our inquiry.

Scientific suggests methods that have already been partially introduced in the multidisciplinary approach outlined above and promise greater precision in dating and understanding the nature and use of artifactual remains of the cult. But we can go further with the basic approach of science. We can formulate hypotheses concerning the Israelite cult on the basis of what we already know and then deliberately structure archaeological research projects to test these hypotheses in order to refine them or reject them in the light of new evidence and new hypotheses. Syro-Palestinian archaeology is too historically oriented ever to be truly scientific, but it could at least become more *systematic* and thus much more productive of data that could be used by theologians and historians of religion with some confidence.

10.4. Conclusion

This admittedly programmatic essay offers more questions than answers. But I have tried to show that the reaction against the proliferation of naive cultic explanations in the past has gone too far the other way,[36] that modern archaeology has vast unfulfilled potential. It may be true that the relatively damp climate of central Palestine and the vicissitudes of the country's long social and political history have conspired to rob us of much of the material evidence archaeology might have produced, such as the remains of the Jerusalem temple and its cultus. It is also evident that some elements of religion do not, in fact, lend themselves readily to archaeological investigation, so that, for instance, without textual data we should be very much in the dark on most matters of religious *belief* and even on certain aspects

---

36. On the excesses of cultic interpretation in the past, see n. 31 above. Yeivin (1973) has sharply criticized more recent archaeologists (who, however, were presumably not religiously motivated), but he is too skeptical. Aharoni was widely accused of a cultic bias in his strategy of fieldwork, and especially in his interpretation of Beersheba, but his instincts were not altogether unsound. Wright's *Shechem: The Biography of a Biblical City* (1965) has also been criticized by both archaeologists and biblical scholars; on this, see my critique in Dever 1980.

of practice such as priestly functions, various festal calendars, liturgy, and sacrificial systems. Above all, it must be stressed that archaeology is not the handmaiden of theology: by definition, it cannot validate theological propositions about the past by confirming the historicity of events as described in the Hebrew Bible.

Archaeology does have unique potential for illuminating actual Israelite religious practice in two directions. (1) First is its ability to penetrate *behind* the later and heavily theologized literary traditions. In doing so, it may yield tangible evidence of popular religion, an independent and invaluable corrective to the establishment view of the texts. (2) Second, archaeology can provide the essential basis for *comparative* studies, for it alone can illuminate neighboring cultures such as those of Late Bronze Age Palestine and Iron Age Philistine and Transjordan,[37] whose religious traditions will probably never be as copiously illustrated textually as those of ancient Israel are by the Bible. If a picture is worth a thousand words, then archaeology is a parallel way of viewing the ancient cult, in no way inferior to textual studies.[38]

Works Cited

Aharoni, Yohanon. 1968. "Arad: Its Inscriptions and Temple." *BA* 31:1–32.
———. 1969. "The Israelite Sanctuary at Arad." Pages 29–36 in *New Directions in Biblical Archaeology*. Edited by David Noel Freedman and Jonas Greenfield. Doubleday.
———. 1973a. *Beer-sheba I: Excavations at Tell Beer-sheba, 1969–1971 Seasons*. Institute of Archaeology, Tel Aviv University.
———. 1973b. "The Solomonic Temple, the Tabernacle and the Arad Sanctuary." Pages 1–8 in *Orient and Occident*. Edited by Harry A. Hoffner. AOAT 22. Neukirchener Verlag; Butzon & Bercker.

---

37. We now have no fewer than two dozen Late Bronze Canaanite temples from Israel (the latest from Tell Kitan, Lachish, and Mevorakh), along with the splendid Philistine temple at Tell Qasile, published by Amihai Mazar (1980–1985) in two volumes in the Qedem series.

38. After this chapter was written, a twelfth- to eleventh-century cultic installation, with a superb bronze figure of a bull, has been found near modern Jenin, in the area of the tribal territory of Manasseh; see Mazar 1982.

———. 1975a. "Excavations at Tel Beer-sheba, Preliminary Report of the Fifth and Sixth Season, 1973–1974." *TA* 2:146–68.
———. 1975b. *Lachish: The Sanctuary and the Residency (Lachish V)*. Institute of Archaeology, Tel Aviv University.
Albright, W. F. 1969. "The Impact of Archaeology on Biblical Research—1966." Pages 1–14 in *New Directions in Biblical Archaeology*. Edited by David Noel Freedman and Jonas C. Greenfield. Doubleday.
Avigad, Nahman. 1953. "The Epitaph of a Royal Steward from Siloam Village." *IEJ* 3:137–52.
Bar-Adon, Pesach. 1975. "An Early Hebrew Graffito in a Judean Desert Cave" [Hebrew]. *ErIsr* 12:77–80.
Barrick, Wilber B. 1975. "The Funerary Character of High Places: A Reassessment." *VT* 25:565–95.
Biran, Avraham. 1974a. "An Israelite Horned Altar at Dan." *BA* 37:106–7.
———. 1974b. "Tel Dan." *BA* 37:26–51.
———. 1980. "Tel Dan—Five Years Later." *BA* 43:168–82.
———, ed. 1981. *Temples and High Places in Biblical Times*. Nelson Glueck School of Biblical Archaeology.
Busink, Th. A. 1970. *Der Tempel von Jerusalem, von Salomo bis Herodes: Eine archäologisch-historische Studie unter Berücksichtigung des westsemitischen Tempelbaus*. Studia Francisci Scholten Memoriae Dicata 3. Brill.
Cross, Frank Moore. 1979. "Two Offering Dishes with Phoenician Inscriptions from the Sanctuary of ʿArad." *BASOR* 235:75–78.
Dever, William G. 1969–1970. "Iron Age Epigraphic Material from the Area of Khirbet el-Kôm." *HUCA* 40–41:139–204.
———. 1971. "Archaeological Methods and Results: A Review of Two Recent Publications." *Or* 40:461–71.
———. 1974a. *Archaeology and Biblical Studies: Retrospects and Prospects*. Seabury-Western Theological Seminary.
———. 1974b. "The MB IIC Stratification in the Northwest Gate Area at Shechem." *BASOR* 216:31–52.
———. 1976. "Archaeology." *IDBSup*, 44–52.
———. 1980. "Biblical Theology and Biblical Archaeology: An Appreciation of G. Ernest Wright." *HTR* 73:1–15.
———. 1982a. "The Impact of the 'New Archaeology' on Syro-Palestinian Archaeology." *BASOR* 242:15–28.
———. 1982b. "Monumental Architecture in Ancient Israel in the Period of the United Monarchy." Pages 269–306 in Studies in the Period of

David and Solomon and Other Essays: Papers Read at the International Symposium for Biblical Studies, Tokyo, December 1979. Edited by Tomoo Ishida. Yamakawa-Shuppansha.

———. 1984. "Asherah, Consort of Yahweh? New Evidence from Kuntillet 'Ajrûd." *BASOR* 255:21–37.

———. 1985. "Syro-Palestinian and Biblical Archaeology." Pages 31–74 in *The Hebrew Bible and Its Modern Interpreters*. Edited by Douglas A. Knight and Gene M. Tucker. Fortress; Scholars Press.

Dever, William G., H. Darrell Lance, and G. Ernest Wright, eds. 1970. *Gezer I: Preliminary Report of the 1964–66 Seasons*. Hebrew Union College Biblical and Archaeological School.

Dever, William G., et al. 1975. *Gezer II: Report of the 1967–70 Seasons in Fields I and II*. Hebrew Union College/Nelson Glueck School of Biblical Archaeology.

Dixon, A. C., et al. 1910–1915. *The Fundamentals: A Testimony to the Truth*. 12 vols. Testimony.

Freedman, David Noel. 1965. "Archaeology and the Future of Biblical Studies: The Biblical Languages." Pages 294–312 in *The Bible in Modern Scholarship*. Edited by J. Philip Hyatt. Abingdon.

Freedman, David Noel, and Jonas C. Greenfield, eds. 1969. *New Directions in Biblical Archaeology*. Doubleday.

Glock, Albert E. 1978. "Taanach." *EAEHL* 4:1138–47.

Graham, Walter C., and Herbert G. May. 1936. *Culture and Conscience: An Archaeological Study of the New Religious Past in Palestine*. University of Chicago Publications in Religious Education: Handbooks of Ethics and Religion. University of Chicago Press.

Graesser, Carl F. 1972. "Standing Stones in Ancient Palestine." *BA* 35:34–63.

Haran, Menahem. 1978. *Temples and Temple-Service in Ancient Israel: An Inquiry into the Character of Cult Phenomena and the Historical Setting of the Priestly School*. Clarendon.

Herzog, Zeev, Anson Rainey, and Shmuell Moshkovitz. 1977. "The Stratigraphy at Beer-sheba and the Location of the Sanctuary." *BASOR* 225:49–58.

Kaufmann, Yehezkiel. 1953. *The Biblical Account of the Conquest of Palestine*. Translated by M. Dagut. Magnes.

———. 1960. *The Religion of Israel: From Its Beginnings to the Babylonian Exile*. Translated and abridged by M. Greenberg. University of Chicago Press.

———. 1970. *The Babylonian Captivity and Deutero-Isaiah*. Translated by C. W. Efroymson. Union of American Hebrew Congregations.
———. 1976. *History of the Religion of Israel, from the Babylonian Captivity to the End of Prophecy*. Translated by C. W. Efroymson. Ktav.
Kelso, James L. 1968. *The Excavation of Bethel (1934–1960)*. AASOR 39. American Schools of Oriental Research.
Lapp, Paul W. 1964. "The 1963 Excavation at Ta'annek." *BASOR* 173:4–44.
———. 1967. "Taanach by the Waters of Megiddo." *BA* 30:1–27.
———. 1969. "The 1968 Excavations at Tell Ta'annek." *BASOR* 195:2–49.
Laughlin, John C. H. 1981. "The Remarkable Discoveries at Tel Dan." *BAR* 7.5:20–37.
Lemaire, André. 1977. "Les inscriptions de Khirbet el-Qôm et l'Ashérah de Yhwh." *RB* 84:597–608.
Loud, Gordon. 1948. *Megiddo II: Seasons of 1935–39*. OIP 62. University of Chicago Press.
May, Herbert G. 1935. *Material Remains of the Megiddo Cult*. OIP 26. University of Chicago Press.
Mazar, Amihai. 1980–1985. *Excavations at Tell Qasile*. 2 vols. Qedem 12, 20. Institute of Archaeology, Hebrew University of Jerusalem.
———. 1982. "The 'Bull Site': An Iron Age I Open Cult Place." *BASOR* 247:27–42.
Meshel, Ze'ev. 1978a. *Kuntillet 'Ajrud: A Religious Centre from the Time of the Judaean Monarchy on the Border of Sinai*. Israel Museum Catalog 175. The Israel Museum.
———. 1978b. "Kuntillet 'Ajrud: An Israelite Religious Center in Northern Sinai." *Expedition* 20:50–54.
———. 1979. "Did Yahweh Have a Consort? The New Religious Inscriptions from the Sinai." *BAR* 5.2:24–35.
Meshel, Ze'ev, and Carol Meyers. 1976. "The Name of God in the Wilderness of Zin." *BA* 39:6–10.
Meyers, Carol. 1976. *The Tabernacle Menorah: A Synthetic Study of a Symbol from the Biblical Cult*. American Schools of Oriental Research Dissertation Series 2. Scholars Press.
Naveh, Joseph. 1963. "Old Hebrew Inscriptions in a Burial Cave." *IEJ* 13:74–92.
———. 1979. "Graffiti and Dedications." *BASOR* 235:27–30.
Shiloh, Yigal. 1979. "Iron Age Sanctuaries and Cult Elements in Palestine." Pages 147–57 in *Symposia Celebrating the Seventy-Fifth Anniversary of the Founding of the American Schools of Oriental Research (1970–*

1975). Edited by Frank Moore Cross. American Schools of Oriental Research.

Stager, Lawrence E., and Samuel R. Wolff. 1981. "Production and Commerce in Temple Courtyards: An Olive Press in the Sacred Precinct at Tel Dan." *BASOR* 243:95–102.

Vaughan, Patrick H. 1974. *The Meaning of bāmâ in the Old Testament: A Study of Etymological, Textual and Archaeological Evidence*. SOTSMS 3. Cambridge University Press.

Vaux, Roland de. 1951. "La troisième campagne de fouilles à Tell el-Farʿah, près Naplouse." *RB* 58:393–430, 566–90.

———. 1961. *Ancient Israel: Its Life and Institutions*. Translated by J. McHugh. 2 vols. McGraw-Hill.

Wright, G. Ernest. 1962. "Cult and History: A Study of a Current Problem in Old Testament Interpretation." *Int* 16:3–20.

———. 1965. *Shechem: The Biography of a Biblical City*. McGraw-Hill.

———. 1969. "Biblical Archaeology Today." Pages 149–65 in *New Directions in Biblical Archaeology*. Edited by David Noel Freedman and Jonas C. Greenfield. Doubleday.

Yadin, Yigael. 1972. *Hazor, the Head of All Those Kingdoms*. Oxford University Press.

———. 1976. "Beer-sheba: The High Place Destroyed by King Josiah." *BASOR* 222:5–17.

Yadin, Yigael, et al. 1961. *Hazor III–IV: An Account of the Third and Fourth Seasons of Excavations, 1957–1958*. Magnes.

Yeivin, Shmuel. 1973. "Temples That Were Not" [Hebrew]. *ErIsr* 11:163–75 (English summary, 28).

Updated Bibliography

Olyan, Saul M. 1988. *Asherah and the Cult of Yahweh in Israel*. SBLMS 34. Scholars Press.

Ackerman, Susan. 1992. *Under Every Green Tree: Popular Religion in Sixth-Century Religion*. HSM 46. Scholars Press.

Bloch-Smith, Elizabeth. 1992. *Judahite Burial Practices and Beliefs about the Dead*. JSOTSup 123. JSOT Press.

Toorn, Karel van der. 1994. *From Her Cradle to Her Grave: The Role of Religion in the Life of the Israelite and Babylonian Woman*. BibSem 23. JSOT Press.

Dever, William G. 1995. "'Will the Real Israel Please Stand Up?' Part II: Archaeology and the Religions of Israel." *BASOR* 298:37–58.

Berlinerblau, Jacques. 1996. *The Vow and "Popular Religious Groups" of Ancient Israel: A Philological and Sociological Inquiry.* JSOTSup 210. Sheffield Academic.

Keel, Othmar. 1998. *The Symbolism of the Biblical World: Ancient Near Eastern Iconography and the Book of Psalms.* Eisenbrauns.

Keel, Othmar, and Christoph Uehlinger. 1998. *Gods, Goddesses, and Images of God in Ancient Israel.* Fortress.

Day, John. 2000. *Yahweh and the Gods and Goddesses of Canaan.* JSOTSup 265. Sheffield Academic.

Hadley, Judith M. 2000. *The Cult of Asherah in Ancient Israel and Judah: Evidence for a Hebrew Goddess.* Cambridge University Press.

Becking, Bob, Meindert Dijkstra, Marjo C. A. Korpel, and Karel J. H. Vriezen. 2001. *Only One God? Monotheism in Ancient Israel and the Veneration of the Goddess Asherah.* BibSem 77. Sheffield Academic.

Nakhai, Beth Alpert. 2001. *Archaeology and the Religions of Canaan and Israel.* ASOR Books 7. American Schools of Oriental Research.

Zevit, Ziony. 2001. *The Religions of Ancient Israel: A Synthesis of Parallactic Approaches.* Continuum.

LaRocca-Pitts, Elizabeth C. 2001. *"Of Wood and Stone": The Significance of Israelite Cultic Items in the Bible and Its Early Interpreters.* HSM 61. Eisenbrauns.

Gittlen, Barry M., ed. 2002. *Sacred Time, Sacred Place: Archaeology and the Religion of Israel.* Eisenbrauns.

Ackerman, Susan. 2003. "At Home with the Goddess." Pages 455–68 in *Symbiosis, Symbolism, and the Power of the Past: Canaan, Ancient Israel, and Their Neighbors from the Late Bronze Age through Roman Palestina.* Edited by William G. Dever and Seymour Gitin. Eisenbrauns.

Dever, William G. 2003. *Did God Have a Wife? Archaeology and Folk Religion in Ancient Israel.* Eerdmans.

Meyers, Carol. 2003. "Material Remains and Social Relations: Women's Culture in Agrarian Households of the Iron Age." Pages 425–44 in *Symbiosis, Symbolism, and the Power of the Past: Canaan, Ancient Israel, and Their Neighbors from the Late Bronze Age through Roman Palestina.* Edited by William G. Dever and Seymour Gitin. Eisenbrauns.

Zevit, Ziony. 2003. "False Dichotomies in Descriptions of Israelite Religion: A Problem, Its Origin, and a Proposed Solution." Pages 223–35 in *Symbiosis, Symbolism, and the Power of the Past: Canaan, Ancient Israel, and Their Neighbors from the Late Bronze Age through Roman Palestina*. Edited by William G. Dever and Seymour Gitin. Eisenbrauns.

Hess, Richard S. 2005. *Israelite Religion: An Archaeological and Biblical Survey*. Baker Academic.

Meyers, Carol. 2005. *Households and Holiness: Religious Culture of Israelite Women*. Fortress.

Ackerman, Susan. 2006. "Women and the Worship of Yahweh in Ancient Israel." Pages 189–97 in *Confronting the Past: Archaeological and Historical Essays on Ancient Israel in Honor of William G. Dever*. Edited by Seymour Gitin, J. Edward Wright, and J. P. Dessel. Eisenbrauns.

Beckman, Gary M., and Theodore J. Lewis, eds. 2006. *Text, Artifact, and Image: Revealing Ancient Israelite Religion*. BJS 346. Brown Judaic Studies.

Bodel, John P., and Saul M. Olyan, eds. 2008. *Household and Family Religion in Antiquity*. Blackwell.

Kottsieper, Ingo, Rüdiger Schmitt, and Jakob Wöhrle, eds. 2008. *Berührungspunkte: Studien zur Sozial- und Religionsgeschichte Israels und seiner Umwelt: Festschrift für Rainer Albertz zu seinen 65. Geburtstag*. AOAT 350. Ugarit-Verlag.

Albertz, Rainer, and Rüdiger Schmitt. 2010. *Family and Household Religion in Ancient Israel and the Levant*. Eisenbrauns.

Ebeling, Jennie R. 2010. *Women's Lives in Biblical Times*. T&T Clark.

Faust, Avraham. 2010. "The Archaeology of the Israelite Cult: Questioning the Consensus." *BASOR* 360:23–34.

Stavrakopoulis, Francesca, and John Barton, eds. 2010. *Religious Diversity in Ancient Israel and Judah*. T&T Clark.

Yasur-Landau, Assaf, Jennie R. Ebeling, and Laura B. Mazow, eds. 2011. *Household Archaeology in Ancient Israel and Beyond*. CHANE 50. Brill.

Meshel, Ze'ev. 2012. *Kuntillet 'Ajrud (Ḥorvat Teiman): An Iron Age II Religious Site on the Judah-Sinai Border*. Israel Exploration Society.

Dever, William G. 2013. "Religion and Cults in Bronze and Iron Age." Pages 285–96 in *The Oxford Encyclopedia of the Bible and Archaeology*. Edited by Daniel M. Master. Oxford University Press.

Albertz, Rainer, Beth Alpert Nakhai, Saul M. Olyan, and Rüdiger Schmitt, eds. 2014. *Family and Household Religion: Toward a Synthesis of Old

Testament Studies, Archaeology, Epigraphy, and Cultural Studies. Eisenbrauns.

Darby, Erin. 2014. *Interpreting Judean Pillar Figurines: Gender and Empire in Judean Apotropaic Ritual.* FAT 2/69. Mohr Siebeck.

Dever William G. 2014. "The Judean 'Pillar-Base Figurines': Mothers or 'Mother Goddesses'?" Pages 129–41 in *Family and Household Religion: Toward a Synthesis of Old Testament Studies, Archaeology, Epigraphy, and Cultural Studies.* Edited by Rainer Albertz, Beth Alpert Nakhai, Saul M. Olyan, and Rüdiger Schmitt. Eisenbrauns.

Dever, William G. 2015. "Israelite Women as 'Ritual Experts': Orthodoxy or Orthopraxis?" Pages 187–201 in *Celebrate Her Hands: Essays in Honor of Carol L. Meyers.* Edited by Susan Ackerman, Charles E. Carter, and Beth Alpert Nakhai. Eisenbrauns.

Hess, Richard S. 2017. "The Religions of the People of Israel and Their Neighbors." Pages 477–502 in *The Old Testament in Archaeology and History.* Edited by Jennie Ebeling, J. Edward Wright, Mark Elliott, and Paul V. M. Flesher. Baylor University Press.

Dever, William G. 2019. "Archaeology and Folk or Family Religion in Ancient Israel." *Religions* 10:1–11. https://doi.org/10.3390/rel10120667.

Faust, Avraham, ed. 2020. *Archaeology and Ancient Israelite Religion.* MDPI. https://tinyurl.com/SBLPress9035h1. (collection of articles first published in *Religions*).

Lewis, Theodore J. 2020. *The Origin and Character of God: Ancient Israelite Religion through the Lens of Divinity.* Oxford University Press.

Ackerman, Susan. 2022. *Women and the Religion of Ancient Israel.* AYBRL. Yale University Press.

11

The Silence of the Text

This essay was written in 1992, by which time I was beginning to publish on religion and cult in ancient Israel (see chapter 10 above). I was also realizing how radically different our portrait was when drawn from our two sources: texts and artifacts (and idea developed further in chapter 13 below). But I had not yet pursued the interplay in detail with specific case studies.

When I was invited to contribute to a Festschrift for Philip King, it occurred to me that 2 Kgs 23 might yield some results—especially on showing how archaeology might provide a real-life *context* for biblical narratives. Phil King had long combined archaeology and biblical studies, so this seemed like a good tribute to him in light of our long and varied associations.

For recent bibliography, see chapter 10 above and the Updated Bibliography (arranged chronologically) at the end of the Works Cited below.

In *The First Historians: The Hebrew Bible and History*, Baruch Halpern observes, "Rightly or wrongly, denying the historicity of Hezekiah's or Josiah's reform has been a reliable cottage industry."[1] Norbert Lohfink previously posed the issue succinctly:

> It remains an open question what kind of historical and sociological reality stands behind the Deuteronomic phenomenon. Was there actually a "movement"? Or are we concerned with "literature," behind which

---

Originally published as pages 143–68 in *Scripture and Other Artifacts: Essays on the Bible and Archaeology in Honor of Philip J. King*. Edited by Michael D. Coogan, J. Cheryl Exum, and Lawrence E. Stager. Westminster John Knox, 1994. printed by permission.

1. Halpern 1988, 26.

stand only a few individuals, be they writers, theologians, or government officials?²

Lohfink then proceeded to raise the explicit question whether the account of the Josianic reform in 2 Kgs 23 could be construed as a reliable source for the history of Israelite religion. He had stated, however, at the outset of his analysis that "archaeology and epigraphy are not of much further help." As a consequence, Lohfink's study becomes mired in minute, internal analysis of the text, without yielding any firmer historical conclusions than innumerable previous studies had. As a recent survey of scholarly interpretations of 2 Kgs 23 points out:

> If laid end to end, the scholarly pages written about Josiah's reform might well reach to the moon. Much has been written, because interpreters long have realized that in Josiah's reform lies the key to Deuteronomy, and in Deuteronomy lies the key to much of the Old Testament.³

It is the contention of this chapter that the skepticism or indecisiveness of most biblical scholars regarding the historicity of 2 Kgs 23 is unwarranted and, further, that recent archaeological data provide for the first time a credible historical-cultural context for this notoriously enigmatic passage in the Hebrew Bible. It would seem obvious, given the increasing attention being paid to archaeology and the ancient Israelite cult in recent years, that someone would have surveyed the rich archaeological data that now illuminate almost every single aspect of the reforms attributed to Josiah. Yet most commentators—even those as recent and as comprehensive as Lowery—ignore the archaeological data altogether.

11.1. Prolegomenon: Text and Artifact

More than simple neglect is involved in biblical scholars' typical exclusion of archaeological evidence in discussing 2 Kgs 23 or any other aspect of the Israelite cult. The most benign explanation of the omission would be that most historians of ancient Israel have been trained not as historians but as

---

2. Lohfink 1987, 459.
3. Lowery 1990, 190.

philologians and thus have been quite naturally preoccupied with analysis of the texts, which do indeed pose sufficient problems in themselves. There is, however, a rather naive historiographical presupposition here, namely, that the biblical texts alone, properly understood, will yield an adequate history. At best, this leads to what Giovanni Garbini and others have rightly characterized as simply paraphrasing the Bible. At worst, biblical scholars have formed an unconscious (?) alignment with the theological biases of the orthodox nationalist, minority parties that shaped the literary tradition in the Hebrew Bible in its final form in the postexilic period (Garbini's "state of psychological subjection"[4]). But philology plus theology does not equal history, as Halpern has shown in his brilliant exposé of historiographic models in biblical scholarship.[5] And since it is becoming increasingly clear that an understanding of the development of Israelite religion is dependent upon working out the larger history of the entity we call Israel, modern scholarship is at an impasse. The crucial question, now widely acknowledged, is how to write an adequate history of Israel. The recent works of Thomas L. Thompson and Gösta W. Ahlström, far from representing the breakthrough that they claim, only prove how serious the dilemma is.[6]

At a deeper level, text-based histories of Israel and of Israelite religion have exacerbated the problem. Since Gunkel and the advent of form criticism, it has been commonplace to state that the biblical texts will yield the kernel of historical truth that they are presumed to contain, but only if they can be located in an appropriate (i.e., original) *Sitz im Leben*. But in practice, the task has been reduced to that of recovering merely a *Sitz im Literatur*. Of course, the Hebrew Bible is literature, but literature is not life, at least not real life; it is, rather, the product of the literate imagination and therefore more fiction than history (although by that account no less true in some sense). It is only archaeological evidence—W. F. Albright's *realia*—that can help to balance the picture derived from texts, by providing external data that have not been subjected to the same editorial process as texts and therefore in principle constitute a more objective witness to events in the past.[7]

---

4. Garbini 1988, 7, 174.
5. Halpern 1988, 3–35.
6. Thompson 1992; Åhlström 1993.
7. See Dever 1990b, 1994a, 1994b, 1994c; Thompson 1987, 25–28; and the several essays in Edelman 1991. Add now, more from the perspective of art history,

Most biblical scholars, however, biased as they are toward texts, have tended to follow Martin Noth in ignoring or denigrating archaeological data as "mute."[8] The obvious point is that artifacts are no more mute than texts: for the student who does not know Hebrew, the Hebrew Bible will appear to be mute. In the same way, if the biblical scholar does not know the language of archaeology, or does not consult the specialist who does know, the material culture record will remain silent (see Knauf 1991, 26). Yet archaeology today can be eloquent, and, as several of us have argued, archaeological evidence can even take precedence over texts in history writing. That is especially true in writing a history of Israelite religion, although no recent work has done justice to the full potential of archaeology today.[9]

A final stricture in this connection is even more serious than neglect or negative assessments of archaeological data: the actual bias against cult that is evident in many works, especially those of Christian scholars. Elsewhere I have suggested that the fault may be due to the influence of the typically Protestant doctrine of *sola scriptura*, which tends to favor the written and spoken word, that is, theology, at the expense of religious practice or ritual and regards overly rational formulations as more normative than emotional or psychological expressions of belief. This elitist approach to Israelite religion, typically male and clerical, may be characterized in terms of a verbal versus visceral gestalt, and it has many shortcomings (Dever 1994a). A refreshing alternative is seen in several recent works on popular or family religion (see definitions below), some of them utilizing

---

Winter 1983; Schroer 1987; Keel and Uehlinger 1998. These recent works contain bibliography to a much larger literature on the problems of relating texts to artifacts in the study of Israelite history and religion—a study that, in my opinion, is just beginning.

8. See Noth 1960, 47–48; Herrmann 1975, 36 n. 25; Rendtorff 1983, 2; J. Miller 1976, 40–48; 1987; Rösel 1992, 74. Cf. Knauf 1991, 26.

9. As discussed below, Smith's (1990) treatment of deities makes a significant beginning, but Albertz's (1992) synthesis comes closest by far to what I envision a history of Israelite religion to be. Yet even Albertz (1992, 1:307–37) deals only with the general literary-historical setting of what he calls the struggle between "official syncretism and poly-yahwism," between "private syncretism and internal religious pluralism." See further Dever 1983; 1987, 209–22; see also references in note 7 above.

much more of the newer archaeological evidence on actual religious practice—several, not surprisingly, by women writers.

What is needed, in my opinion, is a phenomenological or functionalist approach to religion and cult in ancient Israel, using archaeological data to illuminate the biblical texts. Until then, it is the text—not archaeology—that will remain silent, or at least ambiguous. That is certainly true of intransigent texts such as 2 Kgs 23. Instead of embarking upon yet more futile quests for a *Hebraica veritas*, let us seek behind the present text of the Bible (all we shall ever have) a more fundamental *archeologica veritas*, a notion of how it really was in the past. We may never know precisely, but this venture will likely be more fruitful than continually manipulating texts that by now have yielded all the history they contain.

11.2. Descriptions of the Cult in 2 Kings 23: Fact or Fiction?

Much of the critical discussion of 2 Kgs 23 over the past century has revolved around the question of whether or not the Deuteronomistic account of Josiah's sweeping religious reforms, edited into its present form in the exilic period, is propaganda. One's suspicions that the litany of Josiah's successful reform measures in 2 Kgs 23 may be simply a literary convention are strengthened by looking at the parallel passages in 2 Kgs 18:4 regarding Hezekiah and in 2 Kgs 21:1–9 regarding Manasseh. We have virtually the same list—*bāmôt, maṣṣēbôt*, "asherim," the "host of heaven," child sacrifice, magic, and so on—all typifying, of course, precisely the overriding *Tendenz* (one might say obsession) of the later Deuteronomistic Historians.

Let us admit at the outset that the *Sitz im Literatur* of 2 Kgs 23 is propaganda. But what of the *Sitz im Leben*, in real life? The point often missed is that the very force of the polemic against popular cults in the Deuteronomistic History, projected back into the seventh century BCE, is the best argument that they existed at that time—and continued later. Thus far, however, our argument for the historicity of 2 Kgs 23 is based on a commonsense application of form-critical methods to the text alone. Is there any external evidence for the cults that Josiah is said to have suppressed? There is indeed, in the archaeological data. Yet the most recent survey of scholarship such as Lowery (above) reveals that this is a rich lode that virtually no one has mined.

Let us begin with the texts themselves. An initial examination of all the references to what I shall call popular cults in 2 Kgs 23 allows us to group their principal features conveniently into several general categories: (1) unauthorized priests; (2) *bāmôt* and *maṣṣēbôt*; (3) veneration of the goddess Asherah and her cult symbol the asherah; (4) proscribed altars and incense offerings; (5) horse-and-chariot imagery, connected with solar and astral deities; (6) temple prostitution; (7) child sacrifice; (8) magic; and (9) tombs and burial practices.

Further analysis shows that these aspects of popular cults can be distributed into three locales: the Jerusalem temple itself; the immediate vicinity of the temple and elsewhere in Jerusalem; and the countryside. Thus, in the temple the point of contention in the Josianic story was the presence of "vessels" for Baal and Asherah; of "vestments" (or "tent shrines") for Asherah; of shrines/sanctuaries for "male prostitutes"; *'ăšērîm*, or asherah symbols; and representations of horses and chariots. Elsewhere in Jerusalem, the attack on cults focuses on *bāmôt*, *maṣṣēbôt*, incense altars, *'ăšērîm*, child sacrifice, and tombs and rites for the dead. In other cities and in the rural areas, the references are to *bāmôt* and *battê-bāmôt* (often in city gates and dedicated to foreign gods such as Chemosh and Milcom); local, unauthorized priests eating unleavened bread; local altars, sometimes for burning incense to Baal; and offerings to the "host of heaven."

Although the above references to popular cults are relatively straightforward in the Hebrew text of 2 Kgs 23 (apart from a few difficulties; see below), commentators seem curiously reluctant to take these references seriously. Are scholars simply unaware of recent archaeological data? Or is there some hidden theological or other ideological presumption at work, such as that the cult of ancient Judah could not have been that corrupt compared to an idealized pure Yahwism? Whatever the reasons for the neglect, the fact is that every one of the above aspects of the popular cults mentioned in 2 Kgs 23 can now be illuminated by archaeological discoveries, and in some detail.

1. Unauthorized priests. As is well known, the Deuteronomistic tradition regards only the Jerusalem or Aaronide priesthood as legitimate. Nevertheless, among the seventh- to sixth-century BCE ostraca at Arad, where there is a flourishing tripartite temple (see below), there are references to local individuals, no doubt priests, who bear the names of priestly families known from biblical texts (Meremoth, Pashur, and the "sons of

Korah"; note also Ostracon 18, mentioning a *bēt YHWH*, probably not Jerusalem but the Arad temple, contra Yohanan Aharoni). Furthermore, two shallow offering plates, found at the base of the altar in the outer court, are incised with the letters *qoph kaph*, probably an abbreviation for *qōdeš kōhănîm*, "set apart for the priests." At Dan, a fine bronze scepter was certainly used by local priests in the ninth- to eighth-century BCE sanctuary. The above evidence underlines the concern of the Deuteronomistic Historians to discredit all but the Jerusalem priesthood: these were rivals.[10]

2. *Bāmôt* and *maṣṣēbôt*. Much ink has been spilled trying to identify the mysterious *bāmâ* on textual grounds. The archaeological picture, however, is sufficiently clear to enable us to use the evidence to illuminate many biblical texts in more detail (although it was already clear that *bāmôt* were simply raised platforms or outdoor shrines, often associated with Asherah symbols such as trees or wooden poles, standing stones, and altars). A full-fledged ninth to eighth-century BCE sanctuary at Tel Dan, the northern cultural capital, provides us with an excellent example of what an Israelite *bāmâ* probably looked like. The central installation, a massive stone platform approached by steps, no doubt a large outdoor altar, may in fact be the very *bēt-bāmôt* referred to in 1 Kgs 12:31 (probably not an example of a "house on a high place" but rather a "shrine on a high place"). An earlier Israelite cult place, the twelfth-century BCE Bull Shrine in the tribal territory of Manasseh, a hilltop sanctuary with an altar and a standing stone, can also be plausibly construed as a *bāmâ*.[11] Fragments of terra-cotta stands may illuminate the reference in 2 Kgs 23:5 to "burning incense on the high places." Finally, a series of eighth to seventh-century BCE hilltop tumuli west of Jerusalem may well be connected with both *bāmôt* and funerary rites.[12] The congruence between these (and other) actual archaeological discoveries and biblical descriptions of *bāmôt* is adequate, in my opinion, to support their identification of the two, whatever etymological difficulties may remain.

We now know a number of Iron Age *maṣṣēbôt*, which are simply commemorative standing stones erected in cult places. Most instructive is the example of a *maṣṣēbâ* at tenth-century BCE Tell el-Farʿah North, the bibli-

---

10. See Aharoni 1981, 35–38, 115–17; Herzog, Rainey, and Moshkovitz 1984, 12–22; Ussishkin 1988, 155; Biran 1989, 29.
11. Mazar 1982.
12. See Biran 1980, 1986, 1989; Mazar 1982; cf. Holladay 1987, 260–61.

cal capital city of Tirzah, which is actually located in the gate plaza (2 Kgs 23:8). Note also the contemporary *maṣṣēbâ* in the tenth-century BCE cultic structure at Taʿanach. I have already mentioned the *maṣṣēbâ* at the Iron I Bull Site. Finally, there is a *maṣṣēbâ* at the center of the rear wall of the inner chamber (the biblical *dəbîr*) of the ninth- to seventh-century BCE temple at Arad. It may be noteworthy that at two of the three sites listed above, *maṣṣēbôt* are associated with *bāmôt*, just as they are in 2 Kgs 23.[13]

3. Veneration of Asherah. Until recently, biblical scholars had followed the redactors of the biblical text, as well as nearly all later Jewish and Christian commentators, in downplaying the more than forty occurrences in the Hebrew Bible of the term *ʾăšērâ* in its various forms, as though *ʾăšērâ* referred merely to a tree, wooden pole, or some other symbol, not to the deity herself. This remained true despite the obvious fact that in at least half a dozen or so passages in the Hebrew Bible the term must refer not merely to a symbol of the goddess but to Asherah the great Mother Goddess of Canaan herself (including 2 Kgs 23:4, 7), well known from the Ugaritic texts as the consort of El. Today all that has changed, largely as a result of archaeological discoveries. These include especially the eighth-century BCE Hebrew texts from Khirbet el-Qom and Kuntillet ʿAjrud mentioning Asherah as an agent of blessing alongside Yahweh as his consort. Several recent studies now acknowledge the pervasiveness of the cult of Asherah in ancient Israel, from the period of the judges until the end of the monarchy and even into the exilic period—and in official Yahwist circles, as well as in the popular cults.[14] It is no surprise that 2 Kgs 23 refers to "vessels made for Asherah" (23:4) and women "weaving vestments [?] for Asherah" (23:7). In neither case can we interpret these as references to the cult symbol or the like. In the first instance, *ʾăšērâ* is in parallelism with

---

13. See Chambon 1984, pl. 8; Lapp 1967, 19–20; Herzog, Rainey, and Moshkovitz 1984, 7.

14. The bibliography is now extensive, but for Khirbet el-Qom, see Dever 1970, 1984; Zevit 1984; Hadley 1987; Keel and Uehlinger 1992, 199–317. For Kuntillet ʿAjrud, see Meshel 1978a, 1978b, 1979; Beck 1982; Dever 1984; Smith 1990, 85–88; Keel and Uehlinger 1992, 199–317. Several essays in Miller, Hanson, and McBride 1987 discuss both these inscriptions, as well as acknowledging their crucial significance; see P. Miller 1987; Coogan 1987; McCarter 1987; and Tigay 1987. On the cult of Asherah, add Winter 1983; Dever 1984; Hestrin 1987a, 1987b; Olyan 1988; Smith 1990, 80–114; and Hadley 2000.

Baal; if Baal is a deity, so is Asherah. The occurrence of the definite article is almost certainly a Deuteronomic addition, at a later period, when there was evidently a great deal of confusion as to who/what the now-prohibited and largely forgotten 'ăšērâ actually was.

This suggestion is strengthened by the fact that in the second reference to 'ăšērâ (2 Kgs 23:7) the present Hebrew text is corrupt or at least confused, and it obviously was so already by the third century BCE, when the LXX translation was made. The MT has 'ōrəgôt ... bāttîm, the women "wove houses/temples"—an impossibility, unless one takes bāttîm periphrastically to mean "tent shrines." The LXX, however, reads chettiein, and the Lucianic (Lagarde) text has stolas, both of which mean "garment," "tunic," and may presuppose Hebrew kotnôt, "tunic," "priestly garment" (from which the RSV derives "vestments," emending bāttîm to baddîm, "white linen"). Some targums have məkôlîn, "curtains"; Kimchi, perhaps combining several versions, reads "curtain enclosures."[15] Which is the superior text? Is it the LXX, in which case one might argue that "vestments" were being woven for a wooden or metal image of the goddess (as one sees clothed images of the Virgin in Roman Catholic churches)? Or is it the MT, in which case woven tent shrines—perhaps in the ancient (and modern) Near Eastern desert tradition—were being erected as pavilions for Asherah in the temple precincts (alongside the bāttîm of the "consecrated ones" in the same verse)? As for weaving in temple precincts, it may be significant that the eighth-century BCE shrine at Kuntillet ʿAjrud produced more than one hundred examples of linen and woolen textiles, very similar to those mentioned in biblical passages describing priestly vestments.[16] The very persistence of the symbols and imagery of Asherah attests to her real power, namely, her existence in the consciousness of the majority of ordinary folk in ancient Israel and Judah. As Susan Ackerman trenchantly observes, "In the ancient Near East the idol was the god."[17]

To be sure, in 2 Kgs 23:6 a cult symbol of the goddess, rather than Asherah, is implied, something that could be brought out from the temple, burned, and pounded into dust—here probably a wooden image. Not surprisingly, archaeology has not managed to recover any such wooden 'ăšērîm from the Iron Age because of lack of preservation. In some passages

---

15. Cogan and Tadmor 1988, 286.
16. Meshel 1978a, 1978b; Stager and Wolff 1981, 98.
17. Ackerman 1992, 65; cf. Keel and Uehlinger 1992, 203.

(as 2 Kgs 21:7), the image of the ’ăšērâ appears to have been made of metal (*pesel*, "graven image"), probably iron or bronze, but these have not been recovered either by archaeology.

I would argue, however, that the hundreds of ninth- to sixth-century BCE terra-cotta *dea nutrix* figurines (as Albright dubbed them) should be understood as representations of the Mother Goddess, manifestations to bring the reality of the goddess and her power closer to hand. Certainly these are not mourner figurines, like their Late Bronze Age predecessors, nor are they merely toys or the like. These figurines portray the great Mother Goddess of Canaan, primarily as a nursing mother, that is, in one of her primary roles, of ensuring the successful rearing of infants and children. The figurines must, therefore, be associated with Asherah, virtually the only Canaanite fertility goddess still known in the Iron Age in Israel. Anat and Astarte are rarely mentioned in the Hebrew Bible, apparently having coalesced with Asherah, who was undoubtedly assimilated into early Israel from Late Bronze Age Canaan, along with her consort El (later, however, identified with Baal so as to discredit her).

Despite our inability to be certain of the above identification, increasing numbers of scholars are coming to this commonsense realization, which I have long held.[18] If we are right, these common figurines are miniatures of life-sized images of Asherah that once existed throughout ancient Israel and Judah.

There are estimated to be more than three thousand of the terra-cotta figurines, found everywhere but particularly in domestic contexts and also in tombs, where they attest to family religion (see below).[19] A mold for mass producing these figurines, however, found in the tenth-century BCE cultic structure at Taʿanach, suggests that they could also be presented as votives, or used as tokens of sympathetic magic (see below), at shrines. The larger examples of Asherah, either in wood or metal, may all have been destroyed, as the Deuteronomistic History claims. The biblical writers, who as far as we can tell from the terminology never explicitly mention the miniatures, probably tried to suppress them as well, although by chance many have survived. In any case, it was the perceived actual

---

18. See Holland 1977; Dever 1987, 226; 1994a; Winter 1983, 95–199; Schröer 1987, 260–81; Holladay 1987, 276–78; Bird 1990, 1991; Beck 1990; Bloch-Smith 1992, 94–100; Keel and Uehlinger 1992, 380–86.

19. Holladay 1987, 272–80.

existence of Asherah, no doubt in many circles regarded as the consort of Yahweh, that gave these images their awesome power. Thus Josiah would naturally have attempted to purge such images from the temple in Jerusalem, as well as destroying the numerous examples in the countryside. He was foiled, however, by what we now call the formation processes of the archaeological record and also by the persistence of the popular cults that were devoted at least in part to Asherah, the ancient Mother Goddess of Canaan.[20]

4. Proscribed altars and incense offerings. Large altars are now known at many twelfth- to sixth-century BCE archaeological sites, including the Bull Site, Arad (above), and Kuntillet ʿAjrud (benches, which certainly served as altars for offerings, as in Late Bronze Age temples).[21] At Dan, several shovels were found adjacent to the stone altar in the *liškâ* (or biblical "shrine") adjacent to the high place, presumably for burnt animal offerings, as in the biblical descriptions. At Arad, preliminary reports indicated burned animal bones around the large altar in the outer court as well as an oily organic substance on top of the small stone altars at the entrance to the inner sanctum. Unfortunately, inadequate excavation methods and incomplete publication prevent us from being more specific.[22]

The complaint in 2 Kgs 23:5 and 8 about altars and incense burning clearly has to do with local altars that violated the Deuteronomistic attempt at centralization of worship. As for incense burning, it was an accepted part of Israelite worship, according to the Deuteronomistic and Priestly sources, and indeed it is attested archaeologically. In addition to the Arad evidence noted above, we have dozens of small stone horned altars from tenth- to sixth-century BCE Israelite and Judahite sites, which were presumably used for incense burning (among other offerings).[23]

5. Horse-and-rider imagery; solar and astral deities. The reference in 2 Kgs 23:11 to horses and chariots of the sun has sometimes been thought problematic. The allusion to solar and astral worship, however, is clear.[24]

---

20. See Dever 1984; cf. Oden 1976; Olyan 1988.
21. Mazar 1982; Biran 1986, 179–87; Meshel 1978a, 1978b, 1979.
22. Herzog, Rainey, and Moshkovitz 1984, 11–15; cf. Ussishkin 1988; Holladay 1987, 256–57. Cf. Biran 1986, 1980.
23. See Gitin 1992; on incense, Haran 1978, 236–38.
24. See Taylor 1989; Smith 1990, 116; Ackerman 1992, 79–99.

It was possibly of Phoenician or Neo-Assyrian origin, but it was equally likely to have had a continuous local ancestry going back to Canaanite origins in the Late Bronze Age.

The horse and chariot may have a similar pedigree. Miniature terracotta chariot models—usually drawn by horses or oxen and driven by a deity (or a pair of deities)—are well known from Syria throughout the second millennium BCE. They are also attested in Palestine by fragments (wheels, etc.) from the Middle Bronze Age and possibly later. In the Iron Age, however, we have preserved for us only the horse figurines, although these are fairly common in eighth- to sixth-century BCE archaeological contexts.[25]

References in 2 Kgs 23:4–5 to "the sun, the moon, the planets, and all the host of heaven" clearly imply that solar and astral deities were commonly venerated (see above). Archaeological evidence of such cults, however, would not be likely to survive, except in figurative art, and Israelite art is generally thought to have been nonexistent, except perhaps for the ninth- ot seventh-century BCE ivories and seals.

Several members of the Freiburg school have recently challenged the above assumptions, such as Urs Winter, Silvia Schroer, and particularly Othmar Keel, culminating in his *Göttinnen, Götter, und Gottessymbole: Neue Erkenntnisse zur Religionsgeschichte Kanaans und Israels aufgrund bislang unerschlossener ikonographischer Quellen* (with Christoph Uehlinger).[26] Keel's earlier works brought together a surprising array of genuinely Israelite and comparative artistic motifs, especially on hundreds of seals and seal impressions. Keel and Uehlinger, building largely on seals—many of them with horses, bearing sun disks on their heads, or with winged sun disks—argue that by the seventh century BCE Judahite religion was heavily influenced by Phoenician, Aramaean, and Neo-Assyrian solar and astral cults. One might recall even earlier evidence, as seen, for instance, in the winged sun disk carried on the back of a bullock on the tenth-century BCE Ta'anach stand; the moon crescent and stars of the Pleiades on the tenth-century *naos*, or house temple (probably of Asherah),

---

25. Holladay 1987, 265; Bloch-Smith 1992, 101–2; see Keel and Uehlinger 1992, 392–95.

26. Translated into English as *Gods, Goddesses, and Images of God in Ancient Israel* (1998).

at Tell el-Farʻah North; or several tenth- to eighth-century BCE female figurines that are sometimes interpreted as holding a sun disk.[27]

6. Temple prostitution. The interpretation of qədēšîm in 2 Kgs 23:7 as male prostitutes may be open to question. Usage of the feminine form in such passages as Deut 23:16–17 and Hos 4:14 in parallel with zônâ, "prostitute," may suggest a sexual function. The remaining passages, however (as 1 Kgs 14:24; 15:12; 22:47; Job 36:14), simply associate the term with ʾăšērîm, idols, and other "abominations." It is worth recalling that the consonantal text can be read simply as "consecrated ones," that is, temple functionaries, those dedicated to temple service, both male and female. Furthermore, we now have actual archaeological evidence of the use of the term qōdeš for inanimate cult objects such as kraters, platters, and store-jars in eighth to seventh-century BCE cultic contexts at Arad, Beersheba, and Tel Miqne/Ekron.[28] The common notion of cultic prostitution, which seems to derive from somewhat dubious interpretations of the Ugaritic evidence or else from outdated views of the Scandinavian-British myth and ritual school, may be mistaken. The womanat-the-window motif on the ninth- to eighth-century BCE ivories is sometimes taken to represent a temple prostitute, but I think that these scenes are rather to be connected with the female deity who stands in the door or peers out of the window of the terra-cotta naos, or household temple model, of which we now have numerous Iron Age examples (see above; one from Idalion, in Cyprus, has the deity at the window).[29] It must be admitted, however, that ritual prostitution would not have been out of keeping with the overall picture of what we know of the cult of Asherah, given her fertility associations. In any case, we have no direct archaeological witness of cultic prostitution in the Iron Age in Israel or Judah.

It may be significant that the Iron Age Asherah figurines (above) are decidedly chaste in comparison with the typical Late Bronze Age fertility plaques. Full frontal nudity and exaggerated sexual features are replaced by a completely stylized lower body (the pillar base), and only the breasts are prominently modeled. This may suggest that the more overtly sexual

---

27. See Keel and Uehlinger 1992, 1994; Winter 1983; Schröer 1987; cf. Hestrin 1987b; Chambon 1984, 66; Dever 1984, 28; Taylor 1989; Beck 1990.

28. Aharoni 1975, 167; Herzog, Rainey, and Moshkovitz 1984, 12–15; Gitin 1990, 41.

29. Schröer 1987, 519.

aspects of the Canaanite fertility cults were deemphasized in later Israel, so that Asherah was now more mother than consort. But this is largely speculative.

7. Child sacrifice. A number of studies have explored the limited textual evidence for child sacrifice in ancient Israel.[30] There is no direct archaeological evidence, however, nor should we expect any to be preserved—unless, of course, child sacrifice had been practiced on a scale large enough to compare with the well-known Phoenician Topheth at Carthage, where hundreds of cremation urns of children and dedicatory stelae have been excavated.[31] Archaeologically, all we can say is that 2 Kgs 23:10 locates the Topheth in the Valley of Hinnom, south and southwest of the Dung Gate (see Jer 7:31–32; 19:6), which later tradition still remembered as a place of death, desolation, and abomination (Hebrew *gê'-hinnōm* = Greek *geenna*; Latin *gehenna*, "hell"). No systematic excavations have ever been carried out in most of the Hinnom Valley, so the archaeological record is thus far silent. A few Iron Age tombs excavated south of the Jaffa Gate simply confirm the fact that areas outside the city walls were traditionally used for burials (see below).

8. Magic. A number of passages in the Bible reveal that a component of popular cults, going back at least to the period of the judges, was magic in various forms. This included consulting diviners or astrologers for omens, sorcerers for casting spells, mediums for inquiring of the dead, and so on.[32] In the Deuteronomistic tradition, these practices were, of course, proscribed, but there is no reason to suppose that they were rare in ancient Israel and Judah. On the contrary, once again the strong polemic against magic in 2 Kgs 23:24 (and also in regard to the reigns of Hezekiah and Manasseh; 2 Kgs 17:17; 21:5) indicates how widespread it actually was.

The technical terms used by the biblical writers and editors are somewhat vague and ambiguous (perhaps deliberately so), so they do not give us much information on actual paraphernalia of the type that might be recovered by archaeology. Nevertheless, there are classes of ninth- to sixth-century BCE archaeological artifacts, generally overlooked in this connection, that could be adduced as evidence of magic. First, the *dea nutrix*, or Asherah/Mother Goddess, figurines discussed above are sym-

---

30. Smith 1990, 132–38; Ackerman 1992, 117–43 and references there.
31. Brown 1991.
32. Kuemmerlin-McLean 1992.

bols, and these symbols can only have possessed the awesome power that made them popular if people believed that they worked, that is, that they were talismans that successfully identified the devotee with the deity through sympathetic magic. In addition to this evidence, Iron Age tombs have produced significant quantities of other artifacts that clearly were thought to have had magical powers, not only for the dead but also for the living. These include Egyptian-style figurines of Bes, an apotropaic deity who was popular throughout the Levant in the Iron Age; faience Eye of Horus plaques, obviously to ward off the evil eye; and other types of seals (see above), charms, and amulets.[33] A class of terra-cotta models, including beds, thrones, and shrines, surely represents something other than toys and probably denotes again some form of sympathetic magic. Another group of objects includes many types of so-called trick vessels (*kernoi*). These are bowls that are hollowrimmed and allow one to pour out a liquid through one of the typically hollow animal heads attached to the rim. No up-to-date study exists, but it seems that these *kernoi* originated in Cyprus, were brought to Palestine with the Sea Peoples, and continued in use there until the eighth century BCE or so. The *kernoi* are sometimes regarded simply as libation vessels, but the intricate nature of their pouring function suggests to me that they could indeed have been trick vessels, perhaps designed to give an omen, depending on how they were manipulated. Belonging to another category of magical items are *astragali*, or knucklebones, which are not only recovered in small numbers from Iron Age tombs but occur in a hoard of 140 found in the tenth-century BCE cultic structure at Taʿanach, alongside an assemblage of other demonstrably cultic items.[34] These *astragali*, like second/first-millennium BCE Chinese scapulimancy bones, were probably used in divination rites. Another indication of magic is the well-carved Hand of Fatima on the eighth-century BCE Khirbet el-Qom inscription, possibly our earliest example of this well-known good-luck charm. Finally, the seventh-century BCE Ketef Hinnom silver amulet, with the words of the priestly blessing in Num 6:22–24, clearly shows that by then even sacred texts could be used magically.[35]

Also under the category of magic we must include several Iron II tomb inscriptions (below), even though these are not usually considered

---

33. Dever 1984, 25–26.
34. Lapp 1969, 45–57; see Stager and Wolff 1981, 98.
35. Barkay 1986.

as involving magic. The seventh- to sixth-century BCE Khirbet Beit Lei inscription includes not only a formula of praise and blessing but pictographic representations of praying figures.[36] Both the well-known eighth-century BCE Khirbet el-Qom inscription (no. 3) and several of the contemporary Kuntillet ʿAjrud inscriptions include such blessing formulas as "May X be blessed by Yahweh and his Asherah." Uttered by the living, such formulas may be considered simply a part of everyday speech, but I would suggest that, when they were written on the walls of a sanctuary or a tomb, they inevitably took on a certain magical significance. I would argue the same for the abecedaries at Kuntillet ʿAjrud (and elsewhere), which were executed not only as writing exercises but could also be highly symbolic acts.[37] There are other tomb inscriptions, such as Nahman Avigad's Royal Steward inscription, which reads in part, "Cursed be the man who will open this."[38] Surely these curses were thought to influence the living in ways that could only be described as magic. They secured beneficial behavior through the operation of invisible powers that could be symbolically invoked.

Finally, the drawings on the plastered walls and on several large storejars at Kuntillet ʿAjrud have been considered merely as graffiti, but in my view they are nothing of the sort. There was very little such casual art in the ancient world. Nearly all of what we have, even in the minor traditions, is charged with meaning, whether we can always decipher that meaning or not. The ʿAjrud drawings include a tree of life, lions that probably relate to Asherah, the "Lion Lady," the familiar cow suckling her calf, processional scenes, two Bes figures, and an enthroned, half-nude female figure that I have interpreted as Asherah, going with the textual reference to "Yahweh and his Asherah" just above.[39] Some scholars have minimized the significance of the motifs or have even denied that ʿAjrud is in part

---

36. Naveh 1963.

37. Abecedaries are so common, and tend to occur in such singular contexts (i.e., ʿIzbet Ṣarṭah, Kuntillet ʿAjrud [three incomplete examples]), that they can scarcely all be regarded as simply "schoolboy's exercises." Equally unacceptable is the notion of André Lemaire (oral communication) that the abecedaries at Kuntillet ʿAjrud show that this was not a "cult site" but a "scribal school." See also Lemaire 1981.

38. Avigad 1953.

39. Dever 1984.

a cult site. Others, however, have rightly seen that here at last we have, through archaeological discoveries, an evocative glimpse of the popular cults that the religious establishment and the latest redactors of the biblical texts sought to obscure or to suppress entirely.[40] Since religion is not only theology and belief but also practice, then the supposedly superstitious practices at Kuntillet ʿAjrud and other sites are as genuinely a part of ancient Israelite religion as the idealized portrait in much of the Bible—moreso, I would argue.

9. Tombs and burial practices. The references in 2 Kgs 23:16–20 to tombs on the hills surrounding Jerusalem, some of them impressive above-ground monuments, are easily confirmed. Archaeological investigations have brought to light many such tombs from the eighth to the sixth century BCE, not only to the east in the Silwan (Siloam) cliffs, but to the west and to the north of the Damascus Gate. Some of the Silwan tombs are indeed monumental sepulchers, including one bearing the name of "[Sheban]iah, who is over the house."[41]

Elizabeth Bloch-Smith's *Judahite Burial Practices and Beliefs about the Dead* has surveyed the material so thoroughly that little further comment is needed.[42] While we know of the monumental rock-hewn tombs referred to in 2 Kgs 23:16–17, the graves of the common people (23:6) were no doubt simple pit graves and have gone undetected archaeologically. Finally, given the evidence, the looting of tombs and the burning of the bones on the altar (23:16) remain enigmatic, apart from the obvious intent to defile altars that were regarded as illegitimate. All we can say is that many eighth- to sixth-century BCE tombs in Jerusalem were visible and thus vulnerable to robbing or desecration. Perhaps this can be seen simply as an instance of Josiah's attempt to blot out the very memory of noble families who had supported Manasseh, whose reign (2 Kgs 21:1–9) represented all the abominations against which Josiah stood. It is interesting that, after making inquiries about the visible tomb of "the man of God who came from Judah," Josiah spared his tomb (and that of another prophet from Samaria; 2 Kgs 23:16–18).

---

40. See P. Miller 1987, 59; Coogan 1987, 118–20; McCarter 1987, 143–49; in addition to Dever 1987 in the same volume; Ackerman 1992, 66.
41. Avigad 1953; see Isa 22:16, perhaps this very royal steward.
42. Bloch-Smith 1992.

11.3. Toward a Definition of Popular Religion in Ancient Israel

The preceding discussion has shown that all nine aspects of the Judahite cult that Josiah is presumed in 2 Kgs 23 to have reformed can be documented in more or less detail by recent archaeological discoveries. Does that prove the historicity of the passage? Perhaps not, nor is that the purpose of archaeology. I would argue, however, that such archaeological convergence with the text, read on the basis of an appropriate form-critical analysis, does offer a certain kind of corroboration. If nothing else, such external data tip the scales of the balance of probability with which the historian must always work. Beyond that, such a convergence of artifact and text has important, perhaps critical, implications for our understanding of the actual nature of religious belief and practice in ancient Israel, as I shall suggest in summing up.

Elsewhere I have pointed out that nearly all histories of ancient Israelite religion are deficient because they are almost exclusively text-based and thus tend to ignore the sort of rich archaeological data adduced above (and much more).[43] Several recent studies, however, have begun to grapple with the problem by focusing on various aspects of popular religion. Thus Susan Ackerman states at the outset of her seminal work on religion in the sixth century BCE, "The program that is called for here is a rewriting of the history of the religion of Israel so as to take popular religion fairly into account" (her "non-Deuteronomistic, non-priestly, nonprophetic" religion). That is just what I had called for in an earlier programmatic essay on archaeology and cult.[44]

In 1987, John S. Holladay made a significant start by attempting to define nonconformist or distributed worship over against established or statecentralized worship, on strictly archaeological grounds. Other essays in the same volume, *Ancient Israelite Religion*, marked a similar, though far less systematic, revival of interest in popular religion.[45]

Subsequently, several scholars began to take up the challenge of popular religion, including especially Carol Meyers and Phyllis Bird. For Meyers, the key is to explore the neglected role of women in ancient Israelite religion by analyzing the household mode of production, together

---

43. Dever 1987, 210–22; 1990a, 1994a, 1994b, 1994c.
44. Ackerman 1992, 2; see also Dever 1983.
45. Miller, Hanson, and McBride 1987.

with its archaeological correlates in little-excavated domestic areas, and thus to characterize the religion of what I would call "hearth and home." Bird turns away from major communal acts of worship to consider "visits to local shrines, pilgrimages, and individual acts of piety and dedication related to particular needs ... favored by women and better suited to the general rhythms and the exigencies of their lives" (presumably women's concerns focus more than men's on conception, childbirth, and the rearing of children).[46]

Such studies offset the all-too-prevalent biases of male commentators (see above), and they certainly help to balance the picture. But I would caution against setting up a false dichotomy that presumes that men operated only in the realm of public religion (which became, of course, the orthodox, Deuteronomistic version), while women were restricted to private or domestic religion (or mere superstition, in the view of the literary tradition). Jeremiah 7:18 describes a family ritual—probably typical, despite the prophetic and Deuteronomistic prohibition—in which children gathered wood, fathers kindled the fire, and mothers "made cakes for the queen of heaven."[47]

The latest works are Mark Smith's *The Early History of God: Yahweh and the Other Deities in Ancient Israel* and especially Rainer Albertz's magisterial two-volume *Religionsgeschichte Israels in alttestamentlicher Zeit*, now translated into English as *A History of Israelite Religion in the Old Testament Period*.[48] Smith's work, in my view, is the first full-scale treatment of Israelite religion in English that attempts to take popular religion seriously, but even this work is based largely on texts (including virtually all the nonbiblical material), rather than including archaeological discoveries. Albertz gives even more attention to popular religion, distinguishing between state/national (*Volk*) religion, local religion (*Ortsreligion*), and family religion. The latter equals my popular religion—avoiding "folk" because of the possible confusion with *Volk*, which in German connotes "people" in the sense of "national," rather than "popular," as in English. Nevertheless popular religion may be somewhat misleading, since we do not actually know how widespread or popular this alternate vision of Israelite religion (i.e., of Yahwism itself) actually was. Did it appeal only to "the

---

46. See Meyers 1988; 1991, 102–3; cf. Bird 1990, 1991.
47. On the latter, see Ackerman 1992, 5–35.
48. Smith 1990; Albertz 1992, 1994; see also 1978.

uneducated, the lower classes, the rustics, the unsophisticated," as Ackerman phrases the question? Or was such popular religion, far from being an aberrant minority version of official Yahwism, the actual religion of Israel, the norm, rather than the late Deuteronomistic version? Here, then, is the crucial question: What is normative in religion? Who decides, and why?[49]

Whatever the case, I suggest as a working definition of popular religion, for both archaeologists and biblical scholars, the following. Popular religion is an alternate, nonorthodox, nonconformist mode of religious expression. It is noninstitutional, lying outside priestly control or state sponsorship. Because it is nonauthoritarian, popular religion is inclusive rather than exclusive; it appeals especially to minorities and to the disenfranchised (in the case of ancient Israel, most women); in both belief and practice it tends to be eclectic and syncretistic. Popular religion focuses more on individual piety and informal practice than on elaborate public ritual, more on cult than on intellectual formulations (i.e., theology). By definition, popular religion is less literate (not by that token any less complex or sophisticated) and thus may be inclined to leave behind more traces in the archaeological record than in the literary record, more ostraca and graffiti than classical texts, more cult and other symbolic paraphernalia than scripture. Nevertheless, despite these apparent dichotomies, popular religion overlaps significantly with official religion, if only by sheer force of numbers of practitioners; it often sees itself as equally legitimate; and it attempts to secure the same benefits as all religion, namely, the individual's sense of integration with nature and society, of health and prosperity, of ultimate well-being.

The major elements of popular religion in ancient Israel, as we can gather both from substrata of the biblical text and archaeology, probably included: frequenting *bāmôt* and other local shrines; the making of images; veneration of *'ăšērîm* (whether sacred trees or iconographic images) and the worship of Asherah the Great Lady herself; rituals having to do with childbirth and children; pilgrimages and saints' festivals; *marzēaḥ*; feasts; various funerary rites, such as libations for the dead; baking cakes for the "queen of heaven" (probably Astarte); wailing over Tammuz; various aspects of solar and astral worship; divination and sorcery; and perhaps child sacrifice. These and other elements of folk religion are often assumed

---

49. See Albertz 1994; Ackerman 1992, 1.

to have characterized the religion of hearth and home and thus to have been almost the exclusive province of women. That assumption, typically made by male scholars, inevitably carries with it a note of condescension. After all, women in ancient Israel were largely illiterate and marginalized; they played an insignificant role in the sociopolitical processes that shaped Israelite life and institutions.

11.4. Conclusion

The popular cult revealed in 2 Kgs 23 and now corroborated by archaeological evidence, where it has been acknowledged at all by scholars, has usually been regarded as foreign (i.e., Canaanite), syncretistic, heterodox, or pagan—almost always with the presumption (often unstated, even unconscious) that such popular religion is the antithesis of an original Mosaic monotheism or pure Yahwism and therefore less authentic (read "less to my liking").[50]

It is time that such sophistry be set aside, if we are ever to comprehend the religion of ancient Israel and Judah in all its variety and vitality. Religion is not merely what clerics and theologians (or biblical scholars) think people should have believed and done in the name of religion but what the majority actually did. I have shown that the silence of 2 Kgs 23, when amplified by archaeological data, may reveal what the actual religious situation was in seventh-century BCE Judah. Whether or not the

---

50. See further Smith 1990, 145–46, 154–57; Ackerman 1992, 1–2, 215–17; Bloch-Smith 1992, 150. I have used such terms as *Canaanite, syncretism,* even *pagan* (Dever 1984, 31; 1987, 236). But the confusion, or lack of precision, is partly semantic. By *Canaanite,* I do not imply that those features of Israelite religion borrowed from Late Bronze Age Canaan were not then regarded as authentically Israelite; I mean only that they were later and in that sense derivative. If *syncretistic* means "combining differing beliefs in religious belief and practice" (as commonly held), then ancient Israel's religion was indeed syncretistic. Finally, it should be recalled that *pagan* does not necessarily imply a value judgment (certainly not in my view); the word derives from Latin *pagus,* "country," and referred originally to peasants in the countryside, who were slow to convert to Christianity. The "popular religion" discussed here was precisely pagan, i.e., the rural religion of most of Israel and Judah in the monarchy.

Josianic reform was successful is not a matter to be decided here,[51] nor can we justify alignment with the Deuteronomistic view of Yahwism on the grounds that it was this version of the tradition that was vindicated by history (whose history?).

One may choose whether or not to accept the biblical writers' and editors' opinion of what the purported events of ancient Israel's history meant, but the archaeologist or historian must guard against reading modern notions of any kind back into either the textual or the archaeological record. The past was always more complex, more intractable than we think; let it speak for itself, if possible.

Bibliography

Ackerman, Susan. 1992. *Under Every Green Tree: Popular Religion in Sixth-Century Judah*. HSM 46. Scholars Press.

Aharoni, Yohanon. 1975. "Beersheba, Tel." *EAEHL* 1:160–68.

———. 1981. *Arad Inscriptions*. Israel Exploration Society.

Ahlström, Gösta W. 1993. *The History of Ancient Palestine from the Paleolithic Period to Alexander's Conquest*. JSOTSup 146. JSOT Press.

---

51. Kenyon (1971, 120) had tentatively connected her well-known cache of hundreds of broken seventh-century BCE figurines from Cave 1 in Jerusalem with the Josianic reforms, a tantalizing suggestion that, unfortunately, cannot be confirmed. Herzog Rainey, and Moshkovitz (1984, 22–26), following Aharoni, attributed the destruction of the Stratum VIII temple and the new plan of Stratum VII to the reforms of Josiah, but the few reports on pottery of Strata VIII–VII that have been published (1984, figs. 22, 24) are not decisive; see further the skepticism of Holladay 1987, 257; Ussishkin 1988, 155–56. The demise of the supposed horned-altar temple at Beersheba was attributed by the excavators (Herzog, Rainey, and Moshkovitz 1977, 53–58) to Stratum III and was thought to have been due to a destruction by Hezekiah, but Yadin (1976) argued for a Stratum II assignment and thought the destruction due to Josiah. Again, precise historical correlations are, unfortunately, impossible. Finally, Avraham Eitan's excavation of a late seventh-century BCE fortress-sanctuary at Vered Jericho, although published only preliminarily, offers tantalizing hints of a deliberate destruction, i.e., decommissioning; see Shanks 1986. In any case, Susan Ackerman (1992) has demonstrated amply that the popular cults still prevailed in the sixth century BCE (and undoubtedly even later).

Albertz, Rainer. 1978. *Personliche Frömmigheit und offiziele Religion.* Calwer. Repr., Society of Biblical Literature, 2005.

———. 1992. *Religionsgeschichte Israels in alttestamentlicher Zeit.* 2 vols. Vandenhoeck & Ruprecht.

———. 1994. *A History of Israelite Religion in the Old Testament Period.* Translated by John Bowden. 2 vols. OTL. Westminster John Knox.

Avigad, Nahman. 1953. "The Epitaph of a Royal Steward from Siloam Village." *IEJ* 3:137–52.

Barkey, Gabriel. 1986. *Ketef Hinnom: A Treasure Facing Jerusalem's Walls.* Israel Museum Catalog 274. The Israel Museum.

Beck, Pirhiya. 1982. "The Drawings from Ḥorvat Teiman (Kuntillet 'Ajrûd)." *TA* 9:3–68.

———. 1990. "A Figurine from Tel 'Ira." *ErIr* 21:87–93.

Biran, Avraham. 1980. "Tel Dan: Five Years Later." *BA* 43:168–82.

———. 1986. "The Dancer from Dan, the Empty Tomb, and the Altar Room." *IEJ* 36:168–78.

———. 1989. "Prize Find: Tel Dan Scepter Head—Belonging to Priest or King?" *BAR* 15.1:29–31.

Bird, Phyllis. 1990. "Gender and Religious Definition: The Case of Ancient Israel." *Harvard Divinity Bulletin* 20:12–13, 19–20.

———. 1991. "Israelite Religion and the Faith of Israel's Daughters." Pages 97–198 in *The Bible and the Politics of Exegesis: Essays in Honor of Norman K. Gottwald on His Sixty-Fifth Birthday.* Edited by David Jobling, Peggy L. Day, and Gerald T. Sheppard. Pilgrim.

Bloch-Smith, Elizabeth. 1992. *Judahite Burial Practices and Beliefs about the Dead.* JSOTSup 123. JSOT Press.

Brown, Susan. 1991. *Late Carthaginian Child Sacrifice and Sacrificial Monuments in Their Mediterranean Context.* JSOT/ASOR Monograph Series 3. JSOT Press.

Chambon, Alain. 1984. *Tel el-Farʿah I: L'âge du Fer.* Éditions Recherche sur les Civilisations.

Cogan, Mordechai, and Hayim Tadmor. 1988. *II Kings: A New Translation with Introduction and Commentary.* AB 11. Doubleday.

Coogan, Michael David. 1987. "Canaanite Origins and Lineage: Reflections on the Religion of Ancient Israel." Pages 113–24 in *Ancient Israelite Religion: Essays in Honor of Frank Moore Cross.* Edited by Patrick D. Miller Jr., Paul D. Hanson, and S. Dean McBride. Fortress.

Dever, William G. 1970. "Iron Age Epigraphic Material from the Area of Khirbet el-Kôm." *HUCA* 40–41:139–204.

———. 1983. "Material Remains and the Cult in Ancient Israel: An Essay in Archaeological Systematics." Pages 571–87 in *The Word of the Lord Shall Go Forth: Essays in Honor of David Noel Freedman in Celebration of His Sixtieth Birthday*. Edited by Carol L. Meyers and M. O'Connor. Eisenbrauns. Republished as chapter 10 in this volume.

———. 1984. "Asherah, Consort of Yahweh? New Evidence from Kuntillet 'Ajrud." *BASOR* 255:21–37.

———. 1987. "The Contribution of Archaeology to the Study of Canaanite and Israelite Religion. Pages 209–47 in *Ancient Religion: Essays in Honor of Frank Moore Cross*. Edited by Patrick D. Miller Jr., Paul D. Hanson, and S. Dean McBride. Fortress.

———. 1990a. "Asherah Abscondita: The Changing Fortunes of the Great Mother in Ancient Israel, Judaism, and Christianity." Paper presented at the 1990 AAR/SBL Annual Meeting, New Orleans.

———. 1990b. *Recent Archaeological Discoveries and Biblical Research*. University of Washington Press.

———. 1994a. "Ancient Israelite Religion: How to Reconcile the Differing Textual and Artifactual Portraits?" Pages 105–25 in *Ein Gott allein? JHWH-Verehrung und biblischer Monotheismus im Kontext der israelitischen und altorientalischen Religionsgeschichte*. Edited by Walther Dietrich and Martin A. Klopfenstein. OBO 139. Vandenhoeck & Ruprecht.

———. 1994b. "Archaeology, Texts, and History-Writing: Toward an Epistemology." Pages 105–17 in *Uncovering Ancient Stones: Essays in Memory of H. Neil Richardson*. Edited by Lewis M. Hopfe. Eisenbrauns.

———. 1994c. "From Tribe to Nation: A Critique of State Formation Processes in Ancient Israel." Pages 213–38 in *Nuove fondazioni nel Vicino Oriente antico: Realtà e ideologia*. Edited by Stefania Mazzoni. University of Pisa.

Edelman, Dians V., ed. 1991. *The Fabric of History: Text, Artifact and Israel's Past*. JSOTSup 127. JSOT Press.

Garbini, Giovanni. 1988. *History and Ideology in Ancient Israel*. Crossroad.

Gitin, Seymour. 1990. "Ekron of the Philistines, Part II: Olive-Oil Suppliers to the World." *BAR* 16.2:32–41.

———. 1992. "New Incense Altars from Ekron: Context, Typology, and Function." *ErIr* 23:43*–49*.

Hadley, Judith M. 1987. "The Khirbet el-Qôm Inscription." *VT* 37:50–62.

———. 2000. *The Cult of Asherah in Ancient Israel and Judah: Evidence for a Hebrew Goddess*. Cambridge University Press.
Halpern, Baruch. 1988. *The First Historians: The Hebrew Bible and History*. Harper & Row.
Haran, Menahem. 1978. *Temples and Temple-Service in Ancient Israel: An Inquiry into the Character of Cult Phenomena and the Historical Setting of the Priestly School*. Clarendon.
Herrmann, Seigfried. 1975. *A History of Israel in Old Testament Times*. Fortress.
Herzog, Zeev, Anson F. Rainey, and Shmuell Moshkovitz. 1977. "The Stratigraphy at Beer-sheba and the Location of the Sanctuary." *BASOR* 225:49–58.
———. 1984. "The Israelite Fortress at Arad." *BASOR* 254:1–34.
Hestrin, Ruth. 1987a. "The Cult Stand from Ta'anach and Its Religious Background." Pages 61–77 in *Phoenicia and the East Mediterranean in the First Millennium B.C.* Edited by Edward Lipiński. OLA 22. Peeters.
———. 1987b. "The Lachish Ewer and the 'Asherah." *IEJ* 37:212–23.
Holladay, John S. 1987. "Religion in Israel under the Monarchy: An Explicitly Archaeological Approach." Pages 249–99 in *Ancient Israelite Religion: Essays in Honor of Frank Moore Cross*. Edited by Patrick D. Miller Jr., Paul D. Hanson, and S. Dean McBride. Fortress.
Holland, Thomas A. 1977. "A Study of Palestinian Iron Age Baked Clay Figurines, with Special Reference to Jerusalem: Cave I." *Levant* 19:121–55.
Keel, Othmar, and Christoph Uehlinger. 1992. *Göttinnen, Götter, und Gottessymbole: Neue Erkenntnisse zur Religionsgeschichte Kanaans und Israels aufgrund bislang unerschlossener ikonographischer Quellen*. QD 134. Herder.
———. 1998. *Gods, Goddesses, and Images of God in Ancient Israel*. Translated by Thomas H. Trapp. Fortress.
Kenyon, Kathleen M. 1971. *Royal Cities of the Old Testament*. Schocken.
Knauf, Ernst Axel. 1991. "From History to Interpretation." Pages 26–64 in *The Fabric of History: Text, Artifact and Israel's Past*. Edited by Diana V. Edelman. JSOTSup 127. JSOT Press.
Kuemmerlin-McLean, Joanne K. 1992. "Magic: Old Testament." *ABD* 4:468–71.
Lapp, Paul W. 1967. "The 1966 Excavations at Tell Ta'annek." *BASOR* 185:2–39.
———. 1969. "The 1968 Excavations at Tell Ta'annek." *BASOR* 195:2–49.

Lemaire, André. 1981. *Les écoles et la formation de la Bible dans l'ancien Israël*. Vandenhoeck & Ruprecht.

Lohfink, Norbert. 1987. "The Cult Reform of Josiah of Judah: 2 Kings 22–23 as a Source for the History of Israelite Religion." Pages 459–75 in *Ancient Israelite Religion: Essays in Honor of Frank Moore Cross*. Edited by Patrick D. Miller Jr., Paul D. Hanson, and S. Dean McBride. Fortress.

Lowery, R. H. 1990. *The Reforming Kings: Cults and Society in First Temple Judah*. JSOTSup 120. JSOT Press.

Mazar, Amihai. 1980. *Excavations at Tell Qasile, Part One. The Philistine Sanctuary: Architecture and Cult Objects*. Qedem 12. Institute of Archaeology, Hebrew University.

———. 1982. "The 'Bull Site': An Iron Age I Open Cult Place." *BASOR* 247:27–42.

McCarter, P. Kyle., Jr. 1987. "Aspects of the Religion of the Israelite Monarchy: Biblical and Epigraphic Data." Pages 137–55 in *Ancient Israelite Religion: Essays in Honor of Frank Moore Cross*. Edited by Patrick D. Miller Jr., Paul D. Hanson, and S. Dean McBride. Fortress.

Meshel, Ze'ev. 1978a. *Kuntillet 'Ajrud: A Religious Centre from the Time of the Judaean Monarchy on the Border of Sinai*. Israel Museum Catalog 175. The Israel Museum.

———. 1978b. "Kuntillet 'Ajrud: An Israelite Religious Center in Northern Sinai." *Expedition* 20:50–54.

———. 1979. "Did Yahweh Have a Consort? The New Religious Inscriptions from the Sinai." *BAR* 5.2:24–35.

Meyers, Carol. 1988. *Discovering Eve: Ancient Israelite Women in Context*. Oxford University Press.

———. 1991. "'To Her Mother's House': Considering a Counterpart to the Israelite *Bêt 'āb*." Pages 39–51 in *The Bible and the Politics of Exegesis: Essays in Honor of Norman K. Gottwald on His Sixty-Fifth Birthday*. Edited by David Jobling, Peggy L. Day, and Gerald T. Sheppard. Pilgrim.

Miller, J. Maxwell. 1976. *The Old Testament and the Historian*. Fortress.

———. 1987. "Old Testament History and Archaeology." *BA* 49:51–62.

Miller, Patrick D., Jr. 1987. "Aspects of the Religion of Ugarit." Pages 53–66 in *Ancient Israelite Religion: Essays in Honor of Frank Moore Cross*. Edited by Patrick D. Miller Jr., Paul D. Hanson, and S. Dean McBride. Fortress.

Miller, Patrick D., Jr., Paul D. Hanson, and S. Dean McBride, eds. 1987. *Ancient Israelite Religion: Essays in Honor of Frank Moore Cross.* Fortress.
Nakhai, Beth Alpert. 2001. *Archaeology and the Religions of Canaan and Israel.* ASOR Books 7. American Schools of Oriental Research.
Naveh, Joseph. 1963. "Old Hebrew Inscriptions in a Burial Cave." *IEJ* 13:235-56.
Negbi, Ora. 1976. *Canaanite Gods in Metal: An Archaeological Study of Ancient Syro-Palestinian Figurines.* Institute of Archaeology, Tel Aviv University.
Noth, Martin. 1960. *The History of Israel.* Harper & Row.
Oden, Robert. 1976. "The Persistence of Canaanite Religion." *BA* 39:31-36.
Olyan, Saul. 1988. *Asherah and the Cult of Yahweh in Israel.* SBLMS 34. Scholars Press.
Rendtorff, Rolf. 1983. *The Old Testament: An Introduction.* Translated by John Bowden. Fortress.
Rösel, Hartmut N. 1992. *Israel in Kanaan: Zum Problem der Entstehung Israels.* BEATAJ 2. Lang.
Schröer, Silvia. 1987. *In Israel gab es Bilder: Nachrichten von darstellender Kunst im Alten Testament.* OBO 74. Universitätsverlag; Vandenhoeck & Ruprecht.
Shanks, Hershel. 1986. "*BAR* Interview with Avraham Eitan." *BAR* 12.4:30-38.
Smith, Mark S. 1990. *The Early History of God: Yahweh and the Other Deities in Ancient Israel.* Harper & Row.
Stager, Lawrence E., and Samuel R. Wolff. 1981. "Production and Commerce in Temple Courtyards: An Olive Press in the Sacred Precinct at Tel Dan." *BASOR* 243:95-102.
Taylor, J. Glenn. 1989. "Yahweh and Asherah at Tenth-Century Ta'anach." *Newsletter for Ugaritic Studies* 37-38:16-18.
Thompson, Thomas L. 1987. *The Origin Tradition of Ancient Israel I: The Literary Formation of Genesis and Exodus 1-23.* JSOTSup 55. Sheffield Academic.
———. 1992. *Early History of the Israelite People: From the Written and Archaeological Sources.* SHANE 4. Brill.
Tigay, Jeffrey H. 1986. *You Shall Have No Other Gods: Israelite Religion in the Light of Hebrew Inscriptions.* HSS 31. Scholars Press.
———. 1987. "Israelite Religion: Onomastic and Epigraphic Evidence." Pages 157-94 in *Ancient Israelite Religion: Essays in Honor of Frank*

Moore Cross. Edited by Patrick D. Miller Jr., Paul D. Hanson, and S. Dean McBride. Fortress.

Ussishkin, David. 1988. "The Date of the Judaean Shrine at Arad." *IEJ* 38:142–57.

Winter, Urs. 1983. *Frau und Götten: Exegetische und ikonographische Studien zum weiblichen Gottesbild im Alten Israel und in dessen Umwelt.* Vandenhoeck & Ruprecht.

Yadin, Yigael. 1976. "Beer-sheba: The High Place Destroyed by King Josiah." *BASOR* 222:5–17.

Zevit, Ziony. 1984. "The Khirbet el-Qôm Inscription Mentioning a Goddess." *BASOR* 255:33–41.

Updated Bibliography

Hodder, Ian. 1986. *Reading the Past: Current Approaches to Interpretation in Archaeology.* Cambridge University Press.

Dever, William G. 2017. "History from Things: On Writing New Histories of Ancient Israel." Pages 3–20 in *Le-ma'an Ziony: Essays in Honor of Ziony Zevit.* Edited by Frederick E. Greenspahn and Gary A. Rendsburg. Cascade.

12

Archaeology and the Ancient Israelite Cult: How the Khirbet el-Qom and Kuntillet ʿAjrud Asherah Texts Have Changed the Picture

In preceding chapters on ancient Israelite religion, I have referred to my 1969 discovery of the Asherah tomb inscription at Khirbet el-Qom, as well as the Kuntillet ʿAjrud inscriptions found by Zeʾev Meshel a decade later (finally published in 2012 as *Kuntillet ʿAjrud [Ḥorvat Teiman]: An Iron Age II Religious Site on the Judah-Sinai Border*).

The personal details of my recovery of the el-Qom inscription, which later became so well known, have, however, never been told. Meanwhile, the reading of Asherah in both sets of inscriptions by many scholars as a divine name has led to protracted discussions about "Yahweh's consort," as seen in the introduction to chapter 10 and the literature cited there. In light of ongoing controversies, I chose the topic of a divine consort for a chapter in the *Eretz-Israel* volume dedicated to my teacher Frank Cross for my contribution to his early Festschrift. After all, it had been Cross himself who had first piqued my interest in the Canaanite and Israelite cults more than thirty years earlier, so this seemed a fitting tribute.

It may be noteworthy that Cross, who famously dealt with so many Northwest Semitic inscriptions, never commented much on my el-Qom inscription—even though I had showed it to him personally in 1969 when I discovered it (and I also showed it in Jerusalem to W. F. Albright, David Noel Freedman, and Joseph Naveh). His only reference was in an interview in *Biblical Archaeology Review*, where he said that the term *asherah* was not the personal name of a goddess but should be rendered as "shrine," following Albright. I think that Frank, always conservative (in the best sense), had dif-

---

Originally published in *ErIsr* 2 (1999): 9*–15*. Reprinted by permission.

ficulty acknowledging the reality of polytheism in the Israelite cult. But the evidence is now clear (for more recent bibliography, see chapter 10).

It is a special pleasure to dedicate this essay to Professor Frank Moore Cross, who taught me Northwest Semitic epigraphy at Harvard and was one of those who encouraged me early on to enter the field of Syro-Palestinian archaeology. Professor Cross's foresight has resulted in my being able to contribute to both of his Festschriften. In the second one I have chosen to reflect on and to update the discussion of my only venture into Hebrew epigraphy, which by chance brought to light in 1968 the now-famous eighth-century BCE Khirbet el-Qom inscription mentioning "a/Asherah."

12.1. Khirbet el-Qom and Its Inscriptions Revisited

Inscription 3 from Tomb II has by now received so much attention that Khirbet el-Qom itself has been almost eclipsed, as well as the other Iron Age material that was recovered from the site and published.[1] I would remind readers of:

1. The features of the tombs themselves, including the carved head niches on the benches, at the time apparently unique but with parallels later recognized by Gabriel Barkay, Amos Kloner, and myself in the École Biblique tomb in Jerusalem, significantly in the form of a Hathor or "Qudshu-Asherah" wig.[2]
2. The deeply incised representation of a human hand below Inscription 1, which I identified as an early depiction of the later Islamic *khamsa*, or "Hand of Fatima," used as a good-luck sign or apotropaic emblem, a symbol since studied further by Silvia Schröer.[3]
3. The group of inscribed shekel weights. Some of the fractions appeared to be unusual at the time but are now better understood.

---

1. Dever 1969–1970. For convenient bibliography, see now Binger 1997.
2. Long ago I had observed that the eighth century BCE École Biblique tomb in Jerusalem had head niches similar to Khirbet el-Qom, but in the shape of the Hathor wig associated with Qudshu in Egypt and Asherah in Canaan.
3. See further Schröer 1983.

They have been placed in a larger context by recent studies, such as those of Barkay and Raz Kletter.[4]
4. The inscribed decanter, sui generis when I published it but now part of a larger group of Iron II ceramic vessels inscribed in Hebrew and Phoenician bearing the names of the owners.[5]
5. It should also be noted that salvage excavations in the village of Khirbet el-Qom, on the hill above the robbed cemetery, conducted in 1971 by John S. Holladay, revealed an Iron II city wall and a two-entryway gate as well as tenth- to seventh-century BCE occupation.[6]
6. The site has been correctly identified with biblical Makkedah by David A. Dorsey (which is preferable to my tentative identification with Shaphir).[7] The latest addition to our knowledge of ancient Khirbet el-Qom comes from a chalk slab, now in a private collection and recently published by Robert Deutsch and Michael Heltzer. It reads "Bless your stonecutter(s); in this [i.e., the tomb] will rest the elders."[8]

For those who may wish to consult more recent syntheses of what is known of Khirbet el-Qom, I may recommend for the site itself several of my own summaries in standard reference works;[9] for the a/Asherah inscriptions, see such treatments as those of Susan Ackerman and Tilda Binger, with full references to the relevant literature.[10]

---

4. For the most recent comprehensive treatment of the Judean shekel weights, see Kletter 1991.

5. Prior to the publication of the Khirbet el-Qom inscribed decanter, only one other was known, from Kenyon's excavations in Jerusalem (published in 1968). Avigad published another in 1972 and discussed the unusual method of chiseling the letters after firing (Avigad 1972). Another one from Beersheba was published by Aharoni in 1975. In 1994 another was published; for this one and full bibliography, see Deutsch and Heltzer 1994.

6. For Holladay's Iron Age excavations, see Holladay 1971. On the Persian/Hellenistic levels, see Geraty 1975.

7. Dorsey 1980.

8. See Deutsch and Heltzer 1984.

9. For recent resumés, see Dever 1993, 1997.

10. For bibliography, see numerous references in the works cited in n. 1 above.

12.2. Toward a Synthesis on the Reading of Inscription III

While preparing the *editio princeps* of Inscription 3 in Jerusalem in the spring of 1969, I showed photographs and tracings to several leading scholars, including Amihai Mazar, Joseph Naveh, and W. F. Albright, as well as Frank Cross himself. These and other scholars were slow to appreciate the significance of Inscription 3 after its first publication in 1970, until André Lemaire's pioneering rereading in 1977.[11]

It was Lemaire who rescued Inscription 3 from probable oblivion by pointing out that in line 3 we should read "by his a/Asherah." My original notes show that I had originally attempted to read "his a/Asherah," but I suppressed that reading in the final version of my manuscript.

Lemaire correctly put his finger on the crux of our understanding of Inscription 3: the reading of lines 3/4. Line l presents a difficulty only with the second word, evidently *hʿšr*, "the wealthy man," or *hsr*, "the governor," or, alternatively, "the singer." Virtually all scholars have discussed the peculiar seventh "letter" in line 1, which might be read as *ʿayin*, *dalet*, *resh*, or *qoph*. The sign, however, is not entirely right for any of these letters; furthermore, it has been partly obscured by the addition of an extraordinarily long "tail." Naveh and Mittman ignore this letter, so as to yield *hsr*; most others read it as *ʿayin* (despite the comparative difficulty, considering the clearly formed *ʿayin* in line 3), thus *hʿšr*, "wealthy man."[12] I had taken this sign as a *qoph*, however, reading *hqšb*, a *hiphil* imperative of *qšb*, thus yielding "take heed, pay attention to." Not only does this make good sense of the following word *ktbh*, "his inscription," but it would place Inscription 3 within a well-known corpus of Hebrew and Phoenician burial inscriptions that include implicit warnings against disturbing the tomb. Thus the contemporary Royal Steward inscription ends with the warning: "Cursed be the man who will open this!" In publishing this inscription in 1953, Avigad noted several Phoenician examples of such formulas.[13]

I still believe that my original reading has some merit, because it does attempt to read "letter" seven rather than simply discarding it, and it would also provide a clear and well-attested genre. Among the other alternatives, I would prefer reading *hʿšr*, "the wealthy man." Certainly a number of the

---

11. Lemaire 1977.
12. See Naveh 1979; Mittman 1981.
13. Avigad 1953.

eighth-century BCE Khirbet el-Qom tombs *are* elite tombs—in workmanship among the finest ever discovered outside of Jerusalem.[14] The recently published chalk slab inscription noted above, which I agree must have come from el-Qom, with its unique reference to the "stonecutters" who prepared these tombs,[15] would seem to underline the importance of the Khirbet el-Qom cemetery and some of those interred in its tombs. These include our ʿUriyahu in Tomb II, whether he was a comparatively wealthy individual or an official of some sort.

Line 2 has never posed any problems, as it is a formula right out of the pages of the Hebrew Bible: "Blessed be ʿUriyahu by Yahweh." The exact blessing formulae had not been found heretofore in extrabiblical Hebrew texts, although in 1963 Naveh reconstructed in one of the Horvat Beth Loya tomb inscriptions the phrase *hwšʿ* [*y*]*hwh*, "(May) Yahweh deliver (us)."[16] Now, several of the roughly contemporary Kuntillet ʿAjrud inscriptions contain the expression "Blessed be X by Yahweh."[17]

Line 3 is admittedly difficult, and scholars understandably differ on the reading of several letters. As one of the few who has handled the stone slab extensively, I can attest to the fact that several letters are deliberately and deeply overwritten, a problem that does not seem to me to have been sufficiently addressed. This overwriting occurs mostly in connection with the word now read by virtually all scholars as "a/Asherah."[18] That is why I could legitimately read this word differently and thus arrive at a reading that excluded any reference to a/Asherah. Granted that the text does read "a/Asherah" in line 3, the question remains: Did someone try to efface the

---

14. For a full discussion of the Iron Age tombs known to date, see now Bloch-Smith 1992.

15. See references in n. 8 above.

16. Naveh 1963.

17. For syntheses and bibliography on Kuntillet ʿAjrud, see Meshel 1978, 1979; Dever 1984; Hadley 1987. See more recent bibliography and convenient summaries of readings in Binger 1997, 167–79.

18. The best photograph is still the original, published in Dever 1969–1970. One should compare my hand-copy published there with slightly different copies done by Zevit (1984) and myself in 1982. Most of the other commentators discussed here have not seen the stone, and none, to my knowledge, has made a fresh photograph or hand-copy. The major mechanical difficulties lies in (1) several letters in line 3 that have been overwritten and (2) many scratches defacing the stone.

straightforward reading, and, if so, why? I can only suggest that a reference to a/Asherah in connection with the name of Yahweh, in an obvious context of blessing, was becoming a theological problem for some in Judah by the eighth century BCE—as indeed it is for many commentators today, as we shall see presently.

In any case, restoring what is undoubtedly the *original* reading of "a/Asherah" in line 3 yields by common scholarly consensus a phrase that, taken together with line 2, runs something like:

Blessed be 'Uriyahu to Yahweh, and from his enemies save him by his a/Asherah.

The various readings have been conveniently summarized now by Tilda Binger, although her own interpretation of line 3 is idiosyncratic, to say the least ("his light by Asherah, she who holds her hand over him").[19] The overwhelming majority of scholars read Inscription 3 as having to do with 'Uriyahu's being blessed and "saved from his enemies" by some combination of the Israelite deity Yahweh and "his a/Asherah"—the only question being to what or to whom the latter phrase refers.

Lemaire, who as I noted above first drew widespread attention to the el-Qom inscriptions in 1977, was also the first to see in line 3 a reference to Yahweh's "a/Asherah." Lemaire, however, interpreted the term as denoting simply a tree-like symbol relating somehow to the goddess Asherah, as indeed required in most of the forty or so occurrences of the term *'ăšērâ* in the Hebrew Bible. In these instances the asherah is something anathema to the Deuteronomists in particular—a wooden pole or living tree, which, because of its frequent association with "high places" (*bāmôt*) and "standing stones" (*maṣṣēbôt*) that were thought reminiscent of the Canaanite cult, should be cut down, chopped to pieces, or burned up.

A number of more recent commentators have followed Lemaire's "minimalist" interpretation of "Yahweh's a/Asherah," among them John A. Emerton, John Day, Judith M. Hadley, Jeffrey H. Tigay, Mark S. Smith, and Othmar Keel and Christoph Uehlinger.[20] P. Kyle McCarter, however, nuanced the interpretation of the asherah as a "mere symbol" by arguing

---

19. See Binger 1997, 167.
20. See Emerton 1982; Day 1986; Hadley 1987; Tigay 1987; Smith 1990; Keel and Uehlinger 1992, 1998; McCarter 1987.

that at Khirbet el-Qom the asherah was conceived of as a *hypostasis* of Yahweh, that is, neither a deity nor a consort of Yahweh but his "trace" or "cultically available" presence. Yet elsewhere McCarter acknowledges that in the Hebrew Bible and in ancient Israel generally Yahweh had a consort named Asherah, as, of course, El had at Ugarit.[21] This, it seems to me, is wanting to have it both ways. It also begs the question of what a religious symbol is and how it functions. I would insist that the asherah as a tree-like object—a "mere symbol"—would have been *meaningless* unless it mediated to those in the ancient cult the existence, presence, and power of an actual deity, the old Canaanite Mother Goddess Asherah. A symbol (from Greek *symballein*, "to throw together, compare") is any inanimate object that points *beyond* itself to an ontological and ultimate reality, an "outward sign of an inner and invisible reality." To separate the religious symbol from that which it symbolizes, as McCarter and many others do, is to impose upon the past a modern, rational distinction that does violence to what we know of the holistic worldview of ancient Israel and indeed of Canaan and all of the ancient Near East. Such a functionalist, reductionist view of ancient Israelite religion robs it of much of its variety and vitality.

Susan Ackerman has grasped the point when she observes that in the ancient world "the idol *was* the god."[22] Thus I would suggest that the asherah pole/tree would have been perceived as Asherah *herself* by many if not most worshipers in ancient Israel, and *that* constitutes the problem: the widespread presence in popular religion of a consort alongside Yahweh was what led the prophetic and Deuteronomistic writers by the eighth–sixth century BCE to condemn the goddess and anything associated with her. As Saul Olyan has suggested, "Asherah was Yahweh's consort in state religion as well as popular religion in the northern kingdom from earliest times," until later reform movements progressively discredited her, largely by coming to associate her with Baal rather than Yahweh.[23] I concur, and I am therefore puzzled that Olyan should note regarding the clear reference to a/Asherah" at Khirbet el-Qom that "little can be said," that the reference is only to a "symbol" of some sort. In reply to my observation that to interpret the phrase in line 3 as saying something like "May 'Uriyahu be blessed by Asherah and his tree symbol" would be *inexplicable*, Olyan can only

---

21. McCarter 1987, 143–44.
22. Ackerman 1992, emphasis added.
23. Olyan 1988, 23–27.

say: Not so. Yet Olyan's view that "the cult symbol represents the goddess" hardly clarifies the issue, since he misses Ackerman's point and mine here: one cannot *separate* the symbol from the goddess, either conceptually or existentially.[24] It is the *goddess* Asherah who conveys blessings, no matter whether she was conceived as an independent deity by some or simply as one manifestation of Yahweh and his powers. To perceive the issue as one of idolatry is to fall unwittingly into the theological trap of the Deuteronomistic redactors who shaped the late, orthodox literary tradition enshrined in the Hebrew Bible as it has come down to us. Archaeology is valuable precisely because it can enable us to get *behind* this tradition, closer to the original reality.

Several minority opinions may be noted here. Edouard Lipiński, commenting shortly after Lemaire's resurrection of the Khirbet el-Qom inscription, regarded the a/Asherah as a "shrine" of some sort, drawing, however, upon questionable Phoenician parallels.[25] Ziony Zevit, who collaborated with me in 1981–1982 in reexamining and redrawing the stone itself, in the Israel Museum, read ʾašrth rather than ʾašrt + h with the final he understood as the third masculine singular possessive suffix, thus "his a/Asherah," but rather as a *Phoenician* word, that is, the name of the well-known Phoenician feminine deity Ashrata.[26] Although Zevit's reading is ingenious and does indeed deal with the supposed grammatical problem posed by the final possessive he (below), no one seems to have followed his invocation of a Phoenician deity at Khirbet el-Qom. In Zevit's favor, however, is not only the appearance subsequently of inscriptions at contemporary Kuntillet ʿAjrud in the Phoenician script but now also the discovery of several eighth- to seventh-century BCE Phoenician inscriptions at Tel Miqne (biblical Ekron) mentioning offerings for, and even a sanctuary dedicated to, the goddess "Asherat."[27] Thus it seems to me that Zevit's reading should not be arbitrarily ruled out of consideration. Margalit offered what is surely the most imaginative reading, but he inserts an entirely imaginary extra "line" between lines 2 and 3, and this is a flight of fancy that discredits any contribution he might have made.[28]

---

24. Olyan, 1988, 31.
25. Lipiński 1980.
26. Zevit 1984.
27. See Meshel 1978; Gitin 1993.
28. Margalit 1989.

There remain the few scholars who have been bold enough to confront what is to me the obvious reading: "May 'Uriyahu be blessed by Yahweh and saved from his enemies by *his Asherah*," that is, by Yahweh's consort Asherah, acting jointly as an agent of blessing. As long as the Khirbet el-Qom inscriptions were sui generis, scholars might have been justified in being cautious; after all, this was the *first* extrabiblical text to mention what may have been the goddess Asherah herself. But in 1975, Ze'ev Meshel excavated an eighth-century caravanserai, or waystation, at Kuntillet 'Ajrud in the eastern Sinai wilderness on the ancient road from the Mediterranean to the Red Sea, with an attached gateway shrine. The dozen or more Hebrew inscriptions on the plastered walls, on large storage jars, and on votive offerings attracted widespread attention when they were partially published beginning in 1976. By 1978, the catalog of an exhibit at the Israel Museum made many of the inscriptions available to scholars, at least in line drawings. Several of them, especially on Pithos 1, clearly included expressions such as "may X be blessed by Yahweh of Samaria and by his a/Asherah"—an exact, contemporary duplicate of my Khirbet el-Qom Inscription 3.[29] Gradually, and often somewhat reluctantly, it seems, other scholars came around to seeing Asherah not only as a shadowy image but as a deity alongside Yahweh, as his paredros, *all* of them citing the Khirbet el-Qom and Kuntillet 'Ajrud inscriptions. Meshel himself (1979) at least allowed for that possibility, as have much more recent scholars. Patrick D. Miller, Michael D. Coogan, Susan Ackerman, and Tilda Binger do not hesitate to interpret the archaeologically recovered inscriptions, and the texts of the Hebrew Bible as well, as reflecting a full-fledged cult of Asherah in Israelite popular religion.[30]

I recount this brief history of scholarship on the subject only to make an essential point: it was new *archaeological* data that forced biblical scholars to reconsider the nature of Israelite monotheism, of the possible existence of Asherah as Yahweh's consort, and indeed of the entire cult in the light of what we now know of popular, folk, or family religion throughout the history of ancient Israel and Judah. I have recently discussed much of the literature on the latter from an archaeologist's point of view.[31] Here

---

29. See references in n. 17 above.
30. See Miller 1987, 58–59; Coogan 1987, 115–24; Ackerman 1992, 189–93; Binger 1997, 140–41.
31. Dever 1995; see also 1996.

I need only note that the proliferation of recent works on popular religion is due in nearly every case to the recognition that the new archaeological data are relevant and in many cases decisive. Such works would include treatments by John S. Holladay, Carol Meyers, Mark S. Smith, Phyllis Bird, Othmar Keel and Christoph Uehlinger, Susan Ackerman, Elizabeth Bloch-Smith, Karel van der Toorn, Rainer Albertz, Jacques Berlinerblau, Ziony Zevit, and, of course, my own.[32]

12.3. Remaining Impediments

Despite growing recognition among biblical scholars that the discovery of the eighth-century BCE Khirbet el-Qom and Kuntillet ʿAjrud inscriptions mentioning Asherah marks a crucial turning point in our understanding of ancient Israelite religion, a number of scholars remain skeptical, as we have seen. Among some of those that I have noted above, I cannot help but suspect that the hesitation to embrace Asherah (as it were) stems largely from theological sensitivities, whether explicit, unexpressed, or perhaps even unexamined. For some, it is simply unthinkable that Yahweh in ancient Israel and in the Hebrew Bible had a female consort. The widespread abhorrence of such a concept may explain in part why the Kuntillet ʿAjrud inscriptions still have not been fully published or made widely known to the public in Israel, more than twenty years after their discovery. Particularly in North America, many biblical scholars appear to be somewhat ill at ease with the notion of Yahweh having a consort and are either mystified or repelled by the notion of a vibrant, potent Mother Goddess. Whatever the reasons for the continuing resistance to the obvious and overwhelming implications of the archaeological data (not simply the nonbiblical inscriptions discussed here),[33] I do not think that in sophisticated circles there can any longer be cogent *theological* objections.

---

32. Holladay 1987; Meyers 1988; Smith 1990; Bird 1991; Keel and Uehlinger 1992, 1998; Ackerman 1992; Bloch-Smith 1992; van der Toorn 1994; Albertz 1994; Berlinerblau 1996; Zevit 2001. See also Dever 1983, 1984, 1987, 1994a, 1994b, 1995.

33. For the extensive nontextual data on the cult that archaeology has recently brought to light, see Dever 1995; 1996; and 1994, 105–25 and references there.

A few of the holdouts mentioned above advance what appears at first to be a more substantial argument, one based on Northwest Semitic syntax. The *he* at the end of word *'ašrth* is universally taken to be a final *mater lectionis* for ...*tô*, the normal way of representing the third masculine singular possessive suffix in this period, yielding "his a/Asherah." Such usage of the possessive suffix with a personal name is held to be "ungrammatical" by scholars such as Andreas Angerstorfer, P. Kyle McCarter, Jeffrey H. Tigay, and Saul Olyan. Thus, they argue, *'ašrth* cannot refer to a deity by the name of Asherah but only to a symbol, "*the* Asherah."[34] It is true that such usage is rare or perhaps nonexistent in Biblical Hebrew, but I would make several qualifications. (1) A possessive suffix can occur with the name of a deity at Ugarit, as Miller and McCarter have pointed out, thus, *laṭrty*, "my Asherah," and *krtn*, "our Keret."[35] (2) In the later Aramaic of Elephantine, we have the expression ʿ*Anat-yahu*, "face/presence [*pny*] of Baal," that is, Baal's consort—the divine name Baal being in construct relation with the word for face/presence. Of course, such construct relations of nouns with divine names, including Yahweh, are common in the Hebrew Bible, so the *concept* of a deity's "possessing" something or someone is ever-present, even if it is not expressed in precisely the same grammatical construction that we encounter at Khirbet el-Qom and Kuntillet ʿAjrud. (3) Finally, I would suggest, as philologians such as Dennis Pardee already have, that our rules for classical or Biblical Hebrew are to some degree arbitrary, derived as they are largely from the analysis of a living continuous language in its later, formal stages of development.[36] This is not to say, as certain revisionist historians have declared recently, that Biblical Hebrew is a *Bildungssprache*, or artificial literary language of the Persian-Hellenistic era. As hundreds of Iron Age inscriptions, ostraca, and seals written in this supposedly nonexistent Hebrew attest, this is not a reasonable proposition.[37] What I am suggesting is that many of the early Hebrew inscriptions that we now have, such as those scratched in the tombs at Beth Loya or Khirbet el-Qom or the plaster wall *di pinti* at Kuntillet ʿAjrud, do not represent *literary* Hebrew. Thus they may not

---

34. See Angerstorfer 1982; McCarter 1987, 148; Tigay 1987, 175; Olyan 1988, 31.
35. Miller 1985, 208; McCarter 1987, 152.
36. Coogan 1987, 118–19.
37. Davies 1992.

necessarily conform closely to the expected rules of Iron Age Hebrew grammar but are in effect *graffiti*. As a vernacular form of expression, they may have violated formal rules, but they were nevertheless easily intelligible to those in the countryside who were only functionally literate. If this is the case, one problem can be resolved: how to explain the *difficulties* modern, well-trained Hebraists and epigraphers have in deciphering and actually understanding the growing corpus of Iron Age inscriptions that we now have. Why so many *varied* interpretations, when the consonantal text can usually be established with virtual certainty? Perhaps it is because we are more concerned with correct grammar than the ancients were, to the point where overly refined linguistic analysis impedes rather than advances knowledge.

In any case, reading an ancient text or an artifact always requires a certain degree of intuition, empathy, and imagination. It may be that the eighth-century BCE inscriptions at hand have been overanalyzed, overintellectualized, that they mean just what they would seem to the uninitiated to say: "May X be blessed by Yahweh and *his* Asherah." David Noel Freedman not only insists on this, but he thinks that the coupling of the nonstandard (?) possessive suffix with Yahweh's name in the Khirbet el-Qom and Kuntillet ʿAjrud Asherah inscriptions was *deliberate*. It was meant to emphasize the fact that Asherah was *Yahweh's* consort, not Baal's, as the Deuteronomists and other orthodox parties would have had it.[38] I would also stress that the possessive suffix is deliberate but significant in a different way. That is, the writer of the inscription could have put the *he* at the beginning of the word instead, making it "*the* asherah," as frequently in the Hebrew Bible, that is, specifying that the phrase denoted the symbol rather than the deity. But the *he* placed at the end of the word, used clearly as a possessive suffix, seems to me a clear indication that the writer of this inscription intended to specify not "the asherah" but Asherah herself, in contradistinction to most biblical usage. We should recall that in at least seven passages in the Hebrew Bible the term ʾăšērâ clearly refers to the goddess Asherah herself, thus is still understood in the old sense of consort, as in earlier Canaan (see 1 Kgs 15:13; 16:33; 2 Kgs 21:7; 23:4, 7; and also [plural] Judg 3:7; 1 Sam 7:3 [Ashtoreth = Asherah]).

---

38. Freedman 1987.

12.4. Conclusion

In conclusion, I think that it is becoming clearer every day that modern archaeology is at least as revolutionary a tool in biblical exegesis and the writing of histories of ancient Israel as Albright predicted long ago that it would prove to be. It is precisely in the *dialogue between* texts and material culture remains that our best hope for comprehending the reality of life in ancient Israel resides. Our failure to understand very much thus far, however, of Israelite religion lies not so much in faulty or inadequate data of either kind as it does in the narrow, logocentric angle of vision that has characterized most biblical commentators. Fortunately, fresh archaeological discoveries such as those of Khirbet el-Qom and Kuntillet ʿAjrud force us to broaden our perspective. They do so by giving us a rare glimpse into the world of popular religion—the *practice* of religion that characterized the masses in ancient Israel—that texts alone can never provide.

Works Cited

Ackerman, Susan. 1992. *Under Every Green Tree: Popular Religion in Sixth-Century Judah.* HSM 46. Scholars Press.

Albertz, Rainer. 1994. *A History of Israelite Religion in the Old Testament Period.* Translated by John Bowden. 2 vols. OTL. Westminster John Knox.

Angerstorfer, Andreas. 1982. "Aserhah als 'Consort of Jahweh' oder Ashirta?" *BN* 17:7–16.

Avigad, Nahman. 1953. "The Epitaph of a Royal Steward from Siloam Village." *IEJ* 3:137–52.

Berlinerblau, Jacques. 1996. *The Vow and "Popular Religious Groups" of Ancient Israel: A Philological and Sociological Inquiry.* JSOTSup 210. Sheffield Academic.

Binger, Tilda. 1997. *Asherah: Goddesses in Ugarit, Israel and the Old Testament.* JSOTSup 232. Sheffield Academic.

Bird, Phyllis. 1991. "Israelite Religion and the Faith of Israel's Daughters." Pages 97–198 in *The Bible and the Politics of Exegesis: Essays in Honor of Norman K. Gottwald on His Sixty-Fifth Birthday.* Edited by David Jobling, Peggy L. Day, and Gerald T. Sheppard. Pilgrim.

Bloch-Smith, Elizabeth. 1992. *Judahite Burial Practices and Beliefs about the Dead.* JSOTSup 123. JSOT Press.

Coogan, Michael D. 1987. "Canaanite Origins and Lineage: Reflections on the Religion of Ancient Israel. Pages 115–24 in *Ancient Israelite Religion: Essays in Honor of Frank Moore Cross.* Edited by Patrick D. Miller Jr., Paul D. Hanson, and S. Dean McBride. Fortress.

Davies, Philip R. 1992. *In Search of "Ancient Israel."* JSOTSup 148. JSOT Press.

Day, John. 1986. "Asherah in the Hebrew Bible and Northwest Semitic Literature." *JBL* 105:385–408.

Deutsch, Robert, and Michael Heltzer. 1944. *Forty New Ancient West Semitic Inscriptions.* Archaeological Center Publications.

Dever, William G. 1969–1970. "Iron Age Epigraphic Material from the Area of Khirbet el-Kôm." *HUCA* 40–41:139–204.

———. 1983. "Material Remains and the Cult in Ancient Israel: An Essay in Archaeological Systematics." Pages 571–87 in *The Word of the Lord Shall Go Forth: Essays in Honor of David Noel Freedman in Celebration of His Sixtieth Birthday.* Edited by Carol L. Meyers and M. O'Connor. Eisenbrauns. Republished as chapter 10 in this volume.

———. 1984. "Asherah, Consort of Yahweh? New Evidence from Kuntillet 'Ajrud." *BASOR* 255:21–37.

———. 1987. "The Contribution of Archaeology to the Study of Canaanite and Israelite Religion. Pages 209–47 in *Ancient Religion: Essays in Honor of Frank Moore Cross.* Edited by Patrick D. Miller Jr., Paul D. Hanson, and S. Dean McBride. Fortress.

———. 1993. "Qôm, Khirbet el." *NEAHL* 4:1233–35.

———. 1994a. "Ancient Israelite Religion: How to Reconcile the Differing Textual and Artifactual Portraits?" Pages 105–25 in *Ein Gott allein? JHWH-Verehrung und biblischer Monotheismus im Kontext der israelitischen und altorientalischen Religionsgeschichte.* Edited by Walther Dietrich and Martin A. Klopfenstein. OBO 139. Vandenhoeck & Ruprecht.

———. 1994b. "The Silence of the Text." Pages 143–68 in *Scripture and Other Artifacts: Essays on the Bible and Archaeology in Honor of Philip J. King.* Edited by Michael D. Coogan, J. Cheryl Exum, and Lawrence E. Stager. Westminster John Knox, 1994.

———. 1995. "'Will the Real Israel Please Stand Up?' Part II: Archaeology and the Religions of Israel." *BASOR* 298:37–58.

———. 1996. "Qom, Khirbet el." *OEANE* 4:391–92.

———. 1997. "Archaeology and the Religions of Israel." *BASOR* 301:83–90.
Dorsey, David A. 1980. "The Location of Biblical Makkedah." *TA* 7:185–193.
Emerton, John A. 1982. "New Light on Israelite Religion: The Implications of the Inscriptions from Kuntillet 'Ajrud." *ZAW* 94:2–20
Freedman, David Noel. 1987. "Yahweh of Samaria and His Ashera." *BA* 50:241–49.
Geraty, Lawrence T. 1975. "The Khirbet el-Kôm Bilingual Inscription." *BASOR* 220:55–61.
Gitin, Seymour. 1993. "Miqne, Tel (Ekron)." *NEAEHL* 3:1051–59.
Hadley, Judith M. 1987. "Some Drawings and Inscriptions on Two Pithoi from Kuntillet 'Ajrud." *VT* 37:180–213.
Holladay, John S. 1971. "Khirbet el-Qôm." *IEJ* 21:175–77.
———. "Religion in Israel and Judah under the Monarchy: An Explicitly Archaeological Approach." Pages 249–99 in *Ancient Israelite Religion: Essays in Honor of Frank Moore Cross*. Edited by Patrick D. Miller Jr., Paul D. Hanson, and S. Dean McBride. Fortress.
Keel, Othmar, and Christoph Uehlinger. 1992. *Göttinnen, Götter, und Gottessymbole: Neue Erkenntnisse zur Religionsgeschichte Kanaans und Israels aufgrund bislang unerschlossener ikonographischer Quellen*. QD 134. Herder.
———. 1998. *Gods, Goddesses, and Images of God in Ancient Israel*. Translated by Thomas H. Trapp. Fortress.
Kletter, Raz. 1991. "The Inscribed Weights of the Kingdom of Judah." *TA* 18:131–63.
Lemaire, André. 1977. "Les inscriptions de Khirbet el-Qôm et l'Ashérah de Yhwh." *RB* 84:597–608.
Lipiński, Edouard. 1980. "The Goddess Atirat in Ancient Arabia, in Babylon, and in Ugarit: Her Relation to the Moon-God and the Sun-Goddess." *Folia Orientalia* 21:163–74.
Margalit, Baruch. 1989. "Some Observations on the Inscription and Drawing from Khirbet el-Qom." *VT* 39:371–78.
McCarter, P. Kyle. 1987. "Aspects of the Religion of the Israelite Monarchy: Biblical and Epigraphic Data." Pages 137–55 in *Ancient Israelite Religion: Essays in Honor of Frank Moore Cross*. Edited by Patrick D. Miller Jr., Paul D. Hanson, and S. Dean McBride. Fortress.
Meshel, Ze'ev. 1978. *Kuntillet 'Ajrud: A Religious Centre from the Time of the Judaean Monarchy on the Border of Sinai*. Israel Museum Catalog 175. The Israel Museum.

———. 1979. "Did Yahweh Have a Consort? The New Religious Inscriptions from the Sinai." *BAR* 5.2:24–35.

Meyers, Carol. 1988. *Discovering Eve: Ancient Israelite Women in Context.* Oxford University Press.

Miller, Patrick D. 1985. "Israelite Religion." Pages 201–37 in *The Hebrew Bible and Its Modern Interpreters.* Edited by Douglas A. Knight and Gene M. Tucker. BMI 1. Scholars Press.

———. 1987. "Aspects of the Religion of Ugarit." Pages 53–66 in *Ancient Israelite Religion: Essays in Honor of Frank Moore Cross.* Edited by Patrick D. Miller Jr., Paul D. Hanson, and S. Dean McBride. Fortress.

Mittman, Siegfried. 1981. "Die Grabinschrift des Sängers Uriahu." *ZDPV* 97:139–52.

Naveh, Joseph. 1963. "Old Hebrew Inscriptions in a Burial Cave." *IEJ* 13:74–92.

———. 1979. "Graffiti and Dedications." *BASOR* 235:27–30.

Olyan, Saul M. 1988. *Asherah and the Cult of Yahweh in Israel.* SBLMS 34. Scholars Press.

Schröer, Silvia. 1983. "Zur Deutung der Hand unter der Grabinschrift von Chirbet el-Qôm." *UF* 15:191–200.

Smith, Mark S. 1990. *The Early History of God: Yahweh and the Other Deities in Ancient Israel.* Harper & Row.

Tigay, Jeffrey H. 1987. "Israelite Religion: The Onomastic and Epigraphic Evidence." Pages 157–194 in *Ancient Israelite Religion: Essays in Honor of Frank Moore Cross.* Edited by Patrick D. Miller Jr., Paul D. Hanson, and S. Dean McBride. Fortress.

Toorn, Karel van der. 1994. *From Her Cradle to Her Grave: The Role of Religion in the Life of the Israelite and Babylonian Woman.* BibSem 23. JSOT Press.

Zevit, Ziony. 1984. "The Khirbet el-Qôm Inscription Mentioning a Goddess." *BASOR* 255:39–47.

———. 2001. *The Religions of Ancient Israel: A Synthesis of Parallactic Approaches.* Continuum.

13
Folk Religion in Ancient Israel:
The Disconnect between Text and Artifact

As noted in the essay below, I came to know Rainer Albertz in 1993 at a symposium in Bern. Apart from exchanging papers on religion and cult, the main topic, I became acquainted for the first time in any detail with the Freiburg school of art history and biblical studies. Several members of this group were present, including Othmar Keel, Christoph Uehlinger, and Silvia Schröer.

Only in 1998 did their iconographic approach become more widespread in America, with Keel and Uehlinger's *God's Goddesses, and Images of God in Ancient Israel* (Fortress). Schröer had published her *In Israel gab es Bilder* (Frieburg) in 1987, but few American scholars took notice. I began to cite works of the Frieburg school frequently, with high praise, because it was clear to me that both archaeologists and biblical scholars would profit enormously from the new insights in this approach.

In 2009, Albertz and his colleague Rudiger Schmitt convened another symposium on religion and cult in Münster, where I renewed my friendship with Albertz, and we both gave papers (published in 2014). This essay, published in 2008, is an update of my earlier paper in 1993, when I had first met Albertz. I consider it a very great honor to have been invited to publish it in his Festschrift.

Originally published as pages 426–39 in *Berührungspunklte Studien zur Sozial- und Religionsgeschichte Israels und Seiner Umwelt: Festschrift für Rainer Albertz zu seinem 65. Geburtstag*. Edited by Ingo Kottsieper, Rüdiger Schmitt, and Jacob Wöhrte. AOAT 350. Ugarit-Verlag, 2008.

13.1. Introduction

I first met Rainer Albertz at a symposium in Bern 1993, where we addressed the topic of "Yahweh and the Other Gods and Goddesses in the Ancient Near East." My paper dealt with the problem of reconciling what I took to be two differing approaches to understanding the ancient Israelite cult: (1) the textual; and (2) the archaeological, or "artifactual."

I found Albertz among the few biblicists at Bern who seemed to appreciate the problem. He kindly drew my attention to his recently published *Religionsgeschichte Israels in alttestamentlicher Zeit*, which I subsequently reviewed with high praise.[1] It is an honor to be invited to expand our dialogue by returning to the topic of reconciling the differences with new archaeological data, emphasizing the need to explain both historically and theologically what I shall call here the disconnect between texts and artifacts.

13.2. Material Remains of the Cult

In analyzing any religion, a distinction can be made, if only heuristic, between (1) theology, whose locus is almost always found in texts, that is, in Scripture; and (2) practice, which may be reflected frequently, although not exclusively, in artifacts, that is, in what we often call the archaeological record.[2] Both sources of information allow a theoretical reconstruction of the cult, but the resulting portraits may differ considerably. That raises a fundamental historiographical (and theological) issue: Which is the primary source? Further, which portrait is the more authentic? I cannot, of course, resolve such a dilemma here. I can only draw attention to a few instances in which the disconnect is becoming more obvious.

13.2.1. Connections and Disconnections

To put these disconnects in context, it may be helpful to note first that they must be seen in comparison with several places where texts and arti-

---

1. Dever 1994b.
2. My distinction is specifically denied in Keel and Uehlinger 1992, 8–9.

facts do connect. Sometimes the archaeological data appear to reflect just the sort of family religion—"internal religious pluralism" or "poly-Yahwism"—that Albertz has done so much to illuminate.[3] Thus the biblical high places (*bāmôt*), standing stones (*maṣṣēbôt*), food and animal sacrifices (several Hebrew terms), burning incense (*qəṭōret*), votive offerings and vows (*nādār*), and various burial customs are all now reasonably well attested in archaeological remains. This evidence is adequately surveyed elsewhere and need not detain us here.[4] It constitutes what I have called elsewhere convergences, or points at which the parallel lines of textual and artifactual evidence begin to come together. Such convergences point the historian to a synthesis that may yield a reasonably accurate representation of past realities. I am aware that such positivism is no longer in vogue in today's supposedly postmodern world, but, like Albertz, I still defend it.[5] The alternative is, practically speaking, nihilism.

13.2.2. Some Specifics

More significant than these convergences, in my opinion, are several divergences between the biblical texts and the archaeological evidence. The artifacts we now have that are most conspicuously absent (or at least confused) in the Hebrew Bible are the following: (1) small horned altars; (2) ceramic offering stands; (3) *naoi*, or model temples; (4) *kernoi*, or "trick vessels"; (5) amulets, or good-luck talismans; and (6) terra-cotta figurines. We now have dozens, even hundreds, of examples of each of these classes of artifacts, demonstrably Israelite and well dated to the settlement and monarchical period (the Iron I–II Age), and found in clear cultic contexts. The literature is extensive, but I offer a few examples for illustration.[6]

(1) The definitive study of the small horned altars (fig. 13.1) is that of Seymour Gitin, who cites several Israelite examples (in addition to a number of Neo-Philistine ones from Ekron). There are some forty-five in all, ranging from the tenth to the seventh/sixth century BCE.[7] Gitin's argu-

---

3. Albertz 1992, 1:45–60, 143–57, 321–37.
4. See Bloch-Smith 1992; Dever 2005; Gittlen 2002; Lewis 1998; Nakhai 2001; Vriezen 2001; Zevit 2001.
5. Dever 2001b.
6. See, conveniently, Dever 2005 and Zevit 2001, both with full references.
7. Gitin 2002.

Fig. 13.1. Horned altar from Megiddo, tenth century BCE. From Vriezen 2001, fig. 10.

ment that these horned altars were used primarily for incenseburning is persuasive, but I am not as convinced of his attempt to connect these altars directly with the biblical customs of burning incense, that is, the specifically horned variety under discussion.

To my knowledge, none of the biblical texts describing the burning of incense on small altars mentions them having horns. There are twenty-six references to altars with horns (*qərānôt*), but they are always described as large monumental altars. They are said to stand in the wilderness tabernacle (Exod 27:2; Lev 4:17–18) or in the temple in Jerusalem (1 Kgs 1:50–51; 2:38; see also Ezek 43:15, 20; Ps 118:27). The dimensions of the tabernacle horned altar are said to be 3 cubits square and 2 cubits high, or 4.5 feet square and 3 feet high. The dimensions of the Jerusalem horned altar are not given, but it was massive enough that Adonijah and Joab could flee to the temple for sanctuary and cling to the horns of the altar for refuge. In Ezekiel's vision of the restored temple, the dimensions of the altar (somewhat difficult to understand) appear to be even more monumental than those of the tabernacle horned altar.

In any case, the texts specify that these large horned altars were used for animal sacrifice and in the official cult as overseen by the legitimate priesthood. There is nowhere any mention of the burning of incense, small altars, or household shrines. An example of the small incense altar described in Jer 32:29 (see also 19:13) as being used for burning incense on the rooftop has actually been found in the ruins of a fallen late seventh-century BCE roof at Ashkelon, but it is not of the horned variety.[8] In the end, it is not Israelite, nor do the biblical texts cited above specify horned altars.

---

8. Stager 1996, 66*–68*.

In conclusion, the horned altars mentioned in the Hebrew Bible do not correspond at all to the small horned incense altars found in archaeological contexts, whether in size, context, or usage. The biblical writers never mention our altars. Incidentally, there are a few known examples of their large altars—notably, one from Dan and one from Beersheba. Curiously, these cities conventionally mark the borders of Israel, but these altars, as well, go unmentioned in the Hebrew Bible.[9]

(2) Numerous ceramic cult or offering stands (sometimes mistakenly referred to as incense stands) are now well known from various twelfth- to sixth-century BCE Israelite contexts (fig. 13.2). No complete corpus or typological classification exists, but most of these offering stands have several features in common.[10] These include: (1) a square body that appears to model a miniature, multistory temple, with door and windows, parapets, and the like; or, more commonly, (2) a tall cylindrical body that probably represents a stylized palm tree trunk, sometimes complete with drooping fronds; (3) fenestrations or "windows," possibly for wafting burning incense; (4) an open top with provisions for a removable bowl, for food or drink offerings; and (5) limited bas relief iconographic motifs (usually little or none on clearly Israelite examples).

Fig. 13.2. Offering stand from Taʿanach, tenth century BCE. From Vriezen 2001, fig. 11.

Unusual examples are a four-tiered tenth-century BCE stand from Taʿanach (fig. 13.2), with an array of exotic motifs, including many windows (and probably an empty door), a winged sun disc on the back of a quadruped, a tree flanked by two rampant wild goats, lions, several winged

---

9. Biran 1994, 202–3; Aharoni 1974.
10. DeVries 1987; Fowler 1985.

cherubs, and a scene depicting a nude female deity whom I have identified as Asherah, holding a pair of lions by the ears.[11] Another atypical cult stand comes from Israelite 'Ai, of the twelfth–eleventh century BCE, featuring not only numerous fenestrations but also a row of human feet protruding around the base (perhaps signifying the invisible presence of Yahweh).[12]

The use of these cult stands for food and drink offerings is confirmed by the removable bowl on top (sometimes found with the stands), although the fenestrations suggest that incense offerings could also have been made with these stands. Both food and drink offerings are well known in the biblical text, as is the custom of burning incense.[13]

Yet food offerings (probably as a by-product of animal sacrifices) and drink offerings (libations), as well as burnt incense, are connected in the biblical descriptions only with altars, not any kind of cult stands. There is no mention in any biblical text that I know of anything resembling our ceramic offering stands. The biblical writers seem unaware of them, yet the artifacts of the cult are relatively common Iron I–II finds, usually in domestic contexts. What explains this silence of the biblical texts on this aspect of offerings, the descriptions of which are otherwise painstakingly detailed?

(3) We now have a growing corpus of Iron Age *naoi* (or *naiskoi*), miniature terra-cotta temple models. They have a rather long history in the Bronze Age throughout the ancient Near East generally, but the Iron Age group includes Aramean, Phoenician, Edomite-Moabite, and now a few clear Israelite examples. The only intact Israelite example from a well-dated context is the one from Tell el Far'ah North, biblical Tirzah, attributed by the French excavators to Level VIIb, of the mid- to late tenth century BCE (fig. 13.3).[14] It features fluted tree columns with the volutes of the well-known palmette capitals flanking the doorway. Over the lintel above the entrance is a crescent moon and rows of dots that probably represent the stars of the Pleiades. The stylized tree motif has been persuasively linked with the Canaanite-Israelite goddess Asherah (below), while the moon disc and star of the Pleiades motifs are astral symbols usually associated

---

11. Dever 1984; cf. Hestrin 1987a.
12. Zevit 2001, 153–56.
13. Haran 1978; Milgrom 1983; Anderson 1987; Gitin 2002.
14. Chambon 1984, pl. 66.

Fig. 13.3. Terra-cotta temple model from Tell el-Farʿah North. From Chambon 1984, pl. 66.

with the cult of Astarte in the Iron Age Mediterranean world.[15] These *naoi* are clearly portable household shrines, dedicated to a specific female deity wherever we have good evidence, that is, associated or in situ nude fertility figurines.[16]

If the biblical writers are uninformed or ambivalent about horned altars and offering stands, their silence on the subject of the *naoi* is deafening. In none of their frequent condemnations of folk religion—of household and village cults—is there any hint of such model temples, or even of the specific figural representations of the deities that we know were frequently in use with them (on figurines in general, see below). Again, why did these so blatantly "pagan" artifacts escape notice?

(4) Equally exotic are the many bowls with hollow rims known as *kernoi*, often called "trick vessels" because of their peculiar, elaborate facilities for pouring liquids of some sort (fig. 13.4). The Iron Age *kernoi* in Palestine have close parallels and probably antecedents in Cyprus, some as early as the Late Bronze Age. It has been supposed that they were introduced into Palestine by the incoming Sea Peoples, and many of the Iron Age examples are from Philistine or Neo-Philistine sites (e.g., Tell Qasile, Ekron, Ashdod). But there are a few indisputable Israelite examples, dating from the twelfth–eleventh century BCE to the eighth–seventh century BCE.

---

15. Hestrin 1987b; Dever forthcoming; Keel and Uelinger 1992.
16. Dever forthcoming.

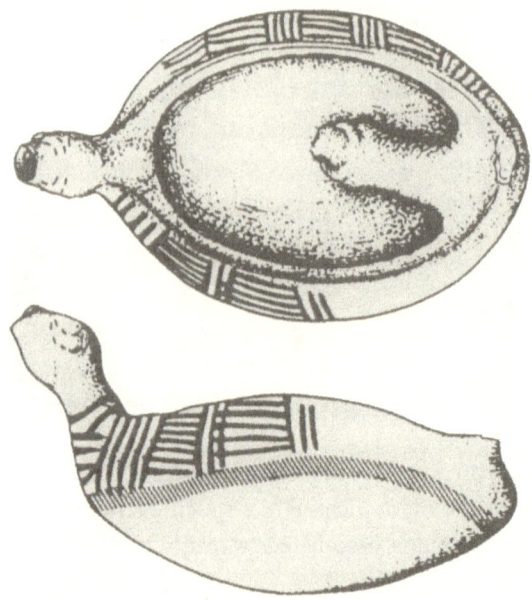

Fig. 13.4. *Kernos* from Tell Qasile, twelfth–eleventh century BCE. From Mazar 1980, fig. 39.

There can be no doubt that these *kernoi*, far from being toys, however amusing, were designed and used for libation offerings. One filled the bowl with a liquid (such as oil, wine, milk, or water), then tilted the vessel so as to fill the hollow rim, and finally tilted it farther so that the attached spouts (animal heads, pomegranates, and the like) poured out the contents. No comprehensive study of these Israelite *kernoi* exists, but I have done a preliminary study in publishing one probably from Khirbet el-Qom (biblical Makkedah).[17]

Once again, the biblical texts are oblivious to these distinctive vessels, even though the libation offering (*nesek*) is frequently described. The paraphernalia used for such libation offerings in the texts are those suitable for official public occasions, that is, elaborate gold and silver vessels such as those used in the tabernacle or temple (Exod 25:29; 37:16). The only possible reference to something like our *kernoi* might be the *qəśôt hannāsek* of Num 4:7, usually translated "cup/bowl for libations." But that reference is generic and cannot be further specified. It may not ever refer to a ceramic vessel at all. Yet simple ad hoc libation offerings could apparently be made

---

17. Dever 2001a.

anywhere: in public, in private, on the roof of a house, and so on.[18] Why the silence of the text?

(5) Amulets of various kinds—small good-luck charms—are common artifacts in Iron Age assemblages (especially in tombs), although they have not been systematically analyzed. The many types of amulets include semiprecious stones that may well have functioned primarily as jewelry but were also employed for their supposed apotropaic powers. More specific functionally are the Eye of Horus and Bes amulets, particularly common in eighth- to seventh-century BCE Judean tombs.[19] The faience Eye of Horus amulets, of Egyptian derivation, are well known in the ancient world for having magical qualities, and the Egyptian dwarf god (or demon) Bes was a deity associated with music, dancing, and even bawdy behavior in the cult. But he also possessed the power to avert evil, especially the hardships risked in pregnancy and childbirth.[20]

Neither Horus nor Bes is mentioned in the Hebrew Bible, despite their popularity in the nonofficial cult. Needless to say, although various forms of magic are tolerated, particularly under priestly supervision, the instruments involved are either not specified in detail or remain somewhat enigmatic. Magical rites are said to employ the ark, the ephod, Urim and Thummim, and teraphim, whatever these may be. Divination may be done with lots (astragali or dice, both attested archaeologically). Then there is hepatoscopy (liver examination), hydromancy, rhabolomancy (divination through the use of a tree, wood, a staff, or arrow), and the invocation of "the Asherah."[21] But the use of good-luck amulets would have been far more popular and widespread, yet the biblical texts, to my knowledge, do not allude to their use for magic.

(6) The ubiquitous Iron Age terra-cotta female fertility figurines, of which we now have as many as three thousand Israelite examples (some two thousand from Jerusalem alone), are our best test case (fig. 13.5). Unlike the above artifacts, these figurines have been extensively studied, even before they occurred so frequently.[22] There are two main types: (1) a

---

18. Haran 1978, 216–34; Dever 2001a, 126–29.
19. See, for examples, Tufnell 1953, pls. 34–36.
20. Wilson 1975.
21. Jeffers 1996.
22. Kletter 1996, 2001, both with references to earlier literature. See also n. 25 below.

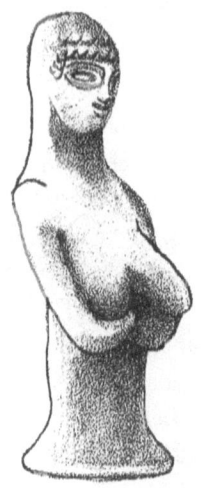

Fig. 13.5. Pillar-base figurine from Jerusalem. From Vriezen 2001, fig. 13.

representation of a nude female figure clutching a circular disc to her left breast, often mistakenly labeled a tambourine (i.e., a frame drum, which we now know it is not), dating from the tenth to the seventh or sixth century BCE; and (2) the more typical eighth- to seventh-century BCE Judean pillar-base figurines, with prominent breasts but a featureless cylindrical lower body that resembles a tree trunk with splayed base.

Albright dubbed these objects *dea nutrix* figurines, assuming that they were used by Israelite-Judean women to secure the favors of the Great Goddess as "Patroness of Nursing Mothers" (thus fertility figurines). He did not, however, specify the goddess—although in ancient Israel she could only have been thought of as either Astarte (Ishtar) or Asherah. More recently, scholars have not only related these figurines specifically to Asherah, but they have been inclined to see them as representations of that deity. That would make them, in effect, not idols but personifications of Asherah, potent symbols that made her palpable, cultically available. I have championed that view, and I am joined by a growing number of both archaeologists and biblical scholars, including Susan Ackerman, John Day, Judith M. Hadley, Raz Kletter, Othmar Keel and Christoph Uehlinger, Karel van der Toorn, and others.[23] To put the admittedly controversial issue succinctly, are these figurines human or divine representations? That is, are they only votives (essentially "stand-ins" for worshipers) or images of a female deity, the Great Goddess herself? (They certainly do not represent Yahweh or any other male deity.)

Those who see the figurines simply as votives point out the lack of any specific iconographic motifs connected with deities: the figurines feature

---

23. See references in Ackerman 2003, 461–65; Dever 2005, 168–208; Hadley 2000, 198–205; Van der Toorn 2004; Zevit 2001, 267–74. Dissenters include Frymer-Kensky 1992; McCarter 1987; Meyers 1988; Miller 1986; Lewis 1998; and Smith 1990. The latter, however, do not necessarily argue that the figurines were only votives, but they do not believe that they can be identified with a specific deity.

only prominent female breasts. Some scholars take the disc at the breast of one type as a tambourine or frame drum, supposedly evidence that this represents a human, that is, a female musician, playing perhaps in a cult scene (for which we do have evidence). But against this view is (1) the fact that it is hard to imagine an Israelite or Judean woman portrayed, or portrayed by others, in the nude, as female deities almost always were in the Bronze and Iron Ages, and (2) a frame drum cannot possibly be played in this position, as several musicologists have pointed out, so this object may better be interpreted as a mold-made bread cake, for which we have ample evidence.[24]

Then there is the matter of context, which in archaeology often is significant, even decisive. Those who hold to the votive theory claim that the figurines are not usually found in clear cultic contexts but rather in all sorts of contexts—in houses, in domestic debris, in tombs, and the like. But this argument loses force if one recognizes that folk religion centers largely on family rituals, as Rainer Albertz was one of the first to show. So cultic items such as the figurines would be widely distributed, not confined to temples or even to village shrines. In any case, the most significant context for the figurines comes from the tenth-century BCE shrine at Taʻanach, where the stand discussed above was found (also an olive press and sheep-goat astragali for divination). Here there was found a mold for making the figurines with disc. It is inconceivable to me that a mere representation of a human figure would be mass-produced in this fashion, especially in what is clearly a local shrine.

All things considered, I regard the female figurines as representations of the goddess Asherah, the existence of whose cult throughout the monarchy is now well documented (above). The argument that she is not, however, a separate deity, but only a "hypostatization" of Yahweh's supposedly female aspects, makes little sense. Asherah, whether "the asherah" or a personal name, is only a symbol? The symbol would have had no efficacy unless it pointed to the reality and presence of the goddess whom it represented.[25]

---

24. The distinguished Israeli musicologist Joachin Braun has shown that these disc-like objects can scarcely be frame drums (Braun 2002, 127–29). He suggests, as I do, that they may represent the mold-made cakes referred to in Jer 44:15–23, describing women who baked cakes for the "queen of heaven" that bore her image; see Ackerman 1992, 5–35.

25. McCarter 1987, 143–49.

I would argue that, in either interpretation above, these figurines functioned somehow in the cult of Asherah, which on present evidence most biblical scholars now acknowledge was widespread. I have recently marshaled the archaeological evidence (and to some degree also the textual evidence) in *Did God Have a Wife? Archaeology and Folk Religion in Ancient Israel* (2005). Whatever the case, as Susan Ackerman has observed trenchantly, "In the ancient Near East the idol was the god."[26] In this view, the figurine—although more a symbol than an idol—was so closely identified with Asherah and her cult that a precise identification is moot. And although it may not be politically correct at the moment, these are connected with fertility in the broad sense of the well-attested desire of women (and men as well) for children—conceived, born, and nursed safely through infancy. Ziony Zevit has rightly called these figurines "prayers in clay," and those prayers were most likely addressed to Asherah the Mother Goddess.[27]

The attempt to connect these female figurines, however interpreted, with the biblical texts is more difficult than with the other cultic artifacts that we have discussed thus far. Ironically, that is because here there are some biblical terms that could conceivably refer to these (or other) figurines. Yet the fact is that a closer examination of all the biblical terms for "figurine," "image," "idol," or similar objects must be ruled out. Both etymology and usage preclude any connection with our Judean pillar-base (or disc-bearing) figurines, even though their eighth- to seventh-century BCE date coincides with the probable date of the initial origin and first redaction of the written traditions.[28] Why do the Biblical writers not mention them—especially in specifically condemning the cult of Asherah, of which these figurines were a common expression?

13.3. The Silence of the Texts

Since Martin Noth's dictum in 1958 that "archaeology is mute" (*stumm*),[29] it has been commonplace for biblical scholars to repeat that charge (untrue,

---

26. Ackerman 1992, 65.
27. Zevit 2001, 274.
28. Dever 2005, 181–83; Zevit 2001, 274–76.
29. Noth 1981, 50.

of course). But in this case, it is the biblical text that is "mute," at least with regard to many of the common physical manifestations of the cult in Iron Age Israel. This phenomenon is by now beginning to be recognized, but I do not find any credible explanation in the literature on biblical scholarship. (Archaeologists seem oblivious to the problem.) Here I will propose four explanations that seem possible to me.

(1) The biblical writers were unaware of the existence of those cultic objects associated with folk religion, presumably because they were elites attached to court and temple circles in Jerusalem (perhaps also because they were all men and thus unfamiliar with, or disposed against, what were regarded as women's cults). That is possible but unlikely, I think. Note, for instance, the detailed condemnation of folk (and here also official) religion in 2 Kgs 23.[30] This passage is characterized by a detailed description of the items proscribed, including specifically "all the vessels" (*hakkēlîm*) made for Baal and for Asherah" (2 Kgs 23:4; Asherah clearly a goddess here). Burning incense is also condemned in 2 Kgs 23, but no reference is made to purging the objects used for these rites.

Also included in the list of things supposedly thrown out of the temple are "horses and chariots dedicated to the sun" and "altars on the roof." Such roof altars, which we actually have, were discussed above. The horses and chariots are reminiscent of the common horse and horse-and-rider figurines that we now know from eighth- to sixth-century BCE Judah. They are probably to be explained by imagery connected with the storm god Baal riding his chariot (or cloud) across the heavens. We actually have Late Bronze Age (Canaanite) examples of horse-drawn chariots, driven by figurines representing a deity (or a pair of deities).[31] So the biblical writers could be quite specific about cult paraphernalia—when they chose to be.

(2) The biblical authors wrote too late to know about these typical Iron Age cult objects, that is, in the Persian or Hellenistic period, when such artifacts were extinct. That, of course, is the argument of the revisionists. But in that case, why do the writers not refer to cult paraphernalia of that era? In any case, the extreme late date proposed by the revisionists is still not accepted by the majority of scholars. In my book *What Did the Biblical Writers Know and When Did They Know It?*, I have shown that, while many

---

30. I have dealt at length with this in Dever 1994c.
31. Taylor 1993.

of the biblical narratives are indeed "stories," the only cultural-historical context for these stories is the Iron Age, not any later period.[32]

(3) The biblical writers were well acquainted with our cult objects, but since they disapproved of them they had no occasion to mention them in describing either official or folk religion. Their silence would then amount to tolerance, if not consent. Yet I find it hard to believe that they would have condoned such things as the female figurines, particularly with their Canaanite associations.

(4) The biblical writers were well informed about all these cult objects, as we would expect. But they deliberately avoided mentioning them because they sought to suppress popular cults that, in their view, were heterodox. In particular, orthodox Yahwists tried to drive Asherah underground, and eventually they succeeded, in the exile and beyond. This is beyond doubt, as scholars now generally agree. But is there any real evidence of such deliberate deception as I am suggesting? There may be.

First, there are hints in the biblical texts themselves. It is well known that many of the forty or so occurrences of the term *ʾăšērâ* are ambiguous. The term can refer either to a goddess by that name or to a tree-like symbol associated with her. Some references are particularly confusing, such as 1 Kgs 15:11–15, which relates how Maacah, the queen mother, "made an *abomination* for Asherah." Earlier translations understood this passage as referring to "making an idol in a grove" (taking the LXX *alsos*, "grove," as the correct translation of *ʾăšērâ*). Thus the confusion perpetuated by the LXX, and even the Vulgate, stems from the original (pre-Masoretic) text.[33]

This confusion, however, is confounded by the other term used in this passage, *mipleṣet*, an enigmatic *hapex legomenon* that means something like "abominable thing" (1 Kgs 15:13 // 2 Chr 15:16; from *plṣ*, "to shudder"). But what was this thing, and why not use one of the many other specific Hebrew terms available (above) for "image"? I make no claim to be a Hebraist, but I would suggest that what we have here is a circumlocution—an oblique way of referring to something that was too repellant to the biblical writers to mention by name. In any case, the term *mipleṣet*, while no doubt an image of some sort of/for Asherah, cannot refer to our terra-cotta figurines, since it was "cut down and burned" (1 Kgs 15:13). In

---

32. Dever 2001b, 23–52, 273–80.
33. LaRocca-Pitts 2001.

this case, it was apparently the wooden tree or pole commonly associated with Asherah and her cult.

The well-known confusion (or obfuscation) of the biblical writers in the use of the term *ʾăšērâ* is also reflected in the fact that, while obviously feminine singular, the word occurs in both the feminine and the masculine plural and even with the definite article, "the Asherah." There are similar difficulties in the use of parallel names for Asherah, such as Ashtaroth and Ashtoreth, both of which appear to be bastardized forms of Astarte.[34] It has even been suggested that Ashtoreth is a conflation of the consonants for Astarte with the vowels of *bōšet*, "shame." While this is speculative, we do have a parallel in the well-known substitution of the vowels of *ʾădōnāy*, "Lord," for "Yahweh" in the Masoretic Text (thus the mistaken later translation "Jehovah"). Thus one would never pronounce either divine name, only its substitute (another circumlocution). One was too sacred, the other too profane.

13.4. Conclusion

If my suggestions have any merit, they would help to explain the curious reticence of the biblical writers regarding some cultic paraphernalia associated with folk religion. By refusing to name these objects, they effectively (and conveniently) deny their existence, for, in the ancient world generally, to name a thing was not only to define it but to confer on it a reality, a tangibility, that it might not otherwise have had. The biblical writers, as well as the final redactors (not to mention later Jewish and Christian commentators), orthodox devotees of an exclusively male deity Yahweh, are reluctant to do that. So while they cannot change the consonantal texts of what is by now becoming Scripture, they can manipulate the text and its context so as to obscure the reality they find too painful to confront.[35] We need no longer be so embarrassed by the "disconnect" between theological ideal and religious reality. Nor do we need to attempt to reconcile the two. The real religions of ancient Israel were, as Rainer Albertz reminds us, diverse and constantly evolving, and archaeology can

---

34. Wyatt 1999.
35. Olyan also raises the possibility of such "willful confusion" (1988, 10).

at last illuminate some aspects of those religions that escape notice in the biblical text.[36]

Works Cited

Ackerman, Susan. 1992. *Under Every Green Tree: Popular Religion in Sixth-Century Judah*. HSM 46. Scholars Press.

———. 2003. "At Home with the Goddess." Pages 455–68 in *Symbiosis, Symbolism, and the Power of the Past: Canaan, Ancient Israel, and Their Neighbors from the Late Bronze Age through Roman Palestina*. Edited by William G. Dever and Seymour Gitin. Eisenbrauns.

Aharoni, Yohanon. 1974. "The Horned Altar of Beer-sheba." *BA* 37:2–6.

Albertz, Rainer. 1992. *Religionsgeschichte Israels in alttestamentlicher Zeit*. 2 vols. Vandenhoeck & Ruprecht.

Anderson, Gary. 1987. *Sacrifices and Offerings in Ancient Israel: Studies in their Social and Political Importance*. HSM 41. Scholars Press.

Andrén, Anders. 1998. *Between Artifacts and Texts: Historical Archaeology in Global Perspective*. Springer.

Biran, Avraham. 1994. *Biblical Dan*. Israel Exploration Society; Hebrew Union College-Jewish Institute of Religion.

Bloch-Smith, Elizabeth. 1992. *Judahite Burial Practices and Beliefs about the Dead*. JSOTSup 123. JSOT Press.

Braun, Joachin. 2002. *Music in Ancient Israel/Palestine: Archaeological, Written, and Comparative Sources*. Eerdmans.

Chambon, Alain. 1984. *Tel el-Farʿah I: L'âge du Fer*. Éditions Recherche sur les Civilisations.

Dever, William G. 1984. "Asherah, Consort of Yahweh? New Evidence from Kuntillet ʿAjrud." *BASOR* 255:21–37.

———. 1994a. "Ancient Israelite Religion: How to Reconcile the Differing Textual and Artifactual Portraits?" Pages 105–25 in *Ein Gott allein? JHWH-Verehrung und biblischer Monotheismus im Kontext der israelitischen und altorientalischen Religionsgeschichte*. Edited by Walther Dietrich and Martin A. Klopfenstein. OBO 139. Vandenhoeck & Ruprecht.

---

36. The dialogue between texts and artifacts is discussed in other branches of historical archaeology as well in Andrén 1998.

———. 1994b. Review of *A History of Israelite Religion in the Old Testament Period, Vol. I: From the Beginnings of the End of the Monarchy*, by Rainer Albertz. *BASOR* 301:83–90.

———. 1994c. "The Silence of the Text: An Archaeological Commentary on 2 Kings 23." Pages 143–68 in *Scripture and Other Artifacts*. Edited by Michael D. Coogan and Philip J. King. Westminster John Knox. Republished as chapter 11 in this volume.

———. 2001a. "Iron Age Kernoi and the Israelite Cult." Pages 119–33 in *Studies in the Archaeology of Israel and Neighboring Lands in Memory of Douglas L. Esse*. Edited by Samuel R. Wolff. ASOR Books 5. Oriental Institute of the University of Chicago; American Schools of Oriental Research.

———. 2001b. *What Did the Biblical Writers Know and When Did They Know It? What Archaeology Can Tell Us about the Reality of Ancient Israel*. Eerdmans.

———. 2005. *Did God Have a Wife? Archaeology and Folk Religion in Ancient Israel*. Eerdmans.

DeVries, LaMoine F. 1987. "Cult Stands: A Bewildering Variety of Shapes and Sizes." *BAR* 13.4:26–37.

Fowler, Mervyn D. 1985. "Excavated Incense Burners: A Case for Identifying a Site as Sacred?" *PEQ* 117:25–29.

Frymer-Kensky, Tikva. 1992. *In the Wake of the Goddesses: Women, Culture and the Biblical Transformation of Pagan Myth*. Free Press.

Gitin, Seymour. 2002. "The Four-Horned Altar and Sacred Space: An Archaeological Perspective." Pp 95–123 in *Sacred Time, Sacred Place. Archaeolgy and the Religions of Israel*. Edited by Barry M. Gittlen. Eisenbrauns.

Gittlen, Barry M., ed. 2002. *Sacred Time, Sacred Place: Archaeology and the Religion of Israel*. Eisenbrauns.

Hadley, Judith M. 2000. *The Cult of Asherah in Ancient Israel and Judah: Evidence for a Hebrew Goddess*. Cambridge University Press.

Haran, Menahem. 1978. *Temples and Temple-Service in Ancient Israel: An Inquiry into the Character of Cult Phenomena and the Historical Setting of the Priestly School*. Clarendon.

Hestrin, Ruth. 1987a. "The Cult Stand from Ta'anach and Its Religious Background." Pages 61–77 in *Phoenicia and the East Mediterranean in the First Millennium B.C.* Edited by Eduoard Lipiński. OLA 22. Peeters.

———. 1987b. "The Lachish Ewer and the 'Asherah." *IEJ* 37:212–23.

Jeffers, Ann. 1996. *Magic and Divination in Ancient Palestine and Syria.* SHANE 8. Brill.

Keel, Othmar, and Christoph Uehlinger. 1992. *Göttinnen, Götter, und Gottessymbole: Neue Erkenntnisse zur Religionsgeschichte Kanaans und Israels aufgrund bislang unerschlossener ikonographischer Quellen.* QD 134. Herder.

Kletter, Raz. 1996. *The Judean Pillar-Figurines and the Archaeology of Asherah.* BAR International Series 636. BAR Publishing.

———. 2001. "Between Archaeology and Theology: The Pillar Figurines from Judah and the Asherah." Pages 179–216 in *Studies in the Archaeology of the Iron Age in Israel and Jordan.* Edited by Amiha Mazar. JSOTSup 331. Sheffield Academic.

LaRocca-Pitts, Elizabeth C. 2001. *"Of Wood and Stone": The Significance of Israelite/Cultic Items in the Bible and Its Early Interpreters.* HSM 61. Eisenbrauns.

Lewis, Theodore J. 1998. "Divine Images and Aniconism in Ancient Israel." *JAOS* 118:36–53.

Mazar, Amihai. 1980. *The Philistine Sanctuary: Architecture and Cult Objects.* Vol. 1 of *Excavations at Tell Qasile.* Qedem 12. Hebrew University of Jerusalem.

McCarter, P. Kyle. 1987. "Aspects of the Religion of the Israelite Monarchy: Biblical and Epigraphic Data." Pages 137–55 in *Ancient Israelite Religion: Essays in Honor of Frank Moore Cross.* Edited by Patrick D. Miller Jr., Paul D. Hanson, and S. Dean McBride. Fortress.

Meyers, Carol. 1988. *Discovering Eve: Ancient Israelite Women in Context.* Oxford University Press.

Milgrom, Jacob. 1983. *Studies in Cultic Theology and Terminology.* SJLA 36. Brill.

Miller, Patrick D., Jr., 1986. "The Absence of the Goddess in Israelite Religion." *Hebrew Annual Review* 10: 239–48.

Nakhai, Beth Alpert. 2001. *Archaeology and the Religions of Canaan and Israel.* ASOR Books 7. American Schools of Oriental Research.

Noth, Martin. 1981. *Geschichte Israels.* Vandenhoeck & Ruprecht.

Olyan, Saul. 1988. *Asherah and the Cult of Yahweh in Israel.* SBLMS 34. Scholars Press.

Smith, Mark S. 1990. *The Early History of God: Yahweh and the Other Deities in Ancient Israel.* Harper & Row.

Stager, Lawrence E. 1996. "Ashkelon and the Archaeology of Destruction: Kislev 604 BCE." *ErIsr* 25: 61*–74*.

Taylor, J. Glen. 1993. *Yahweh and the Sun: Biblical and Archaeological Evidence for Sun Worship in Ancient Israel*. JSOTSup 111. Sheffield Academic.

Toorn, Karel van der. 2004. "Israelite Figurines: A View from the Texts." Pages 45–62 in *Sacred Time, Sacred Space: Archaeology and the Religion of Israel*. Edited by Barry M. Gittlen. Eisenbrauns.

Tufnell, Olga.1953. *Lachish III: The Iron Age*. Oxford University Press.

Vriezen, Karel J. H. 2001. "Archaeological Traces of Cult in Ancient Israel." Pages 45–80 in *Only One God? Monotheism in Ancient Israel and the Veneration of the Goddess Asherah*, by Bob Becking, Meindert Dijkstra, Marjo C. A. Korpel, and Karel J. H. Vriezen. BibSem 77. Sheffield Academic.

Wilson, Veronica. 1975. "The Iconography of Bes with Particular Reference to the Cypriot Influence." *Levant* 7:77–103.

Wyatt, Nicholas. 1999. Astarte. *DDD*, 109–14.

Zevit, Ziony. 2001. *The Religions of Ancient Israel: A Synthesis of Parallactic Approaches*. Continuum.

Index of Biblical References

Exodus		2 Kings	116, 192
25:29	330	12:31	285
27:2	326	14:25	233
37:16	330	17:17	292
		18:4	283
Leviticus		21:1–9	283, 295
4:17–18	326	21:5	292
		21:7	288, 318
Numbers		23	280, 283–84, 286, 296, 299, 335
4:7	330	23:4	286, 318, 335
6:22–24	293	23:4–5	290
		23:5	285, 289
Deuteronomy		23:6	287, 295
23:16–17	291	23:7	286, 291, 318
Judg 3:7	318	23:8	286, 289
Judg 12:5–6	176	23:10	292
		23:11	289
1 Samuel		23:16–17	295
7:3	318	23:16–18	295
8:5	222	23:16–20	295
13:34	177	23:24	292
1 Kings		2 Chronicles	
1:50–51	326	15:16	336
2:38	326		
6–9	64	Job	
9:15–17	17, 23	36:14	291
14:24	291		
15:11–15	336	Psalms	
15:12	291	118:27	326
15:13	318, 336		
16:33	318	Jeremiah	
22:47	291	7:18	297
		7:31–32	292
		19:6	292

Jeremiah (*continued*)
    19:13   326
    32:29   326
    44:15–23   333

Ezekiel
    43:15   326
    43:20   326

Hosea
    4:14   291

Index of Ancient People(s), Places, and Objects

Ahab 114, 177, 206
'Ai 31, 36, 196, 328
Amal, Tel 232
Amarna 150, 155
Aphek 231–32
Arad 145, 232, 254, 257, 259, 266, 284–86, 289, 291
Ashdod 329
Asherah 192, 249–50, 255–58, 261, 266, 284–92, 294, 298, 307–18, 328, 331–37
Ashkelon 170–71, 173–74, 178, 204, 326
Ashtaroth. *See* Astarte
Ashtoreth. *See* Astarte
Astarte 256, 266, 288, 298, 329, 332, 337
Azekah 232
Baal 258, 266, 284, 287–88, 313, 317–18, 335
Batash, Tel 232
Beersheba 145, 232, 255, 257, 259, 261, 269, 291, 300, 309, 327
Beit Lei, Khirbet 258, 294
Beit Mirsim, Tell 232, 264
Bes 293, 294, 331
Bethel 264
Beth-shean 36, 231
Beth-shemesh 232
Bull Site 37, 146, 196, 202, 285–86, 289
Canaanites 23, 151, 188–89, 200, 203, 205
Carthage 292
City of David 126
Damascus 226
Damascus Gate 295

Dan 231, 254–56, 259, 261, 266, 285, 289, 327
Dan inscription 114, 154, 226
David 115, 154, 219, 222, 225–26, 235
Dothan 232
Ebal, Mount, altar 37, 196
Ebla 251, 254
Egypt 171
'Ein-gedi 258
Eitun 258
Ekron. *See* Miqne, Tel
El 37, 202, 256–58, 266, 286, 288, 313
Far'ah, Tell el- (North) 231, 255, 260, 266, 285, 291, 328–29
Far'ah, Tell el- (South) 258
Ful, Tell el- 232
Gezer 5, 7, 16, 23, 84, 170, 171, 173–74, 178, 204, 231–33, 235, 256–57
Gibeon 176
Gilgamesh 225
Giloh 196
Habiru 150, 155
Halif, Tel 232
Hama, Tell 232
Hathor 308
Hatti 170–71
Hazael 226
Hazor 5, 8–9, 23, 202, 231, 233–34, 254–57
Hezekiah 222, 261, 300
Horus 293, 331
Horvat Beth Loya 311
Hurru 170, 171, 174, 178
Idalion 291
Ishtar. *See* Astarte 332

-345-

Israelites 5, 23, 31–32, 38, 54, 114, 135–36, 139, 152, 157, 170, 172–75, 177–78, 180, 185, 188, 192, 196, 200, 203–5, 209. *See also* Proto-Israelites
'Izbet Ṣarṭah 140, 145–48, 196, 200, 235, 294
Jehoram 226
Jericho 84
Jerusalem 1, 115, 117, 126, 147, 219, 226, 231–32, 234, 254–55, 258, 261, 264–65, 269, 284–85, 289, 295, 300, 308, 326, 331, 335
Jezreel 174–75, 205
Joram 226
Josiah 222, 261, 280, 289, 300
Ketef Hinnom 293
Kheleifeh, Tell el- 232
Kinrot, Tel 232
Korah 285
Kuntillet 'Ajrud 249–50, 255, 257–61, 266, 286–87, 289, 294–95, 307, 311, 315–19
Lachish 146, 200, 231–33, 255–56, 260, 270
Maacah 336
Makkedah. *See* Qom, Khirbet el-
Masada 15
Masos, Tel 145, 196
Mazar, Tell 232
Megiddo 5, 23, 85, 231, 233–34, 255, 260, 264, 326
Meremoth 284
Merenptah 139, 169–81, 203–5
Mesha Stela 114, 116
Mevorakh, Tel 232, 270
Michal, Tell 232
Miqne, Tel 291, 314, 329
Mother Goddess of Canaan. *See* Asherah
Omri 115–17, 177, 206, 219
Pashur 284
Philistines 64, 174, 188–89, 235, 258
Proto-Israelites 139, 154, 157, 175, 178–80, 190, 196–97, 199–200, 203–4, 207–8, 230–31. *See also* Israelites

Qadesh-barnea 232
Qarqar 114, 177, 206
Qasile, Tell 232, 270, 329, 330
Qiri, Tel 232
Qom, Khirbet el- 249, 250, 257–58, 266, 286, 293–94, 307–9, 311–19, 330
Radanna, Khirbet 196, 200
Ramallah 147
Ramesses II 155, 174
Royal Steward inscription 294
Samaria 115, 234
Samuel 222
Saul 219, 222, 225
Sea Peoples 156, 293, 329
Ser'a, Tel 232
Shalmaneser III 114, 177, 206
Shasu 150, 155, 204
Shebaniah 295
Shechem 7, 84, 176, 231, 254, 269
Shiloh 146, 196
Shishak. *See* Shoshenq
Shoshenq 233–34
Siloam Tunnel 120
Solomon 117, 219, 225, 233, 235
Tammuz 298
Tananir 146
Tayinat, Tell 254
Ta'anach 7, 231, 255–57, 260, 266, 286, 288, 290, 293, 327, 333
Tehenu 170–71
Tirzah. *See* Far'ah, Tell el- (North) 286
Ugarit 258, 313, 317
'Umeiri, Tell el- 158
'Uriyahu 312–13, 315
Uruk 225
Vered Jericho 300
Yahweh 126, 136, 151, 222, 249–50, 261, 266, 286, 289, 294, 297, 307, 311–18, 324, 328, 332–33, 337
Yanoam 170–71, 178
Yoqneam 232

Index of Modern Authors

Ackerman, Susan   40, 68, 274–77, 287, 289, 292, 295–300, 309, 313–16, 319, 332–34, 338
Ackroyd, Peter R.   58
Adam, A. K. M.   110, 128
Adams, Robert McCormick   228–29, 236, 238
Aharoni, Yohanan   5, 34, 254–57, 260–61, 269–70, 285, 291, 300, 309, 327, 338
Ahlström, Gösta   28, 36
Ahlström, Gösta W.   28, 36, 56, 60, 70, 96–97, 99, 101, 139–40, 154–55, 157–58, 172, 178, 181, 281, 300
Albertz, Rainer   75, 276, 282, 297–98, 301, 316, 319, 323–25, 333, 33–38
Albright, W. F.   6–7, 12, 15–16, 19, 21–23, 48, 74, 83, 88, 103, 124, 224, 230, 251, 263–64, 271, 281, 288, 307, 310, 319, 332
Alt, Albrecht   142
Alter, Robert   90, 101
Amit, Yairah   74
Anderson, Bernhard W.   58, 328, 338
Andrén, Anders   338
Angerstorfer, Andreas   317, 319
Arbino, Gary P.   247
Arnold, Bill T.   76
Ash, Paul S.   243
Avigad, Nahman   5, 258, 271, 294–95, 301, 309–10, 319
Avni, Gideon   149, 164
Bahn, Paul   49
Baker, David W.   73, 131

Baker, Dwight W.   74, 76, 110, 119, 131–32
Bal, Mieke   117
Banks, Diane   75
Banning, Edward B.   149, 158
Bar-Adon, Pesach   258, 271
Barbosa, Marcella   247
Barkay, Gabriel   46, 233, 238, 293, 308–9
Barkey, Gabriel   301
Barnard, Hans   166, 215
Barrick, Wilber B.   259, 271
Barr, James   46, 57–58, 79, 98, 101, 109, 121, 128, 179–81, 187, 209
Barstad, Hans M.   76
Barth, Fredrick   143, 158, 194–95, 209
Barton, John   276
Bar-Yosef, Ofer   8, 11, 19, 86, 101, 141, 143, 149, 158
Bates, Daniel G.   143, 159
Becking, Bob   275
Beckman, Gary M.   276
Beck, Pirhiya   45, 73, 137, 156, 159, 286, 288, 291, 301
Ben-Tor, Amnon   67, 70, 180, 181, 206, 209, 227, 238, 244
Benvenisti, Meir   46
Ben-Yehuda, Nachman   46
Ben-Yosef, Erez   48, 217, 247
Berlinerblau, Jacques   275, 316, 319
Bimson, John J.   136, 159
Binford, Lewis   28, 34, 39, 42, 54–55, 70, 94, 101
Binger, Tilda   308–9, 311–12, 315, 319
Bintliff, John L.   49, 99, 101

Biran, Avraham   21, 51, 71, 103, 214, 226, 238, 255–57, 259, 261, 271, 285, 289, 301, 327, 338
Bird, Phyllis   288, 296–97, 301, 316, 319
Bloch-Smith, Elizabeth   186, 200, 209, 274, 288, 290, 295, 299, 301, 311, 316, 320, 325, 338
Bodel, John P.   276
Boling, Robert G.   63–64, 71
Braun, Joachin   333, 338
Brettler, Marc Zvi   74, 119, 128
Brett, Mark G.   189, 209
Bright, John   227
Broshi, Magen   8, 14, 19, 45, 92, 101, 233, 238
Brown, James Allison   200, 209
Brown, Jonathan M.   48
Brown, Susan   292, 301
Bruins, Hendrik J.   118, 128
Bunimovitz, Shlomo   21, 42, 46, 140–41, 152–53, 159, 191, 195, 199, 209, 216
Busink, Th. A.   254, 271
Callaway, James A.   7
Callaway, Joseph A.   7, 31, 33, 35, 186, 196, 200, 209–10, 214
Calloway, Joseph A.   42
Campbell, Edward F.   7
Carneiro, Robert L.   220–21, 223, 238
Chambon, Alain   286, 291, 301, 328–29, 338
Chancey, Mark   186, 214
Childe, V. Gordon   228–29, 236, 238
Childs, Brevard S.   88, 101
Claessen, Henri J. M.   221, 238
Clark, Douglas R.   46
Cogan, Mordechai   287, 301
Cohen, Ronald   220, 238
Collins, John J.   47, 75, 79, 101, 181, 182
Conkey, Margaret W.   94–95, 101
Coogan, Michael David   103, 183, 214, 243, 286, 295, 301, 315, 317, 320
Cooley, Robert   196, 200, 210
Coote, Robert B.   28, 42, 88, 99, 102, 112–13, 128, 138, 140–41, 151, 154–55, 159, 221, 223, 238
Coudart, Anick   186, 214
Cowgill, George L.   95–96, 102
Coyle, Cameron   247
Cribb, Roger   149, 159
Cross, Frank Moore   6, 11, 13, 19–20, 120, 130, 249, 254, 257, 271, 307–8, 310
Culley, Robert C.   89–90, 92–93, 102
Darby, Erin   277
Daviau, P. M. Michèle   237–38
Davies, Philip R.   55, 60, 62–63, 65–67, 71, 73–76, 98, 102, 107, 109–12, 120–22, 128, 130, 132, 153–54, 157, 159, 169, 176, 180–82, 187, 189–90, 212, 219, 222, 224–25, 227, 236, 238, 243, 317, 320
Davis, Miriam C.   48
Davis, Thomas W.   47
Day, John   75, 210, 275, 312, 320
Day, Peggy L.   92–93, 104
Dee, Michael W.   247
Deetz, James   95
Deist, Ferdinand E.   109, 112, 120, 128
Demarest, Arthur A.   94, 102
Demsky, Aharon   200, 210
Deutsch, Robert   309, 320
Dever, William G.   2, 7–8, 15, 17, 19, 21–24, 26, 31–32, 34–35, 38–42, 46–48, 53, 63–66, 68, 71, 74–77, 82–83, 85–88, 91–94, 97–99, 102, 107–10, 115, 118, 120–21, 123–25, 127–28, 138–43, 145–46, 148, 150–51, 154, 156, 159, 161, 166–67, 170, 172–74, 176–80, 182, 186–91, 194, 196, 198–99, 201–2, 206–8, 210, 216, 223–24, 227, 230, 233–35, 239–40, 243–44, 247, 249, 254, 256–58, 262–64, 267, 269, 271–72, 275–76, 281–82, 286, 288–89, 291, 293–96, 299, 301, 306, 308–9, 311, 315–16, 320–21, 324–25, 328–32, 334–36, 338
DeVries, LaMoine F.   327, 339
Dietrich, Walter   55, 71, 103
Dijkstra, Meindert   275
Dixon, A. C.   264, 272

Index of Modern Authors 349

Dorsey, David A. 309, 321
Dothan, Trude 71
Drinkard, Joel. F. 45
Ebeling, Jennie R. 48, 77, 215, 250, 276
Edelman, Diane V. 43, 71–73, 76, 169, 175–76, 182, 189–90, 195, 205, 211, 225, 240, 281, 302
Eichrodt, Walther 57
Elliot, Mark 77
Ellis, John M. 110, 130
Elon, Amos 46
Emerton, John A. 312, 321
Eshel, Esther 120, 130
Esse, Douglas L. 149, 152, 160
Falconer, Steven E. 228, 240
Faust, Avraham 47, 77, 135, 177, 182, 185–86, 191–92, 199, 209, 211, 215–16, 246–47, 276, 277
Feineman, Peter D. 48
Finkelstein, Israel 16–17, 19, 23, 32, 35, 43, 46, 62, 64–65, 71, 74–76, 97, 103, 107, 112, 117–18, 123–24, 130, 132, 135–36, 139–58, 160–61, 164–65, 169, 175–76, 178, 182, 185–86, 190–91, 195–96, 198–99, 205, 207–8, 211–12, 219, 222, 230, 233–34, 237–38, 240, 243–46
Fischer, Michael M. J. 44, 92, 105
Flanagan, James W. 28, 62–64, 71, 89, 103, 220–21, 223–24, 240
Flannery, Kent V. 220, 240
Fleming, Fleming, Daniel 76
Flesher, Paul W. M. 48, 77
Flight, John 138, 161
Foucault, Michel 111, 130, 181
Fowler, Mervyn D. 327, 339
Frazer, J. G. 86
Freedman, David Noel 2–3, 249, 251, 272, 307, 318, 321
Frei, Hans 98
Frese, Daniel A. 245
Frick, Frank S. 28, 44, 62, 72, 88, 220–21, 223, 240
Friedman, J. 240
Fried, Mortin H. 220–21, 223, 240

Fritz, Volkmar 65, 72, 136, 145–46, 154, 161, 187, 196, 212, 221, 233, 240, 243
Frymer-Kensky, Tikva 332, 339
Gal, Zvi 153, 161
Ganor, Saar 245–46
Garbini, Giovanni 28, 44, 52, 60, 72, 75, 98–99, 104, 108, 123, 130, 281, 302
Garfinkel, Yosef 245–46
Geertz, Clifford 93, 104
Geraty, Lawrence T. 309, 321
Geus, Cornelius C. H. J. de 36–37, 44, 138, 148, 161, 220, 240
Gilman, Antonio 94, 104
Gitin, Seymour 215, 289, 291, 302, 314, 321, 325, 328, 339
Gittlen, Barry M. 124, 275, 325, 339
Glassie, Henry 95
Glock, Albert E. 7, 19, 255, 272
Glueck, Nelson 7, 48
Golub, Mitka R. 246
Goshen-Gottstein, Moshe 59, 72
Gottwald, Norman K. 28–29, 36–37, 43–44, 60, 62, 67, 72, 88–89, 92, 104, 136–38, 141–42, 151, 154–55, 157, 162, 180, 186, 191, 201, 203, 212, 220, 240
Grabbe, Lester L. 74–76, 109, 119, 122, 130, 187, 188, 212, 243
Graesser, Carl F. 255, 272
Graham, Walter C. 85, 104, 264, 272
Greenfield, Jonas 251
Gress, David 108, 110, 130, 181, 182
Gunkel, Hermann 65, 83, 281
Haas, Jonathan 220, 240
Hackett, Jo Ann 120, 130
Hadley, Judith M. 123, 130, 275, 286, 302, 311–12, 321, 332, 339
Hagelia, Hallvard 179, 182
Hallote, Rachel 46, 47
Hallo, William W. 205, 212
Hall, Robert L. 95
Halpern, Baruch 28–29, 36, 44, 52, 54, 62, 63, 67–69, 72, 74, 76, 97, 108–9, 119, 122, 130, 156, 162, 171–72, 180,

Halpern, Baruch (*continued*) 182, 188, 190, 212, 216, 219, 227, 241, 279, 281, 303
Handy, Lowell K. 128, 210, 239, 243
Hanson, Paul D. 36, 43–44, 72, 286, 296, 305
Haran, Menahem 252, 259–60, 263, 272, 289, 303, 328, 331, 339
Hasel, Gerhard 56, 72, 87, 104, 171, 182, 203, 212, 246
Hauser, Alan J. 138, 162
Hawkes, Terence 95
Hayes, John H. 31, 42, 44, 52, 73, 97, 105
H. Darrell Lance 257, 272
Heltzer, Michael 309, 320
Hendel, Ronald 75, 120, 122, 130
Herr, Larry G. 158, 162, 237, 241
Herrmann, Seigfried 282, 303
Herzog, Ze'ev 140–41, 145, 152, 162, 231, 234, 241, 243, 255, 272, 285–86, 289, 291, 300, 303
Hess, Richard S. 76, 276, 277
Hesse, Brian 141, 162, 199, 212
Hestrin, Ruth 286, 291, 303, 328–29, 339
Hiebert, Theodore 135, 166, 215
Highman, Thomas 244
Hitchcock, Louse A. 216
Hjelm, Ingrid 173–74, 183
Hobsbawn, Eric 127
Hodder, Ian 21, 24–27, 29, 38, 44, 49, 69–70, 72, 86, 91, 93–94, 101, 104, 125, 130, 227, 233, 241, 306
Hoffmeier, James K. 47, 73, 76, 119, 132
Holladay, John S., Jr. 17, 19, 23, 44, 86, 104, 123, 131, 199, 212, 233–34, 241, 243, 285, 288–90, 296, 300, 303, 309, 316, 321
Holland, Thomas A. 288, 303
Hopkins, David L. 28–29, 37, 44, 142, 155, 162
Horowitz, Liora K. 216
Hourani, Albert 137
Hua, Quan 247
Hurvitz, Avi 120, 130, 131
Iggers, Georg G. 74
Jacobsen, Geraldine E. 247
Jamieson-Drake, David W. 154, 163, 225, 241
Japhet, Sara 122
Jeffers, Ann 331, 340
Jobling, David 92–93, 104
Joffe, Alex H. 46, 48
Joffee, Alex H. 244
Johnson, Gary L. 8, 20
Jones, Sian 185–86, 193–94, 213
Kaufmann, Yehezkiel 263, 272
Keel, Othmar 275, 282, 286–88, 290–91, 303, 312, 316, 321, 323–24, 329, 332, 340
Keimer, Kyle H. 77, 247
Kelle, Brad E. 76
Kelso, James L. 264, 273
Kempinski, Aaron 46, 145, 151, 163, 196, 212
Kenyon, Kathleen 48, 82, 84, 255, 300, 303, 309
Kessler, Rainer 162, 246
Khazanov, Anatoly M. 86, 101, 141, 143, 149, 158, 161, 163
Khoury, Philip S. 137, 143, 163, 241
Killebrew, Ann E. 2–3, 141, 163, 173, 176–77, 183, 185–86, 213, 215–16, 244
King, Philip J. 279
Kitchen, Kenneth A. 170–72, 174–75, 178, 183
Kletter, Raz 47, 185–86, 191–92, 213, 244, 309, 321, 331–32, 340
Kloner, Amos 308
Klopfenstein, Martin 55, 71, 103
Knapp, A. Bernard 99, 104
Knauf, Ernst Axel 61, 63, 69, 72, 96, 98–99, 104, 154, 163, 245, 282, 303
Knierim, Rolf 66, 72, 83, 93, 98, 104
Knight, Douglas A. 75, 98, 104
Knoppers, Gary N. 119, 122, 131, 243
Kofoed, Jens B. 75
Kolb, Frank 229, 241
Korpel, Marjo C. A. 275

Kostiner, Joseph   137, 143, 163, 221, 241
Kottsieper, Ingo   276
Kramer, Carol   86, 105
Kratz, Reinhard G.   76
Kuemmerlin-McLean, Joanne K.   292, 303
Kuhn, Thomas   5
Kutler, Laurence   48
Kyle, M. G.   264
La Bianca, Øystein S.   89, 105
Lamberg-Karlovsky, Carl C.   82, 105
Lapp, Paul W.   7, 255–57, 273, 286, 293, 303
LaRocca-Pitts, Elizabeth C.   275, 336, 340
Laughlin, John C. H.   266, 273
Lederman, Zvi   146, 163, 186, 196, 212, 216
Lees, Susan H.   143, 159
Lehmann, Gunnar   216, 244
Lemaire, André   76, 120, 130, 216, 245, 250, 258, 273, 294, 304, 310, 312, 314, 321
Lemche, Niels Peter   28–29, 36–37, 44, 52, 60, 62, 72, 74, 76, 88, 99, 105, 107–10, 113–15, 121–22, 131, 137, 139–40, 143, 153–55, 163, 169, 172–73, 176, 178–79, 181, 183, 187–90, 204–6, 213, 219–20, 222, 224–26, 230, 236, 241, 243, 304
Lemert, Charles   110, 131
Leroi-Gourhan, André   95
Levenson, Jon D.   58–59, 67, 72
Levine, Lee I.   109, 131, 175, 183
Lev-Tov, Justin   216
Levy, Thomas E.   89, 105, 180, 183, 216, 244–45
Lewis, Theodore J.   276–77, 325, 332, 340
Lipiński, Edouard   303, 314, 321
Liverani, Mario   75
Lohfink, Norbert   279–80, 304
London, Gloria   39, 44, 140–41, 150, 163
Long, Burke O.   54, 74
Long, V. Phillips   47, 75, 110, 119, 131

Longman, Trevor, III   47, 75
Long, V. Phillips   110
Loud, Gordon   255, 273
Lowery, R. H.   280, 283, 304
Luke, J. Tracy   143–44, 163
Lyotard, Francois   110, 131, 181
Machinist, Peter   107
MacKay, D. B.   141, 163
Maeir, Aren M.   213, 216–17
Magen, Yitzhak   8, 19, 45, 101, 147, 161
Magness, Jodi   141
Malamat, Avraham   131, 175, 183
Marcus, George E.   41, 44, 92, 105
Margalit, Baruch   314, 321
Martin, J. D.   44, 52, 71, 96, 103–5, 138, 163, 224, 334
Marx, Karl   89
Masry, Abdullah H.   11, 19
Master, Daniel M.   2–3, 174, 184, 244
Matthews, Victor H.   46, 143–44, 163
Mattingly, Gerard L.   45
May, Herbert G.   85, 104, 264, 272–73
Mazar, Amihai   2–3, 5, 8, 11–12, 14, 19, 34, 40, 44, 47, 67, 72, 109, 112, 115, 118, 128, 132, 152, 163, 180, 183, 196, 202, 206, 208, 213, 227, 233, 241, 245–46, 270, 273, 285, 289, 304, 310, 330, 340
Mazar, Binyamin   5, 9, 11
Mazar, Eilat   245
Mazow, Laura   250
Mazow, Laura B.   276
McBride, S. Dean   36, 43–44, 72, 286, 296, 305
McCarter, P. Kyle, Jr.   120, 122, 130, 139, 141, 164, 180, 286, 295, 304, 312–13, 317, 321, 332–33, 340
McConville, J. G.   119, 122, 131
McGuire, Randall H.   192, 213
McNutt, Paula M.   171, 183, 186, 213
Mendenhall, George E.   62, 67–68, 73, 138, 151, 155, 157, 164
Meshel, Ze'ev   249–50, 255, 257–58, 261, 273, 277, 286–87, 289, 304, 307, 311, 314–15, 321–22

Meskell, Lynn	49, 112, 132
Meyers, Carol	33–34, 40, 44, 92, 100, 105, 243, 250, 252, 255–56, 258, 261, 273, 275, 296–97, 304, 316, 322, 332
Meyers, Eric M.	2–3, 33–34, 40, 44, 100, 105, 186, 213–14, 252, 273
Milgrom, Jacob	328, 340
Millard, Alan	47, 73, 119, 132, 246
Miller, J. Maxwell	31, 44, 46, 52, 73, 96–98, 105, 126, 132, 154, 164, 186, 214, 282, 295–96, 304
Miller, Patrick D.	36, 44, 286, 304–5, 315, 317, 322, 332, 340
Miller, Robert D., II	186, 214
Misgav, Haggai	246
Mittman, Siegfried	310, 322
Moore, Megan B.	76
Moorey, P. R. S.	46
Moshkovitz, Shmuell	255, 272, 285–86, 289, 291, 300, 303
Mrozowski, Stephen A.	22, 49
Mueller, James W.	147, 164
Muller, Jon	95
Mumcouglu, Madeleine	246
Na'aman, Nadav	62, 65, 71, 136, 144, 152, 154–56, 158, 161, 164, 196, 212, 222, 240, 246
Nakhai, Beth Alpert	123, 132, 250, 275–76, 305, 325, 340
Naveh, Joseph	200, 214, 238, 258, 273, 294, 305, 307, 310, 311, 322
Negbi, Ora	305
Neu, Rainer	137, 158, 164
Niemann, Hermann M.	76
Nietzsche, Friedrich	120
Noll, Kurt L.	171, 177, 183
Noth, Martin	44, 52, 96, 105, 138, 224, 282, 305, 334, 340
Oden, Robert	98, 105, 289, 305
Ofer, Avi	19, 101, 152, 158, 161, 164, 244
Olivier, Laurent	186, 214
Olyan, Saul	250, 274, 276, 286, 289, 305, 313–14, 317, 322, 337, 340
Ortiz, Steven	47, 246, 247
Orton, Clive	233, 241
Paglia, Camille	190, 214
Pearce, Mark	49
Perdue, Leo G.	8, 20
Perevolotsky, Avi	143, 161
Pinski, Valerie	92, 105
Pinsky, Valerie	49
Plicht, Johannes van der	118, 128
Porteous, Norman	58
Porter, Ann	166, 216
Preucel, Robert W.	49, 53, 69, 73, 92, 105
Pritchard, James B.	7, 114, 132
Propp, William C.	216
Provan, Ian	47, 74–75, 117, 132, 223, 241
Rad, Gerhard von	57–58, 98
Rafferty, Janet E.	143, 165
Rainey, Anson F.	6, 135, 166, 189, 214–15, 255, 272, 285–86, 289, 291, 300, 303
Rast, Walter E.	32, 44
Rathje, William J.	95, 105
Redford, Donald B.	171, 178, 183
Rendtorff, Rolf	56, 60, 73, 93, 96, 105, 282, 305
Renfrew, Colin	33, 44, 49, 220, 241
Ricoeur, Paul	90, 105
Rogerson, John W.	89, 105, 120, 132, 137–38, 164
Römer, Thomas	74
Rose, D. Glenn	8, 19–20, 33, 44
Rösel, Hartmut N.	282, 305
Rosen, Baruch	146, 149, 164
Rosen, Steven A.	164
Routledge, Bruce	242
Rowlands, M. J.	220, 240
Rowton, Michael B.	143, 150, 165
Sader, Hélène	158, 165
Sahlins, Marshall	37–38, 45, 201, 214, 221, 242
Saidel, Benjamin	166, 215
Salzman, Philip Carl	143, 165
Sanders, James A.	58, 92, 105
Sapir-Hen, Lidar	216

Index of Modern Authors

Schäfer-Lichtenberger, Christa 118, 132
Schiffer, Michael B. 84, 106
Schloen, J. David 166, 174, 184
Schmidt, Brian B. 47, 75
Schmitt, Rüdiger 276
Schneider, Thomas 216
Schniedewind, William M. 179, 183
Schröer, Silvia 288, 291, 305, 308, 322, 323
Service, Elman R. 220-21, 223, 229-30, 238, 242, 303
Shanks, Hershel 11, 20, 300, 305
Shanks, Michael 41, 45, 49, 92, 106
Shay, Talia 100, 106
Sheppard, Gerald T. 92-93, 103-4, 106
Shiloh, Yigal 8, 12, 230-31, 233, 242, 252, 255-56, 259, 273
Silberman, Lou H. 79-80, 106
Silberman, Neil Asher 2-3, 49, 51, 75, 112, 117-18, 123, 130, 132, 176, 182, 191, 205, 212, 245
Skalnik, Peter 221, 238
Skjeggestad, Marit 139-40, 157, 165
Small, David 51, 74
Smith, Mark S. 282, 286, 289, 292, 297, 299, 305, 312, 316, 322, 332, 340
Smith, Morton 54, 73
Smith, W. Robertson 86, 106
Soggin, J. Alberto 52, 60, 73, 96
Sommer, Benjamin D. 175, 183
Sommerfeld, Walter 246
Sparks, Kenton L. 195, 214
Spieckermann, Herman 76
Stager, Lawrence E. 6, 17, 20, 23, 31-32, 35, 37, 45-46, 64, 73, 100, 106-7, 135, 140-42, 145, 148, 156, 165, 169-71, 174, 180, 183-84, 186, 189, 196, 198-99, 201, 208, 214, 234, 244, 255-56, 266, 274, 287, 293, 305, 326, 340
Stavrakopoulis, Francesca 276
Steen, Evaline J. van der 166, 215
Steiner, Margreet 2-3
Stendahl, Krister 68, 73
Stern, Ephraim 6, 8, 11-12, 14, 20, 27, 34, 45

Strange, James F. 252
Streit, Katharina 246
Sukenik, Eliezer 8
Szuchman, Jeffrey 166
Tadmor, Hayim 287, 301
Tainter, Joseph A. 220-22, 242
Tapper, Richard 137, 221, 242
Tarnas, Richard 108, 132
Taylor, J. Glenn 289, 291, 305, 335, 341
Thomas, Zachary 48, 247
Thompson, Thomas L. 28-29, 45-46, 55, 60-61, 63, 66, 73-75, 83, 97-100, 106-7, 109-10, 114-17, 120, 122, 133, 138-39, 153-54, 157, 165, 169, 172-74, 176, 179, 181, 183-84, 187-90, 192, 205-6, 214, 219, 222, 224-26, 230, 236-37, 241-42, 281, 305
Tibi, Bassam 137
Tigay, Jeffrey H. 286, 305, 312, 317, 322
Tilley, Christopher 41, 45, 49, 92, 106
Toombs, Lawrence E. 7-8, 20, 32-33, 45
Toorn, Karel van der 274, 316, 322, 332, 341
Tramontini, Leslie 246
Trigger, Bruce G. 49, 82, 106
Tufnell, Olga 331, 341
Uehlinger, Christoph 275, 282, 286-88, 290-91, 303, 312, 316, 321, 323-24, 332, 340
Ussishkin, David 8, 17, 20, 23, 45, 47, 200, 214, 234, 285, 289, 300, 306
Van Seters, John 28-29, 45, 52, 73, 97
Vaughan, Patrick H. 259, 274
Vaughn, Andrew G. 244
Vaux, Roland de 255, 263, 274
Vriezen, Karel J. H. 275, 325-27, 332, 341
Wapnish, Paula 141, 162, 199, 212
Washburn, Dorothy 95
Webb, Malcolm C. 221, 242
Weber, Max 88
Webster, Lyndelle C. 247
Weippert, Helga 40, 45, 67, 73, 154-55, 165, 180, 184, 206, 215, 227, 233, 242
Weippert, Manfred 154-55, 165

Wendrich, Willeke 166, 215
Wenham, Gordon J. 110, 119, 131
Westermann, Claus 58
Whitelam, Keith W. 28, 42, 74, 99, 102, 109–10, 112–13, 121, 128, 133, 139–40, 153–55, 157, 159, 165, 169, 174–76, 181, 183–84, 189–90, 192, 204, 215, 219, 221, 223–26, 236, 238, 242
Whitley, David S. 49
Wightman, G. J. 17, 20, 23, 45, 234
Williamson, Hugh G. M. 75
Wilson, John A. 171, 184
Wilson, Robert R. 88–89, 106
Wilson, Veronica 331, 341
Windschuttle, Keith 111, 133, 181, 184
Winter, Urs 282, 286, 288, 290–91, 306
Wöhrle, Jakob 276
Wolff, Samuel R. 160, 247, 255–56, 266, 274, 287, 293, 305
Wood, Bryant G. 151, 165
Wright, G. Ernest 7, 15, 21, 41, 45, 57, 73, 88, 98, 224, 249, 257, 263–64, 272, 274
Wright, Henry T. 221, 242
Wyatt, Nicholas 337, 341
Wylie, Alison 49, 92, 105
Yadin, Yigael 5–9, 11–12, 15–18, 20–21, 34, 43, 46, 49, 233, 242, 255, 256–57, 274, 300, 306
Yardeni, Ada 120, 130
Yasur-Landau, Asaf 191, 195, 209, 276
Yeivin, Shmuel 269, 274
Yurco, Frank J. 155, 165, 174, 204, 215
Zertal, Adam 37, 135, 148, 152, 156–57, 165–66, 196, 215
Zevit, Ziony 46, 62, 73, 113, 122, 124, 133, 245, 250, 275–76, 286, 306, 311, 314, 316, 322, 325, 328, 332, 334, 341
Zubrow, Ezra B. 49

www.ingramcontent.com/pod-product-compliance
Lightning Source LLC
Chambersburg PA
CBHW032149010526
44111CB00035B/1256